DEFENDING AND DECLARING THE FAITH
Some Scottish Examples, 1860–1920

Publication of this book has
been made possible by a grant
from the Twenty–Seven Foundation

DEFENDING AND DECLARING THE FAITH

Some Scottish Examples,
1860–1920

Alan P. F. Sell

Exeter, U.K.
THE PATERNOSTER PRESS

Colorado Springs, U.S.A.
HELMERS & HOWARD

SOUTH AFRICA:
Oxford University Press,
P.O. Box 1141, Cape Town

AUSTRALIA:
Bookhouse Australia Ltd.,
P.O. Box 115, Flemington Markets, NSW 2129

British Library Cataloguing in Publication Data

Sell, Alan P.F.
  Defending and declaring the faith: some
  Scottish examples 1860–1920.
  1. Scotland—Church history—19th
  century 2. Scotland—Church history—
  20th century
  I. Title
  274.11   BR786
  ISBN 0–85364–399–7

Library of Congress Cataloging in Publication Data

Sell, Alan P.F.
  Defending and Declaring the Faith

  Bibliography: p.
  Includes index
  Series 1. Theology, Doctrinal—Scotland—History—19th century
  2. Theology, Doctrinal—Scotland—History—20th century
  3. Theologians—Scotland 4. Apologetics—19th century.
  5. Apologetics—20th century. 6. Church of Scotland—
  Doctrines—History—19th century. 7. Church of Scotland—Doctrines—
  History—20th century. 8. Presbyterian Church—Doctrines—
  History—19th century. 9. Presbyterian Church—Doctrines—
  History—20th century. I. Title.
  BT30.G7S45 1987 230'.52411 87–81387
  ISBN 0–939443–02–3

Set in Garamond by Photoprint, Torquay
and printed in the United Kingdom for
The Paternoster Press, Paternoster House,
3 Mount Radford Crescent, Exeter, Devon
and Helmers & Howard, 1221 East
Madison Street, Colorado Springs, CO 80907, U.S.A.
by A. Wheaton & Co., Ltd., Exeter, U.K.

To Karen

CONTENTS

Foreword

A New Testament writer urges us always to be ready to give an answer to anyone who asks a reason for the hope that is in us. Scotland has had a remarkable succession of churchmen and theologians, in the pulpit and in the universities, who have been eager to declare and defend their faith. If in the sixteenth and seventeenth centuries, during the Scottish Reformation and the covenanting period, they were not afraid of controversy to defend the Gospel of grace and 'the crown rights of the Redeemer' in the political and ecclesiastical arena, in the nineteenth century there was a passionate concern to interpret and contend for the Gospel in the changing cultural and intellectual climate of the day. The first half of the century produced that remarkable trio of Scottish theologians, John McLeod Campbell, Thomas Erskine of Linlathen and Edward Irving who were concerned to call the Church back to the centrality of the Trinity, the Incarnation and the doctrine of the Holy Spirit in their understanding of atonement in proclaiming the universality and 'unconditional freeness of grace'. They wanted to declare God's love for all his creatures and the Headship of Christ over every area of life, in the context of a land which had been for too long dominated by a scholastic Calvinism which had limited God's grace to the elect, and produced a 'legal strain' in Scottish religion. The second half of the century was to produce a galaxy of scholars who were concerned to discern the relevance of such a catholic and evangelical understanding of the Gospel, and interpret it in a world facing the questions posed by evolution, biblical criticism, materialism, naturalism and idealism.

If in an era of imperial expansion, Scottish missionaries were carrying the Gospel to the ends of the earth, theologians were carrying the same Gospel into the realms of philosophy, science and historical scholarship. It may be that with hindsight we can now see that the great missionary pioneers of the era too readily identified the Gospel with Western culture. Nevertheless the Gospel was preached and the Church of Jesus Christ

9

grew. So analogously we might realize today that the apologists of the nineteenth century, in their concern to show the reasonableness of the Christian faith, too readily accommodated the Gospel to Kantian or idealist or evolutionary categories. But nevertheless Christ was proclaimed.

In all ages the Church has sought to proclaim the Gospel in the language and concepts of the time to conquer culture for Christ. If at times she has run the risk of producing syntheses of Christianity and culture, where the Church has been too easily moulded or captivated by contemporary culture, as in primitive gnosticism, none the less she has been right in seeing that there is no area of life which does not belong to Christ, and that the ends of culture and the ends of the Gospel *ought* to be at one. That was the faith of the scholars whom Dr. Sell has so brilliantly presented in these studies. As he says, he has had to be selective. If he has omitted A. B. Davidson, W. Robertson Smith and Marcus Dods in the biblical field, and John Tulloch in his unique contribution to the history of Christian thought, the theologians he has selected show the wide range of apologetic concern and scholarship in Scottish presbyterianism between 1860 and 1920. If John Kennedy of Dingwall was too concerned to keep the Kirk to the old paths, John Caird in his desire to see the continuity between Christianity and idealism, perhaps unwittingly cut Christianity loose from history, by resolving it into ideas. If Flint and Orr were the most learned, Bruce and Denney were possibly more effective in portraying Jesus and the Cross in a theology which could be preached. If Flint and Caird were not active in the General Assemblies of the Church, they were still like Orr, Iverach, Forrest and Denney, staunch churchmen. Whatever their different interests, strengths and weaknesses, they were all men of faith, committed to the defence of the Gospel.

In each study, Dr. Sell has been concerned to let each of his chosen eight speak for themselves. They were intellectual giants in their day, and it would be sad if they were forgotten. Dr. Sell has put us all in his debt by keeping their memory alive and enabling us to enter into this rich inheritance. Was not the prayer of the apostle that we might comprehend with the saints of all ages the extent of the love of God toward all His creatures?

JAMES B. TORRANCE
University of Aberdeen

Preface

For some years now I have been investigating the diversity of ways in which theologians responded to the intellectual challenges of the post-Darwin, pre-Barth period. In *Theology in Turmoil* (1986) I discussed some of the general issues which gave rise to the conservative-liberal debate in modern theology. Elsewhere I considered the way in which Henry Rogers attempted to stem the advancing tide of modern thought within English Congregationalism (*The Journal of the United Reformed Church History Society*, II no. 2, May 1980). The intellectual challenges prompted *Robert Mackintosh, Theologian of Integrity* (1977) to become, in his own words, 'a refugee' from the Scottish confessional Calvinism of his youth to what he regarded as the freer air of English Congregationalism; and they called forth the interestingly diverse reactions of W. B. Pope, Robert Watts and A. M. Fairbairn (*Scottish Journal of Theology*, XXXVIII no. 1, 1985). Even *Alfred Dye, Minister of the Gospel* (1974) has his place as reminding us that to a considerable degree the older thought was perpetuated in England more by the often self-taught and sometimes idiosyncratic preachers of the Strict Baptist and similar kinds than by professional theologians.

In the present work eight Scottish theologians from the same period are studied. I have sought to justify my selection in the Introduction, and need not repeat myself here.

It is imperative, however, that I render thanks—and this I gladly do: to Dr. James Bastable, editor of *Philosophical Studies* (National University of Ireland), who gave me permission to use material on Flint which had appeared in his journal; to Professor Emeritus G. N. M. Collins of the College of the Free Church of Scotland, who kindly loaned his extensive collection of scarce pamphlets by John Kennedy; to Professor James B. Torrance of the University of Aberdeen, who gave much encouragement *en route* to publication, and who contributed the generous Foreword; and to Professor Donald G. Bloesch of the University of Dubuque Theological Seminary who introduced me and my work to Mr. Donald Simpson, the American co-publisher of this book.

11

I am most grateful to Mr. Peter Cousins of The Paternoster Press for his interest in the theme and commitment to the project; and both of us are deeply indebted to the Trustees of the Twenty Seven Foundation Awards and to their Secretary, Mr. Michael Collinge. The generous grant made by this body has made publication possible.

ALAN P. F. SELL
Geneva

CHAPTER ONE

Introduction

If God the Holy Spirit is as vital as Christians believe him to be, and provided that theologians do not wilfully stagnate, then theology will always, and rightly, be in a flux. The reason is not that man's fundamental need of redemption changes, nor that we need to devise a new gospel. But, on the one hand, the way in which the gospel is expressed must take account of the intellectual climate in each successive, changing, age if communication is to take place; in a word, those who sow seed must have some regard to the soil. On the other hand, theologians ought always to be open to the God who, according to the seventeenth-century John Robinson, has yet more truth and light to break forth out of his holy Word. We here examine the responses of eight Scottish theologians to the intellectual challenges of their day. How did they seek to defend and declare the faith?

Not the least of the difficulties confronting the historian and analyst of thought are those concerning *termini* and the selection of thinkers to be discussed. As to the first, we have chosen the period between the landmarks represented by Darwin and Barth as being particularly interesting from the point of view of theological stock-taking. Evolution, biblical criticism, materialism, naturalism, idealism—these, not to mention topics ecclesiastical, were among the matters to be reckoned with. In Scotland, the focus of our attention, a galaxy of theological talent was employed in the work of reassessment and restatement—or, as in the case of Kennedy of Dingwall, was seeking to push back the tide.

In opting for 1860 we by no means suggest that nothing of importance for modern theology happened before that date. On the contrary (to look no further than Scotland), such writings as *The Unconditional Freeness of the Gospel* (1828) by the lay theologian Thomas Erskine of Linlathen (1788–1870) did much to loosen what some were coming to regard as the stranglehold of scholastic Calvinism upon the pulpits of the land. Again, when John McLeod Campbell (1800–1872) took his stand over against the legal strain of Scottish Calvinism, opposed certain forms of penal satisfaction theory, and proclaimed the universality of grace as the *sine qua non* of joyful assurance, he stimulated a line of thought the implications of which are still being variously endorsed and opposed.[1] We cannot, however, embark upon an infinite regress.

Neither can we treat every thinker of significance *within* our chosen period. Between 1860 and 1920 all of the Scottish universities and most of the theological colleges were blessed with theologians of distinction. Moreover, many of these scholars were polymaths. Consequently it is not easy to say, for example, 'Let us deal only with systematicians'. Since some limitation was unavoidable we may perhaps be justified in omitting from major consideration such writers as A. B. Davidson (1831–1902), Scotland's pioneer in modern Old Testament exegesis; his pupil William Robertson Smith (1846–1894); and Marcus Dods (1834–1909)—all of whom published mainly in the biblical field;[2] and John Tulloch (1823–1886), whose major writings were in the history of thought.

We have employed yet a further principle of exclusion: our selection is confined to those of the Presbyterian way. It is not that the other denominations possessed no scholars of repute. They did, though some of their best men—the Evangelical Union/Congregationalist A. M. Fairbairn and the Congregationalist P. T. Forsyth come readily to mind—became exiles.[3] Somewhat less frequently English 'missionaries' such as the Congregationalists D. W. Simon and J. M. Hodgson were received in northern parts.[4] Our purpose, however, is to indicate something of the *variety* of thought to be found within one ecclesiological tradition. Thus we arrive at our selection: Kennedy, Flint, John Caird, Bruce, Iverach, Orr, Forrest and Denney.

Our eight divines were not all of equal academic weight. There can be no doubt that Flint and Orr were the most learned of them all, and the former devoted the larger part of his life to teaching. Orr, Iverach, Forrest and the later Denney all played a considerable part in eccesiastical affairs, while Flint and Caird, though loyal to their Church, were in no sense 'Assembly men'. Again, if Kennedy, Caird and Forrest were in great demand as preachers, their respective styles could not have been more different. Between Flint's penetrating, Bruce's swashbuckling, and Orr's learned apologetic there is a world of difference, while in polemics—and perhaps, paradoxically, in tenderness—Kennedy outclasses his fellows. Kennedy is our example of those parish theologians who never held an academic post, of whom Scotland has produced not a few; and a consideration of the controversies in which he took part will cause us to sketch the ecclesiastical background against which all our divines are to be viewed. Kennedy is further representative of those who understood most of the theological flux they witnessed in the dictionary sense of 'morbid discharge'!

All of the ancient Scottish universities and most of the Presbyterian denominations are represented by our divines. Thus Kennedy, trained at Aberdeen, entered the ministry of the Free Church. Flint, who was brought up in the Free Church, became a minister of the Church of Scotland. He was educated at Glasgow and taught at St. Andrews and Edinburgh. John Caird of the Established Church graduated from, and taught at, Glasgow. The Free Churchman A. B. Bruce was educated at Edinburgh and taught at Glasgow. James Iverach of the Free, and then of the United Free Church, read Arts at Aberdeen and Divinity at Edinburgh, eventually teaching in Aberdeen. Orr and Forrest were both United Presbyterians who became United Free Churchmen at the union of 1900. They were both educated at Glasgow before receiving their theological training at the United Presbyterian Hall, Edinburgh. Orr taught in Edinburgh before proceeding to the Glasgow College, where he was succeeded by Forrest. Denney was among those Reformed Presbyterians (the successors of the Covenanters) who united with the Free Church. He was educated at Glasgow, in which city he later taught.

It would be practically impossible to review every theme on which our thinkers wrote. Each chapter heading incorporates a summary statement of the particular interest to us of its subject. We find that Kennedy, staunchly confessional, is in many ways a seventeenth-century man; Flint, though alive to the swirls of evolutionary thought, is often methodologically reminiscent of Butler. By contrast Caird is the pre-eminent example of a *theologian* who sought to express Christian truth in terms of the prevailing philosophical idealism. Iverach stands on the frontier between theology and science, and while learning from idealism, brings a dose of Scottish common sense to bear upon it. Bruce and Orr pursue the apologetic path—the former more biblically, the latter more historically and dogmatically; and Forrest and Denney probe the christological and soteriological heart of the Christian faith.

The effort expended on this study has been fuelled by the conviction that in regard to any age the attempt to discern theological trends and analyse individual contributions, far from being pejoratively 'antiquarian' is of value in its own right. If, as frequently happens, points of relevance to theology's continuing concerns should emerge, this is a welcome bonus. But the first duty is to allow the thinkers studied to speak for themselves. The fact must be faced, however, that no author comes to past thinkers entirely innocent of presuppositions and expectations. The following bald summary (which unavoidably begs all the important questions) of the present writer's general standpoint may alert readers to the points at which allowances need to be made in what follows.

For good or ill our sympathies are broadly with the Reformed theological tradition. We would emphasize the sovereignty of God in creation and redemption; the priority of grace over law; the necessity of holding together thought concerning the incarnation and that concerning the atonement, and of approaching the question of Christ's person via the consideration of his work; and the continuing work of God the Holy Spirit, by whom the Church is *semper reformanda*. We have no fears of biblical criticism as such (however much some of it may make us squirm!); and our special interest has always been to see what happens to the presentation of the Christian gospel when it engages with diverse intellectual systems. In this latter connection we have argued elsewhere that the 'peril of reductionism' is to be avoided if the theologian's trumpet is not to make an uncertain sound—and it can be avoided by the recognition that 'alien' systems may yield both positive and negative *analogies* which the Christian theologian may employ—but we have never felt that in the last resort it is our part neurotically to guard the ark.[5]

Returning to our eight divines: all of them are now neglected, and some are all but forgotten; such is the fashion-prone nature of theology. Without pretending to offer complete biographies of them we have sought to provide sufficient information to provide the context of their thought. But it is for their thought that we principally return to them. Collectively in their different ways they served their age well. Some of the issues over which they fought no longer survive, but others challenge our neglect. These men do more than interest us. At point after point they come positively to our aid.

CHAPTER TWO

John Kennedy of Dingwall (1819–1884): The Old Paths

'To be behind an age that is drifting away from truth and godliness is the only safe, the only dutiful position.'[1] John Kennedy knew where he stood, and why. He followed the old paths out of intellectual and moral conviction; he was quite unimpressed by the avant-garde of his day. Not indeed that his intentions were negative and reactionary: to him there was nothing more positive than the evangel, and no better expression of Christian truth than that enshrined in the Westminster Confession of Faith (1647). None knew better than he that the tide was against him, but that only made him the more determined to preach the truth as he saw it:

> My style of preaching has been described as antiquated, as ignoring the superior enlightenment of these bright times, as making no use of the wondrous results of recent scientific researches, as therefore, though it might have suited in earlier times, now quite behind the age . . . As I judge the position of the age, I desire my preaching to be behind it; for I think that, in these days, the preacher's work is to be calling back his generation to 'the old paths' in which the Lord was found and followed by the fathers. Nor can I discover any difference between the men of this age and those of another as *sinners*, and I cannot, therefore, see how the gospel which suits the one can be unsuitable to the other. And no one can inform me where I can find a *new theme* given by the Lord to preachers, since the Apostles were sent forth to 'preach *the gospel* to every creature'. And I have utterly failed to see how any method of preaching can be right which differs from that of the great Apostle of the Gentiles, who said that . . . he 'determined not to know anything among' those to whom he preached 'save Jesus Christ and Him crucified'.[2]

John Kennedy earns his place in our volume on a number of counts. Born in Ross-shire, he is the most 'Highland' of our divines. Further, he is our only representative of Scotland's many author-ministers who remained in pastoral charge throughout their careers. Above all, Kennedy is our representative of that confessionalism from which our remaining seven theologians, to a greater or lesser extent, departed. As we watch him in controversy we shall be made aware of the issues which were beginning to stir religious convictions in the land of Knox. Kennedy made his voice heard upon the question of union between the Free Church and the United Presbyterian Church; he waxed eloquent concerning Establishment; his views on worship, on biblical criticism, and on revivalism were widely known, if not universally shared. His silence respecting evolutionary and neo-Hegelian thought is explained by the fact that these had not made their fullest popular impact by the time of his death. Strong though his convictions were on the issues of the day, Kennedy did not rush on to public platforms. On the contrary, he stayed away from them until he could do so no longer. The pulpit was his throne, and he has been called 'the greatest preacher of his generation in Scotland.[3]'

Born on 15th August 1819, Kennedy was the fourth son of the Reverend John Kennedy, minister at Killearnan.[4] His mother was Jessie, daughter of Kenneth Mackenzie of Assynt, to which place Kennedy senior had gone as assistant minister about the year 1806.[5] For some twenty-seven years before his death in 1841 Kennedy ministered at Killearnan, where his neighbour was Dr. John Macdonald of Ferintosh, the 'Apostle of the North'. Kennedy and Macdonald were renowned throughout the North, and hundreds attended their communion seasons. Indeed, the presence of more than two thousand communicants was not unknown at Killearnan. In this godly and zealous atmosphere John Kennedy was reared, and it was said in later years that the mantle of Macdonald had fallen upon him. He attended the parish school at Killearnan, and proceeded to Aberdeen University in 1836. He excelled in Mental and Moral Science and in Chemistry, and graduated M.A. in 1840. In the same year he entered the Theological Hall of the Established Church in Aberdeen. The death of his father in 1841 profoundly moved him in the direction of more-than-formal Christian commitment, and also imposed financial constraints upon him. Accordingly, while still a student, he became tutor to the family of Dr. Henderson of Caskieben. On completing his course a year earlier than normal, he was licensed to preach by the Presbytery of Chanonry in September 1843. The Reverend Alexander Stewart of Cromarty conducted Kennedy's oral examination, and set his trial discourses. Kennedy sided with the Disruption, and in February 1844 he was inducted to his first and only charge, that of the Free Church, Dingwall.[6]

The minister at Dingwall had remained with the Establishment, and Macdonald of Ferintosh was instrumental in gathering a Free congregation in the town. To this new cause Kennedy came, and he never felt it right to leave, though he received calls from Dunoon (1853), Australia (1854), Tain (1857), Renfield, Glasgow (1863), and Greenock (1857 and 1872). On 15th April 1848 Kennedy married Mary (1819–1896), daughter of Major Forbes Mackenzie, at Fodderty, Macdonald of Ferintosh officiating. Of their four children a girl and a boy died in infancy, and twin daughters survived. Kennedy's Sundays at Dingwall included the conduct of a Gaelic service, including a lecture and a sermon, from 11.0 a.m. to 1.30 p.m.; an English service at 1.45 p.m.; and alternating Gaelic and English services on Sunday evenings. (As time went by, and more of the young people spoke English only, the evening services were conducted exclusively in that language.) There were, in addition, separate Gaelic and English prayer meetings on weekdays. All of this, together with catechizing and pastoral work (Kennedy was loved by young and old alike), and an ever-increasing load of guest preaching, demanded all that the sturdy frame of Kennedy could give. In 1849 the Free Church manse was built, and it became a place of refuge for all sorts and conditions of men.

In 1869 Kennedy's health began to give cause for concern, and in 1870 he went to London to recuperate. While there he met the celebrated Baptist preacher C. H. Spurgeon, whom he invited to preach at the opening of the new Free Church building in Dingwall. This event took place on 17th May 1870, Spurgeon preaching on John 7:38,39. So large was the crowd that the evening proceedings took place in the open air. In 1873, following a further period of ill health, Kennedy visited Canada and the United States at the expense of his congregation and friends. He attended the meetings of the Evangelical Alliance in New York, was impressed by the prayers of Charles Hodge, and disquieted by a sermon of Henry Ward Beecher which seemed to him to emphasize the Fatherhood of God at the expense of doctrines of atonement and sin. In the same year the University of Aberdeen conferred its D.D. upon him.

In 1881, diabetes having been diagnosed, his friends sent Kennedy to Europe. After his return, and though never fully fit again, he supported those who in 1883 were resisting the introduction of Sunday services on the Highland Railway.[7] Later in the same year he returned to the continent, visiting Rome among other places. He was taken ill on the way home, and died at Bridge of Allan on 18th April 1884. He was buried in the grounds of Dingwall Free Church on 1st May. The Reverend A. M. Bannatyne, Aberdeen, and the Reverend A. R. Munro, Alness, preached in English in the church; Dr. Aird preached in Gaelic in the open air to a company of thousands. The presence of more than sixty ministers testified to the esteem in which this much-travelled man, pre-eminent as a preacher but also distinguished and loved as Clerk to the Presbytery of Dingwall and to the Synod of Ross, was held. 'His death,' wrote C. H. Spurgeon to Mrs. Kennedy, 'was a loss to the Highlands greater than could have befallen by the death of any other hundred men'.

John Kennedy loved paintings, poetry, Shakespeare, the Puritans; but nothing extra-biblical warmed his heart more than the traditions of evangelical Christianity in the Highlands. The first edition of his book *The Days of the Fathers in Ross-Shire* appeared in 1861, and in 1866 he published his work on Macdonald of Ferintosh, *The Apostle of the North*.[8] The saints of the past were staunchly orthodox; they honoured the Bible, and adhered to the Confession; they did not conform to the ways of the world; they had not succumbed to 'uninspired' hymns and organs; they maintained ecclesiastical discipline; their preaching was God-glorifying, and was in the best sense expository and experimental. For all of this Kennedy applauded them. True, 'They may sometimes have erred, in adding from their own consciousness mere occasional accessories to these essentials, forgetting that the experience of a Christian is not always Christian experience . . . but they were surely right in thinking that Scripture takes cognisance of a region lying in between the objective and the practical. They were wont to speak of *faith* and of *experience* and of *practice*'.[9] On the whole they were doughty defenders of that tradition which Kennedy had no intention of forsaking.

Nothing was more characteristic of Highland religion than the communion season during which, over a period of days, services preparatory to communion would be held. Then would come the communion itself, and the season would conclude with a service of thanksgiving. The Dingwall communion seasons were great occasions, at which Kennedy was assisted by Macdonald of Ferintosh until his death in 1849; by Charles Calder Mackintosh of Tain, whose son Robert was to become, in his own word, a 'refugee' from Free Church Calvinism to English Congregationalism;[10] by Dr. Aird of Creich; and by Messrs. Stewart of Cromarty, Sage of Resolis, Macdonald of Uray, and Mackay of Inverness. Wary of over-much introspection in connection with the individual's approach to the Lord's Table, Kennedy nevertheless regarded the Supper as sealing ordinance, not to be lightly viewed. At the same time, he showed the feeblest believer that 'a sincere *desire* after God was as sure a mark of grace as the strong assurance of the man who could say "I know whom I have believed"'.[11]

At the Friday meeting during communion seasons 'the Men' came into their own. Earnest lay Bible students, their duty on that day was to assist intending communicants in the task of self-examination. Kennedy wrote with affection of such 'Men' as John Munro of Kiltearn, Alexander Ross (Alister Og) of Edderton, Hugh Ross of Kilmuir, and Hugh Ross (Hugh Buie) of Alness, Roskeen and Resolis. The best of 'the Men' were wise and balanced—as the preference of Roderick Mackenzie (Rory Phadrig) shows: 'There were three classes of professors in whom it was very difficult for Rory to see any good; those who, elated with spiritual pride, became disaffected to the stated ministry of the Gospel; the affected sentimentalists who made a parade of their feelings; and those who might be suspected of having all their religion in their heads'.[12] Of the 'Men' who were his own contemporaries, Kennedy was most closely associated with Mr. Duff, who served as catechist at Dingwall for twelve years, before proceeding to Strathconon, and thence to Stratherrick.

Kennedy's roll-call of the ministers of Ross-shire includes James Fraser of Alness, a godly man, whose greatest trial seems to have been that 'A cold, unfeeling, bold, unheeding, worldly woman was his wife. Never did her godly husband sit down to a comfortable meal in his own house . . . .'.[13] There was Charles Calder of Ferintosh, Macdonald's predecessor, an amiable and diligent man: 'Careful in his preparations for the pulpit, and much given unto prayer, he was not often seen abroad among his people; the stern call of duty alone drew him from his study'.[14] Above all, there was Lachlan Mackenzie of Lochcarron, whose powerful mind was matched by his sensitive spirit, and whose strikingly illustrated sermons were long remembered. Born at Kilmuir Wester in 1754, Mackenzie died on 20th August 1819. On his tombstone are the words: 'A man, whose simplicity of manners presented a picture of apostolic times; whose heavenliness of mind still spurned the vain objects of time and sense; whose vivid imagination shed a bright lustre on every subject which he handled; and whose holy unction in all his ministrations endeared him to the people of God, and embalmed his memory in their hearts. His praise is in the churches. His parish mourns'.[15]

'The fathers, where are they?' asked Kennedy in plaintive conclusion: '"Woe is me! For I am as when they have gathered the summer fruits, as the grape gleanings of the vintage; there is no cluster to eat: my soul desired the first-ripe fruit"'.[16] This sense of wistful remembrance of the past, and of mourning over the Zion of the present—a sense which could not be obliterated by fellowship with such evangelical stalwarts as Drs. Martin of Edinburgh, Begg of Newington, and Nixon of Montrose— pervades much of Kennedy's thinking, as our consideration of the controversies in which he became engaged will show.

I

The questions of union between the Free and the United Presbyterian Churches and of the disestablishment of the Church of Scotland were the stuff of which pamphlet wars are made. We shall treat each question in turn.

The briefest résumé of the main landmarks in eighteenth and nineteenth century Scottish ecclesiastical history will enable us to see who the United Presbyterians and the Free Churchmen were, and whence they came.[17] In October 1732 Ebenezer Erskine of Stirling preached his celebrated sermon against the patronage system of the Church of Scotland. For this he was reproved by the Perth and Stirling Synod in 1732, and by the General Assembly in 1733. This led to the formation of the first of the Secession Churches. On 5th December 1733 Erskine, James Fisher of Kinclaven, Alexander Moncrieff of Abernethy, and William Wilson of Perth constituted the Associate Presbytery. Their ranks were swollen by the addition of Ralph Erskine of Dunfermline, Thomas Mair of Orwell, and Thomas Nairn of Abbotshall in 1737, and of James Thompson of Burntisland in 1738. The Associate Synod was formed in 1744.

In the following year the Burgher's Oath controversy flared up. The question was, 'Is it lawful, or is it sinful, for a city burgess to take the oath of loyalty to the established religion of the land?' Ebenezer and Ralph Erskine took the position that it was lawful, and for this they were expelled by the Associate Synod. Thereafter their party became known as the Burghers (Associate Synod), to distinguish them from the Anti-Burghers. The latter group became known as the General Associate Synod from 1788, by which time a secession from *their* ranks had occurred as a result of the Lifter Controversy of 1783–5. Here the point at issue was whether or not the bread and wine should be required to be lifted at the communion service. The Reverend D. Smyton of Kilmaurs, who courted disapproval by his manner of prosecuting the affirmative case, was suspended by the Presbytery. His sympathisers included Messrs. Proudfoot of Leith and Hunter of Falkirk. A Presbytery comprising congregations at Portsburgh (Edinburgh), Denny, and Bellevilla (Stranraer) was formed, which subsequently was united with the Associate (Burgher) Synod.

In 1795 the Burghers began to contemplate the Formula of Subscription and the Westminster Confession, from the point of view of clarifying their position on the questions of the power of the civil magistrate and the status of the National Covenant. The year 1799 saw a further parting of the ways, as the 'Old Lights' divided from the 'New'. Each formed a Presbytery, and the former constituted a Synod in 1805. In the following year the same issues split the Anti-Burghers into the General Associate Synod (the New Light Anti-Burghers) and the Constitutional Associate Presbytery (the Old Light Anti-Burghers). The union in 1820 of the majority of New Lights on both sides brought into being the United Associate Synod of the Secession Church. The remnant of New light Anti-Burghers joined their Old Light counterparts in the Associate Synod of Original Seceders (1827). The majority of the Old Light Burghers rejoined the Church of Scotland in 1839, their remnant uniting with the Associate Synod to form the Synod of United Original Seceders (1842). Finally, in 1847 the United Associate Synod joined with the voluntaries of the Relief Church of 1761 (whose leaders, opposed to the intrusion of ministers upon unwilling congregations, were the deposed Thomas Gillespie of Carnock, and Thomas Boston, who had resigned his charge in 1757) to form the United Presbyterian Church.

Meanwhile in 1843 two further ecclesiastical disputes had come to a head. In the first place James Morison of Kilmarnock, deposed by the United Associate Synod in 1841 for his universalism in respect of atonement, was joined by others in establishing the Evangelical Union, the bulk of whose members united with the Scottish Congregational Union in 1896. Still more important for our purposes was the Disruption of 1843, which resulted in the 'coming out' from the Church of Scotland of what its supporters firmly believed to be the truly confessional part. In their opinion they had left a vitiated Establishment, but they still maintained the Establishment principle. They were the Church of Scotland, Free. On the day of the Disruption their leader, Thomas Chalmers, declared 'We are not voluntaries'. Non-intrusion debates had occupied the ecclesiastical arena ever since 1832, and undoubtedly these were a factor in the unhappy situation. But some have drawn attention to the revivals of the early eighteen-forties as providing the impetus towards the reassertion of the old ways in face of a cool, 'Moderate' Establishment.

The Free Church was joined by the majority of the United Original Seceders in 1852, and by the majority of the Reformed Presbyterian Church (formed from the Covenanters in 1743) in 1876. In 1893 the Free Presbyterians, who were implacably opposed to the Declaratory Act of 1892, seceded from the Free Church. The United Free Church was formed in 1900 by the union of the majority of the Free Church with the United Presbyterians—a possibility which, as we shall see, John Kennedy stoutly opposed. The majority of the United Free Church united with the Church of Scotland in 1929.

The revivals of 1859–60 facilitated such a degree of fellowship between some Free Church and United Presbyterian ministers[18] that a climate favourable to union talks began to be detected. Further, the Scots had before them the example of the union in 1861 of their Australian daughter Churches. At the United Presbyterian Synod of 1861, the question of the possibility of union talks with the Free Church was raised, but the matter was shelved until 1863, when a formal approach to the Free Church was made. Thus began an intense debate. Kennedy was among those appointed to the committee charged with discovering how many points of agreement there were between the two Churches, but he very soon found it incumbent upon him to publish 'no surrender' views which could only accord with the status quo. The Free Church, he said, 'was set on a hill, before the eyes of Christendom, to shed light on the twin truths of the Church's right to be established, and the Church's right to be free . . . Is she to desert that position?'[19]

The weight of Free Church opinion was for the view that the two Churches held sufficient in common to enable union talks to proceed. In the absence through indisposition of Dr. Candlish, Robert Rainy moved a successful motion to that effect in the Free Church Assembly on 30th May 1867. Dr. James Begg, the evangelical stalwart, professed to favour union in principle, but nevertheless argued that since in his view the principles of establishment and endowment were enshrined not only in the Protest of 1843, but also in the Bible and the Westminster Confession, these principles could not be surrendered. He sought to have the matter referred to the Church at large—a move which Rainy construed as rank congregationalism, and as insulting to the competence of the Assembly. The Assembly decision having gone against him, Begg submitted a 'protest' and, together with William Nixon, Julius Wood and James Gibson, resigned from the Union Committee. In 1868 Kennedy likewise tendered his resignation from the Committee. It should be noted that fears concerning the doctrine of the atonement fuelled the opposition to union with the United Presbyterians. Kennedy and others felt that the latter body was advocating a far too liberal understanding of the extent of the atonement. He argued his case in his *Man's Relations to God* (1869), to which book we shall shortly return.

With the passage of time, anti-union attitudes hardened, and even some like Dr. Buchanan who were not averse to continuing negotiations began to feel that matters ought not to be rushed. They feared a possible breach within the Free Church. In 1870 the Free Church Assembly sought the opinion of all Presbyteries on the matter, and although the majority of the findings were favourable to union, the 1871 Assembly resolved to leave the union question on the table, but to encourage local co-operation between Free and United Presbyterian congregations, and to advocate the mutual eligibility of the ministers. Had the outcome been otherwise there might well have been a secession; it was known that Dr. Begg had hired a hall to which he and the anti-unionists could proceed if the need arose.

Kennedy's fears were not calmed, however, and he entered the fray against the mutual eligibility scheme. He published *Unionism and its Last Phase* (1873), the text of what he informs us was the first address to his congregation on the union question. He opens with words which find their echo to this day in those evangelicals who are not enamoured of the ecumenism of the British or World Councils of Churches. He grants that disunity cannot but be distasteful to those who would be peacemakers, but he declared that true peacemakers love God, Christ, purity, truth and the Church more than they love peace: 'They love union, but they *love the Church*, and they know that peace and extension won by selling the truth must be weakness and a snare to her'.[20] The divisions of the Church are 'most grievous'; but 'unite them *as they are*, and do you cure the evil? No; you but add dishonesty to division'.[21] He challenges the voluntary position, and upholds the Establishment principle. Against the view that the latter was not the *constitutional* position of the Free Church, he finds that the Claim of Right (1842) and the Protest of 1843 bear witness to the contrary, and that the Westminster Confession is permeated by the Establishment principle.[22] To those who challenge the invocation of the Confession in this connection, Kennedy replies, 'it is because [the principle] is so thoroughly there that you can have no formal statement of it'.[23]

The question of voluntarism had wider ramifications than might at first sight appear. As Kennedy was writing, the education debate was raging, and the voluntaries denied the right of the government to legislate to provide religious instruction in schools. They argued that the civil magistrate's jurisdiction did not extend to the religious education of the young. To Kennedy this was tantamount to practical atheism: it would, he thought, preclude all legislation concerning the Lord's Day—indeed, it would preclude all legislation based upon the moral law of God. The introduction of organs into United Presbyterian churches gave Kennedy further cause for concern, and when the United Presbyterians began to contemplate the passing of a Declaratory Act which would adjust their position *vis-à-vis* the Confession, Kennedy picked up his pen once more. He felt that the adoption of the Declaratory Statement would mean that the 'distinctive Calvinism' of the Westminster Confession would be 'utterly repudiated' by the United Presbyterian Church, and that thereafter United Presbyterian subscribers to the Confession would be allowed to 'believe as much or as little of it as they are disposed'.[24] He was especially exercised by articles V and VI of the Statement, which he read as expressing the view that voluntarism was to be a term of communion.[25] External opposition notwithstanding, the United Presbyterian Church passed its Declaratory Act in 1879.

II

Whereas the principle of Establishment caused anxiety to some Free Churchmen with regard to the United Presbyterian Church, the question of disestablishment soon began to disturb them with regard to the Church of Scotland. The matter was raised by the latter body. Ever since the Disruption care had been taken to ensure that congregations would approve of the ministers settled over them, and abuses of patronage became more and more infrequent. In 1869 the Established Church petitioned both Houses of Parliament for the removal of patronage. The Moderator of the General Assembly, Dr. Norman Macleod, led a deputation to Mr. Gladstone, who was shrewd enough to see that 'You have borrowed clothes which were fabricated some twenty-five years ago by other brethren of yours for which they suffered, and, most undoubtedly, justice requires that in any change, I should consult the original donors.'[26]

The Patronage Act was eventually passed in 1874, and once again a pamphlet war broke out. Alexander Taylor Innes wrote *The Church of Scotland Crisis 1843 and 1874: and the Duke of Argyll* (1874), and the Duke responded in the same year with *The Patronage Act All That Was Asked in 1843*. It must be said that the Duke here minimises the point that the Free Churchmen of 1843 had not appealed only against abuses of patronage; they had maintained the Establishment principle, and had questioned the purity of the existing Establishment. Now, however, some Free Churchmen, including Rainy, were found saying that the *way* in which the civil magistrate functioned might well vary from time to time, according to circumstances; that in any case the residual, post-1843 Establishment was not the true Establishment on his fellow Churchmen's own admission; and therefore that to press for the disestablishment of *that* body was neither to be disloyal to the Free Church testimony, nor to capitulate to voluntarism. Many were persuaded by Rainy's case, and much ink was spilled by either side. Thus, for example, the Reverend David Ogilvy of Motherwell argued that 'Disestablishment is the necessary sequel of the Disruption, without which the history of the Free Church is an unfinished drama'.[27] On the other hand, Dr. John Adam argued that a return to the Established Church would not make for increasingly effective Christian witness, and would entail the breaking of happy links already forged with the United Presbyterians.[28] Dr. Robert Buchanan, who had supported mutual eligibility as between Free Church and United Presbyterian ministers, was likewise opposed to reunion with the Church of Scotland.[29] Some of those who supported reunion moves recalled the words of Chalmers: 'We quit a vitiated Establishment, but would rejoice in returning to a pure one'; but many felt that by itself the passing of the Patronage Act had not provided that 'independent jurisdiction in things ecclesiastical' for which Chalmers also appealed. Kennedy took the latter view, and his published contribution at this juncture was *The Distinctive Principles and Present Position and Duty of the Free Church* (1875). He here upheld the confessional position on the civil magistrate, maintained the Establishment principle, and argued against union both with the voluntaries and with the existing Establishment: 'We hate the Moderatism that once gave us a stone instead of bread, and oppression instead of liberty, and the Voluntaryism that has in it the blood of France and the taint of Atheism'.[30] In 1876 Kennedy's pamphlets, *The Constitution of the Church of Scotland and Her Relations to Other Presbyterian Churches* and *A Letter to the Members of the Free Church in the Highlands* were published in further prosecution of his case.

In 1877 the General Assembly of the Free Church received an overwhelming majority of resolutions from synods and presbyteries in favour of disestablishment. Begg opposed the idea, while Rainy argued that the *existing* Establishment was against the Claim of Right and the Protest of 1843. He contended that disestablishment would pave the way to an improved situation. Rainy won the day over Begg by 460 votes to 78, and Begg dissented from the Assembly's judgement. At the following Assembly Kennedy seconded Begg's constitutionalist motion, and urged the Assembly not to seek to kill the Establishment, but to cure it, so that it could become the Church of Scotland, free. The pro-disestablishment party charged their opponents with being unrepresentative of the Free Church as it now was, and to this charge Kennedy replied in *A Plea in Self-Defence addressed to the Leaders of the Disestablishment Party in the Free Church* (1878). He further published two lectures under the title *The Establishment Principle; and the Disestablishment Movement*. In the conclusion of the first lecture he summed up his attitude to the Establishment principle thus:

> It is not a mere phrase. It is a great and important reality. It lies at the basis of a Church's right to be free, as well as at the basis of her right to be acknowledged and aided by the State. It rests on the authority, and

bears on the honour, of Christ. It is implied in all that is taught in
scripture regarding the authority of Him who is Governor among the
nations, and King in Zion. The practical acknowledgement of it is
indispensable to a nation's security and welfare. And it is part of our
Church's distinctive testimony, which, without breach of vow, and a
falsifying of profession, cannot be abandoned.[31]

In his second lecture Kennedy recalled a charge once levelled at him that
since he had no personal experience of the Disruption, his attachment to
Disruption principles was inexplicable:

> But I did know something of trial in that sifting time. I was then, on
> the eve of license, living in a manse, which was my brother's, on whose
> kindness I was quite dependent, and which, along with my mother and
> my sisters, I had to abandon. I had to lock the door of the old manse,
> which had been the place of my birth and the home of my boyhood,
> with my weeping mother leaning on my arm, and to accompany her to
> a house, which had for years been untenanted except by birds, with all
> its windows broken, and its floors covered with a thick coating of
> clotted dust, with no prospect before us but pinching poverty during
> the remainder of our days on earth. I had that much experience of a
> Disruption trial . . . [and] it is because the brand, then burnt into my
> heart, abides there still—because I am a Free Churchman and will be
> nothing else—I cannot but protest, with all my heart, against the
> flagrant inconsistency of this disestablishment movement.[32]

The 1879 Assembly resolved to take no action on the disestablishment
question, the fear of the leadership being that further pressure on this
front would drive some Free Churchmen into the voluntary position. But
a year later Rainy was found urging the Assembly to vigorous pursuit of
the disestablishment goal. Kennedy maintained his opposition. In 1882
he was instrumental in securing over eighty thousand signatures on an
anti-disestablishment petition addressed to Parliament, and in the same
year there appeared his *The Disestablishment Movement in the Free Church*.
The rescinding of the Patronage Act, he said, improvement though it
was, did not make the present Establishment a pure Church. On the
contrary, 'the North had the best days it ever had . . . in connection with
the Established Church, when its constitution was far more faulty than
that of the Establishment now is . . . At present the movement of that
church is downwards.'[33] Here we approach the heart of the matter, which
Kennedy argued at all levels. Thus we find him saying that 'from
observation we know that there are in the ministry of the Establishment
ecclesiastical apes, given to mimicry of the English clergy, who are
seemingly quite as innocent of common sense as they are void of grace'.[34]

More serious were Kennedy's objections on liturgical, biblical and doctrinal grounds. We shall consider each area of difficulty in turn, but before becoming enmeshed in theology we should note that by 1886 the divisions within the Free Church were so serious—distinct parties having arisen around Rainy and the successors of Begg respectively[35]—that the disestablishment question could only be left on the table.

In 1864 and 1872 Kennedy came to the fore against the introduction of 'uninspired' hymns into Free Church worship; and in 1883 he presented the General Assembly with a petition signed by 53,000 people, and published a pamphlet, *The Introduction of Instrumental Music into the Worship of the Free Church*. He contended that instrumental music was unscriptural, that hymn singing in moderation was unscriptural, and, in excess (as in revivalism), irrational; and that hymns made for indefiniteness of doctrine.[36] 'Nothing *in* worship is lawful,' he wrote, 'which is "not appointed in the Word"'. Thus, 'we know from the Scripture directory that preaching was the main service in assemblies for public worship. We know also, that spoken, not read, prayers, accompanied the preaching of the Word. We know that the fruit of the lips, unaccompanied by sounds from musical instruments, was the offering prescribed as the service of praise. We know, besides, how the sacraments are directed to be administered. To that rule the Church is bound to adhere'.[37] As for organs, the fact that the United Presbyterians had left the decision concerning the introduction of organs to individual congregations—'a thoroughly unpresbyterian proceeding'—and that one United Presbyterian minister only had seceded from his Church rather than tolerate organs, did nothing to endear that communion to Dr. Kennedy: 'It does rouse one's indignation to hear those who are clamouring for organs called the successors or followers of the Erskines. The first organ peal that awakes an echo in a U.P. Church shall sound, in the ears of any in whom the spirit of the Erskines still survives, as a wail over the grave in which the last relics of their labours have been buried out of sight'.[38]

We may note in passing that many other 'novelties' failed to commend themselves to Kennedy. Looking back from 1879 to the period fifty years earlier he found little to encourage him. There were then no Sabbath schools, now there are; but 'If things were as they ought to be—if all families had a place within the pale of the Church, and if parents were careful and qualified to give scriptural instruction to their children—the gathering of children into a Sabbath school would be quite unnecessary'.[39] As it is, such gatherings become a substitute for the attendance of children at public worship, and encourage parents to deposit their own responsibilities upon the Sabbath school teachers. Again, Christian associations for specific age and sex groups, or for specific purposes, displeased Kennedy as tending towards the fragmentation of the Church, which ought to be an association of families. As for soirées, they 'are becoming an unmitigated nuisance. This sort of thing began in treats for children as inducements to attend, and as rewards for attending, the Sabbath school. But it did not stop there. We now have congregational soirées, at which an annual opportunity is taken of parading the work done, and the money raised, during the past year; flattering speeches are exchanged by those who take kindly to being licked all over with an oily tongue, and a great deal of vapid sentiment is mixed up with exaggerated statements as to success, seasoned with bits of drollery, and interspersed with sensational music. The attempt to sanctify all this by the Word and by prayer is successful only as a sacrilege'.[40] The conversion-mongering of some lay evangelists and the 'Plymouthism' of some religious conventions only added to Kennedy's sense that the foundations were being undermined.

There was not even the cold comfort that the enemy was entirely without. There were breaches in the walls, and some inside were little better than subversives. This was especially the case in connection with the authority of the Bible. Indeed, as far as the 'higher criticism' of the scriptures was concerned, the irony was that this scorpion had been nurtured within the bosom of the Free Church itself. Such, at any rate, was Kennedy's reading of the situation, though, of course, other Free Churchmen took a different view. Thus for example to some, Dr. A. B. Davidson of New (Free Church) College, Edinburgh was responsible for letting some light into biblical studies; to others he was the one who had begun to dispense the poison which made men insensitive to the authority of the Word. Davidson's most famous pupil, William Robertson Smith, was appointed to the Chair of Hebrew and Old Testament Criticism at the Aberdeen College in 1870. While there he wrote on 'Hebrew Language and Literature' for the *Encyclopaedia Britannica* (9th edition). In this article he committed himself to Wellhausen's documentary hypothesis, to the dismay of his more conservative fellow churchmen. Smith's actions were to be considered by the Assembly of 1877, and in May of that year Kennedy wrote, 'I know not what is before us at this Assembly beyond that the Word of God is to be on its trial; a traitor lurking in every breast that will be on the bench, and the power of hell backing all those who would cast dishonour on the inspired Word of God. All I know assuredly about myself is, that I carry the traitor with me in my own bosom. But the Lord is over all'.[41] In the event the Assembly suspended Smith from teaching by one vote, on a resolution proposed by Andrew A. Bonar.

After further discussion Smith was removed from his Chair by the Assembly of 1881, though he was not deposed from the ministry. He proceeded to Cambridge, where his reputation as an orientalist continued to grow, until his early death in 1894.[42]Kennedy stoutly supported Begg in his advocacy of the case against Smith, and published his own views in *A Purteeklar Acoont o' the Last Assembly, by Wan o' the Hielan' Host* (1881).

On the question of advanced biblical scholarship Kennedy found himself in the unusual position of agreeing with Carlyle—by now no lover of organized religion—who asked, 'Have my countrymen's heads become turnips when they think that they can hold the premisses of German unbelief and draw the conclusions of Scottish Evangelical Orthodoxy?'[43] For his part Kennedy lamented that 'not a few of the latest accessions to the ministry must have come to their office with rather unsettled beliefs, and with more respect for the speculations of errant Germans, than for the doctrines of the Confession of Faith, and for the accredited systems of Calvinistic theology'.[44] He found the protracted nature of the Smith case ominous: 'In the first days of the Free Church, its course would have been a very short one; and if dealt with by ecclesiastics, who combined a fervent love of the Bible with firmness and wisdom, it would, at any time and in any place, have been very easily disposed of'.[45] If the United Presbyterians, encouraged by their leader Dr. Ferguson, were repudiating the Confession, the Free Church was weakening the concept of biblical authority. Moreover, the respective positions had something in common: 'It is on the wastes of rationalism they both have entered, though not through the same opening in the fence—the one misshaping the system of doctrine, derived from the Bible, according to the craving of reason unrenewed and benighted, the other degrading the Word of God to a position, in which it shall cease to scare proud men from the mad ambition of being uncontrolled in their beliefs by the will of the Most High'.[46] Kennedy's own view, defended in *The Doctrine of Inspiration in the Confession of Faith*, was that the Confession taught verbal, plenary inspiration because that is what the Bible teaches: 'The Confession does not teach that there is no fixed objective standard of doctrine. Its teaching is to the effect that the written Word in which the Spirit speaks is the one authoritative and unchanging standard, and that the Spirit is the Supreme Judge, who delivers His verdicts in the words of Scripture . . . There can be no more objectless institution in the world than a Church that . . . cares not to defend the oracles of God committed to her keeping'.[47] No enemy of reason as such, Kennedy 'held that the highest flights of reason ought to be submitted in the last resort to the light of revelation—even when reason is admittedly enlightened by the Spirit of God. This is simply to bring the whole man into submission to the will and Word of Christ'.[48]

III

Many of the points we have already noted were repeated by Kennedy in his critique of revivalism. He was against hymns, emotionalism, enquiry room methods—not to mention those compromises of the truth which he was sure were involved when ministers of the Free Church fraternized on public platforms with men of other denominations. The unnamed target of his pamphlet *Hyper-Evangelism 'Another Gospel' Though a Mighty Power* (1874) was the American evangelist Dwight L. Moody, whose British campaign of 1872–5 had captured the headlines. It must be admitted that Kennedy's critique was not of the fairest kind. He had stood entirely aloof from Moody's meetings; he did not name Moody, or provide chapter and verse for the opinions he was ascribing to him; and he took a much harsher view of revivalist excesses that he had taken of some of the more extraordinary phenomena associated with the Ross-shire religion of yesteryear. For all of these reasons, and others, he was criticized by Dr. Horatius Bonar.[49] Bonar also defended those who sympathized with the revival from Kennedy's theological attacks upon them; and here we come to the heart of the matter. Kennedy was not concerned with means and methods alone. Above all he was exercised by what he regarded as impure doctrine.

Kennedy was certain that truly Christian proclamation would have as its primary objective the manifestation of the divine glory. There is far more to preaching than the 'unfolding of a scheme of salvation adapted to man's convenience'. Justice must be done to God's character and claims as lawgiver and judge, as well as to his sovereign power in the dispensation of his grace. Hearers must be shown how, in the light of the doctrine of the Cross, God is glorified in the salvation of a believing sinner; and those who profess to believe must be cautioned against antinomianism.[50] In elaboration of these points Kennedy argues that a free gospel is not one that suits the sinner's disposition: it is one that meets his real needs, as well as honouring the divine nature. Neither our works nor our faith save us; all is of God's grace. To suggest that we are saved by believing is to place belief on a par with other works; it is to fall into legalism. Further, it leaves very little for the Holy Spirit to do—that is, it bypasses the need of regeneration, something which natural, sinful man can never do. Again, faith in the substitutionary arrangement which makes salvation possible must not be placed above faith in the One who glorified God, and in whom alone we have redemption: 'A true sense of peace with God there cannot be, unless a sinner, assured that God was glorified by Him who died on the cross, can, with reverence of His glorious name, approach Him in the right of the crucified and exalted Jesus, having hope of acceptance in His sight'.[51] Having found peace with God the believer's life should bear fruit. But now works will be the *evidence* of faith.[52]

On the question of the offer of the gospel Kennedy was quite clear. Among the elements of that preaching which in times past God blessed was 'A clear, unhesitating proclamation of the gospel call to every sinner, as giving him a warrant to come for a free and full salvation to Christ, and assuring him that every coming sinner shall be saved, and leaving all excuseless who refuse to come.'[53] The introduction to Kennedy's sermon on Isaiah 45:22 provides an example of Kennedy's actual practice in this matter. Having announced the text 'Look unto me, and be ye saved', Kennedy said, 'You cannot possibly place yourself outside the range of this authoritative command unless you can prove, either that you are a fallen spirit or that you are beyond the confines of the earth. You cannot prove the former, for you are now in the flesh, a human being having soul and body; and it is equally futile to attempt to provide the latter, for you at this moment occupy a portion of the earth where this congregation is now assembled.'[54] Again, Kennedy applauded Macdonald of Ferintosh for the free way in which he offered the gospel:

> While never losing sight of God's sovereignty in dispensing his grace, he never hesitated to proclaim his good will to all. He believed on the same authority the electiveness of God's covenant purposes, and the indiscriminateness of his gospel calls . . . It is strange that those who believe the doctrine of election and who preach it, and who also believe, and in their teaching insist on, the necessity of regeneration in order to faith, should be deemed incapable of honestly, heartily and hopefully inviting sinners, in the Lord's name, to Christ. Surely it is the man, who has made his election sure, and who, in the light of that doctrine, sees his salvation secured by the immutable purpose of Jehovah, who feels himself, above all others, under obligation to declare the will of God, whatever it may be; who, above all others, regards salvation as worth the offering and worth the having . . .[55]

Kennedy offered Christ to all comers. He did not encourage undue introspection; he did not suggest that the gospel was only for 'sensible sinners'; and he was no antinomian. A High Calvinist he was; a Hyper-

Calvinist he was not.[56] As he reflected on much of the preaching of his day, Kennedy lamented that

> Hazy utterances as to objective truth, and strong and one-sided enforcements of the practical, in general cover the whole area of the teaching. If there be a description of Christian exercise given, it is the unattainable that is set forth, and conformity to that is enforced in a legal spirit. It would be difficult to tell whither men with broken credit, and with broken hearts, could go to find what would meet their cases and remove their fears. Men with whole skins might be trained, under the staple preaching of the times to perfectionist dreamings, and to zealous bustle in proselytising work; but, for aid in godly living and in preparation for heaven, there is but little that can be expected to avail.[57]

The points just made are resumed in Kennedy's most sustained and least controversial piece of theological writing, *Man's Relations to God Traced in the Light of 'The Present Truth'* (1869). A brief summary of this now scarce book will expose the kernel of Kennedy's theology. He begins by speaking of 'Man, as created, in relation to God'. God is the omnipotent creator; man is his creature. Man belongs to, and lives in, God. Not indeed that any 'pantheist haze must be allowed to lie over the relation in which, as dependant creatures, we stand to Him who made us'. Man is not a mere creature; he is rational and, sadly, he is sinful. Man knows God's revealed law, and is judged by it. 'I cannot but be overawed by the wrath of such a Judge', says Kennedy, 'but were He less rigorous I could not revere Him'. In reaction against those who were inclining to an over-sentimentalized understanding of the Fatherhood of God, Kennedy denies that God is Father by virtue of the fact of creation: 'The relation of fatherhood would impose conditions which cannot consist with the free exercise of God's sovereignty'. The point he here seeks to safeguard is that if God saves, it is because he wills to do so; he does not save because he can do no other. The idea that God is the father of fallen man is to him 'revolting'. Men become sons of God by the adoption of grace, and this is the work of the Holy Spirit who 'makes them sons by creating them anew in the image of God'.

The chapter on 'Man, as fallen, in relation to God' opens somewhat ambiguously, '*All* the image of God is effaced from the soul of fallen man', whereas on the other hand there is still some light: there is still man's conscience. But whence comes this, and how could the totally (i.e. absolutely) depraved sinner recognize them? Kennedy in fact appears to think that sin affects every part of man's life, and not that man is absolutely apart from God. Be that as it may, man is a covenant breaker, and by refusing perfect obedience to God he has, in Adam, broken the covenant of works and forfeited life. But a new relationship between God and his elect has been constituted by the covenant of grace, which builds upon, but does not annul, the covenant of works. Christ is the federal Head of the elect; he is not 'the Brother of the sons of Adam, but of the "seed of Abraham"'.

Turning next to 'Man, as evangelized, in relation to God', Kennedy argues that the gospel is addressed to 'children of wrath' whose proper relation to God cannot be restored by a revelation of grace, but only by a work of grace. The gospel is to be proclaimed to all, but the preacher may not declare that God loves all who hear it: he loves his elect alone. We are not assured of the love of God until we are in Christ, and to bring us to him is the Spirit's work. 'It is "Christ crucified" that is preached in the gospel . . . in His death He finished a work by which God's justice was satisfied, His law magnified, and His name glorified on earth. By His death he sealed the everlasting covenant of grace, and procured a right to all its blessings for those whom the Father gave him.' From this anchorage Kennedy criticizes those who espouse the double reference theory of the atonement, namely, the view that the virtue of what Christ did on the Cross is sufficient for all, but that in fact the elect alone benefit from it. Kennedy finds this position to be inconsistent, unscriptural and opposed to the Westminster Confession. He is especially suspicious of the underlying motive of the theory in so far as 'To tell men that Christ died for all, and that this is the basis on which the call is founded, is to quit hold of all that is distinctive in Calvinism in order to command the sympathies of a heart unrenewed . . . If men believe that Christ died for many whose sin He did not bear, whose surety He was not, and whose redemption He did not purchase, they are adrift on a current which may carry them down to Socinianism . . . How sad it is to hear men, sworn to Calvinism, declare that without this theft from the Arminian stores they could not preach the gospel at all!' In a nutshell, 'Our relation to the gospel is such, that it cannot be ours till we are in Christ through faith; that we are required by God to accept of it in Him; and that it shall infallibly be ours if we believe in His name'.

Kennedy's concluding chapter is entitled, 'Man, as in Christ, in relation to God'. All who are in Christ have been born again. 'Regeneration precedes and produces faith.' The Spirit dwells in the believer, and thus God is glorified, the saint is sanctified, and Satan is mortified. True Christians are justified: 'the righteousness wrought out by Christ, their Surety for them, has been imputed to them by God'. They are now free, though it is a narrow path they must walk between legalism on the one hand, and antinomianism on the other. By the act of adoption a new relationship is made as between the believer and God: 'Regeneration makes the loved one a living soul; justification removes all that intercepts him from the grace of God; adoption secures to him the place and privileges of a child of God; the Spirit of adoption introduces him in gospel light through Christ to his Heavenly Father, and develops in him the disposition of a child; and the Holy Spirit, by His work of sanctification, makes him what his Father would have him to be.' The believer's sonship is not, however, the same as that of Christ. He is Son *by right*; Christians are sons *by adoption*. Such sons may have trials here below, but they are eternally secure; and even now they enjoy 'the foretastes of such rest and happiness at last, as shall leave to the child no more to desire, and to the Father no more to bestow'.[58]

No doubt much might be said in criticism of Kennedy's position as here summarized. That there are difficulties attaching to the federal theology cannot be denied: were there two covenants, or one only? Again, may we not hold that God *is* Father of all by virtue of creation, but that not all are true sons?[59] Is it not possible that Kennedy's doctrine of the decrees exercises too much control over his doctrine of God's fatherhood? But our main purpose has been to allow Kennedy to speak for himself, and to make plain the traditional confessional stance from which those to be treated in subsequent chapters were, to a greater or lesser extent, to depart. We hope too that it has become plain, against caricatures of Calvinism, that Kennedy's practical and experimental interests were strong. In this he stood in the line of the best of the Puritans. Dry-as-dust systematics had no greater appeal to him than did revivalist emotionalism. He struck a balance, but it was a balance grounded in the Bible and guarded by the Confession. He held to the eternal Sonship of Christ,[60] and to particular redemption.[61] It must be said that at times his polemicist enthusiasm carries him away, and leads him to overstate his case. It is, for example, difficult to reconcile Kennedy's statement to the effect that the United Presbyterians bring 'the name of God into disrespect' because their Statement leads us to think that 'God loves us while we are yet in our sins, and away from Christ'[62] with Paul's declaration that 'God shows his love towards us in that while we were yet sinners Christ died for us'.[63] We may wholeheartedly agree, however, that 'the faith that is unto salvation can only be produced by the quickening Spirit of the Lord'.[64] Once quickened and sealed, the believer is with Christ for eternity.[65] Meanwhile, 'The privileges of the Church on earth are their's [*sic*]. There they lead a colonial life, under the law, and under the King of glory, till they are prepared for the kingdom of glory, for that is already their's. They are heirs of God and joint heirs with Christ already'.[66] The message of Kennedy and of others like him was summed up thus by a writer in *The British Weekly* of 1st June 1888:

> That was what the Highland preachers meant by dwelling on election and Divine sovereignty. *The seeking was all on Thy side.* It was inconceivable that man could choose God; God must choose man. The practical test of the doctrine was, 'Did it exalt God and abase man?' Hence, no stress was laid on any merit in man. Salvation was all of grace. The elect in whom Christ still survives lived through burdened and shadowed years striving against sin. The law in the members was the crook in the lot only to be cured by death. Assurance of God's love was a privilege for the few, and by them not to be vaunted of. Jaunty, superficial, easy-going religion was of no account at all.[67]

IV

When John Kennedy read the signs of the times, he read danger.[68] Against these dangers he reacted by word and pamphlet. He was, however unwillingly, a polemicist. But we hope that we have shown that he was so much more besides. His overriding intention was to proclaim the truth *positively* and thereby to glorify God. However much he may, on occasion, have over-played his hand, or inadequately guarded his flanks, we can see—even from the printed page—why some called him *the* preacher of his generation. The following passage on the Father's drawing (John 6:44) is not untypical of Kennedy at his best:

> *The Father's Drawing.* This is, and must be *gracious, attracting,* and *effectual* . . . *Gracious,* beyond all conception, must be the drawing which brings into a relation of everlasting union that sinner to His glorious Son . . . And it is drawing by *attraction.* He who comes is *'made willing'* in a day of power . . . There is no *dragging* though there is drawing. It is *attraction,* not *compulsion,* that overcomes the sinner, into submission, and wins his acquiescence in the terms of the gospel. The drawing is and must be *effectual.* No power can successfully resist the drawing of the Father . . . The wildest rebel He can subdue, the most ignorant He can enlighten, the most hostile He can make friendly, the most oppressed He can deliver, the man who has been longest 'dead in trespasses and sins' He can quicken 'together with Christ', and the most timid He can 'persuade and enable' to embrace Jesus Christ as He is freely offered to us in the gospel.[69]

These may be the cadences of yesteryear; but this is not 'crude' or 'harsh' Calvinism. It is more than the human face of Calvinism. It is basic Christianity, and as such there are many who can gratefully say 'Amen' to it.

CHAPTER THREE

Robert Flint (1838–1910):
Theism and Theology in Tension

'A great man's failures teach more than a little man's successes.' So wrote
F. D. Maurice of Francis Bacon,[1] and we find it appropriate to apply the
judgement to Robert Flint,[2] whose *Theism* (1877) comprises the Baird
Lectures delivered at Glasgow, St. Andrews and Edinburgh in the spring
of 1876. Flint admits of no straightforward classification, either in respect
of his thought or of his influence during his lifetime. On the one hand, he
was keenly interested in the evolutionary and scientific thought of his day,
while on the other hand he owed his methodology in large part to the
eighteenth century. Again, although *Theism* passed through eleven
editions between 1877 and 1905, it received but the briefest notice in
Mind,[3] a journal to which from its first issue in January 1876 Flint
contributed articles and reviews. In a word, Flint seems to have been
respected—even admired—by his philosophical contemporaries, but not
followed by them. He swam against the fashionable idealism of his day,
adopting a stance which some, no doubt, deemed to be *passé*. (Philosophy
being the fashion-prone subject it is, Flint is not necessarily the worse for
that). Nevertheless, his impact upon many thoughtful churchmen who
rejoiced at the way in which Flint enlisted the aid of science in *defence* of
the faith was considerable.

To a greater degree than any of the other divines here under review,
Flint *was* his books and sermons. A devoted (and unmarried) scholar, he
was not at all an ecclesiastical 'assembly man', and his close friends and his
extra-curricular activities were few. Born the son of a farm overseer on
14th March 1838, he went to school at Moffat, and thence to Glasgow
University, where like some others in his day he excelled without
graduating. After serving as a lay missionary in Glasgow, and as assistant
to Norman MacLeod the younger at The Barony Church, Flint ministered
at the East Church Aberdeen (1859–62). From 1862–64 he was minister
of Kilconquhar, Fife. He held the Chair of Moral Philosophy at St.
Andrews (T. H. Green being among other candidates for the post) from

1864–76, and was Professor of Divinity at Edinburgh from 1876–1903. He lectured on the Stone and Croall foundations, and was appointed to the Baird Lectureship in February 1874.

Although we shall here concentrate upon the first set of Baird Lectures, cautioning ourselves that they were but a part of Flint's effort in natural theology which also included the second set of Baird Lectures, *Anti-Theistic Theories* (1879), and the Croall Lectures on *Agnosticism* (1903), we may not fail to note his monograph on *Vico* (1884) and his impressive works, *The Philosophy of History in France and Germany* (1874) and the more comprehensive *History of the Philosophy of History* (1893). Flint died on 25th November 1910.

I

According to his biographer Flint opened the first course of Baird Lectures dramatically with the question, 'Is there a God, or is there not a God?'[4] The first sentence of *Theism* reads, 'Is belief in God a reasonable belief, or is it not?'[5] Flint intends to answer both questions affirmatively. He is convinced that feeling is incompetent to provide firm grounds for religious belief: *knowledge* of religion's object alone will suffice. But if there be no God, religion is a delusion or a mental disease; and if believers do not investigate the theistic question they will not *establish* their right to their beliefs (He does not advance the unwholesomely elitist view that unless all believers conduct personal theistic investigations they have no right to their beliefs).

Undoubtedly the books of the Bible do not set out to *prove* God's existence, they rather assume it; but they do 'refer us to the world and our own hearts for the means and materials of proof'.[6]

The moral no less than the ontological implications of the theistic question are of great importance, for if an almighty, all-wise, all-holy God exists, it is a great misfortune if men do not know him, and a serious moral fault if they do not wish to know him. Further, there is the question which lies behind all scientific enquiry: 'Does the world explain itself?' To this question theism returns a negative answer. The convergence of the ontological, moral and scientific questions brings Flint to his definition of theism: 'Theism is the doctrine that the universe owes its existence, and continuance in existence, to the reason and will of a self-existent Being, who is infinitely powerful, wise, and good'.[7] The term 'theism' is thus not synonomous with 'religion', and may be properly applied only to Judaism, Christianity and Islam. Indeed, in our society we owe the greater part of our theism to Christianity; consequently the independence which natural religion currently claims from revealed religion is the independence 'of one who has grown ashamed of his origin'.[8] Flint grants that a purely rational philosophy cannot demonstratively prove the truth of the theistic claim, but it can do two very important things: it can adduce arguments in its favour, and it can counter polytheism. In *Theism* the former task is attempted, and Flint endorses Whately's view that 'the only way to avoid credulity and incredulity . . . is to listen to, and yield to the best evidence, and to believe and disbelieve on good grounds'.[9]

Before we pronounce upon the worth of any particular religion, whether theistic or not, we must, says Flint, have some idea of what religion itself is. His suggestion, tentatively expressed, is that 'religion is man's belief in a being or beings, mightier than himself and inaccessible to his senses, but not indifferent to his sentiments and actions, with the feelings and practices which flow from such a belief'.[10] A perfect religion is one which 'presents an object of worship capable of eliciting the entire devotion of the worshipper's nature, and at the same time of ennobling, enlarging, refining, and satisfying that nature'.[11] As far as Flint is concerned reason cannot rest in polytheism, for its impetus is ever to reduce things to a unity and to serve but one master. Nor will pantheism satisfy, for there the personality of the divine is denied, and communion is replaced by absorption. Christian theism alone gives a true representation of God, and in Christianity alone do we find the means whereby the sinner may enjoy fellowship with the holy God. Our religious understanding is open to development, but genuine progress will be that which is consonant with the Bible's final revelation. By contrast, Comte's deification of humanity and Strauss's deification of the universe leave us *lower* than they found us. These preliminaries completed, Flint comes to his main argument.

By 'proofs of God's existence' Flint means the grounds of our belief, and he is persuaded that a religion without such grounds is a poor thing indeed. In the wake of the Kantian onslaught upon the traditional proofs, a major work of rehabilitation requires to be performed, and Flint cannot understand those theologians who *rejoice* to see the old proofs demolished because, so they say, a place is then made for faith. After all, 'The proofs of God's existence must be, in fact, simply His own manifestations . . . They can neither be, properly speaking, our reasonings, nor our analyses of the principles involved in our reasonings'.[12] What men do is to draw the theistic inference from God's multifarious manifestations of himself in instances of causation, intelligence and righteousness. Apart from these manifestations we should have no basis for the theistic conclusion; and each of the areas within which God manifests himself provides the starting-point for one or more of the theistic arguments. The chief service which the speculative reason affords to religion is that it prevents the latter from becoming a 'degrading anthropomorphism'.[13] Although the theistic inference may be analysed into its components it is in itself synthetic. The mind is capable of embracing its principles in a single act. Thus 'The various theistic arguments are, in a word, but stages in a single rational process, but parts of one comprehensive argument'.[14]

The term 'inference' is of crucial importance to Flint. We have no a priori knowledge of God—or of our friends either, for that matter.[15] But the evidence for both friends and God is clear. While 'worldliness and prejudice and sin may blind the soul'[16] to the facts which demand the theistic conclusion, it remains the case that 'our entire spiritual being is constituted for the apprehension of God in and through His works'.[17] To rest upon intuition and to shun inferential argument is, Flint avers, 'the merest dogmatism'.[18] He does not deny that the apprehension of God involves intuition, but the apprehension itself is so readily analysable into simpler elements that we may be quite certain that it is not itself an intuition. The point against the evidential value of feeling is reiterated, and the suggestion that there can be such a thing as a self-authenticating belief is trounced—we can believe only what we know, or think we know. Not indeed that we can ever know completely. Man is both like and unlike God. He is sufficiently like God to know him, but unlike him in not possessing perfect knowledge: 'We can *apprehend* certain attributes of God, but we can *comprehend*, or fully grasp, or definitely image, not one of them . . . Man is made in the image of God, but he is not the measure of God'.[19]

His foundations laid, Flint proceeds to discuss the arguments for God's existence, turning first to the cosmological way. He argues that contemporary science makes it easier rather than harder to show that 'nature is but the name for a effect whose cause is God'.[20] How did the universe come to be as it is? he asks. 'Did the atoms take counsel together and devise a common plan and work it out?'[21] Clearly, they did not. As for those who have posited an infinite regress of causes rather than a single cause, Flint, by means of rhetoric rather than of solid argument, contends that they 'have all, without a single exception, allowed themselves to be led by [the principle of causality] to a first cause and not to an eternal succession of causes. They have all believed what they say they ought to have disbelieved . . .'[22] Observation and reason combine to require one uncaused cause of infinite power, which is both transcendent over the universe and immanent within it, and which is a rational will.

The conviction that 'The complex and harmonious constitution of the universe is the expression of a Divine Idea, of a Creative Reason'[23] is next explored by means of a detailed discussion and defence of the argument from order. The manifestation of order, we are assured, provides ground for belief in a Supreme Mind; and such a mind is required if mathematical truths, which are laws of the physical universe, are to be realized in the physical realm. Support is drawn from astronomy, chemistry, geology, palaeontology, biology and zoology; but quite apart from these, 'The mere existence of originated minds necessarily implies the existence of an unoriginated mind'.[24] As for mankind *en bloc,* 'History viewed as a whole teaches the same truth on a wider scale. An examination of it discloses a plan pervading human affairs from the origin of man until the present day . . . [Man's widespread ignorance of, and lack of conformity to the plan notwithstanding] the order, progress, plan of which I speak, have been slowly and silently but surely built up'.[25] For all that, the argument is *to* rather than *from* design. We are back with inference once more. The alternative is to assume design before we seek it, thereby landing ourselves in circularity.

Flint is well aware of the criticisms which have been levelled against the teleological argument, and he rebukes Hume, Kant and Mill for supposing that since the teleological argument does not stand alone it is of no value at all. He grants that the argument may do no more than suggest a former (i.e. orderer) rather than a creator of matter; but so long as we do not expect the teleological way to stand in isolation from other approaches we are entitled to adduce other considerations against that pernicious eternal mind/eternal matter dualism which is the consequence of the objectors' position. Again, when Mill suggests that our observation of the universe can at best sustain only the view of the deity as limited, Flint replies that

> Infinite power and wisdom must necessarily work 'under limitations' when they originate and control finite things; but the limitations are not in the infinite power and wisdom themselves—they are in their operations and effects. According to Mr. Mill's argument, infinite power could not create a finite world at all: only a finite power could do so. That surely means that a finite power must be mightier than an infinite power; and that . . . is surely a plain self-contradiction, a manifest absurdity.[26]

Neither chance nor necessity can act independently of mind, and since matter cannot create order, mind must, and does. Flint rebuts the alternative view in two pages of rhetoric which end thus:

Were these glorious works composed by the mere jumbling together of atoms, which were not even prepared beforehand to form things, as letters are to form words, and which had to shake themselves into order without the help of any hand? They may believe that who can. It seems to me that it ought to be much easier to believe all the Arabian Nights.[27]

Reverting to argument, Flint complains that those who deem law to be the fount of order evade the problem, for law *is* order. Nor does Comte's approach answer the case, for when, with him, we have noted phenomenal development, we have reached process only, not cause. As for Darwinianism, far from demolishing Paley's argument, it has confirmed it—as we shall see.

We come next to the moral argument for God's existence. Morality testifies (mark the word) to God's existence and character. The force of moral considerations has been appreciated by Kant, Hamilton, Newman and Schenkel, though Flint would resist any suggestion that conscience is the exclusive faculty through which we meet God. In fact we never directly meet, or immediately intuit, God through conscience: 'Morality is the direct object of conscience; God can therefore only be the presupposition or postulate of conscience'.[28] The authority of conscience is a delegated authority. Moreover, its authority is violated by the sinful soul to the soul's own hurt. Yet, 'as a matter of fact, our race does on the whole advance, and not recede, in the path towards good',[29] and for this God alone is ultimately responsible. Flint counters objections to his belief that God is wise, benevolent and just, and we shall return to his treatment of these objections shortly.

The arguments thus far expounded 'are not merely proofs that God is, but indications of what He is. They testify to the Divine existence by exhibiting the Divine character'.[30] Even when combined, however, they do not 'yield us the full idea of God which is entertained wherever theism prevails'.[31] In particular, 'They do not prove Him to be infinite, eternal, absolute in being and perfection'.[32] Enter the a priori argument; and Flint is in no doubt but that the correct procedure is to move from a posteriori to a priori considerations, and not vice versa: 'to get from the ideal to the actual may be impossible, and is certain to be difficult; whereas, if we have allowed facts to teach us all that they legitimately can about the existence, power, wisdom, and righteousness of God, it may be easy to show that our ideas of absolute being and perfection must apply to Him, and to Him only'.[33] Flint discusses a number of a priori arguments, finding Kant's attack upon Descartes inconclusive, and Clarke's anti-deistic argument at the very least a *reductio ad absurdum* of the sceptical

position. He reiterates his view that the a posteriori arguments need to be
supplemented by 'this intuition of the reason—infinity',[34] and it is quite
clear that for him this is a practical and not simply a theoretical necessity:

> The heart can find no secure rest except on an infinite God. If less than
> omnipotent, He may be unable to help us in the hour of sorest need. If
> less than omniscient, He may overlook us. If less than perfectly just,
> we cannot unreservedly trust Him. If less than perfectly benevolent, we
> cannot fully love Him. The whole soul can only be devoted to One who
> is believed to be absolutely good'.[35]

For all its worth, as Flint's tenth and final lecture proclaims, 'Mere
Theism [is] Insufficient'. The Westminster Confession is right when it
declares that nature and providence 'are not sufficient to give that
knowledge of God, and of His will, which is necessary unto salvation'.[36]
Only when theism is allied with revelation can the appeal of atheism,
polytheism and pantheism to ordinary minds be thwarted. For in the last
resort the difficulty is not with man's opinions, but with his sin. 'Mere
theism might have sufficed us had we remained perfectly rational and
perfectly sinless; but those who fancy that it is sufficient for men as they
are, only make it evident that they know not what men are . . .
Philosophy found out *many truths,* but not *the truth.* It did not disclose the
holiness and love of God—discovered no antidote for the poison of sin—
showed the soul no fountain of cleansing, healing and life'.[37] A worthy
religion may be built only upon the gospel. The 'gods' of Comte, Strauss,
Spencer and others will not suffice. We can know God as sinful beings
need to know him only through Christ, and the greatest deficiency in
creation and ordinary providence is that nothing in either can be shown to
have *cost* God anything. The most ignorant person who accepts God's
revelation in Christ is 'infinitely wiser than the most able or learned man
who trusts solely to his own wisdom apart from Christ's revealed work and
will'.[38] The former partakes of infinite wisdom; the latter must bear the
punishment of the foolish.

II

Our first impression on re-reading *Theism*—and in particular its
appendices, which numbered forty-one by the time the tenth edition of
the book appeared—was that we were in the presence not only of an able
man, but of a learned man. Flint was a polymath, trained at Glasgow at a
time when learning was more important than certificates. (Although he
was a distinguished student, and the recipient of many prizes, Flint did

not enter for degrees—they were bestowed upon him later.) It was characteristic of him that in a prize essay on Cartesianism Flint should have indicated some twenty relevant works in French and Latin which were conspicuous by their absence from the University Library.[39] Certainly Flint more than fulfilled Professor James Lindsay's requirement that 'Independence should come *after* knowledge, and not court the Nemesis of independence *of* knowledge'.[40] Flint's methodology was as broad as his knowledge. In his own words, 'The truths which lie *between* the sciences are as real and have equal claims to attention as the truths *within* the sciences',[41] and *Theism* provides evidence of his quest of inter-disciplinary harmonization in the interests of truth. It was on account of his catholicity of spirit that J. K. Mozley placed Flint in the line of the Alexandrines and Aquinas rather than of the Reformers, and especially Luther.[42]

Whereas we have discovered none who would deny Flint's breadth and depth of thought, by no means all have followed him in every detail of argument, or endorsed his methodology. Thus, for example, Lindsay considered that Flint's exposition of his view (that nature is an effect whose cause is God) left the door too wide open to the deistic tendency—though Lindsay did grant that in Flint's *Encyclopædia Britannica* article on 'Theism' the emphasis was more directly placed upon contingency and immanence.[43] Again, we have already noted the way in which Flint counters by rhetoric those who deny that the universe had a beginning in time. He asserts rather than substantiates his claim that such a beginning is absolutely necessary, thereby employing the first cause (whose existence he sets out to prove) as the means of halting the infinite regress. Further, as Professor Pringle-Pattison noted, he argues from the mutability of effects within the universe to the conclusion that the universe as a whole is an effect in the same sense, and this 'is an example *in excelsis* of the fallacy of Composition'.[44] As C. S. Peirce expostulated, 'Universes are not as plentiful as blackberries'.[45] Even if he had explored contingency more fully than he did, it is not clear that Flint would have had much to offer to those who, like Russell, refuse to raise the question of origins, and content themselves with saying, 'I should say that the universe is just there, and that's all'.[46] (But who *can* say much to those who place such simple trust in brute facts?) It might have been more interesting to have seen how Flint would reply to Spinoza, who, according to Flint's contemporary John Caird, maintained that God's nature as infinite, and his existence beyond the world of time and space, rendered the category of causality inapplicable to him.[47]

We found Flint's treatment of the teleological argument and his attempted rehabilitation of Paley particularly interesting if, in the last resort, unsatisfying. This section of *Theism* was the more refreshing because in our own time so many have criticized Paley for failing to answer Hume's anti-teleological case which appeared in the *Dialogues* published twenty-seven years *before* Paley's *Natural Theology* (1802), and because comparatively few today would go as far as Fr. Copleston in opining that it is 'an exaggeration to suggest . . . that his line of thought is worthless'.[48] Paley, as is well known, utilizing an already hoary illustration, held that as we infer a designer from our study of a watch, so the universe bears witness to its having been intelligently and purposively designed. Objections to this view, to the effect that our observation of the world does not necessarily lead us to conclude to *one* designer only, or to a designer worthy or our worship, are beside the point as far as Flint is concerned. To him, teleological considerations do not stand alone any more than do cosmological, moral or a priori considerations. He will extract what he needs from the teleological argument, and make good its deficiencies from elsewhere. He seeks to protect Paley from the charge of deism, and in Appendix Note **XXIV** he enlists the aid of Sir William Thompson in this cause. In his address to the British Association in 1871, the latter denied that Paley intended us to understand that the world was made as a watchmaker makes a watch, or that God from outside of the universe set the universe in motion.[49] The inference is more important to Flint than the terms of the analogy, and his case is that from the ordered universe we infer an intelligence which is responsible for the order; we do not immediately intuit a purposive designer. We argue to, rather than from, design:

> While. . .it is legitimate and even necessary to illustrate the design argument by references to human inventions, the numerous and immense differences between the works of man's art and the processes of nature must not be overlooked; and there is no excuse for saying that they have been overlooked. It is precisely because the universe is so above anything man has made or can make, and because vegetable and animal organisms are so different from watches and statues, that the argument in question leads us to a divine and not to a merely human intelligence. It implies that both the works of God and the works of man are products of intelligence; but it does not require that they should have anything else in common.[50]

Dr. Alfred Caldecott could not believe that all teleologists would be content with Flint's treatment of the case. On the contrary: 'Dr. Flint's treatment will be regarded as an abandonment of the Teleological Argument by those who think that the absence of ends is not compensated for by insistence on order, and that his condemnation of analogy takes away what mankind in general mean'.[51]

Unlike Sir Leslie Stephen, to whom evolution 'opposes the greatest difficulty to the teleological argument',[52] Flint understands the evolutionary lesson as reinforcing the wonder of the intelligence with which we have to do; and, in any case, to him 'Creation is the *only* theory of the *origin* of the universe. Evolution assumes either the creation or the self-existence of the universe'.[53] To Flint, who cannot account for order apart from intelligence, the choice is clear. That small if sometimes vociferous army of rationalists were to proclaim the contrary view well into the twentieth century: 'Modern science does not point to a beginning of the scheme of things. The consensus of opinion is entirely the other way. So far as we know, the ultimate cause [of the universe] recedes for ever and ever . . .'[54] The psychology, whether of affirmation or denial, seems remarkably similar at this point.

Perhaps the greatest difficulty in Flint's teleological case is one which applies to all such cases, and which is parallel with Russell's objection noted above. Flint's substitution of concern with order for concern with design avails nothing in face of the kind of argument which F. D. Maurice had already opposed to Paley himself when he said that Paley

> *began* with the recognition of a Person. The confession of a great designer fastened itself to that confession. He assumes that the process is reversed. Given a designer, you must accept a person. The answer is one of experience and fact. It lay before him and behind him. The most intelligent naturalists of his day—the men who had seen most of these evidences of design—did *not* rise to the belief of a person; the Father was not there; the Creator could not be detected. What signified it that the watch lay on the road? The watch suggests a watchmaker to those who bring the thought of their own nature with them, who have need of one to whom they can refer themselves; it does not contain in itself the maker; its springs move without him.[55]

Flint, however, with his cumulative approach to the arguments, holds a priori considerations in reserve, as we have seen. To the fact of evil, which, as Mill roundly declared, told decisively against the teleological argument, we shall return shortly.

Before leaving the cosmological and teleological arguments, both of which lead us back to the question of creation, we would note Flint's maintenance of the creator–creature distinction. If it be true, as some have alleged, that he did not altogether satisfactorily guard against deism in his statement of the cosmological argument, we must grant that he was not bowled over by deism's fashionable opposite, post-Hegelian absolute idealism. Immanentism had not so overcome him as to foster any tendency towards pantheism. His criticism of absolutism was twofold:

> The philosophy of the Absolute was, on the whole, a great advance towards a philosophical theism. And yet it was largely pantheistic, and tended strongly towards pantheism. This was not surprising. Any philosophy which is in thorough earnest to show that God is the ground of all existence and the condition of all knowledge must find it difficult to retain a firm grasp of the personality and transcendence of the Divine and to set them forth with due prominence . . . [Absolutism] regarded too exclusively the necessary and formal in thought, trusted almost entirely to its insight into the significance of the categories and its powers of rational deduction. Hence the idea of the Divine which it attained, if vast and comprehensive, was also vague and abstract, shadowy and unimpressive'.[56]

For all that, and especially in view of Flint's ultimate recourse to the a priori, both Lindsay and Caldecott were surprised that his rationalism could permit him to rest so near, and yet so far away from, the fully transcendentalist position.[57] We believe that the explanation of this degree of ambivalence and of Flint's resulting 'loneliness, alike as a man and a thinker',[58] is to be found above all in his indebtedness to certain pre-Kantian and typically Scottish influences, and notably in the influence of Reid. Certainly Flint gave no encouragement to those who, in the interest of obliterating the distinction between the natural and the revealed, were tempted to make God as dependent upon man as man was upon God, thereby paving the way for that variety of popular liberal theology which, for example, thought of the kingdom of God as man's achievement rather than as God's gift, and which, at its worst, almost envisaged God as saying to man, 'Apart from you I can do nothing'.

Again, while (as we shall see) Flint was carried along by evolutionary thought in the direction of an over- or perhaps prematurely optimistic view of man, his doctrine of creation prevented him from falling into that trap which some more recent process theologians have found opening before them, and which prompted Professor Glover's remark, 'Where process philosophy is theistic, it tends toward either deism or pantheism, neither of which is consistent with the Christian doctrine of creation'.[59] Flint would surely have agreed, and, moreover, he would have been in sympathy with his Edinburgh successor, John Baillie: 'The mess into which our modern idealists have so often landed themselves has come from their discarding the idea of creation which Christianity had introduced into Western thought, and their consequent reduction of the fundamental Christian distinction between the created and the uncreated to the pagan (both Greek and Indian) distinction between the apparent and the real'.[60] No doubt Baillie had in mind, *inter alia*, the work of Flint's contemporary F. H. Bradley, whose *Appearance and Reality* (1893) attempted the reversal of all our ordinary understandings of what phenomena are real, and of whom his sardonic foe F. C. S. Schiller declared that he had been received into 'the bosom of the Absolute' in a manner reminiscent of 'the fabled "rope trick" of the Indian jugglers'.[61]

In the course of developing his moral argument Flint makes a number of telling points, as even Caldecott was forced to admit.[62] We were struck by the reiterated suggestion of the importance of the ethics of belief. Just as Descartes before him had declared that such matters as the soul and God are so clear that they *ought* to be believed in, and that refusal so to believe was culpable,[63] so Flint held that, in the words of Thomas Chalmers,

> Man is not to blame, if an atheist, because of the want of proof. But he is to blame, if an atheist, because he has shut his eyes. He is not to blame that the evidence for a God has not been seen by him, if no such evidence there were within the field of his observation. But he is to blame if the evidence have not been seen, because he turned away his attention from it . . . To resist God after that He is known, is criminality towards Him; but to be satisfied that He should remain unknown, is like criminality towards Him.[64]

Flint does not deny that religious belief is 'in a great measure conditioned and determined by character',[65] but man remains, within certain limits, responsible and accountable for his belief. He recognizes that however successfully the theistic arguments are stated, they may not be accepted, and feels that the conditioning undergone by character is the main reason for the hiatus between evidence and belief. Theologians may feel that there is a need at this point to include a reference to the fact of sin (which Flint elsewhere acknowledges), and to the operation of God the Holy Spirit as illuminator—concerning whom Flint is almost completely silent in *Theism*, except by implication. He does, indeed, commend G. T. Ladd for underlining that fact that 'The truth becomes ours only as a gift from without',[66] and that 'The pure in heart shall see God; they that obey shall know of the doctrine; the things of the spirit are spiritually judged of;[67] and he applauds the insight of Theophilus that 'if there be any sin in man, he cannot see God'.[68] Of course, we must ever remember that it is the acceptance or rejection of an argument, *not* the argument's validity or invalidity, which may be affected by sin. With all this the framers of (Flint's) Westminster Confession were quite familiar 'Although the light of nature, and the works of creation and providence, do so far manifest the goodness, wisdom, and power of God, *as to leave men inexcusable;* yet they are not sufficient to give that knowledge of God, and of his will, which is necessary unto salvation'.[69]

In the course of his discussion of the moral argument Flint produces some telling points against Kant, to whom the fashionable idealism of his day owed so much. Flint is worth quoting fairly fully at this point, both because of what he says, and by way of providing a specimen of his style of argumentation. He is opposing Kant's view that conscience is competent apart from reason to lead a man to God, and he notes that Kant fully realized that *his* argument was open to the same line of attack wherewith he had, to his own satisfaction, disposed of other approaches. Indeed,

He saw all this as clearly as man could do, and it is marvellous that so many authors should have written as if he had not seen it; but certainly he might as well not have seen it, for all that he was able to do in the way of repelling the objection. His reply amounted merely to reaffirming that we are under the necessity of associating the idea of a Supreme Being with the moral law, and then qualifying the statement by the admission that we can know, however, nothing about that Being; that as soon as we try to know anything about Him we make a speculative, not a practical, use of reason, and fall back into the realm of sophistry and illusion from which the Critical Philosophy was designed to deliver us. In other words, what he tells us is, that the argument is good, but only on the conditions that it is not to be subjected to rational scrutiny, and that no attempt is to be made to determine what its conclusion signifies. It seems to me that, on these conditions, he might have found any argument good. Such conditions are inconsistent with the whole spirit and very existence of a critical philosophy. And it is not really God that Kant reaches by his argument: it is a mere moral ideal—a dead, empty, abstract assumption, which is regarded as practically useful, although rationally baseless—a necessary presupposition of moral action, but one which tells us nothing about the nature of its object'.[70]

Such strictures notwithstanding, Flint in no way minimized the importance of conscience. We may say that he regarded it as being on a par with feeling. Eclectic as ever, he endorsed Chalmers's view that conscience is 'so distinct and authoritative a voice on the side of righteousness'[71] that it testifies to its giver, God. Conscience cannot, however, stand alone—and for this insight, which placed him apart from the powerful ethical idealism of the day, James Lindsay commended him.[72] As for the emotions, Flint anticipated some of the latter-day charges of psychologism which have been levelled against some who stand more or less in the line of Schleiermacher. While recognizing (in his

Encyclopaedia Britannica article) that Schleiermacher, Ritschl and others had provided a necessary corrective to hyper-intellectualism by reminding us that 'God is to be known, not through mere intellectual cognition, but through spiritual experience, and that no dicta as to the Divine not verifiable in experience, not efficacious to sustain piety and to promote virtue, to elevate and purify the heart, to invigorate the will, to ennoble the character, to sanctify both individuals and communities, are likely to be true',[73] his view in a nutshell was that 'neither the head nor the heart is a competent witness. . .when the one is dissociated from the other.[74]

Turning to the ontological argument, we cannot fail to notice how much more Platonic idealism appealed to Flint than did its post-Kantian namesake: 'My belief . . . is, that Platonism is substantially true; that the objections which the empiricism and positivism at present prevalent urge against its fundamental positions are superficial and insufficient; that what is essential in its theory of ideas, and in the theism inseparable from that theory, must abide with our race for ever as a priceless possession'.[75] Thus inspired, he defends Anselm against Gaunilo by arguing that whereas 'Mere existence is not a predicate . . . specifications or determinations of existence are predicable',[76] and that all that the argument requires is that reality, necessity and independence of existence are predictables. Against Kant's criticism of the second form of Descartes's a priori argument (to the effect that God cannot be thought of as a perfect being unless he is thought of as necessarily existing) Flint contends that in asserting either 'there is no God' or 'there is no triangle', we *imply* rather than annul the idea of God or triangularity. Hence Kant is at fault in supposing that having denied the need of the subject one may without contradiction deny the need of the existential predicate. Despite all their difficulties, Flint upholds the importance of the a priori arguments. They are to him vital in contributing the notion of infinity to the cumulative case for theism, and he had no qualms about concurring with an unnamed writer who said of these proofs that 'they will never be despised so long as speculative thinking is held in repute'.[77]

Uneasiness lingers, however, and thus it was that in response to Flint's *tentative* assertion that it may be that the a priori proofs 'concur in manifesting that if God be not, the human mind is of its very nature self-contradictory'.[78] Caldecott could reply, 'That anyone could come so directly in face of the Transcendental position and describe it so clearly and yet come to no decision upon it is strange'.[79] Elsewhere Flint could extol the speculative reason as leading us to the absolute Being (and not merely to the Father, King, and Judge), thereby standing as a bulwark against anthropomorphism.[80] We reiterate our suggestion that Flint's ambivalence is traceable to the influence of his philosophic roots which caused him to value the help which the a priori proofs could afford, while he balked at the departure from common sense which they could inspire.

Having briefly commented upon the arguments, we would offer some further reflections upon Flint's case before turning to the crucial methodological question. As we view Flint's *Theism* today, we cannot but feel that by comparison with the almost neurotic passion for analysis which has been bred in us during a half-century in which speculative thinking has been to put it mildly, by no means universally held in high esteem, Flint on occasion sits somewhat lightly to conceptual analysis, and nowhere more so than in respect of the terms 'proof' and 'fact'. Concerning 'proof', while recognizing that the proofs will not and should not lead to an intellectually coerced belief in God, the fact remains that Flint occasionally speaks as if they do possess demonstrative validity. Thus, for example, he can write, 'All the essential principles of mental action, when applied to the meditative consideration of finite things, lead up from them to Infinite Creative Wisdom'.[81] In view of remarks of this kind we are not surprised to discover that one of Flint's own pupils, himself a Professor of Systematic Theology, should have been tempted to state his own position over against a *misunderstanding* of his teacher's:

> I do not hold that we arrive at our knowledge of God by way of the 'theistic proofs'. Dr. Flint held that so emphatically that he made these 'proofs' the basis of his elaborate and carefully considered classification of the Divine Attributes. I hold that all real knowledge of God is always a knowledge of Him and He impresses Himself on us somehow in the totality of His Being. . .I do not hold that a rationally demonstrable 'Natural Theology' is the sure foundation on which we erect a superstructure of Christian conviction. Dr. Flint regarded all his writing and thinking as part of one great comprehensive argument establishing a logically convincing proof of the existence of God and at the same time furnishing much sure and certain knowledge of His Nature.[82]

As we have seen, Flint takes 'proofs' in one sense to be God's self-manifestation; in another sense he understands them as grounds of belief; and occasionally he suggests, but he does not strictly hold, that they are rationally watertight and compelling logical demonstrations of God's existence. Further, by way of mitigating Dr. Dickie's assertion of Flint's devotion to natural theology, we would advert to Flint's reminder to the members of the British Association to the effect that 'we must know God, and love Him, before we can see Him in natural things with any clearness or to any profit. I deny not that Nature may in some small degree lead us to look aright on the Gospel; but I affirm that in a far higher degree the Gospel is needed to make us look aright on Nature. Awaken, through Christ's death, the love of God within me, and then all Nature will speak to me of God; otherwise she will hardly speak to me one intelligible word. The Gospel must give me the requisite intelligence and the requisite interest'.[83] Thus, when Dr. Dickie writes of the proofs that they are not, 'taken by themselves, capable of creating belief in God. But they do confirm and strengthen an already existing belief',[84] he is underlining his mentor's position and not, as he thinks, dissenting from it.

Following Flint's encyclopaedia article it really should not have been so easily possible for thinkers to repeat the charge that he was a narrow intellectualist. The following statement from that article could scarcely make his position clearer: 'the idea of God is not one which can be rightly apprehended merely through intellect speculatively exercised or operating on the findings of science. It requires to be also apprehended through moral experience and the discipline of life. Neither individuals nor committees can know more of God as a moral being than their moral condition and character permit them to know'.[85] For Flint, as for others before and since, the theistic arguments have a cumulative force. Thus,

> It is sophistry to attempt to destroy them separately by assailing each as if it had no connection with the other, and as if each isolated fragmentary argument were bound to yield as large a conclusion as all the arguments combined. A man quite unable to break a bundle of rods firmly bound together may be strong enough to break each rod separately. But before proceeding to deal with the bundle in that way, he may be required to establish his right to untie it, and to decline putting forth his strength upon it as it is presented to him.[86]

Sadly, he nowhere really answers Kant's objection against the cumulative approach to the effect that the arguments all reduce ultimately to the untenable ontological argument. In other words, what if all we have is not a bundle of rods, but just one rod, and that a weak one? Finally, he does not show how his idea, that the proofs confirm *what* God is as well as providing evidence *that* God is, escapes the charge of the selective eisegesis of notions acquired from other, generally scriptural, sources. Flint's clearest affirmation of the proofs as indicative of the character of God appears in the final chapter of his *Agnosticism* (1903).

As for the term 'fact', it would be undeniably anachronistic to reprimand Flint for not having rebutted the unduly constructed understanding of facticity which was purveyed by sundry empiricists and positivists during the nineteen-twenties and thirties. But his very innocence *vis-à-vis* the complexities of this term strikes us, and reminds us of the need to give the most serious attention to it in any present-day theistic enterprise. We need to defend an idea of facticity which will admit not only the facticity of such 'phenomena' as faith, repentance, forgiveness, agape, and the like, but which will at least raise the question whether, apart from the presupposition of God, we may properly apprehend any facts at all. This question in turn raises the question as to the presence or absence, or degree, of common ground between believer and unbeliever—and with that we are face to face with the methodological issue.

III

Flint's *Theism* is not a complete natural theology, and none knew this better than the author himself. It is not simply that, as Dr. Caldecott complained,[87] one pro-theistic consideration of importance, namely the aesthetic, is here omitted (though it is dealt with elsewhere[88]); it is rather that, as Flint himself explains, a *system* of natural theology would comprise the following: an account of the evidence for belief in God's existence; a refutation of anti-theistic claims; a delineation of the character of God; and an history of theistic speculation. He continues, 'The first theme is the subject of the present work. The second theme is so far, discussed in its companion volume. [This was *Anti-Theistic Theories* (1877), Flint's second series of Baird Lectures, which were even better attended than the first.] The other two themes have not been touched, except at points where slightly doing so could not be avoided.'[89] In fact, Flint subsequently made good his self-confessed gaps, covering the history of theism in his encyclopaedia article, and the character of God in numerous sermons and addresses, some of which were published.[90] He also gave what many, including R. M. Wenley,[91] considered to be his best thought to his full-scale treatment of *Agnosticism*. There can be no doubt that at a time when so many Christians—and by no means only the unlettered—were bewitched by the Higher Criticism, bothered by Darwinianism, and bewildered by Spencerian agnosticism, Flint appeared (and was even caricatured as) a knight errant in defence of the faith once delivered. In a letter to Flint, Principal Sir William Geddes spoke for many: 'In the great battle which you have been fighting and fighting so well, I trust you will find ere long a multitude of coadjutors and the tide turning in favour of Idealism and the Eternal Verities'.[92] It will be our own contention, however, that Flint was, if anything, too indebted to too many thinkers to be entirely satisfactory or consistent in his theistic stance. We shall suggest that while he fully appreciated the necessity of revelation, he does not fully allow for it in his system; indeed, his markedly a posteriori approach, which sits uneasily with his Platonic predilections, accounts for the ambiguity in his method—a method influenced on the one hand by the Scottish common-sense school of philosophers and by Butler, and on the other by his aversion to that pantheism to which he thought some varieties of fashionable idealism led as a final resting place. We shall observe too the man behind the method, for Flint's temperamental inclination to Moderatism, which made him in some ways so different from his predecessor at both St. Andrews and Edinburgh, Thomas Chalmers (architect of that Free Church into whose ministry Flint could *not* in conscience enter), is too important to be overlooked.

Flint's philosophical antecedents were in some ways inhibiting to any fully-fledged revelational Christian philosophy. There was in the first place Thomas Reid (1710–96)[93], who in attacking the theories of ideas propounded by Locke, Hume and Berkeley—the cumulative result of which, he thought, was an untenable subjectivism—sought to ground a new empiricism in a divinely bestowed common sense (which is by no means the 'instinct of the common herd') whose presence cannot adequately be accounted for as long as God is left out of account. This type of thinking was influential not only in Scotland, but in France and Italy, and it is no coincidence that among Flint's writings is one on the Italian philosopher Vico (1668–1744), whose ideas had in some respects anticipated those of Reid.[94] Although Reid spoke of 'original and natural judgements' which are 'the inspiration of the Almighty' and the gift of nature,[95] he did not, despite his ministerial status, treat of theological themes in detail. This was the age of Scottish Moderatism when 'men of wide culture—like Blair, Carlyle, Robertson, and Reid—left theology utterly alone'.[96] The increasing provincialism of much subsequent Scottish philosophy (of which Dugald Stewart's psychology is an example), which would not permit a just estimate of such men as Kant, Hegel, and others,[97] drew forth Flint's polymathic protest that although Stewart's psychology was 'the only psychology worthy of the name' it suffered through being 'unconnected with the past through learning'.[98]

But if philosophy at home was provincial, we have already seen that Flint made but sparing use of the findings of some from abroad, notably those of Schleiermacher. He could not overlook the claim of natural theology as easily as did Schleiermacher; and in his strictures against 'feeling' he approaches that horror of enthusiasm which characterized Reid and the eighteenth century Moderates and Deists alike, and which, together with his a posteriori starting-point links him with the English-

man 'with whom one is constantly tempted to compare Flint',[99] Joseph
Butler (1692–1752).

Although at first impressed by Samuel Clarke's a priorism, Butler later
opposed it in favour of a more empirical *method*. We do not go so far as to
say that he forsook a priorism for empiricism, for his conversion was less
than complete. He was, for example, quite happy to join the Deists in the
unargued assumption that nature required a causative power. In fact
Robert Mackintosh was not wide of the mark when he wrote,

> On the whole . . . Butler in personal conviction is an intuitionalist,
> wavering towards the idealism of his age; but in argument he is an
> empiricist, trying to reason every question as one of the given facts.
> None the less, in the issue, it is the very element which goes beyond an
> appeal to facts—it is the depth and purity of Butler's moral nature—
> which fascinates the reader, and wins praise from Matthew Arnold or
> Goldwin Smith or even Leslie Stephen. [100]

The first part of this judgement could be made of Flint: and just as
Butler's method was an attempt to defeat, as far as possible, the Deists on
their own empiricist ground (unlike Lord Herbert of Cherbury, Butler's
deistic contemporaries, standing as they did in the wake of Locke, were
not defenders of the doctrine of innate ideas[101]) so Flint in his turn was
anxious, as we have seen, to claim the latest scientific advances as evidence
for the truth of theism. He thought, in fact, that the design argument had
been greatly strengthened by the findings of the Darwinians. [102] The
second part of Mackintosh's judgement, when placed alongside a comment of Professor Ramm, and considered in relation to Flint's possible
underemphasis upon the aesthetic, underlines a further 'eighteenth
century' characteristic of Flint. Ramm writes that 'One could deduce from
Butler that the universe was ordered but never that it was beautiful. One
could assume that the religious man was thoughtful but never that he was
emotional'. [103] If this is over-statement, it is over-statement which makes
a point.

The Butler-Flint approach in theistic philosophy raises three main
questions: Will probability suffice? What common ground is there
between believer and unbeliever? How are God's revelation and man's
deepest needs to be accommodated? Clearly in Butler, and somewhat less
clearly in Flint (because he holds a priori and revelational considerations
more obviously in reserve, and is more manifestly ambivalent than
Butler), one detects the conviction that the wise man proportions his
belief to the evidence; and that given the ambiguity of the phenomena
which confront him in the world and in his own mind, he settles for

probability rather than for absolute certainty concerning the theistic question. No doubt some of the criticisms of Butler are wide of the mark. For example, to those who say that on occasion by throwing caution to the winds we secure a more favourable result than we would have done had we acted more prudently, Butler can reply that probability is but a *guide*, and that it is invoked at all precisely because absolute certainty will for ever elude us. There are other criticisms, however, such as Lindsay's response to a typically Butlerianism assertion of Flint: when Flint asserts that 'A rightly regulated mind is one in which evidence is the measure of assent; or, in other words, in which assent is proportional to evidence',[104] Lindsay declares, 'This position is still too much in accord with eighteenth century Deism and nineteenth century Natural Theology in its intellectualistic stress. One can hardly help feeling how impossible it is for the thought of our time not to take more account of the part played by the subjective factors, than is involved in such a stress of "evidence"'.[105] John Caird had made the same point against Butler: 'the mental attitude of the evidential school is a false one. Genuine religious conviction can never be the result of a balancing of logical arguments; it cannot be a belief produced by a series of external proofs, and which implies no relation of the spirit of man to the thing believed'.[106] We have already seen, however, that Flint had another side to him, and that he was aware of the limits of intellectualism. (Not that this prevented his pupil Dickie from referring in the preface to another of his books, *The Organism of Christian Truth* (1931) to Flint's 'purely intellectualistic view of the nature of religious knowledge'). But this ambivalence in Flint is but symptomatic of a yet deeper ambivalence.

Butler—and Flint in so far as he follows Butler's method—presupposes that Christian and deist, Christian and humanist, occupy common ground *vis-à-vis* the theistic question, and thus there is some point in arguing. But at the same time Flint knows that his method will never produce demonstrative certainty, and can at best remove certain intellectual obstacles to belief. He would have agreed with his contemporary John Caird that those who believe truly in righteousness and goodness will not be content to join the adherents of the evidential school in assigning these to the realm of the probable, as distinct from the demonstrably true.[107] But to have given due weight to this insight would have entailed an approach much more akin to that which John 'Rabbi' Duncan sketched— an approach from which Flint's methodological (though not his convictional) stance precluded him:

> I postulate God, and out of this postulate any philosophy I have emerges . . . We do not infer his being from what we are. We cannot

rise to him thus. But He is himself within us . . . Revelation apart, I am a sceptic, *i.e.* I am a philosophical sceptic.[108]

The criticism that from the natural one may not rise to the supernatural by argumentation had, of course, been levelled at Flint, and he answered those who would have preferred a more scripturally based argument thus:

> Now it would, perhaps, be possible to construct an argument of this kind which would not be justly censurable as reasoning in a circle. Such an argument would require, however, so much preliminary explanation, and would be received by so many persons with suspicion and aversion, that it is to be feared it would be rather a weakness than a strength in a vindication of theism. It can hardly be necessary to say that no doubt or disparagement is cast by this statement on the self-evidencing character of Scripture and of Christianity to those who already believe in God, or to those whose religious susceptibilities are vivid.[109]

Three comments require to be made on this. First, may it be that the kind of circularity here feared is unavoidable and does not adversely affect the theist's case, for 'When we are arguing on behalf of an absolute authority, then our final appeal must be to that authority and no other . . . [the Christian] believes that God made men to think in terms of *his* circularity, rather than in terms of some competing circularity'?[110] Secondly, the fact that many persons will be suspicious of the kind of argument in question is no reason for not attempting to construct such an argument; indeed, if such an argument is the only viable one, then not to make the attempt is to capitulate before one begins. Thirdly, Flint begs the question by supposing that his preferred method is truly viable; yet in other places he admits that it is not entirely satisfactory, and we have quoted enough of his own words to show that he would not be out of accord with the contemporary Calvinist Cornelius Van Til who has written that 'the attempt to find God in the world without looking through the eyes of Christ is fruitless, not because the world does not reveal God (it continually shouts of the existence of God to men), but because men need new eyes!'[111] All of which underscores the methodological question and raises the theological issue.

Although in some ways Flint echoes the eighteenth century, in other respects he is decidedly of his own age. He remains selective, however, suspecting immanentism, and utilizing evolutionary thought. It is perhaps not without significance that the 'vogue' theology of the latter part of the nineteenth century shared with Butlerian (High Church) and Wesleyan (evangelical) Arminianism—the 'vogue' theologies of a hundred

years earlier—a generally optimistic view of man's ability to elect God
and to go on to perfection. Both ascribed to man a measure of autonomy
which made it easier to think of sins as errors, rather than of sin as a
radical, alienating rupture of the God-man relation. Thus Flint can argue
that God is not the author of sin, while granting that he permits evil; he
can say that freewill is the indispensible condition of moral agency, and
that God limited his own freedom in creating men free.[112] There is much
here that requires to be unpacked. No doubt we may not make God the
author of sin, but are there not dangers in speaking of God's permission of
sin? May it not be implied that God reluctantly permits something
which he cannot control, or could not foresee? This would be to impugn
his omniscience and his omnipotence. What of the analysis of 'freedom'?
The notorious ambiguities of this term remain unconsidered by Flint,
who appears to have the 'liberty of indifference' chiefly in mind. What,
however, of the Reformed emphasis upon the bondage of the will, and the
consideration advanced by Paul, Luther and Calvin that man, though
having free agency, is not truly free until his will is unchained? We
suspect that the inhibiting factors upon Flint at this point derive from
that mixture of eighteenth-century and evolutionary influences to which
we have drawn attention. Thus, although, as Whewell pointed out,[113]
Butler and Paley differed from each other in that the former paid more
heed to conscience, the latter to utility, they shared the optimism of their
times, and that less-than-radical view of sin that went with it. The
eighteenth century flavour of the following is unmistakable: 'as men may
manage their temporal affairs with prudence, and so pass their days here
on earth in tolerable ease and satisfaction, by a moderate degree of care: so
likewise with regard to religion, there is no more required than what they
are well able to do, and what they must be greatly wanting to themselves,
if they neglect'.[114]And when Paley writes that 'It is a happy world after
all. The air, the earth, the water, teem with delighted existence',[115] one
cannot prevent a slight shudder as one contemplates the ammunition he
was unwittingly giving to such later rationalists as Vivian, who prefers
red to dwell upon 'nature red in tooth and claw'.[116] As Maurice said, 'A
divine being who could only be approached and worshipped in sunshine
and on gala days was one eminently suited to the temper of the eighteenth
century'.[117]

Maurice's own century was not, however, altogether guiltless, as we
have said. Under the influence of evolutionary thinking Flint can write:

> the system of God's moral government of our race is only in course of
> development. We can see but a small part of it, for the rest is as yet
> unevolved. History is not a whole, but the initial or preliminary

portion of a process which may be of vast duration, and the sequel of which may be far grander than the past has been. That portion of the process which has been already accomplished, small though it be, indicates the direction which is being taken; it is, on the whole, a progressive movement; a movement bearing humanity towards truth, freedom, and justice.[118]

Professor Hick quotes this passage as an example of 'the spacious and optimistic spirit of upper-class life in Victorian England' [*sic*],[119] and rightly proceeds to remark upon the value of the necessary corrective to it which was to be provided supremely by P. T. Forsyth, in considerably darker times, in his *The Justification of God* (1917). It appears that Flint's optimism kept him from a sufficiently radical understanding of the nature of sin, and for this reason he could go as far as he did in Christian philosophizing without recourse to sin's remedy. Nowhere is this clearer than in his discussion of evil. For all his strictures against Mill, he does not, in setting forth his own theodicy, make much of the Cross-Resurrection event. For our part we cannot believe that such an omission leaves us with the choice between a more Christian and a less Christian answer to the problem; we seem to be left with no adequately Christian answer at all. If it be thought that in making this complaint we are guilty of blurring the distinction between natural and revealed theology, so much the worse for the distinction. Most of Flint's inhibitions at points crucial to the presentation of the fully Christian position seem to arise from too careful a compartmentalization at this point. No doubt Flint proceeds thus in the interest of finding an area of common ground on which the apologetic task may be conducted. We cannot resist the feeling, however, that he had taken rather more notice of Paul and Calvin in these matters, and rather less of Aquinas and Butler, he would have reached a more satisfactory conclusion.

It is at this point that the contrast between Flint and his predecessor Chalmers is revealing. Granted that evolutionary thinking had not made its full impact in Chalmers's day, and notwithstanding the influence of Butler upon him, the fact remains that the acknowledgement of the gravity of sin, and of the need of a truly sovereign remedy, caused Chalmers to abhor Moderatism, and to align himself with that most Calvinistic of churches. Nor is it without significance that, like Forsyth after him, Chalmers emphasized the holiness of God in his writings. The holiness of God was, he remarked, a theme which 'occurs but rarely in any of the expositions of Natural Theology',[120] and he maintained that to a man confronted by God's holiness on the one hand and his own sin on the other, the message of natural theology was grossly inadequate. That Flint knew this too is clear from his sermon to the British Academy in which he declared that those who would place undue reliance upon nature as a guide to God 'forget, in particular, these two things about man—the gross darkness of his mind, and the deep perversity of his heart!'[121] We suggest that he does not take sufficient account of these factors himself in the outworking of his method—indeed, that his method militated against his so doing. Yet the remedy was within his grasp. When writing in opposition to the undue exaltation of confessional affirmations he said that 'The only true basis of Christian theology is the original revelation of God in Christ; not the impression which it has produced on the minds of a society of fallible men'.[122] Sadly, and despite his insistence that 'theism has come to mankind in and through revelation',[123] we cannot feel that this insight, though at the heart of his experience, was accorded its due place in the construction of his system. We can see why this was; it was not simply that he was a child of his age; in some important respects he was not that. We are nearer the mark if we attribute his deficiencies to his being, as befits a polymath, a child of more ages than one.

IV

Flint's learning was prodigious, and much of his work is truly illuminating and delightfully written. He did well not to yield to the pantheizing tendencies of post-Kantian immanentist thought, and to keep his head during a period in which a naturalistically-inspired optimism in man was not uncommon. Again, his warnings concerning the pitfalls in the path of those who, in the wake of Schleiermacher and Ritschl, pursued uncritically the subjectivist way, were entirely appropriate. On the other hand we, at this distance, have learned to be somewhat more hard-headed than was Flint concerning such matters as the alleged cumulative force of the arguments for God's existence, the analysis of 'fact' and 'proof' and so on. But these are points of criticism made with benefit of hindsight. Much more important are the questions which Flint's approach thrusts to the fore as we contemplate (if we so dare!) our own constructive task.

We have seen that there is an ambivalence in Flint's work which results from the tension between his methodology and his religious convictions. His methodology, so largely that of eighteenth-century natural theology, inhibits his legitimate use of the data which his religion provides. Hence for example, as we saw, his attenuated account of the problem of evil, and his too easy (methodological if not altogether convictional) assumption of common ground between believer and unbeliever. Two fundamental questions are thus forced upon us. First, in holding the deliverances of revelation in reserve, so to speak, is the Christian philosopher working with one hand tied behind his back? Secondly, having regard to the fact that many varieties of theism, including Flint's, presuppose common ground between believers and unbelievers, what are the ethical and epistemological implications of that renewing of the mind which is God's gift in response to man's plight—a plight which results, *inter alia*, in that inadequacy of theism which was well summed up by Dr. Lovell Cocks: 'It does not fail in principle but only *de facto*. It fails not because, being finite, man is *non capax infiniti*, but because, being a sinner, he loves the abstractions he can admire and manipulate rather than the living Truth that menaces his egoistic pride'?[124]

If the answers we give to these questions are such that we have no further confidence in old-style natural theology, a series of huge questions immediately follows: Are we inevitably imprisoned in a circle of revelation? If not, what kind of common ground is envisaged between believer and unbeliever? If so, what becomes of the Church's apologetic task— can we testify only, and never rationally commend? No doubt as we address ourselves to these questions we shall quickly discover that it is much easier to fail ignominiously and disastrously than nobly and valuably—as, we believe, did Robert Flint.

CHAPTER FOUR

John Caird (1820–1898):
Apostle of Continuity

'There was no thought on which he more constantly dwelt than that of the unreality of the hard divisions which are often made between one part of life and another, between faith and reason, between the church and the world, between the religious and the secular life in any of its forms.'[1] These words of Edward Caird upon his brother are entirely to the point. If ever there was a theologian whose thought—whether in the classroom, in print, on a platform, or in the pulpit—was all of a piece, that theologian was John Caird. The theme of union is the thread which holds all else together. We find it in the sermon, 'Religion in Common Life', (Romans 12:11), preached before Queen Victoria at Balmoral in 1857, and published only at her request.[2] Here Caird opposed that false compart-mentalization which would divorce religion from the rest of life. The same theme is to be found in his posthumous Gifford Lectures on *The Fundamental Ideas of Christianity* (1900), which close with an affirmation of faith in 'the Father of all spirits' from whom there can be no separation; and it informed his last public utterance, delivered on 13th April 1897 to his Glasgow students, in which he dwelt upon that wider unity of knowledge of which their particular courses of study were but a part.[3] From first to last, the divine-human continuity and its outworkings was his theme.

Caird's approach found a ready response from the idealist philosopher Henry Jones, who said of him that 'he still seems to me, in one respect at least, to stand alone: in his matchless power to present those deep truths, on which the world of spirit securely rests, in so clear a light that, more and more as time rolls onward, they shall become the sure possession of the common mind of man'.[4] Others, however, were by no means as content with Caird's general stance. Dr. Macleod, writing from the standpoint of confessional Calvinism, regretted that Caird 'bowed his neck to the yoke of German Idealism', and that both he and John Tulloch 'extended scant hospitality to the Theology that they had pledged themselves to teach and to defend'.[5]

A summary statement of our own judgement upon Caird may not come amiss. Caird is undoubtedly a master of majestic prose, and the more majestic he is, the more dangerous he becomes. For we are so easily carried along by the cadences of an earlier generation, which are the more delightful because of their now quaint air, that unless we remain alert we can fail to heed the nagging suspicion that all is not well. The most intriguing thing about Caird is the challenge which a careful reading of his works presents to detect *what* is not well, and why. The matter is more complicated, and hence more interesting, than might at first glance appear. It is not simply that Caird fastens on to Hegelianism and presents an attenuated Christianity as a consequence. It is rather that there is an inconsistency in his work of which he himself seemed to be unaware. His theme of union, continuity—his greatest debt to Hegelian idealism— ought to have made him less orthodox than at times he sounds. There are attenuations in Caird's presentation of the gospel, but from one point of view we might have expected more; and, conversely, the more orthodox assertions which he does make are, in his work, unsupported by those christological and historical facts which alone can bear their weight. At crucial points his metaphysic is at war with his theology.

I

The bare facts of Caird's career may briefly be related.[6] He was born the eldest of seven brothers at Greenock on 15th December 1820. After schooling, notably from Dr. Brown, an enthusiastic classicist and disciplinarian, he went to work in the office of his father's engineering firm at the age of fifteen. With his father's blessing he proceeded to Glasgow University in 1837, and became a prizeman in Mathematics and Logic. In 1838 he returned for a year to his uncle's foundry, but on the deaths of his father and uncle their respective businesses were sold. Caird returned to the University, graduating M.A. in 1845. A lonely, shy student, he worked extremely hard, and the various prizes he won, and the satisfactory results he gained in Latin and Hebrew, were a tribute to his industry rather than evidence of intellectual brilliance. Among his few student friends were Duncan Weir, who was to become Professor of Hebrew at Glasgow, Archibald Watson, Robert Graham, and John Paisley. It is not without significance that Caird's theological Professor during his days at the Glasgow Divinity Hall was Alexander Hill, son of Professor George Hill of St. Andrews—a leading Moderate of his day. Alexander had been elected to the Chair in 1840, despite the candidature of no less a person than Thomas Chalmers. During Caird's course, the Disruption of 1843 (led by Chalmers) occurred, and the Church of Scotland, Free, came into being.[7] Caird's family circle was affected by the Disruption in that an aunt of his 'went out'.

Caird was ordained on 18th September 1845, and for eighteen months he ministered at Newton-on-Ayr, whose minister had seceded, taking most of the congregation and all but one of the elders with him. In 1847 Caird answered a call to Lady Yester's Church, Edinburgh, where he was inducted on 6th May. For two years he ministered to a growing and appreciative congregation, which included a fair proportion of professional and business men and students. When it became clear that his health would not stand the strain of this demanding sphere, Caird removed to Errol, Perthshire, where he was inducted on 4th October 1849, and where he remained until 1857. While here he read widely; he learned German; he was instrumental in establishing a Girl's School of Industry, whose object was to instruct working-class girls in housekeeping, domestic crafts, and the like. The school was opened in 1856, and after the first four weeks the roll numbered about one hundred girls. It was as minister of Errol that Caird preached before the Queen in 1855, and no less a person than Dean Stanley described the published sermon as 'the greatest single sermon of the century'.[8] Originally preached at Errol, the sermon was polished and delivered before the Lord High Commissioner during the 1854 General Assembly of the Church of Scotland, before it reached the ears of the Queen. So impressed was Victoria that on 7th December 1857 she appointed Caird one of her Chaplains-in-Ordinary.

On the last Sunday of 1857 Caird preached his first sermon as minister of Park Chapel, Glasgow, whose call he had accepted in preference to one from St. George's, Edinburgh. In June 1858 he married Isabella Glover, the daughter of the Reverend Dr. Glover of Greenside Church, Edinburgh.[9] Three years later his University conferred its D.D. upon him.

Caird's professorial career began in November 1862, when he was appointed to the Chair of Theology at Glasgow. Of his teaching the Reverend Dr. M'Adam Muir said, 'He presented as clearly, as sympathetically, the argument which he sought to controvert as that which he sought to establish . . . He disliked negative teaching: he was constructive, not destructive; he contented himself, as a rule, with enunciating truth, leaving the error to die of itself'.[10] Another of his students, Dr. Strong, wrote that 'His aim from first to last has been the same—to place theology on a rational basis—to bring our thinking on the greatest of all subjects into line with our thinking on other subjects of serious import—thus to give theology a philosophic or scientific basis, and to harmonize, if not to identify, natural and revealed religion'.[11] It is also worthy of note that of all the Reverend Professors, Caird alone gave his students homiletic advice. About three years after Caird's accession to the Chair of Theology, his brother Edward was appointed Professor of Moral Philosophy. For the next twenty-eight years they worked side by side, until Edward became Master of Balliol, Oxford.[12]

In 1868 John Caird proposed the award of the degree of D.D. to John McLeod Campbell, who had been deposed from the ministry of the Church of Scotland in 1831 on account of his universalism; in 1870 he gave the address at the opening of the new University buildings on Gilmorehill; and on 7th March 1873 he succeeded Thomas Barclay (1792–1873) as Principal of the University.[13] This post was in the gift of the Crown, but the University Senate had unanimously petitioned for Caird's appointment. In 1883 the University of St. Andrews conferred its LL.D. upon him, and in the following year Edinburgh University awarded him its D.D. He gave twelve lectures as Gifford Lecturer at Glasgow (1890–91), and had given a further eight in 1896, when a stroke prevented his completing the course. Caird presided over University affairs with distinction, but eventually felt that the time had come to resign. His resignation would have taken effect from 31st July 1898, but in fact he died in office on July 30th. He was buried in Greenock cemetery on Wednesday 3rd August, his successor, Principal Story, representing the Queen.

Although he was of a naturally retiring disposition and had few intimates, Caird's heart was warm. He grieved for the lot of the oppressed. Thus, when Glasgow City Council refused to open the East End Palace to the working people on Sundays he expostulated, 'Could they not offer them *this* brief refuge from the wretchedness of their narrow and crowded and noisy, and too often fireless hearths? Oh! the prejudice and bigotry of men!'[14] At a more personal level people found him to be a rock during the necessities of life. One of his Glasgow parishioners testified that 'His visits when I was ill were like those of a messenger of God'.[15] The extent to which this man, who had no children of his own, mentioned children in his sermons is also noticeable: 'The loftiest intellectual elevation, indeed, is nowise inconsistent with a genial openness and simplicity of nature; nor is there anything impossible or unexampled in the combination of a grasp of intellect that could cope with the loftiest abstractions of philosophy, and a playfulness that could condescend to sport with a child'.[16] Nor was Caird so 'metaphysical' as not to have noticed the responses of men to pastoral visitation: 'Habitual coarseness or impropriety of speech or conduct are for the nonce kept out of sight, and good-company manners produced for the occasion. When the minister of a parish makes his rounds, the children are smoothed into decorous trimness of dress and demeanour, the house is swept and garnished, the Bible is brought out, and everything puts on a Sunday look till he goes away'.[17]

Caird shrunk from, rather than sought, the limelight; and of his mental gifts it has been said that

> His intellect was not of a sparkling order, and his mind, though clear, evinced the qualities of a crystal rather than a diamond . . . It ground slowly, though, like the mills of God, it ground exceeding small . . . Accumulating knowledge and distilling it into wisdom, he could pour forth torrents of eloquence to the world, but he never said a really witty thing in his life . . . He had not that intuitive and penetrating mind which, darting and flashing, clear and swift and sharp, can drive home almost by instinct to the heart of a problem.[18]

As a preacher, Caird could always entrance the ear. At times he could reach right to the heart: 'I experienced what I had never heard before,' said one of his Glasgow hearers, 'a sermon which pierced my heart like a sword, and brought me face to face with a Saviour robed with love and not with dread'.[19] At other times, truth to tell, he could leave his people far behind: 'There are times when one thinks Dr. Caird the very apostle for the age, and other times when one cannot make out what he is preaching'.[20] Dr. Warr supplies a supportive incident: '"Was he no' graun' the day?" asked one elderly worshipper of another as together they left the portals of Errol kirk. "Ay", came a fervent assent; "but did ye un'erstaun' him?" "Un'erstaun' him?" echoed the first speaker—"I wadna presoom!"'[21]

On the other hand, Caird's *intentions* were practical enough, as in the reply he gave when D. W. Forrest asked him what kind of theme he should take for his first University sermon: 'Give us something practical and helpful', replied the Principal, 'we are tired enough of reconciliations of science and religion'.[22] Dr. Macmillan of Greenock confirms the point: 'His sermons . . . were more religious than theological, more practical than devotional. They were distinguished for their philosophic breadth, and their intense sympathy with all the struggles and sorrows and sins of humanity'.[23] Caird might almost have been describing himself when he wrote of Erasmus, 'Though of blameless life, and though there is no reason to question the sincerity of his religious belief, his piety was certainly of the rational rather than the emotional order, devoid of anything approaching to enthusiastic feeling, and in his theology the dogmatic element was ever subordinated to the moral and practical'.[24]

His own practical interests, combined with his distaste for controversy and his broadly tolerant spirit, lay behind much of the anguish he aroused in some hearts. He could not place confessional Calvinism above ethical interests as he saw them, and the result was that many missed much of the familiar 'language of Canaan' in his pulpit utterances. As Edward Caird said, 'he dwelt less upon doctrines about Christ, and more upon the idea of identification with him as a living person; less upon atonement by his death, and more and more upon unity with him'.[25] From the standpoint of conservatism, his were sins of omission:'Can it be that in seeking harmony he has lost the keynote and the *motif?* . . . Dr. Caird is half a Puritan, but the Hellene comes in. He has been much in company with Goethe and Arnold. One may say that he has just missed being a poet such as Arnold but with more warmth. Do these spirits help a preacher to convert sinners and build up believers? . . . Dr. Caird is on the holy mount; he has entered into the cloud and has said, "Master, it is good to be here" . . . the life of man consists in the love of this Holy, the service of this True God. Is it not enough? It is not. Puritanism will have the soul, and the soul cries out for the risen and redeeming Christ'.[26]

Caird's support of McLeod Campbell caused further consternation, as did that ecumenical openness which enabled him to welcome nonconformist students to his classes; to open the University pulpit to Anglicans and nonconformists; to deliver the St. Andrew's Day lecture in Westminster Abbey in 1874; and to supply for the Seceder Dr. Joseph Leckie at the Ibrox Church during Leckie's last illness.[27] As if all this were not enough, Caird contributed two sermons to the Scottish Broad Church volume, *Scotch Sermons* (1880), edited by Professor William A. Knight of St. Andrews.[28] The preface somewhat over-optimistically described the volume as comprising 'a few specimens of a style of preaching which increasingly prevails among the clergy of the Scottish church,' and declared the homiletic methods employed to be 'in harmony with the results of critical and scientific research'. All of which, in the prevailing intellectual climate, was 'fighting talk'. Many believed that the coal magnate James Baird inaugurated the Baird Lectureship with the specific intention of counteracting the teaching of Caird, and no student of Caird ever held a theological Chair in Scotland.

Caird's typical attitude towards conservatism emerges in a letter written on 24th November 1862, on his appointment to his Glasgow Chair:'It is very kind of you to warn me of the censorship to which, in common with every man who ventures to think or speak one word out of the routine jargon that stands for thought and faith with so many, I am subjected. I must lay my account with that, but I shall not needlessly provoke it. I have not the shadow of a wish for notoriety, not certainly for notoriety of that kind. My only desire is to work out of sight, and to do my share of the world's work, quietly and usefully'.[29] He experienced, like Erasmus of old, the difficulties which beset the thinker who lived in a time of transition:

> A thinker, a man of ideas, imbued with the pure and ardent love of knowledge, and therefore hating obscurantism and all its brood of vices, intellectual and moral, he has yet no sympathy with the rôle of the vulgar partisan, and the coarse weapons of party warfare excite in him nothing but disgust. He cannot be false to his own growing convictions, or refuse to follow where the lights of science and speculation seem to lead him, even though it be to the uprooting of cherished associations and the subverting of venerable institutions; yet, on the other hand, there is a side of his nature to which the very antiquity of such institutions appeals, as something imposing and sacred; and where it is possible to breathe new life into the symbols and traditions of the past, he will have no hand in their destruction.[30]

The following are examples of the kind of statements which would disturb Caird's more conservative brethren: 'The gentle virtues are not plants that bloom only on the soil of orthodoxy. They flourish, with a wonderful disdain of ecclesiastical restrictions, on the unhallowed domain of heresy; nay, sometimes are found blossoming into a strange luxuriance on the outlying wastes of heathendom'. 'The essence of religion is something more catholic than its creeds.' 'Theological systems in their merciless dogmatism have found in the sphere of intelligence and moral life a principle of supernatural selection as absolute as that of nature, and only differing from it for the worse in being purely arbitrary and capricious. The heaven of the theologian, like that of nature, has been a heaven only for the few . . . ' 'There are many good people to whom it seems to be the most pious and reverential attitude towards divine revelation to say, "Here is a book the divine authority of which has been proved by miraculous credentials, and every word that is contained in it I will, therefore, implicitly accept and believe" . . . But, however humble and reverent such language may sound, it is, I make bold to say, the language, not of faith but of unbelief . . . For that faith for which Christ calls . . . can say, "This is the truth of God; I see it, I believe it, I know it, and though heaven and earth should come together to disprove it, my faith in it would not be shaken"'. At the same time, Caird declared his aversion to 'latitudinarian indifference to truth';[31] and he could lament the fact that such older latitudinarians as Dr. Hugh Blair all but obliterated the distinction between Christianity and the non-religious world.[32]

Ought not Caird, perhaps, to have raised the questions of confessional subscription and revision in the Church courts? It was not in his nature to do so. He never spoke in the General Assembly; when he was Moderator of the Perth Presbytery from November 1851 to April 1852 he attended only two out of the six meetings held; and according to tradition, he absolutely refused nomination for the Moderatorship of the General Assembly. Among the advantages which Caird saw in his accepting Park Church, Glasgow in preference to St. George's, Edinburgh, was that the former 'is, moreover, a church unconnected with the Presbytery—I mean not a Parish Church—and I hate Presbyteries; but in St. George's I should be forced to attend them'.[33] Though in favour of the Establishment principle, Caird was by no means persuaded of the divine right of Presbytery:

> The Church and Church arrangements do not exist for themselves; they are but means to an end . . . I would maintain that we cannot expect to find in the Bible any rigid, uniform and unalterable form of Church government . . . The ideal of a Church platform which commends itself to all but bigots is that, not which presents the longest array of articles and points of belief drawn out with the most keen-eyed logical subtlety and minuteness, but that which under a creed or confession of the simplest form—enunciating but those grand facts and verities of God, of Christ, of sin, of salvation, on which the great mass of Christians are agreed—can comprehend the largest range of opinions in the sympathies of a common faith and love.[34]

If others could not, or would not, see this, then the Erasmian spirit can only 'stand by in amused pity till the din be done'.[35]

We may properly conclude this section by referring to some of the positive points which recur in Caird's sermons. We find, firstly, a thoroughly traditional understanding of the doctrine of regeneration. Man does not save himself: 'Religion is from beginning to end the work of the Spirit of God.'[36] And the end of religion is 'to produce character, to make men holy, and loving, and pure'.[37] True religion affects everything: 'It goes with you, or should go, to the shop, the plough, the anvil, and takes cognisance of what passes there; and the idle servant, the dawdling, trifling workman, the man who wastes his time and hangs listlessly over his work, sins against religion just as certainly as the man who neglects prayer or seldom opens his Bible'.[38] Nor are religious convictions to be lightly won. It is an aspect of Christian manliness that it does not blindly

follow an authority, but is ever questing after the truth: 'Salvation by
implicit belief or assent on bare authority to a set of doctrines that lie
outside of reason and conscience, is a degrading notion; it is a notion
which transforms God's Word into a spell; it is idolatry of the letter that
killeth, but desecration of the spirit that giveth life . . . Brethren,
religion is the manliest of all things . . . Its language is that which babes
may lisp, but it is also that which the lips of sages may not disdain to
utter'.[39]

   Caird was not among those liberals who sat loosely to the idea of the
wrath of God. There is, he declared, 'the anger of justice, moral
indignation, the condemnation and hatred of sin which a good and holy
nature must feel'.[40] But the law is interpreted by love, and 'what law
cannot do, Christ does'.[41] He is the response to our prayer,'Come, O my
Saviour, for sorely I need thy presence: my thoughts are confused, my
affections languid, my purposes weak and wavering. Come, O my
Saviour, and with thee my whole being shall grow bright and strong!'[42]
He is the One to whom we may ever come: 'Open the door of your heart to
Him, and He will come in to you and bless you'.[43] Having come, we are
secure for this life and the next. Believers know that 'be heaven what or
where it may, they will never find themselves unprepared for it who, filled
with undying faith in Christ's promise, have in life and death identified
their own happiness with the cause for which he lived and died, the final
triumph of the kingdom of light and love, the kingdom of Christ in the
world'.[44] And all this because of what is offered to us in Christ:

> 'There is balm in Gilead; there is a Physician there.' No case beyond
> His intervention; no soul so far gone in sin as to baffle His skill. Open
> your whole heart to Jesus. Tell Him all your case. Confess at His feet
> every hidden grief, every secret sorrow, every untold guilty fear. He is
> ready to hear and help. He is infinitely able to save to the uttermost all
> that come unto Him.[45]

Hence,

> Though my sin cannot be literally unsinned, though the past is
> irrevocable, though no moral act once done can ever be annulled, yet
> surely in this my trembling heart may find the rest for which it craves—
> the assurance that the past may be forgotten, and that sin is blotted out
> by an act in which its guilt is most fearfully condemned and expiated—
> when I behold the very God who is Law, Righteousness, Absolute
> Justice, in human form offering Himself up to the death to save me.[46]

II

The most comprehensive account of Caird's philosophico-theological stance is to be found in his Croall Lectures for 1878–9, *An Introduction to the Philosophy of Religion* (1880; 2nd edn. 1900). In this section we shall attempt an outline of this work, noting as they occur points for future reference. Then in the concluding section we shall discuss certain crucial themes in more detail, with reference to Caird's entire corpus, and in relation to Christian claims.

The presupposition of the philosophy of religion is that 'religion and religious ideas can be taken out of the domain of feeling or practical experience and made objects of scientific reflection'.[47] It is not denied that there is knowledge implicit in feeling, but philosophy elicits a 'higher' form of knowledge than this. Philosophy admits no limits to its range of activity: 'Whatever is real is rational, and with all that is rational philosophy claims to deal . . . Its vocation is to trace the presence and the organic movement or process of reason in nature, in the human mind, in all social institutions, in the history of nations, and in the progressive advancement of the world'.[48] Philosophy lifts us out of individuality, and searches for absolute truth; it seeks 'to bind together objects and events in the links of necessary thought, and to find their last ground and reason in that which comprehends and transcends all—the nature of God Himself . . . [Hence] in the explanation of religion philosophy may be said to be at the same time explaining itself'.[49]

A number of points need to be made here. First, we see clearly the neo-Hegelian idealistic stance. The real is the rational; reason is organic in all things; the evolutionary note is sounded. Secondly, the role of philosophy is declared to be the quest of objective, absolute truth. We are far removed indeed from those more recent understandings of philosophy according to which it is merely a discipline in which we raise at one remove analytical questions concerning what we are saying about what is or is not the case. Caird is after knowledge, and he expects philosophy to yield it. Furthermore, and again *pace* much recent philosophy *and* theology, he asserts the common interests of philosophy and religion. To him the God of religion is the Absolute of philosophy, and we shall have to see later whether this view leads him towards any unfortunate attenuations of the gospel. Thirdly, we begin to see signs of that methodological inconsistency to which we referred at the outset. Thus, on the one hand Caird seeks to *work up to* God. But on the other hand he speaks of God as the source as well as the consummation of all thought and being.[50] We seem to have here the seeds of two different methodologies. But on balance it is perhaps correct to say that Caird's emphasis is upon the latter. Thus, for all his strictures against pantheism, he can say that 'All thought of God must be pantheistic in this sense, that it starts from the presupposition that God is all'.[51]

Caird properly notes that those who wish to dispute philosophy's role must employ philosophy in order to do so, and then he mentions three more specific objections to his programme: that finite and relative human knowledge cannot comprehend the infinite and absolute; that the organ of religious knowledge is not reason, but faith; and that since religious truth is authoritatively revealed, human reason is not competent either to discover or to criticize it. Caird proceeds to review these objections in turn.

In discussing the relativity of human knowledge Caird grants that the objects and methods of religion are not the same as those of the physical sciences: 'the objects of religious knowledge cannot be perceived by the senses, or generalised out of the facts and phenomena which sense perceives'.[52] But it by no means follows that 'human knowledge is absolutely limited to things finite and phenomenal, that thought cannot transcend the objects which exist in space and time . . .'[53] The case of those who argue to the contrary must be carefully examined, for they claim to have exposed an illusion to which some of the best minds have been wedded. Caird takes Spencer as a prominent exponent of the relativity of human knowledge, and finds him inconsistent in wishing to maintain both the relativity of human knowledge and the Unknowability of an Absolute which is *known* to exist. As for those who, like Mansel, have welcomed Spencerian agnosticism as making an opening for faith, they are equally misguided. Caird's view is that the One who lies beyond our knowledge is, though unknown, not unknowable.

Caird next reviews the intuitionist position which appears here as a theory of 'innate ideas', there as a 'Philosophy of Common Sense'; and, characteristically, he begins by granting its strengths. Intuitionists take the force of the fact that our reason can never comprehend God. However, since philosophy does not aim at a *religious* result, there need be no conflict between religion and philosophy. More serious is Caird's protest against that psychologism to which supporters of immediacy are prone. He feels that the choice between sensationalist and empiricist theories on the one hand, and intuitionist theories on the other is by no means exhaustive, 'for the highest explanation and justification is given to any idea or element of thought when it is shown to be a necessary moment of the universal system, a member of that organic unity of thought, no part of which is or can be isolated or independent, or related to any other accidentally or arbitrarily, but wherein each idea has a place or function involved in its own nature and in its necessary relations to all other ideas and to the whole'.[54]

So we come to the suggestion that the ideas of revelation and science are reciprocally exclusive. Caird accepts that 'a God who does not reveal Himself ceases to be God'—in other words, that 'revelation is the necessary presupposition of religion.'[55] Even so, revelation is not necessarily exclusive of the activity of reason. Those who set reason and revelation at variance land in the paradoxical state of recognizing the ultimacy of reason, for 'We are to conclude a thing to be true *because* it seems absurd, and to believe it *because* it seems impossible'.[56] But the human spirit cannot be so divided. If absolute but contradictory principles were to exist side by side, we should need 'a higher umpire than both to decide between them, or thought and knowledge are reduced to chaos.'[57] Some, following Leibniz, have said that the content of a revelation, though not contrary to reason, may be above reason. But if we can posit an absolute limit to thought, ·we have already virtually transcended that limit. Further, what lies beyond reason is the irrational, or the non-sensical; and finally, 'The revelation of a mystery, in the sense of a doctrine altogether transcendent, relating to things outside the sphere of finite thought, is self-contradictory'.[58] Positively, 'It is only because the content of a revelation is implicitly rational that it can possess any self-evidencing power, or exert any moral influence over the human spirit'.[59]The moral is that 'if the contents of revelation be no longer regarded as above reason, then human reason not only may seek, but ought to seek, all the light which reverent and thoughtful investigation can throw upon them'.[60]

Caird next turns to a consideration of the necessity of religion. He does not mean that every man is necessarily religious, or that the religious ideas of all men or of all ages are coincident. Rather, he holds that there is an organic, developing religious experience which has its basis in what is involved in man *qua* man, namely, 'the transcendence of all that is finite and relative and the elevation of the finite spirit into communion with an Infinite and Absolute Spirit.'[61] Finite knowledge as such is illusory and false; true knowledge 'contains in it an absolute or infinite element, apart from which the whole complex of finite knowledge and experience would be reduced to chaos.'[62]

Clearly, Caird cannot be other than staunchly opposed to materialism and to positivism; nor does he think those theists wise who counter such 'isms' by the declaration that there *must* be a Creator, Designer, Governor of the world—for such a God is of the deistic kind, an occasional visitor.

The way to controvert materialism is to show that whereas materialists profess to exclude mind, they tacitly presuppose it at the outset; and that their master-key of mechanical causality is 'inapplicable to organic or vital phenomena',[63] for intelligence is involved therein. Negatively, we cannot seek the explanation of a highly complicated system in its lowest factor; positively, 'To prove the necessity of religion, it must be shown that the elevation of the human spirit above the finite, that upward movement of mind, which is involved in religion, is contained in the very nature of mind, is necessary to mind as mind'.[64] Thus Caird works towards his conclusion that 'all human knowledge . . . will be seen to rest on or involve the presupposition of the unity of knowing and being, or of a unity which embraces all thought and existence'.[65]

Caird proceeds to apply this principle to a number of the traditional topics in philosophy of religion. He accepts the failure of the theistic proofs as logical demonstrations, but reads them as 'expressions of that impossibility of resting in the finite and of that implicit reference to an Infinite and Absolute Mind, which we have seen to be involved in our nature as rational and spiritual beings'.[66] We need not follow his arguments in detail, but something of the flavour of his approach is suggested by this comment on the design argument: 'Even if the argument were otherwise unexceptionable by which we infer a design in each of the innumerable instances of adaptation with which the world abounds, yet a thousand finite designers would never make up the idea of that Being, of whom and through whom and to whom are all things';[67] or by this on the ontological argument: 'The true meaning of the Ontological proof is this, that as spiritual beings our whole conscious life is based on a universal self-consciousness, an Absolute Spiritual Life, which is not a mere subjective notion or conception, but which carries with it the proof of its necessary existence or reality'.[68]

This leads Caird to an examination of the religious consciousness, in which—against any compartmentalizing suggestions—he asserts the unity of man's spiritual life, and finds thought to be, at least implicitly, the omnipresent and underlying principle. Admittedly, 'ordinary thinking consists, for the most part, of generalised images, of conceptions derived from the outward and phenomenal world, and charged more or less with the inherent characteristics of their sensuous origin . . . [Such thinking] may suffice for practical piety, but it is insufficient for the purposes of philosophy'.[69] In particular, it cannot solve the contradictions to which ordinary thought is prone, or 'give organic connection and unity to the objects with which it deals.'[70] Enter the philosopher, to show us that unlike the natural world, the spiritual realm 'cannot be conceived of as made up of individual things independently existing and only externally related to each other'.[71] With a touch of *ad hominem* argument Caird avers that

> What, for any sober thinker, idealism does mean is, that both mind and matter, self and not-self, intelligence and its objects are, taken in isolation, nothing more than abstractions, that they have no conceivable existence save in opposition and therefore in relation to each other, and that a self which does not refer itself to that which is not-self, a not-self, which is not for a self, is as much an impossible notion as an inside without an outside, an upper without an under, a positive without a negative. Thought or self-consciousness is that which at once posits and in its own higher unity solves the contradiction.[72]

Formal logic, while it may 'dissect and exhibit in isolated detail the various members of the organic whole of truth' cannot reproduce the living unity of the whole.[73] A higher method of reconciliation is required. What is required is real unity, not merely that formal unity which we have when particulars are embraced under a general conception. 'This deeper and truer universality is that which may be designated *ideal or organic universality.*'[74]

At this point Caird immediately confronts the trap of pantheism, and in view of the criticisms made of neo-Hegelianism, not least by such theologians as Iverach, we ought in fairness to hear his own words:

> The attraction of Pantheism and of pantheistic systems of philosophy lies in this, that they meet the craving of the religious mind for absolute union with God and of the speculative mind for intellectual unity. But while Pantheism gains by the sacrifice of individuality and responsibility in man, by depriving the finite world of reality and reducing Nature, Man and God, to a blank colourless identity, a true philosophy attains in another and deeper way. It gives us a principle in the light of which we can see that God is all in all, without denying reality to the finite world and to every individual human spirit, or without denying it except in so far as it involves a life apart from God—a spurious independence which is not the protection but the destruction of all spiritual life.[75]

As a thinking, conscious being, man lives 'in the atmosphere of the Universal Life'.[76] The idea of the infinite, which man cannot but entertain if his idea of the finite is not to be an abstraction, 'is simply the idea of God as Absolute Spirit.'[77] The challenge before man is not to suppress his nature, as in asceticism, but to find his lower nature transformed so that it can be the expression of that higher nature which is his by virtue of his participation in the life of the Absolute Spirit. By the path of morality we may approximate to the ideal, but what we really need is religion's proclamation of a present, helping, real God. In Him and with Him the contradiction between the ideal and the actual vanishes: 'Oneness of mind and will with the Divine mind and will is not the future hope and aim of religion, but its very beginning and birth in the soul'.[78] Not indeed, that we have yet arrived. There is progress in the religious life, but it is not 'progress *towards*, but *within* the sphere of the infinite'.[79] But to which religion should we owe allegiance? Caird has no hesitation in affirming Christianity as being the religion which meets 'the unconscious longings of heathendom.'[80] Christianity takes up into itself the scattered rays of light in the old religion and transforms them—it is not that the old is the mechanical and efficient cause of the new—so that God is known 'not merely as an Omnipotent Power and Will above us, but as an Infinite Love within us'.[81]

III

Unlike some philosophers, John Caird did not become interested in the subject because of doubts and difficulties concerning his inherited beliefs. Rather, his philosophical foundations were reached when he sought to determine the implications of his faith. He *had* faith, but he could not rest content with unreasoned faith. 'Philosophy', he came to see, 'is simply the intelligent study and apprehension of human experience'.[82] And, as we have seen, his profound conviction was that that experience begins and ends in God.

Sir William Hamilton's relativistic epistemology and its Mansellian development appalled Caird, while Hegel, although relatively seldom mentioned in his works, gave him the stimulus he needed to order his own convictions. Caird's fundamental attitude was religious. He had, as Henry Jones said, a 'sense of the majesty of the natural and spiritual order in which man is placed, and, what is much more rare, of the surpassing splendour of the intrinsic endowment of man, as spirit'.[83] As Jones admirably put it, Caird's view was that 'the natural world and natural truth rest upon the spiritual world and spiritual truth, and these latter stand impregnable forever *in their own right*. Grasping the material realities of the outward world, confronting the hard, sad facts of human history with the unflinching directness of the Materialist and Pessimist, he was led by what seemed to him to be the unerring processes of necessary thought, to pronounce that these facts and the whole realm of nature culminated in spirit, and were explicable only in its light'.[84] The theologian's task is to take the truths of religion, which are true to life, and 'to mould all the separate elements into a consistent and systematic form'.[85]

As far as Caird was concerned, neither sensationalism nor materialism were true to the facts. The former could not accommodate the sceptic himself, for, as in Hume, 'A scepticism which evaporates all thought, evaporates at the same time the sceptical evaporator.'[86] The latter begs the question by overlooking the fact that '*You cannot reach mind as an ultimate product of matter and force; for in doing so you have already begun with mind*; the earliest step of the inquiry involves mental forms, and it is only in terms of mind that the problem you are investigating can be so much as stated'.[87] Hegel's great advantage over Kant, according to Caird, was that he pursued Kant's suggestion, that knowledge of the objective world is relative to the self-consciousness of the individual, to its logical conclusion in his assertion of the continuity between the human and the divine spirits. Indeed, Caird testified that he had been 'more largely indebted' to Hegel's *Philosophie der Religion* than to any other book.[88] This continuity finds its supreme expression in Christ. Hence, 'A philosophy . . . which pretended to deal with man in his spiritual nature and relations without taking cognizance of the person and life of Christ, would be leaving out of sight the one all-important element of its investigations, neglecting the key to its deepest problems'.[89]

Caird's idealism, like Hegel's, is one in which all oppositions are resolved in an Absolute conceived as immanent. Contrary to what is sometimes supposed, Hegel and the absolutists have no interest in denying the reality of the phenomenal world. They are not, as in Berkeleian idealism, claiming that reality depends for its existence on its being perceived. What is claimed is that the various aspects of reality together comprise a system. In this sense the real is the rational. That Caird does not set out to flout ordinary experience, and that he acknowledges the limits of that experience, is plain from the following remark: 'All our knowledge of nature, let it be conceded, is derived from experience. But experience itself depends on something that is not given by sensible experience, and without which it could not exist . . . isolated sensations are not knowledge'.[90] The activity of the rational self-consciousness cannot be excluded.

But with the implication of a prior synthesis, we seem to be verging upon that other idealism, the Platonic. There are, indeed fascinating oscillations in the thought both of Hegel and of Caird between the stuff of the world and the world of the forms. This is very much connected with

that combination of empiricism on the one hand and presuppositionalism
on the other which we noted in the first chapter of *An Introduction to the
Philosophy of Religion*. Caird was nowhere more Hegelian than in his high
opinion of man's intellect, and in his commitment to the evolutionary or
developmental ideas with which much of the fashionable science of his day
seemed to be in harmony.[91] Let us look at each of these aspects in turn.

   'Christianity and Idealism', wrote Edward Caird, 'were the two poles of
my brother's thinking, and the latter seemed to him the necessary means
for interpreting the former. He had, therefore, the strongest repugnance
for all theories that divorced faith and reason . . .'[92] This is confirmed by
John Caird's own reply to a note of congratulation on his Croall Lecture: 'I
shall be satisfied, if it leads some few who are in doubt on the highest
matters, to see that Christianity and Christian ideas are not contrary to
reason, but rather in deepest accordance with both the intellectual and
moral needs of man'.[93]

   Caird echoes Hegel, who had taught that while religion yields only
imaginative representations (*Vorstellungen*) of ultimate reality, philosophy
discovers exact concepts (*Begriffe*). For Caird, ordinary language cannot
rise to the task of expressing spiritual truth, and *faith* can do no other than
use the language of the phenomenal world when referring to the spiritual.
Reason, on the other hand, 'translates the necessarily inadequate language
in which thought represents spiritual truth, into that which is fitted to
express its purely ideal reality.'[94] Now this seems to us to have a decidedly
aristocratic air about it—especially given Caird's declared aim of holding
faith and reason in balance. We may agree that not every believer needs to
be a philosopher or a theologian,[95] but there is a strongly gnostic
suggestion in the words just quoted that what is revealed to philosophers
is superior to what is revealed to babes. Indeed, the philosopher is said to
be able to express spiritual truth in 'its purely ideal reality' (whatever that
may mean). Let him try! Does not pantheism lurk in the suggestion, in so
far as the philosopher would need to be able to think God's thoughts *with*
him, and not merely after him? Happily, Caird elsewhere takes a less
exalted view: 'Man is a mystery to himself; how can he think to
comprehend God?'[96]

   As we have already seen in passing, Caird, in seeking to hold reason and
faith together, fights on two main fronts. First, he is opposed to those
who would advocate a blind deference to authority, whether Bible,
Church or sacerdotal priesthood. In his Memorial Address, Henry Jones
expressed his concurrence with Caird by saying that to bow to authority
was a counsel of despair, for 'the faith it leaves to us is tainted with a
deadly scepticism'.[97] In Caird's own words, the glory of the gospel is that

'It speaks not to the ears merely or the senses, but to the hearts and consciences of men. It addresses mankind, indeed, with a voice of absolute authority, but its authority is not the mechanical authority of force or arbitrary will, but that authority which is the most majestic and irresistible—the authority of reason and righteousness over all rational and moral intelligence.'[98] It follows that theological propositions, dogmas, articles of faith, assemblies of divines—none of these avail to produce Christian experience, though they are important as interpreters of that experience where it exists.[99]The human mind does not excogitate its faith; rather, 'in the deepest sense [religious truths] are congenial to man's nature'.[100] Here, once again, is that 'naturalness' which flavours the writing of an apostle of continuity such as Caird. His mind is not, at crucial epistemological points, disturbed by the thought of the noetic effects of sin.

Secondly, Caird is in opposition to those who, like Mansel, would welcome the divorce of reason and faith on the ground that now faith could have its head. Caird would have agreed with Seth that when reason and faith were treated as two distinct organs, 'we are upon unsound ground, and mischief lurks not far distant'.[101] (What Caird would have made of those latter-day Barthians who, in relishing the divorce of reason from faith, played into the hands of the positivists, we can only speculate.[102]) Once again Jones accurately summarises Caird's position:

I find him . . . one who believed that faith is to be confirmed by *means of knowledge*, that the inheritance of traditional virtue and truth received from ages past is no bequest under a dead hand, but the means and the condition of new enterprises from which the human spirit will return with richer argosies of truth . . . it is possible for the frank intelligence and open trustful soul to search in the great book of nature and of spirit, written for their behoof by the finger of God, and to see inscribed therein, not mere contradiction or chaos, but the immutable laws of a spiritual order, a manifestation of the mind and majesty of God, which shall the more command and entrance the intelligence and heart of man, the more simply and humbly and sincerely he seeks to possess its inexhaustible truths.[103]

This is not to deny that we begin with faith; but having begun there, we advance to science: 'faith is but implicit reason, reason working intuitively and unconsciously, and therefore without reflection or criticism of its own operations'.[104] In fact, if faith is the first resort, it is also, in a profound sense, the last: 'The Bible is no philosophy. Its glorious truths are to be apprehended not by the critical intellect but by the humble and loving heart . . . The logic of the heart, in one word, may overleap the logic of the head'.[105]

We turn now to the evolutionary motif in Caird's thought. He holds that precisely because of the divine-human spiritual continuity, there is activity, movement, development in the universe. Consonantly with this, man's thought progresses and deepens: 'Far above the agitation and strife of man's petty passions, far above individual cares and interests that seem for the moment so important, never hasting, never resting, onward through the ages, the life of thought and knowledge advances to its goal.'[106] Negatively, this is why the human spirit may not be constricted by the creeds of yesteryear; positively, it informs the Christian's attitude towards other belief systems. Christianity's relation to these is not of the iconoclastic, but of the refining and re-contextualizing kind, as we have seen. Here as elsewhere the immanentist thrust of Caird's philosophy is unmistakable, and the vexed question of pantheizing tendencies cannot but be raised.

From the point of view of Christian theology the main deficiencies of pantheism are that it threatens the status, and even the real identity of the individual; and that it so implicates God in the world as to make it easy for man to regard himself as divine, and difficult to exonerate God from actual moral responsibility for man's sin. In a word, pantheism grievously blurs, if it does not altogether obliterate, the creator–creature distinction.[107] It is not without significance in this connection that William James predicted that Hegel's philosophy would 'probably have an important influence on the development of our liberal form of Christianity. It gives a quasi-metaphysical background which this theology has always been in need of.'[108] Certainly the blander, more sentimental liberal extremes, of which echoes may yet be heard—'God needs you as much as you need him'—need some kind of defence!

But there is *pantheism* and there is *panentheism*. The former more or less crudely tends towards the identification of God and the world, or, as in Spinoza's case, abstracts God from the world; the latter claims that God is unexcludable from any part of his creation: that everything exists in God. Undoubtedly the emphasis in Caird's writings as in subsequent process theology, is in favour of the latter view. Indeed, he launches upon a sustained attack upon Spinoza's pantheism in his *Spinoza* (1888), and in many other places too. The nub of his criticism is as follows:

> Spinozism is, from one point of view, the ambiguous result of two conflicting elements—a self-identical, undetermined substance which is all in one, and a world of finite individualities, each of which has a being and reality of its own. It is the obvious intention of the author to

bring these two elements into the unity of a perfect system . . . But the relation between the two elements is only asserted, never demonstrated. The absolutely undetermined is, by its very definition, precluded from going forth out of itself into a world of finite determinations; and if we start from the latter, they can only be brought back to the former by the destruction of their finitude, and their absorption in the infinite all.[109]

As for cruder pantheisms, Caird expostulates: 'Go to nature in your times of spiritual darkness and trouble, when an awakened conscience perturbs you, when the haunting memory of sin fills your soul with anguish and foreboding, and with the same unmoved and unpitying aspect she confronts your wretchedness.'[110] Far from deifying the world, pantheism's germ of truth is its declaration of 'the nothingness and insubstantiality of the things that are seen and temporal . . . For it is not so much by the affirmation, but by the negation, of the finite that the idea of the infinite first reveals itself in the human spirit'.[111]

For Caird, as for Hegel, Absolute Spirit is such that by its immanent working it can transcend and unify opposites; and Caird never tired of asserting (mark the word) that far from our being absorbed, we fully come into our own only when we are at one with God as Absolute Spirit. Pantheism's gravest defect is that it expunges rather than explains the existence of the finite world.[112] Caird, then, is no more in favour of pantheism's god than of deism's separated, arbitrary deity and the dualism therein implied. But *can* he preserve human individuality and divine transcendence? Can he preserve the creator/creature distinction? There is no doubt that he wishes to. Thus he declares that 'In *Christianity* and the Christian idea of God, we reach a conception which embraces and *does full justice* to the elements both of unity and difference . . . In the idea . . . of God as infinite Self-consciousness or Self-revealing Spirit, we attain to the conception of an Infinite Being who *neither limits nor is limited by the finite world*, but reveals or realizes Himself therein; and, on the other hand, of a finite world which is *neither absorbed in, or irreconcilably opposed to*, the Infinite . . .'.[113] But he can also declaim in such a way that the important qualifications just italicized by us are lost: 'immersion in the natural is absorption in the divine, and even the wildest orgies of sensual excess may be part of the homage rendered to the object of worship, seeing that in yielding ourselves up to nature we are yielding ourselves to God'.[114] It is not easy at this point to feel certain that transcendence survives the onslaught of immanence. The final paradox in that event is that our thought equals God's, and we have a materialism as pernicious as any of the varieties of materialism which Caird so ably attacked.[115]

We in no way wish to deny the closeness of the believer to his God. We endorse Caird's view that Christ 'tells us of a oneness with God so absolute that we may be said to be *in* God and God in us . . .'.[116] We even agree that we become truly free when we are thus in God.[117] But Caird somehow seems to make it all too automatic. Such union is, we believe, by grace through faith. Any sort of union with a *holy* God whom we have flouted is torment apart from that. Here we approach the methodological crux of the matter. Caird does not clearly make the distinction between the metaphysical and the moral to which we have just alluded. This is because his idealism makes the thought of divine-human ontological continuity uppermost in his mind. Certainly, if man were in no way akin to God, he could not respond to God; and the Christian doctrine of the *imago dei* is intended to assert that metaphysical link. But, on the other hand, if man were not distinct from God he could not flout God, he could not sin. Both ideas must be maintained, but the preponderating idea of unity in Caird's mind precludes the accuracy which the real situation warrants. Caird moves from the presupposition of the unity of all things in Spirit, and then seeks to work up to Christianity as the culminating expression of this unity. Now we have nothing against presuppositions, but we wonder whether Caird's is sufficiently *Christian*. We are aware how notoriously difficult it is to work in distinctively Christian insights and emphases if a supposedly 'neutral' basis has served at the starting-point. In this connection the verdict of Professor H. M. B. Reid upon Caird is very much to the point:

> Anselm's words, used as the motto of the 'Introduction to the Philosophy of Religion' (*negligentia mihi videtur, si postquam confirmati sumus in fide, non studemus quod credimus intelligere*) indicate Caird's strong bias to the intellectual side. But Anselm's words cannot be adopted literally by a Protestant thinker, because they subject the intellect to a yoke at the outset; the man who has been confirmed in the faith may zealously seek to understand it, but it remains the faith of his confirmation hour. He cannot travel beyond that. Caird indeed held that no philosophy deserving of the name would exclude anything essential to religion. But that itself is a presupposition as much as Anselm's *Credo ut intelligam*.[118]

Again, we may observe that Edward Caird was not convinced that his brother had taken the full measure of the impact of Hegelianism on the Faith:

> Perhaps he did not realize—I say this only to indicate a difference between us which was never completely settled in all our discussions— how great must be the transformation of the creed of Christendom,

before, in the language of Goethe's well-known tale, the hut of the fisherman can be transformed into the altar of the great Temple of Humanity . . . If he committed an error it was . . . that he followed Hegel in believing that the whole structure of dogma, as it had been developed by the Church, could be re-interpreted by philosophical reflection, without any essential change.[119]

James Denney, as we might expect, was even more vigorously certain that *Edward* Caird was starting in the wrong place:

The last unprofitable labour I have done was to read Edward Caird's Gifford Lectures. That put me in mind of a remark by a wiser man than Law: 'After that in the wisdom of God the world by its own wisdom knew not God, it pleased God to dispense with philosophers, etc. etc., and to save the world in an absurd way'. The philosophers, however, are irreconcilable still, and think themselves in a position to patronise Heaven. It is pitiful.[120]

Further, and precisely because of his less than fully Christian presupposition, John Caird cannot do justice to the historical. We thus have the uncanny feeling that, somehow our participation in the Infinite is secure; that at the same time our growth into the Absolute is gradual; and that all is guaranteed—even inevitable. Now this cannot but make such a phenomenon as the Cross-Resurrection event appear somewhat redundant. No doubt this phenomenon can teach us all manner of things, but our union with God is there irrespective of it. Accordingly, it is not easy to see how the idea of regeneration, to which, as we saw, Caird subscribed, can really be full-bloodedly present to his mind. Certainly full account is not taken of it in his epistemology. Similarly, although he can say that 'although to fallen man sin has become a second nature, it is never to be forgotten that the make and structure of his being is not for sin, but for holiness',[121] his presupposition of continuity does not allow this insight concerning *fallen* man's actual condition to emerge clearly in his metaphysic. Again, he can happily invoke those biblical verses which testify to the believer's mystical union with Christ—the very verses, incidentally, with which, as we shall see, Denney had most difficulty—but he cannot so easily accommodate the doctrine of creation *ex nihilo*. Finally, his doctrine of the Trinity is much more like Hegel's than like that whose seeds are to be found in the New Testament. Of Hegel's Trinity, H. R. Mackintosh said that it amounts to this: 'as pure abstract idea God is Father; as going forth eternally into finite being . . . God is Son; as once more sublating or cancelling this distinction, and turning again home enriched by this outgoing in so-called self-manifestation or incarnation, God is Holy Spirit. Such a Trinity, clearly, represents that which is in no sense eternal but only coming to be; it has no meaning, or even existence, apart from the finite world. It is a dialectical triad, not Father, Son and Spirit in any sense in which Christian faith has ever pronounced the three-fold Name'.[122] With Caird's bold asertion that 'The Trinity is the distinctively Christian idea of God',[123] we may agree; but that he himself was not altogether satisfied with his treatment of it is clear from his remarks at the end of a course of lectures on the subject: 'I thought that I should find in the formulae of the Hegelian philosophy a solution of the high mystery of the Trinity. I feel, I am bound to confess, that I have failed to satisfy my own mind. That philosophy seems to me, with my best efforts to apprehend and state it, to fall away, either on the one hand into pantheism, or, on the other, into a dualism that has disappointed my hope'.[124] How infinitely preferable is such candour to the thunderings of a pretended omniscience!

It remains briefly to show how Caird's inadequately Christianized presupposition of continuity adversely affects his treatment of other major Christian doctrines. In the first place, his notion of revelation as not once-for-all given, but developing, cannot but threaten the idea of the finality of Christ. The once-for-allness of Christ's work does not emerge clearly from Caird's writings. No doubt Caird's approach seems to be open and hospitable, but how can he be sure, on his organic, plastic principles, that the supremacy of Christ, to which he *does* adhere, may not be engulfed by its opposite with a view to a further process of harmonization and development? Next, it is consistent with the principle of continuity that (as Professor Paterson observed) when Caird speaks of immortality, the centre of gravity in the discussion is not the concept of justification, which is only incidentally touched upon, but that of the blessing of union with God.[125] The same point may be made in relation to sinful man's need. Caird says, 'If . . . we think of God as the Creator of man, as calling into being finite spiritual natures distinct from Himself, we see also that it is the very principle and essence of such natures to renounce their finitude, to quell in themselves the self that divides them from God, and to return not into pantheistic absorption, but into living union with Him from whom they came'.[126] Just like that! We hardly seem to be reading about actual man as he is; the necessity of atonement is undermined; and there is no notion that sin is anything other than an unfortunate deficiency to be expected in the finite. On the other hand, in a more homiletic moment, Caird takes a much more radical view of the nature of sin: 'Sin is a malady which affects the very organ by which itself can be detected; it creates the darkness amid which it injures us, and blinds the eyes of its victim in the very act of destroying him . . . Guilt and sin separate the soul from God as the widest wastes of untravelled space could never separate'.[127] It is difficult to resist the conclusion that the metaphysics are in tension with the religion. Not surprisingly (given Caird's presupposition) when he speaks of the restoration which man requires, the intellect is much more to the fore than is the will.[128] In any case, to Caird, with his developmentalist approach, 'the discord which sin has introduced is but the transition step to a more glorious harmony'.[129] Far be it from us to deny that God can turn the wrath of man to his praise: the Cross-Resurrection event is *the* paradigm of this *par excellence*. But firstly, it is difficult on Caird's principles to deny that sin is a *necessary* step on the path towards the good; whereas, as James Orr will make plain to us, sin is that which ought never to be. Secondly, Caird's notion of the path to perfection has a 'Pelagian' ring about it which coheres with the 'automatic' atmosphere within which, as we have seen, we seem to be operating. Consequently, the graciousness of grace is minimised: 'Not what I am by nature constitutes my true spiritual life, but what, in the exercise of my own throught and will, *I have made myself to be*.'[130] No doubt such talk struck a chord with liberals of the more 'heroic' kind, but what now of sin's disabling power, and of the need of regeneration? What indeed of Caird's insight, later expressed, to the effect that 'there is a sense in which the atoning work of Christ is a thing achieved for us apart from any effort on our part'?[131] Thirdly, Caird's comparative weakness on God's transcendence, together with his continuity principle, prompt him to say that 'the discord . . . in which sin consists must be the discord of an infinite with a finite element, both of which are in our own nature . . . '.[132] We do not have holy God over against sinful man. Rather, we have man at odds with himself—or (why not on these principles?)—God at odds with himself. The finite-infinite account of sin does scant justice to the fact of inter-personal dislocation, and this, surely, is of the essence of sin's tragedy. With almost uncanny calmness Caird can say of Christianity that 'Its essential truths are not foreign to man's nature or contradictory to it, but true to that which is deepest and most real in man'.[133] No doubt, if 'man' here is 'ideal man'. But of 'natural man' the reverse is the case; he it is who wilfully suppresses what he knows of God; he it is who shakes his fist against God; he it is who needs a Saviour. And what of Caird's Saviour? The New Testament gives us 'the story of divine wisdom dwelling on earth in human form'; Christ's Cross reveals the 'sublime triumph of trust in God and love and hope for man'; and herein is 'good news from heaven for all mankind'.[134] We do not seem to have here Christ the atoning Saviour, but simply Jesus the epitome of trust and other worthy qualities. This 'good news' could as well have been written with invisible ink. Elsewhere however (and how often have we had to say this!), Caird borrows a different answer to the question 'What does Christ *do* about sin?' In fact, he borrows it from James Orr. Christ, he declares, rendered satisfaction to righteousness for us.[135] The exemplification of eternal principles accords best with Caird's metaphysics; his borrowing from Orr is indicative of a theology which ever and again in his writings strives, but just fails, to gain mastery.

We should not wish to be thought of as offering an entirely negative judgement on a considerable thinker. Many of Caird's insights are of abiding worth. His case against the privative view of evil is cogent; we welcome his denial of the hard and fast distinction between natural and revealed theology; we applaud his detailed discussion of Spinoza. But we choke on his principle of continuity. His vision was grand, but his gospel was inadequately rooted in the life and work of Christ—or, more accurately, his philosophical presupposition did not allow him to take the full measure of the gospel in his system.

CHAPTER FIVE

Alexander Balmain Bruce (1831–1899): Seeing and Showing Jesus

'Two things are urgently required of us modern Christians: to see Jesus truly and to show Him just as we see Him.'[1] To the former of these tasks A. B. Bruce brought his exegetical linguistic skills; to the latter he applied his apologetic and literary gifts. Not for him the mere handing on of a legacy from the past; he was an adventurer in the faith who hoped that the results of his own spiritual quest would benefit others. He was, to use his own word, 'modern' in a way that Kennedy, and even Orr, were not. Methodologically, he was not as obviously 'eighteenth-century' as was Flint; nor was he as penetrating philosophically. Open to new thought, he was not bowled over by it, and, in particular, he resisted the neo-Hegelian path which his contemporaries, the brothers Caird, made so attractive. Well versed in the history of Christian thought, he did not carry the weight of learning of an Orr. Faithful to his Church, he was not the all-round theological educator-cum-ecclesiastical–statesman that Iverach and Forrest were; and he was not so resolutely and pungently dogmatic as was his pupil Denney. Bruce spoke of what he knew; he was agnostic where he could be no other. His very honesty caused him to be regarded as a 'troubler of Israel' by some of the more conservative members of his Church.

Bruce was born at Aberargie in the parish of Abernethy, Perthshire, on 30th January 1831.[2] His father, David Bruce, was a farmer who was forced to resign his post because he 'came out' at the Disruption of 1843. The family removed to Edinburgh, and Alexander, whose schooling had been at Auchterader parish school, entered Edinburgh University at the age of fourteen. In later years he was wont to chuckle over the fact that he had gained higher marks in mathematics than the distinguished mathematician James Clerk Maxwell. But from the first his own sense of call was to the Christian ministry, and in 1849 he entered the Free Church College, Edinburgh. While there he laid the foundations for his life's work—and that not intellectually only, but emotionally too. If ever there was a professional apologist who had more than an imaginative sympathy with those assailed by doubt, that apologist was Bruce. D. F. Strauss's *Life of Jesus* (1835–6; revised 1864), with its denial of the historicity of the gospels, shook him to such an extent that he seriously questioned whether or not he should proceed to ordination. He derived little help from his staunchly Calvinistic mentors, but was heartened by the preaching of Oswald Dykes, and by the writings of F. W. Robertson of Brighton. From these he learned that the evangel could be retained without sacrificing the intellect. A further hero of his was Carlyle, who on Bruce's own admission taught him—perhaps at times too insistently, we feel—'to read the gospels as a polemic against pharisaism'.[3]

Already a number of things begin to become clear. We can for example see why, in his last book, Bruce should write, 'It does not suit my temper to speak oracularly. I am content to occupy the humble position of one who feels keenly the pressure of the question'.[4] We can see how ideally he filled the role of one who aimed 'to secure for Christianity a fair hearing with conscious or implicit believers whose faith is stifled or weakened by anti-Christian prejudices of varied nature and origin.'[5] This aim governed most of his preaching, teaching and writing, and that the apologist had himself stood where the doubters and weak of faith stand is further underlined in a letter he wrote to a young minister, Mr. Macellar of Gourock: 'I was in your case for years, diseased at once in body and mind, each acting on and intensifying the other . . . I have doubted the whole supernatural system of truth, the incarnation, the atonement, the resurrection of Christ and of men in general, the future world, the inspiration of Scripture, and been indescribably miserable. Now I have attained to the full assurance of understanding, to the acknowledgement of the mystery of God and the Father, and of Christ; and so will you. Meantime, get up the tone of your body, and do nothing rashly'.[6]

Bruce was troubled not only by intellectual doubts, but also by ecclesiastical strife. When in later years he (concurrently with Professor Marcus Dods) was challenged by the Free Church Assembly to justify some of the opinions expressed in his *The Kingdom of God; or Christ's Teaching According to the Synoptical Gospels* (1889), he recalled that when he went to University, two years after the Disruption, 'I made my escape from the strife of the Churches to the teaching of Jesus, where I saw in its brightness and unearthly beauty the Christian ideal . . . I am not greatly concerned to defend all I have said . . . Call [the offending passages] one-sided, severe, pessimistic; all true, possibly, and more. But that is only one side. The other is, I have been looking at the Church in the dazzling light of the King and the Kingdom.'[7] Small wonder that he should write two years later, 'One who had, after a spiritual struggle, at last got himself grounded in the essentials of the Christian faith may be left to adjust his relations to the community of believers the best way he can'.[8] His struggles, intellectual and ecclesiastical, had given him a sense of proportion. More importantly, they had driven him to Jesus.

On leaving theological college Bruce held two assistantships—at Ancrum and Lochwinnock—before being called to Cardross, Dunbarton-shire, in 1859. His predecessor there, Mr. Macmillan, had been deposed by the General Assembly and had left behind a congregation of divided loyalties. Under Bruce's ministry wounds were healed, and harmony restored. In 1860 Bruce married Jane Hunter, daughter of James Walker of Fodderslee, Roxburghshire. In 1868 the Bruces removed to Broughty Ferry, and in 1871 Bruce published his first book—the fruit of his gospel studies and expository ministry—*The Training of the Twelve*. With characteristic humility he declared that he did not publish because he thought he had spoken the last word on the subject. Far from it: 'it was the voice of the stern prophet Death that brought me to decision . . . In one brief fortnight I followed to the grave three beloved relatives: my aged godly father, my son, and my brother's wife. When all the mournful duties of that sad season were over, I felt impelled to proceed at once with the publication of this work . . . thankful to find escape from sorrow in hard work, and obtaining the requisite leisure in consequence of the fever which carried off my child making me for a time as a leper, separated from the congregation of the Lord'.[9] The book was very well received, and in 1874 Bruce was appointed Cunningham Lecturer. *The Humiliation of Christ* (1876), Bruce's most doctrinal work, was the published fruit. Before the book appeared, Bruce had in 1875, been appointed to succeed Principal Patrick Fairbairn of Glasgow Free Church College in the Chair of Apologetics and New Testament Exegesis. In the same year his own University conferred its D.D. upon him.

Bruce remained in Glasgow for the rest of his days, but his fame spread far and wide. His students and colleagues loved him, and his services were much in demand. On a number of occasions he visited the United States, and was Ely Lecturer at Union Theological Seminary, New York, in 1886. He wrote for *The Expositor* and for *The Expository Times*, and the list of his books is long. A number of his works enjoyed successive editions, and his *Apologetics; Or, Christianity Defensively Stated* (1892) was into its tenth thousand by 1927. Bruce helped to popularize the work of others by his joint editorship, with Canon T. K. Cheyne, of *The Theological Translation Library*, and his term as Gifford Lecturer at Glasgow (1896) was a fitting climax to his distinguished teaching career. His lectures were published as *The Providential Order of the World* (1897) and *The Moral Order of the World* (1899).

Though not an ecclesiastical statesman, Bruce was ever loyal to his Church. He was a great admirer of Thomas Chalmers, and it was perhaps the memory of Chalmers which inspired his highly important Assembly speech of 1873. He argued that the existing Establishment rendered impossible the formation of a truly national Church. He encapsulated his sentiments in an addendum to a motion, which was carried. Always eager to advance the cause of Christ, he gave £100 of his Gifford Lectures fee to the Glasgow Church Planting fund, and he served as convenor of the Church's Strangers' Committee—a body charged with the responsibility of pursuing the lapsed and the luke-warm with pastoral care. Above all, he rendered notable service (of which John Kennedy would by no means have approved!) by his advocacy of instrumental music in worship, and by his convenorship of committees which produced the *Free Church Hymn Book* (1882) and its successor, the *Church Hymnary* (1898). In the preface of the former book the Committee's purpose is given as being 'the advancement of God's glory in the praise of the sanctuary'.[10]

Many regretted that Bruce was not called to the Moderatorship of the General Assembly. No doubt the 'indiscretion' of the Dods-Bruce case, to which we have already referred, was in part responsible for this. Professor Clow surmises that the *Modern Church*, a weekly paper in which Bruce, 'the most catholic-minded man in Scotland', sought to provide a platform for a variety of views, may have deepened the sense of hostility which so pained Bruce during the case. But there was no arrogance on Bruce's part, and he did not patronize those less able than himself. He was a humble man, and to Clow we owe testimony as to the quality of Bruce's devotional life, which was evidence by his death-bed utterances on the Kingdom of God, and by an engaging habit: 'Anyone who sat near his desk might have seen a line of single letter written boldly on a slip of paper before him. What were they? They were the first letters of a sentence of prayer. O s. o. T. l. a. T. t. ('O send out Thy light and Thy truth') was a favourite line. His custom was to rise early, and as he began his work he wrote out some such appeal to God, and as the hours passed he lifted his eyes and murmured his prayer for help'.[11]

With the memory of Kennedy and Begg in our minds it is not difficult to understand why Bruce was 'suspect' in some quarters. He was temperamentally unsuited to hyprocrisy, and could not affirm what he did not believe. He did not speak in terms of the old dogmatic (though his speech could be blunt enough!), and his fellow-feeling with doubters and seekers was intense. Thus, in his Gifford Lectures, in welcoming free theological enquiry, he said, 'it is not so much a matter of course that a theologian by profession should sympathise with the desire for free unfettered inquiry in this region of thought. Nevertheless I do'.[12] Again, he was quite ready to say when his knowledge had run out, and he refused to indulge in speculative dogmatics. On the question of the millenium, for example, while recognizing that some students of the Bible felt able to tell us all about it, he preferred 'to confess my ignorance and remain silent.'[13] And for those who sought to impose less-than-necessary belief upon others, Bruce had very little patience. He was quite prepared to let men begin where they could, and grow at their own pace. This emerges, for example, in his comment upon the parable of the Pharisee and the publican. He draws out the moral to the effect that God exalts the humble, and humbles the proud, and then says of this lesson, 'Let us not despise it because it is elementary, and does not belong to the more specific doctrines of Christian theology on the subject of justification. Let those who do not feel at home in these doctrines, and to whom perchance they appear not only mysterious but unreal, lay this elementary ethical truth to heart, and it will be at least one lesson learnt on a very important subject'.[14]

The fear of Pharisaism, ever at the back of Bruce's mind, remained with him throughout his professional life. In his first book he averred, 'Orthodoxy will not save the church any more than ecclesiastical dignitaries—priests, bishops, cardinals, popes. The temple which endures for ever is founded on Christ, the Rock of ages, and built up of "lively stones"'.[15] And in his penultimate book he averted to the danger inherent in the contrary approach: 'it is hard to say who really believes when disbelief is interdicted under heavy penalties. Prudence takes the place of conviction, and make-belief becomes the order of the day'.[16] 'When', he sighed, 'will young men and old men, liberals and conservatives, broad Christians and narrow, learn to bear with one another; yea, to recognize each in the other the necessary complement of his own one-sidedness?'[17] And he ruefully remarked that 'There are always a sufficient number of prosaic, order-loving disciples, to keep their quixotic brethren in due check'.[18] Far better, however, to face up to the legalists than to become like Nathanael, whose difficulty in believing that any good thing could come out of Nazareth showed that 'He timidly allowed his mind to be biased by a current opinion originating in feelings with which he had no sympathy; a fault common to men whose piety, though pure and sincere, defers too much to human authority, and who thus become the slaves of sentiments utterly unworthy of them'.[19] The Kingdom of God is a Kingdom of liberty, not of oppression; of truth, not of orthodoxy; and of moral truth, not of legalism.[20] This is not to say that Bruce favoured so easy a tolerance as to admit to Church fellowship those of all beliefs or of none. In his view,

> The hope of the future seems to lie neither in a creedless Church nor in a Church clinging superstitiously to all traditional dogmas, but in a Church which has the will and the wisdom to distinguish between the essential and the non-essential in religious belief, between catholic Christian certainties and matters of doubtful disputation; in other words, between *doctrines of faith* and *theological dogmas* . . . The Church is now weak, and among the causes of her weakness are *doubt, division,* and *dogmatism.* To renew her youth, and make a fresh start in a career of victory she needs *certainty, concord,* and a *simplified creed.*[21]

Bruce's own statement of the more essential truths of revelation is as follows:

> God manifested as a Trinity through the Incarnation of Christ, and the mission of the Comforter. Men found by God lost, impotent, dead, alienated,—lifted up by His grace into a region of holiness and blessedness; forgiven for the sake of Him who was crucified for sin; admitted to intimate fellowship with God, and made partakers of eternal life; united into a holy commonwealth, in which they are related to God as sons, to each other as brethren, exhibiting in their mutual converse the communion of saints, and, as a spiritual society, having for their high vocation to bring about the consummation of the desires which Jesus taught His disciples to cherish for the advancement of God's glory, the coming of His kingdom ever more extensively, and the doing of His will on earth as it is done in heaven.[22]

So concerned was Bruce to commend the essentials—and that to all age groups—that he tried his hand at a Christian Primer: 'It is my desire that the children also may see Jesus "with open face". Existing catechisms do not accomplish this good object. In them Jesus is seen only through the somewhat opaque veil of theology. I do not quarrel with theology, but it should come last not first. Theology is for full-grown men, not for children'.[23] Certainly, Pharisaism is 'an ungenial soil in which the gospel of the kingdom had little chance of taking root . . . How certain that the kingdom of heaven will draw few citizens from the ranks of Pharisaic society, and what poor citizens even the few are likely to make!'[24]

The attitudes thus expressed did not endear Bruce to those whose consciences smote them at the charge of Pharisaism. But it would be wrong to convict all his opponents of that sin. Some might have agreed that 'Many, in fact, have left the Church in order to become Christians'.[25] They would have endorsed Bruce's view of Christ's doctrine of man to the effect that we should 'look for the most aggravated types of moral degeneracy from the divine ideal of manhood, not among the irreligious, but among the inhumanly religious'.[26] They might even have granted that the Reformers were open to the criticism that in their zeal to oppose merit, and to make grace all, they drained faith of its moral contents.[27] But the sincerely confessional could not rest content with an approach to the Bible which enabled Bruce to say that whereas 'From the Calvinist's point of view, it may appear waste in the Saviour to die for more than the elect', Jesus's own attitude was, 'I die for every human creature, because all men are My brethren and God's prodigal children.'[28] Above all, they abhorred the way in which Bruce invoked Jesus's aid against the doctrine of predestination:

> He did not think of the elect as chosen to an exclusive salvation, or as enjoying a monopoly of divine favour . . . The aim is universal human salvation, and the elect of any age are God's agents in the execution of the beneficent plan. If any are unsaved, it is a miscarriage for which God is not responsible, and which wrings from the Redeemer's heart tears of bitter regret . . . [particularists if they exist] belong to an elect that has lost its savour, and is fit only to be trampled under foot.[29]

All the issues raised in the last paragraph, together with such fears as that Bruce was being unduly influenced by sceptical German scholars, were mingled in the Dods-Bruce case. Dods and Bruce had earlier displeased their more conservative brethren by their support of William Robertson Smith during the controversy of 1878–80. Now the College Committee found that although there were regrettable statements in Bruce's *Kingdom of God*, there were no grounds for a heresy charge. Dr. Ross Taylor and Principal Rainy adopted the same position in the Assembly of 1890. The Assembly concurred, and many heaved a sigh of relief that the battle for biblical criticism was won in the Free Church. Not, indeed, that all were satisfied at the outcome, but even among those who were not, few could have remained entirely unmoved by Bruce's statement, which included the following words:

> In the closing passage of its special report the College Committee recognize the 'intellectual vigour' of my book. I thank them for the compliment. But I must take leave to say that it is a small thing to me in connection with such a work to be complimented on my ability. The question is, Have I seen Christ and helped others to see Him? . . . I have been trying all my life to see Jesus and to show Him; and if I have failed, it will be small consolation to be told that I have written with considerable ability.[30]

It was on the basis of his understanding of the mind of Christ that Bruce reflected on everything else. We may profitably complete our picture of him by drawing together some of the observations scattered throughout his books. As we might expect of an anti-Pharisee, Bruce made much of the inwardness of faith. Outward observance, whether ritual or moral, will not suffice. Genuine repentance is an 'indispensable condition of citizenship' in the Kingdom of God.[31] Humility is required too. In fact, 'the struggle for religious name and church place and power may be more respectable than the struggle for physical livelihood, but it is not less, but rather more, ungodly'.[32] The Kingdom is one of righteousness, hence the need of repentance; and of grace, hence the need of faith. The Kingdom is God's gift, and faith is the means of its appropriation.[33] Bruce insisted that Jesus 'did not regard faith as an isolated faculty separate from reason, and still less as opposed to reason, but rather as a function of the whole mind exercized on religion';[34] and he was equally convinced that works should follow faith: 'Surely meditation on the life and death of Christ ought to be as wings, helping us to soar to the mountain heights of duty; or as military music, inspiring courage, banishing fear, and causing us to march to battle and hardship and danger with a light step and a gay cheerful spirit!'[35] Few went further against antinomianism than Bruce. His was a robust faith, and in his ethic, moral resentment against ungodliness took its place alongside mercy.[36] Unconditional service was in his ethic too, and it inspired his criticism of utilitarianism, which 'tends to trimming and time-serving; it is the death of heroism and self-sacrifice; it walks by sight, and not by faith; it looks only to the present, and forgets the future; it seats prudence on the throne of conscience; it produces not great characters, but at best petty busybodies'.[37]

Undeniably the ideals of Christianity are high, but they are not so high that we should faint before the attempt to realize them. It is sadly the case that 'To many, the creed which resolves all religion into impracticable ideals is very convenient. It saves a world of trouble and pain; it permits them to think fine thoughts, without requiring them to do noble actions and it substitutes romancing about heroism in the place of being heroes'.[38] The Christian way is a way for heroes; and those who walk it have something better to encourage them than the Socinianizing interpretation which makes Christ say, 'I have overcome the world, therefore so may ye' if you follow in my steps. Rather, the true Christian assurance is that 'Christ's victory is the victory of His followers, and ensures that they too shall conquer'.[39] The emphasis is upon what he has done, before it is upon anything which we may do. It was the error of the

Pharisaic that they placed all the emphasis upon our obedience; and the same tendency made itself felt in that 'huge and mischievous mistake', the ascetic theory of Christian virtue.[40] The fundamental error of asceticism is that it 'strikes at the root of all faith in a providential presence of God in human history. God is only in the monk's cell, the devil is everywhere else'.[41] In one sentence Bruce embraces three of his major aversions. He speaks against the perversion of Christian truth 'into forms of error kindred in appearance, utterly diverse in spirit; as, for example, of spiritual authority into priestcraft, of salvation by grace into Antinomian licence, or of self-denying devotion into a gloomy asceticism'.[42]

Bruce was not afraid to apply his critical powers to the Church as he found it, and not least to the Church's ministry: 'my sympathies are very strongly with the advocates of a learned ministry. In my view, what we have to complain of is, not that the Churches have adopted this as their ideal, but that the ministry turned out of their theological seminaries can only by courtesy be described as learned. What we need is not less learning, but a great deal more and of the right sort. At the same time, it has to be acknowledged that the programme involves dangers. Learning may kill enthusiasm, and transform the prophet into a rabbi!'[43] The ministry should aim rather at exhibiting

> the many-sided wisdom of God in the gospel. The result will be a faith to which Christ is wisdom by being at once righteousness, sanctification and redemption; . . . a Christ for us and a Christ in us; a Christ who died in our stead, and a Christ with whom we die daily; a faith which will work through fellowship with Christ in His sufferings to the effect of making us Christlike as surely as it will rest upon Christ as the Saviour from sin.[44]

Evangelism is not enough; there must be edification,[45] and, sadly, 'the melancholy history of many hopeful religious movements is this: many converts, few stable Christians; many blossoms, little fruit coming to maturity'.[46]

When we turn to questions of church order, we find Bruce's catholicity and tolerance in full display. He cannot agree that the New Testament infallibly and for all time prescribes one form only of church government. Jesus provided for the Church 'no ecclesiastical constitution, issued no authoritative instructions concerning forms of church government, clerical offices and orders, or even worship'.[47] In any case, 'The Church is only a means to an end. It is good only in so far as it is Christian. There is no merit or profit in mere ecclesiasticism. Whatever reveals the true Christ is of value and will live. Whatever hides Christ, be it pope, priest, or presbyter, sacraments or ecclesiastical misrule, is pernicious, and must pass away . . . Christ will ever remain . . . and the kingdom of God will remain, a kingdom that cannot be moved'.[48] Bruce supported all movements towards clearing the ecclesiastical undergrowth, and uniting Christians of all kinds.[49] Apart from anything else, this would discomfit refugees from ecclesiastical discipline:

> Fugitives from discipline are always sure of an open door and a hearty welcome in some quarter . . . One who has become, or is in danger of becoming, as a heathen man and a publican to one ecclesiastical body, has a good chance of becoming a saint or an angel in another. Rival churches play at cross purposes, one loosing when another binds; so doing their utmost to make all spiritual sentences null and void both in earth and heaven, and to rob religion of all dignity and authority. Well may libertines pray that the divisions of the church may continue, for while these last they fare well![50]

Since all of Bruce's views were coloured by what he has seen of Jesus, we must next ask, 'What had he seen?', and then turn to the question of the means by which he sought to commend Christ to others.

I

> On the idea we cherish of the Divine Being it depends whether our religion is to be a bane or a blessing, emancipating or enslaving, in moral tendency elevating or degrading. Come then to Christ's school, all ye who desire the true knowledge of God. Learn of Him how to think of God, man, and their relations. His doctrine solves all vital problems: the problems of past sin, of present duty, and of future destiny.[51]

Bruce took his own advice and went to the school of Christ. His studies convinced him that we do have reliable knowledge of Jesus. Christianity 'is essentially a historical religion',[52] and we have adequate records of its establishment. The Jesus whom the gospels reveal is, moreover, the Christ. Arnold's view that the correspondence between the prophetic ideals and the Jesus of history is simply a remarkable coincidence, is tantamount to the claim that there is no providential order whatsoever. As the materialist stood in relation to the physical constitution of the universe, so did Arnold in relation to history.[53] Jesus *was* the long-expected Messiah, but he had his distinctive and (to Zealots and Pharisees alike) unacceptable way of being the Messiah. He was one who would conquer by love and truth. His Messianic claims were clear: he was judge, saviour, revealer of God. Though humble in spirit, he was the Lord, and he demanded the utmost loyalty and obedience from his followers. Himself sinless, he was competent to forgive the sins of others.[54] The title 'Son of Man''announced a Messiah appointed to suffer, richly endowed with human sympathy, and destined to pass through suffering to glory'.[55] The title 'Son of God' proclaimed that filial consciousness from which the Messianic consciousness flowed.[56] As they reflected upon Christ's resurrection victory, Paul and the other early Christians could not withhold from Jesus the title 'Lord'. In a phrase often attributed to Ritschl, Bruce says that 'Jesus has for the Christian consciousness the religious value of God'.[57] But that Bruce did not intend to languish in subjective idealism is plain from the many passages in which he asserts the historicity of the gospel narratives; and we have already seen that he did not divorce reason from faith.

We may build upon these general remarks by reference to Bruce's most solidly doctrinal work, *The Humiliation of Christ*. It was typical of Bruce's robust, heroic attitude that he should declare that while those who would treat of Christ's divinity should proceed with reverence and caution, a dash of audacity was also required. He recognized that in placing Christ's state of humiliation in the dominant place he was embarking upon a comparatively novel path in Christology. True, some Reformed theologians had made more of the idea of Christ's humiliation than its formal position in their schemes suggested, but Lutheran scholars had 'constructed their Christology in utter defiance of the doctrine of humiliation, making the Incarnation, in its idea, consist in a deification of humanity rather than in a descent of God into humanity, and investing the human nature of Christ with all divine attributes, even such metaphysical ones as are commonly regarded and described as incommunicable,[58] It has been left to the kenoticists, themselves not uninspired by the desire to heal the Lutheran-Reformed breach, to bring the theme of Christ's humiliation to the fore.

A great advantage of beginning from the humiliation is that we are brought directly to the ethical heart of Christology. Metaphysical, speculative Christologies quite fail us here—so it was, for example, that in the eighteenth century 'the Trinity and kindred dogmas were quietly dropped out of the living belief of the Church, though retained in the written creed . . . If the great thought, under whose guidance we advance, do not conduct us to new discoveries, it will at all events redeem the subjects of our study from the blighting influence of scholasticism'.[59] Bruce proceeds to expound Philippians 2:5–9, finding in it 'a clear reference to an act of condescension on the part of the pre-existent Son of

God, in virtue of which He became man'.[60] Schleiermacher is adversely criticized for objecting to the idea of humiliation on the ground that it implies the pre-existence of Christ, and that this would both threaten the unity of Christ's person, and do violence to the absoluteness of God. But to Bruce, 'The glory of God consists not simply in being high, but in that He, the highest and greatest, can humble Himself in love to be the lowest and least. The moral, not the metaphysical, is the highest, if not the distinctive, in the Divine Being'.[61] Thus in Philippians we do not have simply the claim that Christ was made man. We have the claim that he *took* servile form and suffered. As Bruce elsewhere put it, 'Patripassianism is not wholly a heresy'.[62]

Bruce draws the following inferences from the text: Christ, the pre-existent Son, humbled himself; that this entailed a change of state, though not of personality; that Jesus did not cease to be the Son; that His life on earth was a life of service; and that in all that He did He was a free agent.[63] To these insights of Paul, the writer to the Hebrews adds the important considerations that Christ's nature is one with ours—sinfulness excepted—and that His humiliation is an aspect of His glorification, 'For while it is a humiliation to *die*, it is glorious to taste death *for others*; and by dying, to abolish death, and bring life and immortality to light'.[64]

Bruce proceeds to review the history of Christology, judging matters from his ethical point of view. Thus, while fully appreciating the motives which led to the composition of the Chalcedonian formula, he found the statement deficient. He correctly understood the assertions of the creed—that Christ was truly God and truly man, 'of the same substance with the Father as to His divinity, of the same substance with us as to His humanity'—to be a *via media* between the Nestorian view that there were two persons in Christ, and the Eutychian view that there was but one person and one nature in Christ, and that that nature was, even in its humanity, predominantly divine. He applauded the fact that the formula, together with Leo's *Tome*, addressed originally to Flavian, Patriarch of Constantinople, laid down two fundamental propositions, providing for both Christ's unipersonality and His duality of natures. But they did not help men to see how this might be; nor did they show what belongs to the person and what to the natures, nor, in particular, to which of the two the will of Christ is to be assigned. The way was thus opened to the Monophysite, Monothelite and Adoption controversies.

Bruce does not delay over these controversies; indeed, it must be said that he does not have much by way of original historical scholarship to offer in this book. But by keeping to the theme of Christ's humiliation, he does illuminate doctrine. For example, he finds a line from Cyril of

Alexandria (d. 444) through John of Damascus (c. 675–749) to the Lutheran theologians, all of whom proposed a one-sided theory of the communication of attributes: 'There is no kind of communication by which the divine nature becomes partaker of the humiliation of humanity, corresponding to that by which the human nature becomes partaker of the glories of divinity'.[65] Reformed theologians, on the other hand, followed Aquinas in emphasizing the distinctness of the two natures in Christ's person.

The divergent answers given by Luther and Zwingli to the question 'How is Christ present at the Lord's Supper?' gave rise to a long and unhappy controversy between the Lutherans and the Reformed. Luther emphasized the ubiquity of Christ's body, while Zwingli regarded the Supper as a memorial meal with Christ present in a spiritual sense only. Within the Lutheran camp there were those who, with Johann Brentz (1499–1570), dispensed with the axiom *finitum non capux infiniti* on the ground that it ruled out a real Incarnation; and those who followed Martin Chemnitz (1552–1586) in emphasizing the pervasion of the human by the divine. Bruce sums matters up thus: 'According to Brentz, Christ in His state of humiliation not only *could* use, but *did* use, and *could not help* using, His majesty as a communicated attribute of His human nature; only in that state the use was dissembled, hidden; while in the state of exaltation it is open. According to Chemnitz, Christ in the state of humiliation *could* use majesty in, through, and with His humanity, and *sometimes did* use it to show the fact of possession; but generally he did not *wish* to use it'.[66] The compromise Formula of Concord (1577) succeeded only in fuelling succeeding disputes. Its gravest weakness concerned 'the relation of the majesty communicated to the human nature of Christ, by the personal union, to His earthly state of humiliation. It seemed to teach at once full possession and secret use; full possession and prevalent abstinence from use; and not only partial use, but even partial and defective possession'.[67]

Bruce brought a number of charges against the Lutheran Christology as a whole, of which the most serious is that it robs us of a real Incarnation: the divine attributes are communicated to human nature, but not vice versa; 'God is not at liberty to descend; He can only make man ascend: Incarnation means not God becoming man, but man becoming God'; and the real humanity of Christ's nature is put at risk.[68] He granted that 'The old Lutherans were not Pantheists, nor did they look on the historical Christ as an ordinary man; but their Christology was undoubtedly of such a character, as to make it possible for modern Pantheistic Christologies to lay claims to orthodoxy with a show of plausibility'.[69]

Whereas the Lutheran theologians underlined the majesty of Christ's humanity, the Reformed emphasized its reality. Moreover, 'In the Reformed view, Incarnation and exinanition were practically one'.[70] Not surprisingly, the Reformed theory was more historically rooted than its more speculative rival. Bruce's sympathies were clearly with the Reformed, though he does note objections to that position—especially the accusation that in Reformed theology the divine and human natures of Christ are simply glued together like two boards, without any real communication. The way out, he believes, is by the assertion of the *moral* union of the divine and human natures which, he grants, are metaphysically far apart. This is consistent with Reformed teaching to the effect that the Son of God really emptied himself at the Incarnation, and that Christ's humanity is, apart from its sinlessness, like that of all other men in all other respects.

Out of the friction between the Lutheran and Reformed christologies, and inspired by the desire for closer concord between the two branches of Reformation Christianity, there developed the emphasis upon *kenosis*. As Bruce remarks,

> You may reach the kenotic position from the Lutheran territory along the path of the *communicatio idiomatum*, simply by the inverse application of the principle; teaching with reference to the earthly state of Christ a communication of human properties to God, instead of a communication of divine properties to man. You may reach the same position from the Reformed territory along the path of the *exinanitio*, to which the Logos became subject in becoming man, by assigning thereto a positive meaning, and converting the Reformed *occultatio* or *quasi-exinanitio* into a real self-emptying of divine glory and divine attributes.[71]

Bruce passes in review the kenoticism of Thomasius, Gess, Ebrard, and Martensen. We cannot describe his criticisms in detail, though we recognize the great service which Bruce performed in fostering the discussion of these men in Britain, and we find this the most closely analytical section of his book.[72] Of more importance for our present purpose are the clues to Bruce's own attitude towards the kenotic question.

Bruce welcomes the fact that kenoticism presupposes the orthodox doctrines of the Trinity, and of the pre-existence of Christ; but he regrets the fact that some kenoticists have tended in the direction of subordinationism, and thinks that the problem as to why the Son and not the Father became incarnate is one which besets all christological theories, and is best left alone. He welcomes the kenotic emphasis upon the real, historical humanity of Christ, and applauds the attempt to do justice to the divine love as manifested in the Incarnation. He enters the important caveat that although the historical phenomena may to a large extent be the same in both the orthodox and the Socinian systems, 'the moral and theological significance of the phenomenon is *toto coelo* different. The Christ of the kenosis is God self-humbled to man's level; the Socinian Christ is man exalted to the highest human level. The conceptions of the Deity cherished by the two systems are equally diverse. The God of the one system is self-sacrificing love; the God of the other system is a Being who cannot descend from the altitude of his metaphysical majesty'.[73] Finally, Bruce will not allow that a priori refutations of kenoticism, based upon considerations of the divine immutability, are in order: 'It is wiser in those who believe in revelation to be ready to believe that God can do anything that is not incompatible with His moral nature, to refuse to allow metaphysical difficulties to stand as insuperable obstacles in the way of His gracious purposes, and so far to agree with the advocates of the kenosis as to hold that He can descend and empty Himself to the extent love requires'.[74]

At the same time, Bruce is acutely conscious of grave objections to kenoticism, and considers that the attitude of suspended judgement is perhaps the most appropriate one to adopt. For, when challenged as to what is happening to the person of Christ in the *kenosis*, some resort to the theory of two life centres in Christ; others speak of a gradual Incarnation; others of a depotentiated Logos. But Bruce declines to believe that it is necessary to support any of these views. He considers that if we ask ourselves how much we really know, and to what extent the Bible enables us to pronounce upon these matters, we discover that we know little more than Paul and the letter to the Hebrews teach us, and that the more speculative christological theories can obscure such elementary truths as 'the unity of the person, or the reality of the humanity, or the divinity dwelling within the man, or the voluntariness and ethical value of the state of humiliation'.[75]

Bruce turns next to modern humanistic theories of Christ's person, of which he finds five main types. First, there are the thoroughgoing naturalists, F. C. Baur (1792–1860) among them. Their theories founder in particular on the character of Jesus, who was not conscious of, nor could he be accused of, sin. Secondly, there are those who inconsistently banish the supernatural from the physical sphere, whilst retaining it in the ethical, so that they can confess Christ's sinlessness. This is the position of the Unitarians Channing and Martineau, and also of Schleiermacher. To Schleiermacher Christ must be both a historical individual and the one in whom the ideal of humanity is fully realized. But here we have 'a supernatural element in a creed which is predominantly influenced by a naturalistic, Pantheistic spirit'.[76] Pantheism and theism mingle in Schleiermacher's thought, and we may be grateful that his Moravian blood prompted that inconsistency in his theory which enabled him to assert the sinlessness of Christ. Third, there is the variety of naturalism espoused by Ewald (1803–1875) and Keim (1825–1878). Theoretically they are with the out-and-out naturalists in proscribing miracles; emotionally they are with those who find Christ's life and character extraordinary and wonderful. Christ is a mere man, and yet in every way exceptional. Fourth, popularizing liberals such as Haweis shun the miraculous, return to the life and teaching of Jesus for inspiration, find it possible to echo Peter's confession at Caesarea Philippi, and yet they are so innocent of dogmatic intentions that they cannot bring themselves to say what they mean by it all. Finally there are those who are naturalists, not on speculative grounds, but on exegetical. Of these Beyschlag (1823–1900) is representative. While not denying that Christ is the realized ideal of humanity, Bruce finds Beyschlag's exegesis misleading because it is conditioned by his philosophical prejudices. In particular Beyschlag idealizes the title 'Son of Man' in such a way as to threaten the reality of Jesus's humanity; and when he does speak of Christ's birth he does so against so ambiguous a doctrine of pre-existence as to rule out Christ's condescension altogether: he was 'sent in the sense of being born into an existence which dates from birth'.[77]

Having considered the physical aspects of Christ's humiliation, Bruce turns to the ethical. After discussing the theological contributions (and contortions) of thinkers from Hilary of Poitiers (c. 315–367) to Edward Irving (1792–1834) on the question of Christ as the subject of temptation and moral development, Bruce returns principally to the letter to the Hebrews, and presents his case for the view that the holy one was subject to moral development. He was like us in that He was tempted; He was ethically unlike us, in that He did not yield: 'The exalted Christ is regarded by the writer of this Epistle as one now morally perfected; the earthly state of humiliation is regarded as a school of virtue, in which Christ had to learn, and did thoroughly learn, certain moral lessons; the experience of temptation is viewed in the light of a curriculum of ethical discipline, designed to make the tempted One master of certain high heroic arts, the arts to be mastered being those of *Patience, Obedience,* and *Sympathy*'.[78]

Bruce comes finally to the official, or soteriological, aspects of Christ's humiliation. We shall, however, reserve our consideration of Bruce's soteriology for the next section, and close this by noting some criticisms which have been offered of his view of Christ's person. The crucial question is, 'Does Bruce minimise Christ's divinity?' We have thus far found no evidence that he does; on the contrary, he declares in the clearest possible terms that Christ is the divine Son of God. There are, it must be admitted, sentences which tell in the opposite direction. Thus for example two reviewers of Bruce's work on the synoptic accounts of Jesus, *With Open Face*, felt uneasy on this score. The first writes, 'our Lord's Godhead is practically ignored. Professor Bruce does indeed speak of "the Divine loftiness of His character" . . . but he refers to Him as "a Son of God, if not in the metaphysical sense of theology, at least in the ethical sense of possessing a God-like spirit", and the general tone of the book is not calculated to give the slightest idea that He who is being described is personally the Eternal Son of God, of one Essence with the Father'.[79] The second declares, '*Jesus* was both human and divine, and in Him the divine was more than Professor Bruce seems able to find it. We are not even so sure as we used to be that the better way to come to Jesus is to come by the Man of Nazareth. The greatest of all the evangelists would have us approach from the other side: "In the beginning was the Word" . . . Indeed it is the oldest way of all . . . And when we find our God in Christ, how easy to pass to the Carpenter. But how hard it always seems to have been to rise from the Carpenter to "My Lord and my God" '.[80] These comments are just, as far as they go. Bruce was not a man to indulge in eisegesis, and his very caution may have inclined him on occasion to see less in a text than was actually there. But if we put all his works together, the sinlessness, the pre-existence, the divinity of Christ are all affirmed, if not *always* closely argued—though the whole thrust of *The Miraculous Element in the Gospels* (1886) is to make plain that the union in Christ of the eternal Son of God and the perfect Son of Man is the *one* miracle.

The enigma is partly explained, then, by the fact that his method was to fasten upon one thing at a time, thereby overlooking balancing judgements and qualifying factors. Robertson Nicoll went further in a letter to Marcus Dods: 'I never feel', he said, 'that Bruce deals in a really *scientific* way with matters of scholarship'.[81]Considerations of aptitude, temperament and starting-point mingle, and not the least influential consideration is Bruce's fear that dogma concerning Christ's divinity may serve us ill: it may act 'as a veil to hide the true Jesus from the eye of the soul. The only faith concerning Jesus as the Divine Lord worth possessing is that which springs out of spiritual insight into its historical basis, and is charged with ethical significance. Such a faith calls Jesus Lord by the Holy Ghost, and is legitimate, wholesome, and fruitful in beneficent effects'.[82]

But what perplexed Bruce's critics most of all was his posthumously published article on Jesus in the *Encyclopaedia Biblica* (1901). The fact that he collaborated with Professor Schmiedel of Leyden (against whom Denney rampaged in letters to Nicoll) did little to allay the fears of some. Nicoll himself went so far as to say that 'Words have no meaning if Schmiedel does not deny the sinlessness of Christ, and certainly Bruce goes a long way in that direction'.[83] This, we feel, is to over-state the position, though we can see why, in the hey-day of attenuating theological liberalism, some should be especially on their guard. They would be disquieted by the statement that Jesus thought of himself as 'the representative of all who live sacrificial and redemptive lives'; and by the superficially Harnack-like view that we are only now beginning to understand Christ's 'radical doctrine of the dignity of man'.[84] But here again, Bruce says one thing at a time, and it is the absence of qualifications which enables opponents to drive the knife in.[85] Bruce was not a great systematizer, but nor did he ever deny the divinity of Christ— least of all when that divinity was conceived in ethical terms.

We have noted one critic who would have favoured a more God-ward starting point, but Bruce, as we have seen, was governed by his desire to locate Jesus in history. For our part we would take our cue from the Cross-Resurrection event, and accordingly, we shall be particularly interested to discover what Bruce has to say of the work of Christ.

II

In Bruce's first work, *The Training of the Twelve*, we find numerous references to the death of Christ, and we shall refer to some of these. We shall in addition refer to what Bruce regarded as his trilogy: *The Kingdom of God* (1889), *St. Paul's Conception of Christianity* (1896) and *The Epistle to the Hebrews* (1899). Finally, we shall draw attention to some of the theological issues raised in the chapter on the soteriological aspects of Christ's humiliation in *The Humiliation of Christ*.

From the very first, Bruce took a generous view of the work of Christ. Referring to the anointing at Bethany[86] he says, 'It symbolized a similar characteristic of Christ's good work as the Saviour of sinners. *He* did *His* work magnificently, and in no mean, economical way. He accomplished the redemption of "many" by means adequate to redeem all . . . Christ could not save any unless He were heartily willing to save all, for that willingness is a part of the perfect righteousness which it behoved Him to fulfil'.[87] Not indeed that redemption is automatic, or without cost.

Christ's death was 'the natural effect of fidelity to righteousness in an unrighteous world'.[88] He antagonized the supporters of the status quo by exposing the pseudo-righteousness of the scribes, by fraternizing with the poor and despised, and by defying Rabbinism—that 'moral system in which virtues and sins were alike artificial'.[89] From the attitude of Jesus towards his work—so different from the attitude of Zebedee's ambitious sons—we learn that his aim was to gain sovereignty through ignominy. Far from asserting his own rights, he voluntarily gave himself as a ransom. Of all this the Lord's Supper is the sign and the seal.[90] It follows that Levitical sacrifices are redundant; that the Law is internalized; and that the Church should be characterized by humility, thankfulness and brotherly love. This much Bruce learns of the meaning of Christ's death from the teaching and ministry of Jesus. His death is 'a sin-offering, atoning for guilt, and purchasing forgiveness of moral debt'.[91] Compared with the orthodox view of Christ's death, the Socinian alternative is poor indeed: 'In that scheme pardon has no real dependence on the blood of Jesus: He died as a martyr for righteousness, not as a Redeemer for the unrighteous . . . A Socinian God, who pardons without atonement, is destitute alike of a passionate abhorrence of sin and of a passionate love to sinners'.[92] The God communed with in the Lord's Supper is very different: 'The Lord's Supper commemorates the Lord's *death*; points out that death as an event of transcendent importance; sets it forth, indeed, as the ground of our hope for the pardon of sin; and finally exhibits Christ the Lord, who died on the cross, as all to us which our spirits need for health and salvation— our mystic bread and wine'.[93]

Turning to Paul, Bruce finds that the apostle's thought concerning Christ's death revolves around two axes: the idea that God publicly exhibits Jesus in his death in a propitiary capacity; and the idea that Christ was made a curse and sin for us, that we might become curse-free and sinless.[94] The death of Christ both reveals and averts the divine wrath, and behind it all is God's loving purpose. 'Christ's *whole state of humiliation* was the λύτρον, the resulting benefit for us is ἀπολύτρωσις.'[95] The death of Christ, objectively considered, achieves the redemption of humanity from legalism; subjectively viewed, it achieves the believer's status as a son of God. The objective state of privilege is transmuted into a subjective experience by faith.

To the insights of Paul the author of Hebrews adds the profound thought that we need, and have, a great High Priest. Leviticalism, with its sacrifices and sacerdotalism, failed to deal with human sin, 'the great separator'.[96] Already in the gospels, in Jesus's self-sacrifice and solidarity with sinners, we have indications of his priestly ministry, but the author of Hebrews does not think of Christ's death in terms of one stereotype only. Jesus died once, as we all do (9:27); he died as one who bequeaths an inheritance (9:16); his entire ministry together with the crucifixion was a discipline which he underwent (2:10); since, though sinless, he dies, the connection between death and sin is broken (2:14,15); and by his priestly act of self-sacrifice he perfects those who are sanctified (10:14).[97] For this writer, salvation includes not only pardon of sin, but nearness to God (12:14), loyal obedience to Christ (5:9), a priestly life of thanksgiving and service (13:15,16), and heaven. Indeed, 'the death of Christ, though occurring in this visible world on a hill called Calvary, essentially belongs to the heavenlies. As an act of the Spirit, it was and is a sacrifice performed in the heavenly sanctuary. As an act of an Eternal Spirit, it has no exclusive connection with a certain point of time in human history. It is eternal, and, like Christ Himself, is the same yesterday, today, and for ever'.[98]

Bruce had a particular affection for the letter to the Hebrews. To him it was the first apology for the Cross, and that in two ways: it is an apology 'first and chiefly, for the cross which Jesus bore, and second and subordinately for the cross that came to Christians in connection with their profession of faith in the Crucified One'.[99] In his most doctrinal work he emphasized the truth about Christ which was so clearly grasped by the author of Hebrews: 'while as a Priest He is our representative, as a sacrifice He is our substitute'.[100] From this anchorage Bruce launches out against all those who would think of Christ as representative only, and not as substitute. Here we have the germ of the mystical theory of the atonement, or what Bruce prefers to call the theory of redemption by sample. This theory, prominently espoused by Schleiermacher, includes Christ as an object of his own priestly action. In sanctifying himself he sanctifies mankind, and so presents 'the whole lump holy to the Lord'.[101] A number of Fathers (including Hilary) advocated this theory, and in the nineteenth century it was propounded by both Mencken and Irving, with the qualification that Christ sanctified but a *portion* of the corrupt mass of humanity. Bruce grants that in a sense Christ was holy for himself as well as for us, but he cannot allow that Christ died for himself as well as for us: 'As a Priest, acting in His own interest, He simply ensured that He should continue what He *was—holy*. As a Priest, acting for us, He ensured, by His holiness in life and death, that we, the unholy, should be holy in God's sight—"accepted in the Beloved"'.[102] Bruce's second complaint against the theory of redemption by sample is that it returns hazy answers to a number of vital questions: 'Does the sample really sanctify the whole lump in God's sight? or does it merely exhibit a result which has to be reached in every individual member of the race, which it somehow helps us to reach, and which, when realized, or foreseen as realized, is the ground of God's judgement in accepting us as holy?'[103] In so far as proponents of the theory incline towards the latter view, they are prey to the temptation to seek the necessary aid in sacramental grace, a prospect at which Bruce is characteristically alarmed: 'This recourse to sacramental grace as the mainstay is, in my view, a confession of failure. It is the mountain labouring and bringing forth a ridiculous birth. It is more and worse. The *reductio ad absurdum* of a certain theory of redemption, it is at the same time a melancholy perversion and caricature of Christianity'.[104]

Bruce passes in review certain other modern theories of the atonement including that 'eccentricity of a devout author', the theory of McLeod Campbell (1800–1872):

> The idea of a confession made by a perfectly holy being, involving *all* the elements of a perfect repentance, *except* the personal consciousness of sin, is certainly absurd enough. It is either the play of Hamlet without the part of Hamlet; or, if the repentance have any real contents, then the remark of a Transatlantic critic is most pertinent: 'After having implied that Christ repented of the sins of the race, we do not see why Mr. Campbell should object to the theory that He was punished for these sins.'[105]

So Bruce comes to his conclusion. He can see some merit in the prophetic view of the atonement (e.g. that of Ritschl), according to which Christ, our fellow combatant, reveals the truth that fellowship with God is independent of outward circumstances; in the moral influence theory of Abelard and Bushnell, according to which the self-sacrificial love of Christ inspires us to our spiritual good; and even in the theory of redemption by sample in so far as it emphasizes Christ's solidarity with the race. Again, the view that Christ was not only sacrificial Priest but victim cannot be excluded, even if we may not press it as far as did McLeod Campbell. But the catholic theory of redemption teaches above all that the atonement is not merely a subjective, but an objective matter.[106] Although this theory has not always been well served by its friends, it is here, more than anywhere else, that Bruce stands. Indeed, 'on the one hand, it is a presumption in favour of the Catholic doctrine, that it does not require to negative rival theories, except in so far as they are exclusive and antagonistic; and, on the other hand, one may hope that theories which have even a partial truth will bless their advocates by the truth that is in them, connecting them in some way with Him who is the fountain of life, and initiating a process of spiritual development which will carry them on to higher things'.[107]

III

Having now discovered what Bruce saw when he viewed the person and work of Christ, we have finally to ask, 'How did he seek to commend Christ to those who doubted, or entertained less-than-helpful views?' In other words, 'What form did his apologetic take, and on what principles was it based?'

In 1886 Bruce published a course of lectures which he had delivered in the Presbyterian College, London, under the title *The Chief End of Revelation*. In the preface to the first edition of this work he set down his two 'ruling motives' thus: 'One is, that in many respects the old lines of apologetic argument no longer suffice either to express the thoughts of faith or to meet successfully the assaults of unbelief. The other is, that the Church is not likely again to wield the influence which of right belongs to her as custodian of the precious treasure of Christian truth, unless she show herself possessed of vitality sufficient to originate a new development in all directions, and among others in Doctrine; refusing to accept as her final position either the agnosticism of modern culture, or blind adherence to traditional dogmatism'.[108] In the preface to his second edition, Bruce noted that some critics, appreciative of his expository powers, advised him to remain in that field, and to leave apologetics alone. Bruce's reply was characteristic of the man:

> it would be a somewhat unheroic proceeding in one having any apologetic talent, to confine himself to the comparatively easy task of the expositor. It would be to shun the perils of a search for the straying sheep, and abide securely in the fold with the ninety and nine that need no special care. I am glad to think that I am deemed one able to lead the flock of believing men to the green pastures of Holy Scripture, but I trust also that I am not without some capacity to seek and find the erring and doubting; and I should be ashamed of myself if I were not willing to try, even at the risk of being assailed as a traitor to the faith by men not accustomed to distinguish between sectional opinions and the Catholic verity.[109]

Thus undeterred, Bruce proceeded to state his view of the apologist's task: 'His vocation is neither to confound infidels nor to gratify the passions of coarse dogmatists, but to help men of an ingenuous spirit, troubled with doubts bred of philosophy or science, while morally in sympathy with believers'.[110] He reiterated this view in his major work, *Apologetics*, underlining the fact that his foe is not 'the dogmatic infidel who has finally made up his mind that Christianity is a delusion, but anti-Christian thought in the believing man's own heart'.[111] To attempt to do battle with dogmatic unbelief is futile, and it is out of place for an apologist to be a partisan of dogmatics. Rather, the apologist 'regards himself as a defender of the catholic faith, not as a hired advocate or special pleader for a particular theological system'.[112] He may thus expect to satisfy neither the thoroughgoing unbeliever, nor the dogmatizing believer. In this spirit Bruce goes to work, and we find that his method is governed by two positive and two negative motives. Having accorded a paragraph to each we shall be in a position to offer a résumé of Bruce's view of the presuppositions of Christianity.

Positively, then, Bruce intends to follow the scientific method, and this entails two things. First, he must protest against the 'unscientific' exclusion from consideration of man's moral sense, religious insights, and faith. We have to proceed from man, as he fully is, to God.[113] To be scientific means 'that what we say about God is to rest on observation of the world we live in—of nature, of man, of human history—and to consist of such statements as may be verifiable by such observation. It excludes nothing which belongs to the world in any department, therefore nothing which belongs to the religious history of humanity, therefore not the Hebrew and Christian sacred literatures which occupy a prominent place in that history'. The second point immediately follows: The scientific spirit 'excludes the use of these literatures as authorities, but not as *witnesses*'.[114] Here, once again, is the attitude which fuelled the Dods-Bruce Case: the Bible is to be regarded in the same way as any other literature, and criticized accordingly.[115] We are to be as impartial as possible, though even the man of science has his guiding hypotheses;[116] and our aim, above all, must be to see Jesus as clearly as we can, and then to exhibit what we see. It is sadly the case that 'Men are not permitted to see Jesus with open face, but only through the thick veil of a dogmatic system'.[117] Thus for example against traditional confessionalism Bruce can say, 'The doctrine of a Fall may or may not be true'.[118] But we do him an injustice if we miss his positive emphasis to the effect that 'The revelation recorded in the Scriptures is before all things a self-manifestation of God, as the God of *grace*',[119] and if we forget what he is guarding against: 'Put the book foremost in your idea of revelation, and you almost inevitably think of revelation as consisting in words, doctrines'.[120] In reality, what is at the heart of the gracious, supernatural revelation (though not to exclusion of words) is the saving *activity* of God.[121]

The second positive motive is that Bruce intends to speak to his age. For him this means attending to history and adopting the evolutionary theme.[122] We use the term 'theme' advisedly, because at no point does

Bruce thoroughly examine the *theory*—or *theories*—of evolution. Nevertheless, the laws of growth, and the slow-but-sureness of development and progress, are ideas which continually recur in his writings, and we are not surprised to find that the reference is frequently to the ethical realm: God is educating his people.[123] The combination of the evolutionary theme with the historical method enables Bruce to illustrate this point in countless ways, not least in *The Moral Order of the World*. He here reviews Buddhism, Zoroastrianism, Greek and Stoic thought, Biblical and modern thought—all with a view to showing Christ as the culminating revelation of moral values; Christ, whose watchwords were 'Nature God's instrument, and, Growth the law of the moral as of the spiritual world'.[124] As to the reliability of the crucial biblical texts, Bruce is persuaded that 'To open-minded men neither unduly dogmatic nor unduly sceptical, a sufficient knowledge of the historical Jesus will not seem unattainable'.[125] God's work continues and 'Evolution [is] simply God's method of communicating to man the light of reason and the sense of duty. Surely a worthy ending of the long process of world-genesis!'[126] On occasion, under the impetus of evolutionism, Bruce sounds like a typical liberal optimist: 'the world is marching on towards the desired consummation with the certainty of a law of nature'.[127] Elsewhere, he recognizes that although the outcome is assured, God's Kingdom will come through conflict and sacrifice: 'This prospect will not satisfy extreme optimists',[128] but neither should it drive us to Schopenhauer and the gods of modern pessimism.[129]

The first negative motive is that Bruce's Jesus-centred stance prompts his dissatisfaction with the older theism. He finds less of value in the theistic arguments than did Flint. Indeed, it cannot be said that he discusses the arguments in great depth. Even so, and despite a tendency to subjectivism in his writings, Bruce is no irrationalist. On the contrary, he trounces Benjamin Kidd's view that reason is 'the most profoundly individualistic, anti-social, and anti-evolutionary of all human qualities';[130] for this would make religion but the antidote to man's egoism, and would imply that reason and religion have nothing in common. Bruce sees here the positing of an intolerable psychological dualism which implies a constant warfare between man's reason and his religious instincts; and he will have none of it. It is, moreover, 'a dualism unknown to Greek philosophers and Christian apostles, who knew of a conflict between flesh and spirit, but never dreamed of reason and religion being deadly foes'.[131] For his part, Bruce asserts the harmony of faith and reason—as, he believes, did Jesus.[132] Although not over-enamoured of the old 'proofs', Bruce can find a good word to say for natural theology: 'If Christ's doctrine of God be true, there ought to be something in the world to verify it . . . . The bankruptcy of natural theology is a gratuitous proposition'.[133] Paul was right when he claimed that the heathen world lacked not the capacity, but the *will* to know God. Moreover (and here we revert to Bruce's scientific motive), 'This is the reasonable view still for men who walk in the light of modern science. In view of man's place in the cosmos, it is a priori credible that there is a revelation of God in nature [however "dim and rudimentary" it may be[134]], and that man in the exercise of his cognitive faculties is capable of deciphering it.'[135] At the same time, Bruce regards the traditional division of territory between natural and revealed theology to be artificial and unhelpful. We cannot proceed so far in our reasoning, and *then* introduce revelatory considerations. On the contrary, 'Whatever we discuss, whether it be the being of God, or the reality of a righteous benignant Providence, or the certainty of a life to come, it ought to be felt that the discussion is carried on in the interest of the Christian faith'.[136] Consistently with this he expresses regret that 'Even Butler could write such a sentence as this: "For though natural religion is the foundation and principal part of Christianity, it is not in any sense the whole of it"';[137] and he quotes Mark Pattison with approval: 'The defect of the eighteenth century theology was not in having too much good sense, but in having nothing else besides'.[138] The upshot is that Bruce does not deny that, for example, the heavens declare the glory of God, but he does not think that we can argue from the stars to God. Indeed, the fact that many unite in believing in God while differing as to which proofs are valid and valuable suggests that 'the belief in God is antecedent to evidence, and that in our theistic reasonings we formulate proof of a foregone conclusion innate and inevitable. How otherwise can it be explained that men who have demolished what have passed for the strongest arguments for the theistic creed are not content to be done with it, but hold on to the conviction that God is, on grounds which to all others but themselves appear weak and whimsical?'[139] Bruce's procedure is to begin from the datum that God *is*, and then to expend his energies in discovering what *kind* of God he is.[140] In the process we return yet again to the evolutionary theme, for Bruce maintains that by reason of that 'wider teleology' which encompasses both the physical and the moral, and which evolutionary thought justifies, we may begin from man himself, and not from those external considerations concerning motion, causation, design, and the idea, on which the earlier 'proofs' turned.[141] But to repeat: man, for Bruce, is always man seen in the light of God's supreme revelation in Christ. His starting-point, if we may be clumsily brief, is theistic-Christo-anthropological.

Bruce's second negative motive is the exclusion of all theories which would undermine what he has seen in Jesus. In the course of his writings he levels charges against numerous isms which do violence to Christianity. We have already noted some religious isms to which he did not take at all kindly—Pharisaism, Leviticalism, and the like; and we have noted his dislike of the extremes of optimism and pessimism. But now we must briefly advert to certain philosophical viewpoints to which he stands firmly opposed. First, Bruce abominates agnosticism in all its forms: 'The agnostic position is fatal, or at least most hostile, to all earnest Christian faith',[142] for it forbids us to discover truths concerning God from nature, history and the human soul and if we cannot do that any higher revelation is incredible if not impossible: 'The Christian doctrine of God, to be valid, must be a hypothesis which all we know tends to verify'.[143] The materialism and naturalism which underlie much agnosticism are repeatedly repudiated by Bruce. He finds the materialist unable to account for life on the physical side, or for morality on the ethical; and as for materialists who, like Strauss, adopt a religious stance, 'The trouble is, that for one who has discarded a living God it is difficult to think so well of the world as is necessary for the sincere practice of this new cult'.[144] The fundamental challenge to the materialist, and the one to which he has no satisfactory reply, given his presuppositions, is to account for mind.[145] The naturalists for their part are roundly condemned. Their error (and here Baur is a favourite target) is that they begin by presupposing the impossibility of the miraculous.[146] This, to Bruce, is quite illegitimate, though he grants that miracles cannot be used as *evidence* for the existence of God, as in some older theisms.[147] What then of those who, while believing in God, entertain defective views of him? In this connection Bruce opposes dualism, which denies the all-embracing providence of God;[148] deism, which tends towards a fatalistic doctrine of providence, a Pelagian view of salvation, and a pagan view of immortality;[149] and idealism. This last variety of thought was very much in vogue in Bruce's day—indeed, he worked but a stone's throw from the Cairds. Idealism was particularly threatening to the faith as far as Bruce was concerned. It was not that he objected to the notion of immanence, so highly favoured by the idealists. On the contrary, he can say that 'It is vital that we conceive of God as immanent in the world, and unceasingly active throughout the whole history of its genesis, the ultimate cause of all that happens'.[150] Nor is the immanence of God in any way incompatible with his transcendence;[151]indeed, 'It would crown the apology of Providence if we could conceive God, nor merely as an onlooker, but as a participant in the vicarious suffering by which the world is redeemed and regenerated.

This we may do under the doctrine of immanence'.[152] For all that, the immanently ideal Christ of such philosophers as T. H. Green (1836–1892) was not the Jesus of whose historicity Bruce was so sure.[153] The pantheizing tendencies of speculative theism are resolutely to be opposed. Pantheisms of all kinds, whether Spinozistic or Hegelian, founder on the historical Jesus; for pantheism's deity is too vague to be a satisfactory object of worship, its view of man is degrading in that it deprives him of genuinely free action, and its doctrine of evil, according to which evil is a stage on the way to the good, makes nonsense of all moral distinctions.[154] History is not to be escaped from, either by the idealistic way, or by the experience-centred way of which Schleiermacher was the prophet. We *know* God in Christ and therefore

> I do not wish, if I can help it, to worship an unknown or unknowable God called the Absolute, concerning whom or which all Bible representations are mere make-believe, mere anthropomorphism; statements expressive not of absolute truth, but simply of what it is well that we should think and feel concerning God. I am not disposed to subject my idea of God to the category of the Absolute, which, like Pharaoh's lean kine, devours all other attributes, even for the sake of the most tempting apologetic advantages which that category may seem to offer. A poor refuge truly from unbelief is the category of the Absolute![155]

Having enumerated the motives which influenced Bruce's apologetic method, we come full circle to what were to him the main ingredients of the Christian world view. We should remember that these ingredients are not manufactured a priori;[156] rather, they are distilled from the biblical text. Bruce's determination to proceed from man to God (i.e. as far as the *kind* of God is concerned: God himself is the datum with which we begin), requires him to take a noble view of man. Man is one for whom God cares 'in all samples of his common humanity, whether good or bad'.[157] Neither must we take a low view of God—as for example does Schopenhauer, with his God of mindless will.[158] The Christian revelation of God in Christ encourages a balanced view of man and God; it neither defies man nor cheapens God. This revelation is a revelation of grace, and this grace 'is exhibited as the *Kingdom of God*, as the *Righteousness of God*, as *unrestricted Fellowship with God*, and as *Eternal Life*'.[159] So it is that 'In proportion as the Bible humbles men [*sic*] by its picture of his natural condition, it exalts him by the prospect it holds out before him'.[160] We have already given Bruce's summary of 'the more essential truths of the revelation of grace'.[161] The authority for these truths is neither Bible nor Church. The final authority is Christ himself.[162]

It was said of Bruce's second series of Gifford Lectures that 'It is a preacher's book, not a philosopher's'.[163]There is truth in the judgement: we feel that we are in the presence of a seer rather than of a tough-minded philosopher. But in fairness to Bruce we should remember that he took seriously the requirement of Lord Gifford's will that the Lectures should be for popular consumption; and we should also recall Bruce's intention in all his apologetic work not to meet dogmatic agnosticism or atheism, but to clear the way for puzzled theists.[164] Even so, we cannot help but feel that at time Bruce wins his victories too easily—and that generally means too rhetorically. But every thinker has the faults of his virtues, and Bruce would no doubt feel that while much latter day philosophy of religion is acute and painstaking, it is dull and lacking in conviction.

Bruce had his convictions, and he expressed them clearly. Certainly Warfield goes too far in saying that Bruce's 'later works illustrate all too vividly the wrong impression that the gospel for an age of doubt should preferably be a doubting or even a doubtful gospel',[165] though we can understand why a Princetonian rationalist and upholder of biblical inerrancy should express himself thus against Bruce. But another way of reading the situation is to say that to an age in which many Christians had the vague feeling that all was not well with the Faith because of the onslaughts of alien isms and of the higher criticism of the Bible, Bruce spoke a confident, courageous and hopeful word. He encouraged the doubting and the intellectually perplexed to realize that Christianity's enemies could be routed without recourse to 'ostrich' methods, and by holding the real Jesus before men he offered them that apart from which there is no Christianity worthy of the name. If we have any complaint against his method, it is that he did not sufficiently probe his presuppositions. Had he done so he would almost certainly have recognized the need for a greater emphasis upon the work of the Holy Spirit as guide into truth, and would have thrown into prominence the question of the existence or otherwise of common ground between believer and unbeliever.[166]

Let it be granted, then, that Bruce was not the greatest technical scholar, the most penetrating philosopher, the most learned historian of doctrine, the most comprehensive systematizer. In all of these respects he was outclassed, for example, by James Orr. But few sought more ardently to see Jesus and to show him to others. The comment of an Anglican scholar is just: 'It is in his devotion to the Gospels and to the Person revealed in them that he stands out as a great religious teacher, as also in the moral fervour which forms a kind of luminous atmosphere for what he has to say'.[167] In fulfilling his own terms of reference, Bruce was a considerable apologist: 'The apologist', he wrote, 'is most successful when he offers to others as aids to faith thoughts which have first helped himself'.[168] That he struck a chord in many hearts is seen by the testimony of Dr. Lewis Muirhead, who said that, helped by Bruce, many 'came to see in the man Jesus the glory of God'.[169]

In his first book Bruce declared that 'The apostolic character . . . must combine freedom of conscience, enlargement of heart, enlightenment of mind, and all in the superlative degree'.[170] Bruce, we may say, went a long way towards fulfilling his own specification. Certainly, he knew whom he had found. When asked to speak to a group of humble folk in a mission hall he said, 'There is only one thing I should like to say: for myself I have an entire love for the Lord Jesus Christ, and with all my heart I hope that you may come to be able to say the same'.[171]

CHAPTER SIX

James Iverach (1839–1922):
Theologian at the Frontier

'Like Saul, the son of Kish, he is head and shoulders above his fellows, massive in proportion to his stature . . . His slow and stately step—the body moving as a whole—reflects his deliberate and safe thinking. He is undoubtedly, as Dr. Chalmers would say, "a man of wecht" in more senses than one. The grit and braininess so characteristic of many of Caithness' sons are his in a conspicuous degree. His very longevity with its unimpaired vigour has carried him far, and helped him to attain slowly but justly to the high position he occupies.'[1]

So wrote a former student of his then octogenerian College Principal, James Iverach. Dr. Reith spoke of feeling in Iverach's presence 'like a novice at the feet of a rabbi who had not taken, but had been given all knowledge for his province', and 'like an adoring but nervous worshipper of Olympian Zeus'.[2] Those of us who have Iverach's books and *curriculum vitae* only before us can infer the accuracy of the description, and can understand the feeling. Iverach made haste slowly. 'Deliberateness' is the key word in his life and thought. Born at Halkirk in 1839, he did not appear in print until 1884. He wrote no 'young man's' book; nor, having produced his first work did he spend the rest of his days finding fresh ways of saying the same thing. On the contrary, something of the variety of his interests is suggested by the fact that in 1884 he published not one, but three books: *Is God Knowable?*, *Jonathan Edwards*, and *The Philosophy of Mr. Herbert Spencer Examined*. Not indeed that Iverach never retraced his steps; Spencer, for example, makes quite regular appearances in the Iverach corpus, but this might be excused by saying that Spencer wrote much and listened little! Iverach's next two books were those in which he came to terms with the currents of evolutionary thought that were swirling around him: *The Ethics of Evolution Examined* (1886) and *Evolution and Christianity* (1894). In 1896 there appeared his *multum in parvo*, *The Truth of Christianity*. By now he was contributing to *The Expositor*, *The Expository Times*, *The Hibbert Journal*, *The Spectator*, and the *Aberdeen Free*

Press. Articles in Hastings's *Dictionary of Christ and the Gospels* and *Encyclopaedia of Religion and Ethics* were to follow.

It was not until 24th May 1887 that Iverach was called by his Church, the Free Church of Scotland, to be Professor of Apologetics and Exegesis of the Gospels at its Aberdeen College. His was no meteoric rise up the academic ladder. Rather, as befits one called to blend the academic role with that of the training of ministers, he had acquired solid pastoral experience, first at West Calder, where he was ordained in 1869, and then at Ferryhill, Aberdeen (1874–87). To these churches, 'my own people', and to the members of Pollockshields West United Free Church, he dedicated his collection of sermons, *The Other Side of Greatness* (1906).

If the pastoral foundations were well laid, so too were the academic. Iverach graduated M.A. at Edinburgh, and proceeded to New College for his theological training. At the University he excelled in Mathematics and Physics, winning the medal of Peter Guthrie Tait's class. In later years he recalled Professor Tait in his University Commemoration Sermon preached in St. Giles' Cathedral on 7th July 1911: 'Nor can I ever forget my debt to one of my teachers, the best teacher I have ever known, who first enabled me to recognize the unity of this universe, who told me and enabled me to see that there was a great objective order, fixed as the stars, deep as the firmament, regular as the seasons, and that it was our business to find that order and submit to it'.[3] But from others, not least from Campbell Fraser, he learned that 'truth was not only an objective standard but also an inward reality. It was a property of things, it was also a spiritual quality'.[4] The seeds of a metaphysic are here.

In the latter half of his long life a number of honours came Iverach's way. Aberdeen University, in whose vicinity he ministered and taught for so long, honoured him with its D.D. The University of New York, which had on 15th April 1895 accepted a bequest of fifteen thousand dollars from the American Institute of Christian Philosophy, invited him to become the first Charles F. Deems Lecturer. Iverach discharged this duty in April 1899, and the lectures were published under the title *Theism in the Light of Present Science and Philosophy* (1900). Within his Church Iverach was honoured too. In 1894 he was chosen to present Principal Rainy's portrait to New College on behalf of former students.[5] In 1905 he became Principal of what, since the union of 1900, had been the United Free Church College, Aberdeen, and at the same time he exchanged his Chair for that of the late Principal Salmond, in Dogmatics. The future of the College had been under discussion in the Church. Some felt that the maintenance of three colleges was more than the Church should be asked to bear. On accepting the Principalship Iverach's characteristic word was,

'I might respectfully hint to my brethren that they should speak a little less of the College, and pray for it a good deal more'.[6] In 1907 Iverach's teaching duties were changed again, when he became Professor of New Testament Language and Literature once more. He had published on such biblical themes as *St. Paul, His Life and Times* (1890) and *The Life of Moses* (20th thousand, 1947).

Called to his Church's highest office, Iverach was Moderator of the General Assembly, 1912–1913. The addresses he delivered in this capacity are to be found in *The Christian Message*, and their very titles, 'Our Heritage' and 'Our Outlook' epitomize their anchored, yet ever questing author. During his Moderatorial year Iverach became the first of a succession of United Free Church Moderators to pay official visits to the General Assembly of the Church of Scotland. He longed for union, and he worked tirelessly on committees concerned with it; and although he did not expect to live to see the consummation, he was sure that 'What the Lord has begun, He will surely finish in His good time'.[7]

In the Spring of 1919 a 'remarkable gathering' was held in Aberdeen to mark Principal Iverach's ministerial jubilee. The congratulations and good wishes of the university were conveyed by Professor George Adam Smith. A year later Iverach resigned his Chair, remarking that in view of the number of subjects he had taught over the years, he was more a syndicate of Professors than a Professor. He continued as Principal until his death on 6th August 1922. At his last speech to the United Free Church Assembly, in 1921, something of the pawkiness of his humour was displayed. In reply to James Barr, whose pro-Voluntary argument rested on the erroneous belief that men should for ever mouth the old words however much circumstances had changed, Iverach told a story: there was 'a northern farmer who was driving his gig across a burn by a ford. The stream was in heavy spate, the pony got "laired", and the farmer had considerable difficulty in extricating it. Later in the year, when being driven to the ford, now a small trickle, the pony balked, and the farmer said, "Toot, beastie; I doot yer memory is better than yer jidgment!" (Uproarious laughter in Assembly)'.[8]

Iverach did not reach quick or easy solutions. He worried at problems, he patiently teased out arguments. It must be said that some of his works bear the marks of the obverse of this worthy caution in that they lack form and quantitative balance. In both book and sermon he could spend so much time on preliminaries that weighty matters were crowded together at the end, or even omitted altogether. Thus for example the reviewer of his *Descartes, Spinoza and the New Philosophy* (1904) justly complained that 'The more theological part of Spinoza's writings and the main part of his political philosophy are untouched, while the account of the last three fifths of the *Ethics*,—which are admitted to be "of great importance" . . . —is "extremely brief", only about the same amount of space being given to it as to the early *Cogitata Metaphysica*.[9]

Iverach's patience and refusal to dogmatize without due deliberation made him an ally of any who were in danger of falling foul of the more rigidly conservative thinkers within the Church. The supreme example of this is his support of William Robertson Smith, his Aberdeen colleague, to whose case we have already referred.[10] In an address to his students Iverach recalled this incident, and drew the moral:

> I remember when I was in a minority, and did not think certain views to be heretical which appeared to be heretical to many of my brethren. There are many questions which ought to be discussed in the Press, in the current literature of the time, which ought not to be matter of discussion in Church courts. [How different this from the spirit of John Kennedy.] . . . I am glad for one that the Church did not condemn the law of gravitation . . . nor has the Church ever condemned evolution, though certain forms of the theory appear to be antagonistic to any form of the Christian faith. On such questions as these the Church should keep an open mind . . . [11]

In connection with the Dods-Bruce case Dr. Reith, to whom Iverach's intellect was 'perhaps the richest, the most subtle and the most versatile in the whole Church', later recalled that 'A few survive who remember, and still speak of with bated breath, a devastating speech of his in the Free Assembly more than forty years ago' in which he defended the culprit biblical scholars.[12] In a sermon on 'Things which are of real worth' Iverach lamented that 'with us in Scotland very often correctness of creed, orthodoxy of belief, takes the place of faith working by love'.[13] But he also knew that 'there are some truths of which the Church is sure, on which she has spoken with no uncertain sound, on which she feels that her life is based, and opposition to which she cannot safely tolerate'.[14]

Iverach was the third son of James Iverach of Halkirk. He married Margaret, daughter of Donald Macdonald of Thurso, by whom he had one son and four daughters. For our final glimpse of Iverach the man we reproduce something which he said to the Aberdeen University Debating Society. It speaks volumes concerning the humility of a considerable intellectual who yet remembered his starting-place. He thinks of the student new to the University and to its Debating Society:

> Let us see him as he enters the debating hall and listens to the oration, flowing and free, of a senior student who has won his freedom, and wonders if ever he can reach the same facility and freedom. I remember

my own experience, and have a sort of creepy feeling as I recall it. I had not spoken in public when I was called to second in a debate. I had prepared a speech which I was firmly persuaded would bring down the house, and would place me in the foremost ranks of the dialectic. Well, I managed to get up and move to the desk from which the young orators spoke, and then the room appeared to have extended to a vast distance, the faces of the members appeared to recede until they were invisible, the chairman hovered over the scene as if he were in a cloud, and the words would not come, and I had simply to sit down with a mind in unutterable confusion.[15]

That the confusion was not permanent is amply illustrated by Iverach's thought, to which we now turn.

I

In an end of session address to his students Principal Iverach said, 'You may in masterly fashion justify the ways of God to man, you may pulverize all the isms—materialism, atheism, agnosticism, and all the unorthodox theologies which have been or are afloat in the world—and you will never advance one step towards the goal of the Christian ministry. I do not undervalue the service of pulverizing. But I never apologize in the pulpit. I proclaim, I announce, I warn, I set forth the promises of God. I am a man with a message . . . which is first given to me, but which I have made bone of my bone and flesh of my flesh'.[16]

This passage prompts a number of comments. First, we heartily endorse Iverach's distinction between apologetics and preaching. We shall review his apologetics in this section and his preaching in the next. Second, we note the final clause which is reminiscent of what Iverach elsewhere calls 'Butler's wise saying that things are not offered to our acceptance but to our acquisition'.[17] Third, the declaration 'I do not undervalue the service of pulverizing' is a splendid example of understatement: he valued pulverizing highly, believing as he did that it is just not *rational* to stop short of Christianity; and, what is more, he took obvious delight in the work, slaying his foes with many an ironic *tu quoque*, and more than once ridiculing the ploys of an opponent by utilizing the very words from the latter's mouth and drawing an absurd conclusion from them. If, when he was preaching, 'There is always a gleam in the eyes; latent awhile, it shoots forth with some ironic reference . . .'[18] that gleam was doubly bright when he was defending the faith. A reviewer's comment upon Iverach's Bible Class Primer, *The Truth of*

Christianity is just: 'He cannot write for infants, it is true. But young men will easily comprehend him. And it is to them that his strength will make its most victorious appeal'.[19] Iverach was an intellectual warrior; a theological frontiersman. He sallied forth to do battle against the two most potent isms into whose service the evolutionary theme had been pressed: naturalism and absolute idealism. He sought to defend faith's rationality, and to uphold the rights of personality. Let us see how he went about it.

In Iverach's day no frontiersman could fail to recognize that 'Evolution is the working hypothesis of most scientific men at the present time'.[20] As such it had to be reckoned with by Christian apologists, and Iverach went to great pains both to utilize the benefits of the evolutionary stance in the service of the Faith, and to warn of the dangers to which an uncritical acceptance of particular evolutionary theories could lead. He was quite sure that Darwin's theory of natural selection, 'with its limited range and carefully guarded statements',[21] was a good working hypothesis. No longer was it necessary or possible for Christians to maintain that each species was specially and immutably created by God at the beginning of time: 'the creeds of Christendom simply affirm that God is the Maker of the world and all that is in it, and does [*sic*] not say anything about the way and manner in which He made them . . . if evolution can tell us anything of the method of creation and the order in which the different forms of life appeared, then we ought to rejoice in it'.[22] The idea of organic evolution, in particular, has helped us to see life whole; the 'eternal' cause of Paley has been replaced by an immanent rational principle, and this is a great gain.[23] There need be no conflict between science and faith, 'For the concern of science is with the force itself and its way of working, and not with the origin and cause of it'.[24] Thus, 'we do not interfere, in any way, with the work or the method of mechanical science, when we take their results and show that they may be read in another fashion'.[25]

Iverach was quick to apply his critical powers to evolutionism of the vaguer kind. 'There seems to be a hazy idea in the minds of many', he said, 'that if a start can be made in chaos, and afterwards a cosmos appears, a solution of the problem of creation has been obtained'.[26] Again, he observed that some used the term 'natural selection' in an inconsistent manner. From being used of the notion of the elimination of the 'unfit' it comes to be used, surreptitiously and illegitimately, as the label of a *cause*.[27] Some, having happily employed the profoundly anthropomorphic idea of natural selection, proceed to charge Christian talk of a Creator and Maker with being 'unscientific' because anthropomorphic![28] Above all,

'What a large part chance has to play in the theory of evolution, and how diligently its advocates seek to conceal its working!'[29] Caprice used to be attributed to the waywardness of imperfect personal beings, but now it is postulated as being inherent in the universal, with the result that when new varieties require to be explained, recourse is had to freaks of nature and lucky accidents. On all of which the quasi-deism of Wallace, whose God intervenes only when self-adjusting forces have failed, is no improvement at all.[30] Iverach contends that 'To me creation is continuous. To me everything is as it is through the continuous power of God; every law, every being, every relation of being are all determined by Him, and He is the Power by which all things exist. I believe in the immanence of God in the world . . .'[31]

If evolutionary thought *per se* held no terrors for Iverach, he was convinced that the work of Herbert Spencer (1820–1903) rested upon the shakiest of foundations, and required to be opposed. Spencer maintains that 'organic evolution consists in a change from the homogeneous to the heterogeneous'.[32] He fails, however, to explain how this happens, or, indeed, how it *could* happen: 'A finite form of the homogeneous', counters Iverach, 'is really destructive of his hypothesis. For the finiteness of the form postulates a difference between the homogeneous and its environment; and as that difference is both continuous and active, it will not allow the homogeneous to exist. The very notion of a finite homogeneity is self-destructive'.[33] Spencer further errs in elevating a generalization of science, that of the conservation of energy, to the status of an ultimate principle, the persistence of force. The idea of persistence, however, is *not* yielded by science, and 'It is eminently unreasonable to abstract from the various kinds of force which we know, only one phase or aspect, and credit that abstraction with the infinite variety of the system . . . We make bold to say that no physicist will recognize the scientific doctrine of energy in the strange presentation of it given by Mr. Spencer, while a mediaeval schoolman would hail it with delight as an old friend with a new face. *Ex nihilo nihil fit* is the older maxim, which has been renamed the persistence of force, and raised to the position of universal datum, from which all else is deduced'.[34]

Iverach was no less puzzled by Spencer's persistent desire to explain the higher in terms of the lower. From the homogeneous cell he can obtain all the complexities of animated being! How can this be?

One has sympathy with those who labour at an impossible task. It is hard on one who has undertaken to explain evolution in terms of the distribution of matter and motion to arrive at a stage where matter fails, and then to be compelled to deal with super-organic evolution.

Hard, also, to have to speak of subject and object, and of other conceptions which decline to be subjected to a process of distribution and redistribution of matter and motion. We can but express our sympathy, and pass on to the conviction that the source of explanation lies not where they are seeking it. What has appeared in the process of evolution was there in the source from which evolution flowed. And what has appeared is a revelation of the living energy from which all things proceeded.[35]

Spencer's position feeds his agnosticism, for if we can only explain by what is below us, how can we know what is above?[36] Yet—perversely—how useful the Unknowable is to Spencer, and what a great deal he can tell us about it! He knows that time, matter, space, time and force are all forms of the Unknowable; hence it must be the case that 'if the Unknowable is manifested, so far as it is manifested it can be known'.[37] Yet Spencer will not permit religion to know its God! Iverach is the first to regret that some invoke religion in order to explain away intellectual difficulties, but Spencer is no less guilty, for he uses the Unknowable 'as a convenient storehouse for the warehousing of difficult problems'.[38]

We have concentrated upon Iverach's criticism of Spencer because it was so searching and so prolonged. But we should not overlook the fact that he preferred his fundamental charge more widely: 'The primitive nebulosity of Professor Huxley, the lifeless chaotic mass of Professor Karl Pearson, the absolutely homogeneous of Mr. Spencer . . . do not serve the purpose of those who introduce them to our notice. They do not help us to pass from the indeterminate to the determinate, and they do not help us to get intelligence out of what is not intelligent. Every problem presented by the present complex universe is presented also by the primitive nebulosity'.[39]

Iverach was persuaded that since the universe was intelligible to rational beings it was itself rational, and that 'each new discovery is a fresh testimony to theism, and each new law found in phenomena is only a fresh argument for God—for intelligence as the source of order and the only ground of law . . . the postulation of a Supreme Intelligence cannot be tested by experiment, because it is assumed by all experiments . . . We have not put the intelligibility into the world; we find it there'.[40] Herein resides the distinction between man and all other animals. They are acted upon by their environment; he can investigate, understand, and purposively and socially act upon his surroundings.[41] And with the mention of the idea of purpose we come to a further phase of Iverach's criticism: naturalistic evolutionists cannot allow for purpose in the universe, and they violate man's personality by reducing him to one who can take no initiatives, but can only react to circumstances. What is needed is that the story of natural evolution be supplemented by the story of moral and spiritual and religious evolution.[42] Both naturalistic and (as we shall see) idealistic versions of evolutionary theory founder on the rock of purpose. As he sardonically says, 'Even Hegelian evolution, which is a greater and higher thing than Darwinism, leaves us without a future, and its outlook is bounded by the life that now is. Indeed the highest product of evolution in the hands of Hegel seems to be a Prussian at the beginning of the present century—a respectable product of evolution certainly, but one that does not seem to have exhausted the resources of civilization'.[43] A worthier teleology is required.

But we have already moved beyond Iverach's response to evolutionary thought in general, and have stumbled upon the metaphysical principles underlying it, and the ethical principles implicit in it. This will become clearer if we turn at once to a series of articles Iverach wrote on 'Pantheism', having regard first to metaphysical matters.[44] Iverach declares that

> That form of Pantheism which Greek materialism elaborated appears today in the evolutionary Pantheism of Spencer and Haeckel, while the Pantheism of the Upanishads appears in absolute idealism, which regards the universe as an experience of a single life, or the expression of an Absolute Self-consciousness. While the modern forms gather up in themselves the historic gains of former explanations, they owe their precise shape mainly to the influence of Kant . . . [Kant's] restriction of knowledge to phenomena, and his recognition of things in themselves as lying beyond knowledge, laid the foundation on which the structure of Agnosticism has been built up.[45]

From the side of naturalism, Spencer posited the Eternal Energy as the source of all, thereby courting the disapproval of some who had welcomed the agnosticism of his *First Principles* (1862). He had now, they held, simply restored the 'metaphysical and theological ghosts which they thought had been banished for ever'.[46] He inconsistently tried to give an Unknowable to the agnostic, and an eternal, albeit immanent, cause to the theist. The eternal is thus merged with the world, and has no meaning apart from it. But this is precisely the end result of the *absolute idealistic* tendency too. For here too the creator/creature distinction is obliterated; the only difference is that under idealism all reality is said to be spirit.

Kant is once more the fountain-head. He argued that in order to experience an object, both intuition and understanding come into play. They are transcendental principles; that is, they are implicitly in experience in general. They become explicit by the process of transcendental deduction. Now whereas Kant's transcendental categories had no application beyond experience, Fichte, Schelling and Hegel pursued them further by positing a Mind as the standard by which to test the adequacy of experience, and by seeking that perfect system to which, they thought, the categories pointed. In this way the subject/object distinction, which lies at the basis of human knowledge, was transcended; the world became the other of God, and as necessary to him as he was to it. Iverach counters, however, that from Kant's analysis of consciousness in general we may not infer one single intelligence for which all things are. This is the false step which the absolutists take, and thus they land in a pantheistic unity.

As we have already seen, the writings of Edward and John Caird are notable examples of the attempt to describe Christianity in terms of absolute idealism. Edward Caird went so far as to say that Hegelianism is 'but Christianity theorized'.[47] In Iverach's opinion, much may be learned from the attempt so to express Christian insights, but in the last resort the attempt fails:

> Never in the history of human thought has the identification of the world-idea with the idea of God been presented in so alluring and persuasive a form as at the present hour . . . Never has philosophy insisted so strongly on the truth, beauty, and worth of the highest ideals of religion as under the inspiration of Hegel, one of the greatest, if not the greatest, of philosophical thinkers. But while we gladly admit and, indeed, assert this, and much more than this, we must sadly turn to our own path and take up the burden of our own work; for the idealistic philosophy makes religion to be simply an aspect of itself, and does not leave us with a God into whose fellowship we may enter, in whose service we may find perfect freedom. For we can come to Him, and He can come to us, only by the way of the works He has made, by the institutions He has founded, and by the ways of the universe which is His only manifestation. We need a God who can speak to us, and if He cannot speak directly to us, the greater and better part, the flower and fruit of religion will wither and die.[48]

Iverach could not stand by while Edward Caird 'calmly annexed' the sphere of revelation and made it part of the natural process.[49] Indeed, he went so far as to say that 'It is recognized now by all Christian apologists worthy of the name that to defend Christianity with Hegelian weapons is to surrender at the outset all the distinguishing marks of Christianity. It transforms Christianity beyond all recognition. Facts disappear, doctrines vanish, experience distinctively Christian is evaporated, and we are left with nothing save the ideas disembodied in the religion. History and Fact are merely scaffolding useful for the introduction of the Ideas, but as soon as the ideas are there the facts may usefully disappear'.[50] Edward Caird's *Evolution of Religion* was an able attempt to translate Christianity into the terms of our modern experience, but Iverach warned that 'such translation must not leave out the essential facts'[51]—as he was sure Caird did. History apart, we would do well also to remember that the great contribution of the Hebrews to our thought of God was that he is *distinct* from the world.[52] Further, and with a clear debt to the Old Testament, 'The Christian conception of God insists that in Him there is no becoming, in Him there is no realization of Himself . . . Now all idealistic, all pantheistic theories assume that God is in the process of realization, and that the evolution of the world is the evolution of God'.[53] But if God suffers under absolute idealism, so too do men; and with a refreshing dose of Scottish common sense Iverach thunders, 'There must be room in the world for a system of self-conscious beings, for they are there . . . A pantheistic scheme does not recognize the uniqueness of the self'.[54]

Iverach was never happier than when running abstractions to ground. His most serious objection to abstractions—whether to 'the monstrous self-consciousness of the Hegelian school, the impersonal will of Schopenhauer, and the unconscious intelligence of Hartmann';[55] to 'scientific intelligence', 'will', 'feeling', or Spencer's 'force'—was that they conduced to the depersonalization of man. A prominent forerunner of modern abstractors was Descartes, who having set mind over against body left men the task of conjoining them once more.[56] What Iverach sought was a theory which took account of *all* the facts. He was quite content to join T. H. Green in the declaration that we live in a rational universe, and we may know it; but he could not endorse a world view which left out of account the facts of religious experience and the deliverances of revelation.

Our knowledge of God is real, though not exhaustive. It is ours because gradually over the centuries, and decisively in Christ, God has been making himself known. We could not manage without such a revelation, for God's ways are not our ways, and his thoughts are not our thoughts.[57] Nor is the problem simply one of magnitude; it is one of sin. 'Many hindrances there are on Christ's view to the communication of God to His creation; but the main hindrance is that men are not pure in heart.'[58] Hence the theistic arguments, though 'of supreme value as indications of some of the ways by which He may be known',[59] are not conclusive demonstrations of God's existence. God comes to man in Christ; Christ redeems thought and life; and *these* are the facts which do not merely require to be taken into account. Rather, these facts provide the perspective from which all science and philosophy must be viewed.[60] If

God is as he is, and has done what he has done, it is just not rational to persist in unbelief. Iverach's complaint against Balfour was that while some of his conclusions were worthy, he had reached them by an impossible, naturalistic route which required him to deny the rationality of faith.[61]

We turn now to the ethical implications of evolutionary naturalism and of absolutism. Iverach was sure that neither of these isms could do justice to morality, since neither did justice to the nature of man. His presupposition here is that personality is the highest category we know, and his charge is that naturalism reduces man, while absolutism loses him and plays havoc with man's moral convictions. As we might by now guess, Spencer is the focus of Iverach's anti-naturalistic onslaught.[62] Spencer's doctrine of man is erroneous. He conceives of man as the recipient of a series of nervous shocks; these shocks induce consciousness, and eventually, as a result of a succession of such shocks, moral intention emerges. This leads to the view of man as an aggregate of feelings. Iverach's counter-attack turns upon the considerations that the moral cannot originate in the physical; that Spencer overlooks the influence of man's inheritance and education; and that man cannot be reduced to an aggregate of feelings: the ethics and psychology implicit here are quite misguided. As to the psychology, 'Consciousness . . . is indefinable. Like all ultimates we must simply accept it as the condition of explaining all else, itself remaining unexplained. It may not be identified with the sum of its states, any more than we can identify a real whole with the sum of its parts. For, after we have summed up the parts, there remains unaccounted for the wholeness of the whole'.[63] As to the former, Spencer would leave us with no will. Indeed, it is difficult to see how he can truly have an ethic at all—descriptive ethics alone ought to be open to him, for his principles—notably his belief that there is no self, but only naturalistically produced states of consciousness—cannot consistently accommodate the idea of obligation. Undeterred, Spencer attempts to derive morality from the laws of life, and from the physical order. It is, thinks Iverach, a forlorn hope.

In order to advance his cause Spencer derives all he can from the theory of evolution. He is optimistic that the utilitarian sanction of pleasure, though so far incompletely successful, will in the future, when the organism is fully adjusted to the environment, promote conflict-free life. Iverach perceives at once that the evaluative judgement, 'better', has here been surreptitiously battened to the concept 'more evolved'. Iverach has three points to make here. Firstly, 'We are not helped by the criterion of Mr. Spencer that right conduct is the conduct that is most evolved. The immoral sentiments are as evolved as the moral. There is a great deal of definite, coherent heterogeneity in the burglar and the thief . . . both in their badness and in their goodness [men] seem to transcend the cosmic order'.[64] Second, men need an ideal, and 'There is no ethical ideal like the ideal of Jesus of Nazareth, realized in His own life and set forth in His teaching'.[65] Third, this ideal radically revises our ethical attitudes, however 'evolved'. Evolutionary ethics cannot incorporate Christ unless it can show either 'that the moral ideal of Christianity is just what we ought to expect in the time and place and circumstances of its origin, and that its origin and character are not exceptional; or it must show that it is not of a kind fitted to be the highest ideal of humanity in every age and time. Either task seems impossible'.[66]

Absolutism's hold upon ethics is no less sinister. In his balanced way Iverach both praised and blamed T. H. Green. He thought it a great gain that Green had emphasized the importance of personality as the essential feature of human nature, and that he had not overlooked the social implications of that feature: 'How great a gain this is we shall readily understand if we reflect that scarcely any book on English psychology has ever touched on the question of personality. As a rule, English psychology discusses faculties as if they had an existence apart from the self'.[67] Among the advantages accruing from Green's approach was the fact that now, the question of the freedom of the will could more profitably be discussed. Previously the question had been treated as if it were a question in dynamics or mechanics; and then 'an undetermined will was a monstrosity, and an irrational absurdity', while 'a will absolutely determined by the strongest motive . . . leaves to such a will no ethical meaning'.[68] In this connection Iverach had earlier taken Jonathan Edwards to task. He regretted that Edwards had approached the question of the relation of divine sovereignty to human freedom from the philosophical side, and that he had not taken the force of the point that man's creaturely freedom is different from man's freedom as sinful, fallen creature. Concerning the latter, Reformed theology has a definite opinion; it leaves the former question open, as between determinists and libertarians. More unsatisfactory still is Edwards's illegitimate abstraction of the will from the other faculties: 'His argument becomes meaningless when you substitute for the action of the will the action of the person, and when you get away from abstractness to the concrete realities of life'.[69] At this point Hegel and his followers did well to teach that freedom, the possession of self-conscious beings who can form and realize ideals, is self-determination.[70]

Sadly, however, this gain upon which Green capitalizes in his theories of history and of knowledge does not inform his ethics: 'We venture to suggest that here Green has not been faithful to his own principle . . . Self-consciousness in his ethical system tends to vanish, and is replaced by a universal self, which is sometimes set forth as that which thinks in all thinkers . . . The attempt to unify the divine and human subject seems to destroy the reality of both'.[71] But by far the most disturbing feature of all in pantheizing ethics is the minimizing of the fact of evil. Thus for example Royce can say, 'The very presence of ill in the temporal order is the condition of Perfection in the eternal order'.[72] Iverach is better pleased by Frederic Harrison's view that 'No force can amalgamate in one idea tornadoes, earthquakes, interstellar spaces, pestilences, brotherly love, unselfish energy, patience, hope, trust and greed'.[73] Precisely because pantheism affords all of these a home in the Absolute, all our customary and right distinctions between right and wrong are obliterated; and 'Any philosophy which obliterates moral values, and which apologizes for ugliness, evil and sin, and makes these to be essential to the perfection of the eternal order, is under the necessity of revising its procedure, and of bringing its conclusions into something like harmony with the moral convictions and apirations of mankind'.[74]

These aspirations find their culmination in Christ. But let us proceed step by step through Iverach's positive account of Christian ethics. He begins with a lofty view of man—lofty because man alone among the animals can reason, know God, and mould his environment. Indeed, 'Man's environment is largely made by man'.[75] To man alone belongs personality, but personality is not simply given. Individuality is given, but personality is won: 'To other beings the law of their life is given; man has to subject himself to law, and to choose the highest law to which he will subject himself'.[76] Other creatures and agencies are contributory to this achievement of personality. Not only the Sabbath, but science, the state, and so on, were made for man.[77] But Christ is *the* man, the ideal in whom all other ideals, intellectual, moral, aesthetic and religious, find their fulfilment: 'The perfect human Personality reveals to man how to show reverence to what is above man, love to all his equals, and benevolence to all that is subject to him. He has shown it in His own action, and inspires it in those who trust Him'.[78] As he contemplated *the* Personality, Christ, Iverach reflected 'To me the difficulty is not whether personality should be predicated of God, but whether so great a word should be a predicate of man'.[79]

In the idea of growth into true personality lies the true teleology, and ethics and theology cannot be other than teleological.[80] At this point both Descartes and Spinoza failed. Descartes's doctrine of external causes working on minds excluded the idea of purpose; and although Spinoza's treatment of the development of man's emotional life is teleological enough, he loses teleology when he makes man's essence to be pure intelligence, thereby losing touch with experience.[81] In his own contemplation of man's end, Iverach characteristically shunned abstractions. For all his emphasis upon personality, he thought that 'the individual' was an abstraction, for man is a being in relation to others. Equally, he was sure that those who, like Benjamin Kidd, spoke of the social organism, were also guilty of an abstraction.[82] He ever tried to keep his feet on the ground; to interpret real experience; to remember the real world. And when he realized, as he invariably did, that man's ideal in Christ is perfect, and that man's actual performance is abysmal, he returned naturally to the One who, as well as ideal, is Saviour; for the person who has Christ 'has a motive for living, an aim for life, strength by the Holy Spirit to bear and do, and hope to crown and reward his efforts . . . it will become more apparent as time rolls on, and experience widens, that Christian Ethics are the only true scientific Ethics'.[83]

II

'All through he is the skilful reasoner, Scottish every bit . . . he is also the skilful preacher . . . The whole affair is full of character, and he is happiest when he has a long platform to patrol and can move from side to side, looking into the assembly and dropping sentences, now quietly, now with resonant firmness, out of an iron-grey beard . . . Professor Iverach is a realist . . . he analyses, but to the exhaustion of humbug, not of honest human emotion'.[84]

In treating of Iverach's work as an apologist we have already had cause to set forth the main burden of his message, for while there is no need for apologetics in the pulpit, there can be no satisfactory apologetics without affirmation. But now we must think of Iverach in a somewhat wider way: not simply as Professor of Apologetics and author of philosophico-theological works, but as preacher, pastor, trainer of ordinands. All his work in these areas was grounded upon the conviction which informed his apologetics, namely that Christianity places us in touch with reality:

> The Gospels stand well all the tests of Reality. The life recorded here must be real, for no one could have invented it. The Personality also is Real, for He is so unique as to pass beyond the bounds of human imagination. The help He gave to men, and gives to them, is real, and

the truth He taught has been verified a thousand times over in the heart and conscience of men, and in their life and conduct.[85]

It was this real Christ who must be proclaimed. Iverach exalted preaching, and delighted to address his students upon their homiletic task and privilege. In particular he underlined the source of all true preaching: 'You may be learned in all the culture of the world, you may have selected from these systems what you have reacted against and appropriated in your own life, yet if you have not had the vision of God you can never effectively witness for Him, you can never say what every true preacher ought to be able to say, I believe and therefore preach'.[86] For Iverach, preaching was something quite other than the mere conveying of information from one mind to another; the whole personality was to be involved:

I assume that the preacher really is preaching, not reading an essay, not filling up time. He is there living, palpitating, bringing to bear on the people the stored-up power of his whole life, focussing into that moment the thinking of a lifetime, pouring out on them the tide of emotion called forth by the situation and by the time which may be a time of decision for those who hear, rousing them by the flood of passion for their well-being, a passion that has grown with his growth and strengthened with his strength, and has now become a rushing tide that sweeps the people into conclusions which shall affect them to eternal issues . . . If we come forth fresh from fellowship with Christ, our people cannot but feel the glow and power which must be ours if we have been with Jesus. We may not be conscious of it ourselves, but others shall know it. Moses wist not that his face shone, but the people knew it.[87]

What, then, was the heart of the preacher's message? In Iverach's words,

We believe in God the Father, and His Son our Saviour and Lord, in the inspiring Spirit, in the forgiveness of sins, in the Kingdom of God, and in the life everlasting. These things are at the heart of the Christian message, they form the burden of the Christian revelation, as they form the basis, however far from complete realization they may be, of our Christian civilization. . . . It is something worth while to be able to say to men that God is their Friend who has loved them with a wiser, deeper love than ever they have borne towards themselves. It is surely something to be able to say to people that the cross of sacrifice has been planted within the innermost circle of the divine life, and to be able to assure men that the Son of God loved them and gave Himself for them. It is a story which has broken the hardest hearts, a story which yet has power to lead men from sin to righteousness, from darkness unto light, from lostness to salvation, from death unto life.[88]

Iverach did not write extensively on pastoral work, but he said enough to make it clear that he viewed the work of ministry as all of a piece: 'there is a good deal to be said regarding a minister's relation to his people, which really is only a continuation of what he is to them in the pulpit. For a minister is not two men, one man in the pulpit and another out of it. He is one man in the pulpit and out of it'.[89] Nor is the minister an isolated agent. He is a representative of the whole Church; he testifies to the common faith. But, speaking as one who had lived through the period of 'heresy' trials and Declaratory Acts, Iverach hoped (in most un-Kennedy-like fashion) that in any similar debates in the future the Church would 'frankly face the situation, leave her Confession as a valuable historical document in its historical position, and set forth her creed as the real faith of the living Church at the hour when it is promulgated'.[90] This was by no means to say that the line may not be drawn *anywhere*. Iverach certainly would not 'select the moral maxims and stray religious truths from other religions in order to demonstrate the redundancy of revelation. Nor would he see reason dethroned. Religion 'must satisfy reason, the conscience, and the affections. And all these demands are satisfied in Him who is the Way, the Truth and the Life'.[91]

In pulpit as in classroom, Iverach set forth Christ as the ideal. But 'if it were the part of Christianity merely to set forth high ideals before men, if it did no more, it would be a counsel of despair. The Sermon on the Mount would be no Gospel, no glad tidings to me, if I were to take it by itself, for I could never unaided rise to the height of the righteousness that exceeds . . . But, then, He who described that ideal and bound it on me has promised that He will come to my help, and pour into my broken life the fulness of His own life'.[92] *Of course* we have to work out our own salvation; but we can only do it when the statutes have become songs, God's requirements inward impulses.[93]

A reading of Iverach's sermons will convince the most sceptical that this pulveriser of isms had the heart of a child. He writes movingly on the tenderness of God: 'Gather together all that you can think of love and tenderness, sum it up till it surpasses all that you can imagine, and even then you fall immeasurably short of the great reality of the tenderness of God'.[94] Finally, in a passage in which he gives his own testimony, Iverach noted a lack in the preaching of his day:

> I have noted an absence of the eternal note in our modern preaching. I have noted also that preachers too often forget that Christianity is a religion of redemption, and sin and forgiveness are dealt with less thoroughly than of old. But on this I do not dwell, but I should like, ere I close, just to say this, that Christ has made life and immortality

luminous, so luminous that they shine on our daily life and daily work; and it is simply wilful blindness on our part if we refuse to allow the thought of them to have a practical influence on our walk and conversation.[95]

III

At a time when some were being bowled over by evolutionary thought, James Iverach neither shirked the issues which that thought raised, nor lost his head. New thought, by itself, held no terrors for him. He was quick to welcome the findings of the scientists, though he reserved the right to view their presuppositions from the standpoint of Christian faith. He rightly saw that as far as the findings of science were concerned there was no need of conflict between scientists and Christian believers. Similarly, he learned what he could from absolute idealism—he did not find it easy to learn from naturalism—but he insisted that these isms were in some ways not scientific enough. Neither naturalism nor absolute idealism, though for different reasons, paid sufficient attention to personality; and neither could give an adequate account of the *facts* of the Christian faith and experience. His pupil's judgement was sound: 'The brightness of his Christian faith, inherited and then made his own, could not be disintegrated by the ever-growing complexities of the Spencerian evolution, nor obscured by the dazzling cloudbanks of Hegelian speculation. The torch was indeed shaken, but the more it shook the more it shone'.[96]

On the other hand, Iverach showed himself to be a child of his time in respect of the atmosphere (rather than assertion) of inevitability which attaches to his expectation that theology is *par excellence* the unifier of the knowledge and the experience of men. Thus for example while working hard to remove the terrors to the faithful inherent in the doctrine of evolution, he did not really face up to the logical difficulties which arise in so far as scientists and theologians tell different stories about the *same* things.[97] He sought a reasonable and reasoned statement of the faith, and one which was true to Christian experience. For all his admiration of Butler, he was no slavish eighteenth-century apologist. On the contrary, his grasp of the centrality of personality, with its concomitant of immanence, made him sceptical of Paley's 'externalism'; and he was careful not to claim too much for the theistic arguments. We welcome Iverach's reassertion of the creator–creature distinction, and are persuaded that where this distinction is obliterated man is on the way to becoming lost in something that is less than God. Pantheizing gnosticisms still stalk theology's stage, and they owe more to the absolute idealism which Iverach queried than is sometimes realized.

From the point of view of arrangement of material, Iverach did not always present his case in the most balanced way; and sometimes it is not altogether clear for whom he is writing. The prime example of this is *Descartes, Spinoza and the New Philosophy*, which is too slight for the scholar and too laden with Latin quotations for the general reader. Again, sometimes he was too prone to swashbuckle, as a reviewer of *St. Paul: His Life and Times* observed; 'If he sometimes raises, rather unnecessarily, giants (mostly of German extraction) in order immediately afterwards to knock them on the head, yet he always *does* knock them on the head'.[98]

But in another sense, Iverach was perhaps the most balanced of all the divines we are considering. He went out to the frontiers; he hewed from the rock. He was effective in writing, in classroom, in pulpit, in Assembly. Perhaps his very versatility makes him the most forgotten of our divines. But he can still teach us, and not the least important lesson we may learn from him is that concerning the need to shun abstractions, and to make our philosophico-theological method accord with the realities of the Christian life.

CHAPTER SEVEN

James Orr (1844–1913):
The Ineradicability of the Supernatural

In May 1897 James Orr addressed the Jubilee Synod of the United Presbyterian Church on 'The Contribution of the United Presbyterian Church to Religious Thought and Life'. 'If I were asked', he said, 'to name the characteristic of the type of piety which has prevailed in our Church from the Seceders down, I should say that it lies in the union of thought and life—in the upbuilding of a strong, earnest intelligent Christian manhood; rugged, stern, rude in husk, perhaps, but with a sweet kernel within; the kind of stuff Covenanters were made of, and which furnishes the material for stable and reliable characters everywhere'.[1] If we add the phrase, 'massive in frame, massive in intellect', we have an excellent description of James Orr himself, of whom his colleague Denney was one day to write, simply and poignantly, 'he was a big man by the grace of nature and of the Gospel too, and his removal makes a great void'.[2] But something remains to be said. Thus far Orr might appear formidable—even aloof, especially if we also have a sight of his resolutely Victorian portrait. It is not, therefore, inappropriate to note that there was a touch of whimsy about him. We are strangely comforted by the knowledge that this doughty champion of the evangelical cause, who was in his element when graciously battling for the Gospel's sake, could also entertain the young with skilfully and gleefully executed conjuring tricks.[3]

The son of Robert Orr, engineer, James was born in Glasgow on 11th April 1844. He was left an orphan at an early age, and was brought up by relatives. On leaving school he was apprenticed to the book-binding trade, but encouraged by such men as Drs. James Ker and Fergus Ferguson, he began to think in terms of the Christian ministry. His home church was Parliamentary Road United Presbyterian, Glasgow, and from there he was sent forward, first to the University of Glasgow, where he graduated with first class honours in Philosophy under Edward Caird, whose favourite pupil he was, and also found time to work for the Glasgow City Mission. In 1868 he proceeded to the United Presbyterian

Divinity Hall, Edinburgh, where his professors were Harper (Systematic and Pastoral Theology), Macmichael (History of Doctrines), Eadie (Biblical Literature and Exegesis) and Cairns (Apologetical Theology). He graduated B.D. of Glasgow and later, in 1885, he became one of only two men ever to gain Glasgow's D.D. by examination, under the revised regulations of Principal Caird's day.[4]

On leaving the Divinity Hall Orr served for some months at Trinity Church, Irvine, as *locum tenens* to the minister, Dr. W. B. Robertson; and in 1874 he accepted the call to East Bank United Presbyterian Church, Hawick. Here he remained for seventeen years, preaching, tending his flock, serving the wider community, and all the while pursuing his philosophical and theological studies. In 1891 he became the first holder of the Kerr Lectureship, of which *The Christian View of God and the World* (1893) is the permanent fruit. The same year saw his appointment to the Chair of Church History at the Divinity Hall in Edinburgh, where he remained until the revised arrangements necessitated by the formation of the United Free Church in 1900 prompted his transference to the Chair of Apologetics and Systematic Theology at the Glasgow (ex Free Church) College, in succession to A. B. Bruce.[5]

By now Orr was widely known both at home and overseas. He examined in Philosophy for Glasgow University; he lectured on German theology at Chicago in 1895; his Elliott Lectures at Allegheny (1897) were published under the title *The Progress of Dogma* (1901); and three lectures originally given at the Mansfield College Summer School, Oxford, in 1894 were repeated as the Morgan Lectures at Auburn, New York in 1897, and subsequently published under the title *Neglected Factors in the Study of the Early Progress of Christianity* (1899). In 1903 Orr delivered the Stone Lectures at Princeton, which appeared as *God's Image in Man* in 1905, and his book on *The Problem of the Old Testament* (1906), submitted in proof, won the Bross Prize of Lake Forest College, Illinois, for 1905. In April 1907 he gave a course of lectures to the Bible Teachers' Training School, New York, and these were published in the same year as *The Virgin Birth of Christ*. To most of Orr's other writings we shall in due course refer. Meanwhile we note his contributions on Exodus, Deuteronomy, II Kings, and Hosea to *The Pulpit Commentary*; his editorship of the five-volume *International Standard Bible Encyclopaedia* (1914) and his essays in *The Fundamentals*, that series of booklets published at the expense of the American layman, Lyman Stewart between 1910–1915. The purpose of this series was to defend the evangelical faith, to oppose and expose rationalistic biblical criticism, and to trounce such sects as the Mormons.[6] Among Orr's other contributions were those to Hastings's *Dictionary of the*

Bible and *Encyclopaedia of Religion and Ethics*, and to such journals as *The Expositor* and *The Expository Times*.

A convinced conservative himself, Orr was tolerant of the right of others to differ from him. Thus, for example, he rose to the defence of Fergus Ferguson when the latter, an advocate of credal revision, was formally charged with violating the United Presbyterian Church's doctrinal standards;[7] and he sided with Dr. Ross Taylor against Drs. John Smith and John McEwan in defending the right of George Adam Smith to retain his Chair while publishing such 'advanced' views as were to be found in his *Modern Criticism and the Preaching of the Old Testament* (1901).[8] In the latter case Orr seconded Rainy's Assembly motion, which was carried by 534 votes to 263.[9] This was the last of that series of trials which began with the proceedings against Robertson Smith, and included the Dods-Bruce case—a fact which caused some to heave a sigh of relief, and others to feel confirmed in their view that the 'downgrade' was irreversible. Reflecting afterwards on the Robertson Smith case, Dr. Leckie wrote 'James Orr was always a generous soul; and, if he disliked "heresy", he disliked intolerance still more'.[10]

Orr's geniality and zeal for harmonious relations found a further outlet in the *Union Magazine*, which he jointly edited with James Denney.[11] He longed for the healing of the rifts within Scottish Presbyterianism, and was one of four[12] who had drafted the United Presbyterian resolution of 1896, to the effect that that Church's desire for union with the Free Church was unabated (that is, despite an abortive approach made in 1893). The resolution was carried unanimously, and in the opinion of one writer this was 'the critical step in the whole movement'.[13] Two years later Orr proposed in the United Presbyterian Assembly that the findings of the Joint Committee be accepted, and an unanimous verdict once more ensued. Rainy (of the Free Church) was present for the vote, and although his motion on the matter did not have so easy a passage in his own Assembly, the desired result was forthcoming, and the way was clear for the union of 1900.[14]

The United Free Church was still in its infancy when a still wider union was contemplated, and we find Orr on the side of those who, in the Assembly of 1903, approved of the successful move to explore union possibilities with the Established Church, provided that nothing should be acceded to which would threaten the proper freedom of the Church. Indeed, this proviso formed the substance of an Assembly amendment proposed by Orr himself.[15] As time passed, Orr became increasingly apprehensive, and at the 1912 Assembly he proposed that the Union Committee be instructed to investigate the extent of agreement between the two parties on the questions of Church-State relations and endowments. He was motivated in this by his high regard for the principle of equity.[16] Denney's assessment was that 'Orr thinks those who are keen for union are trying to square the circle, and does not seem to see what he is trying to do is to circularize the square'.[17] Be that as it may, it was rightly said that Orr's 'intellectual power, his profound scholarship and his fine Christian character, coupled with his commanding stature and the quiet dignity of his manner, lent great weight to all his utterances in the Assembly'.[18]

Eager as he was for the healing of breaches, Orr could never forget the rock whence he was hewn. In the Jubilee address to which we referred at the outset, he recalled the scholars and hymn writers of his Church. He observed that 'In hymnody, too, our Church was pioneer, and even in that special sign of modern culture in Church worship—the organ!'[19] (Compare John Kennedy's opinion of the United Presbyterians on that score reported earlier!) But he declared that the special genius of those in the Secession and Relief traditions was the preaching of the pure gospel. This had lain behind the evangelical awakening of the eighteenth century, and it had prompted that dedicated service to the wider community—missions, Bible Society work, the anti-slavery movement, of which the nineteenth century had seen so much. It had taught the nation the meaning of spiritual religion, and it had fuelled the quest of the freedom and independence of the Church. Indeed,

> The Distruption of 1843—the noblest ecclesiastical event of the century, as I regard it—was but the vindication, in this respect, of the principles of the Seceders. Men talk of National Religion. It is the Church, like ours, which is free from the State by which I hold national religion can most effectually be advanced. I honour the State Church for everything great and good in it, but it is not among its glories that it has ever been a pioneer of progress. It cannot in the nature of things be. Its guns are spiked. In the great forward movements of the century, in the struggles for reform and freedom, its influence has as a rule been cast against, as that of the Free Churches has been cast for, progress.[20]

James Orr died, leaving a widow, on 6th September 1913. He was succeeded at the College by D. W. Forrest, himself of United Presbyterian stock. In his Inaugural Lecture Forrest paid the following tribute to his predecessor:

> No one who is acquainted with Dr. Orr's writings can fail to be impressed by the great range of his knowledge, alike in philosophy and theology. There were few systems of thought with which he was not

familiar: and his accuracy was as remarkable as his range. Nor did this
learning over-weight or suppress his individuality. He possessed a
speculative gift and a logical acumen which made him a powerful
critic. He was in no sense a traditionalist, if by that is meant one who
adheres to accepted doctrine, because it has become consecrated by
time. If he kept to the broad lines of the evangelical dogmatic, it was
because after the fullest investigation they approved themselves to his
own judgement: and the grounds of that judgment he was well able to
state. But I may be forgiven if . . . I dwell rather on the fine qualities
of his personality, the simplicity of his nature, the absence of all
pettiness or pretence, and above all the courage and fidelity with which
he applied to all social and national questions the Christian principles
of justice and compassion.[21]

J. H. Leckie was more succinct, but no less accurate: 'The last great
theologian of the old evangelical type, he was worthy of his ancestry and
an honour to his Church.'[22]

I

We have already remarked that James Orr was a conservative in theology,
but that slippery term requires careful elucidation. Orr's was no
unthinking, narrow traditionalism. If he ended, more or less, with the
faith of his fathers, it was because, having departed thence for argument's
sake, he had returned to base, after slaying numerous foes *en route*. He was
in no sense one who needed the security of the blinkered. On the contrary,
he was at his best when judiciously dissecting the views of those who were
far removed from him in spirit. Indeed, we might say that of all our
divines, Orr's interests were the most catholic. Certainly, in detailed
knowledge of the Christian thought of the ages he outclassed them all.
This was the stock-in-trade of his Edinburgh Chair, and it provided the
backcloth, and gave much of the perspective to, his work in Apologetics
and Systematic Theology at Glasgow.

Scholarly though Orr was, his practical intentions were never far below
the surface. Thus for example in his lucid survey of *The Progress of Dogma*
he said, 'I am to ask whether there is a recognizable law in the progress of
dogma, and, if there is, what help it affords us in determining our
attitude to theological system now, and in guiding our steps for the
future. This is a question, surely, as practical as it is pressing'.[23] At once
he faced the challenge, current then as now, that dogma is nothing but an
impediment to faith; that dogma divides where Christ would unite. His

answer was that doctrines, however nebulous, are unavoidable, for Christianity has its *content*. Not for him the slogan, 'Christianity is not creed, but life'; or the view that religious faith is a matter of the heart only; or the fond but erroneous belief that we may have facts devoid of interpretation.[24] Again, Orr counters those who contend that if dogma is not redundant, its actual course has been pathological in so far as the original idea of Christianity has been obscured by alien influences. In this connection he conducts a running battle with Harnack's view that the original Christianity was sorely misunderstood by those who unwarrantably 'Hellenized' it, and that what is required is a return to the immediate impression of the historical Christ upon us, in order to the construction of a new theology, free from unhelpful metaphysical presuppositions. Orr's method is to criticize what Harnack says, and then to attach the (metaphysical!) principle on which he says it.

In the first place, Harnack unjustifiably throws all the emphasis in the development of dogma upon the first three centuries, thereby, for example, overlooking the epoch-making character of Augustine's theology.[25] Such exclusions enable Harnack to focus upon two areas: the alleged shortcomings of the apologists, and the insight of the Gnostics. As to the former, Harnack maintained that the apologists asserted the doctrines of natural religion—God, immortality and virtue—and that to them such facts as the Incarnation and Resurrection had value only as attesting those natural beliefs. Orr cannot agree. He grants that the apologists suited their approach to their pagan audience; and he reminds us that antagonism to Christians was often prompted by the non-compliance of the latter with the established worship of the day, and not by doctrinal motives. To this extent replies to charges would not need to be of a doctrinal character. Nor does Orr deny that the apologists *do* declare the following truths of natural religion: 'the being, unity and spirituality of God; His free creation of the world, and its dependence on Him for continued existence; His providence and moral administration; the reality and immutability of moral law; the certainty of a day of judgement, and of a future state of rewards and punishments'.[26] But these doctrines are '*very real parts of the Christian system*. A truth does not cease to be Christian because it is also in accordance with reason, though this would seem to be the presupposition of much of the criticism of the apologists'.[27] Even so, the apologists (*pace* Harnack) do more than simply repeat the truths of natural religion: though Orr is bound to admit that at times they do blunt the edges of Christian truth.[28] Thus, Justin recognizes, '*if inadequately*, the weakening of the powers of human nature through sin, and speaks of man in his fallen state as the child of necessity and ignorance'.[29] Accordingly, there is substance in the charge that the apologists dwell too much on the Christianity as being a 'new philosophy', and their methodology leads them to concentrate on the rationally defensible.[30]

As for the Gnostics, Orr cannot share Harnack's view that they are 'the first theologians' inasmuch as they achieved the Hellenizing of Christianity on its religious side; for 'There is a theology which keeps true to the basis of Christian facts . . . and there is a theology, the centre of gravity of which lies outside of Christianity altogether, which would subvert these facts, and dissipate Christianity into a cloudland of human imaginations'.[31] The latter type is exemplified by Gnosticism. Orr did not quarrel with the Gnostic's questions—Whence came matter, and evil? How came man to be, and is he redeemable?—but he profoundly disagreed with his answers, among them the idea of a distinction drawn between the framer of the universe, the Demiurge, and the God of the Old Testament. Again, to the Gnostic, 'Christ Himself is either a celestial Being, an Æon, who appears in a phantasmal body among men for their redemption (Docetism), or is the earthly Jesus, with whom the higher power temporarily associates itself '.[32] Despite the dangers of Gnosticism, the controversy yielded benefit in that 'it compelled the Church to provide itself with . . . bulwarks against the inroads of unauthorized speculation, which not only served the immediate end of safety, but were of abiding value'.[33]

We may note in passing that Orr elsewhere makes out an impressive case for the view that in the relationship between Christianity and paganism, influence was exercised by *both* parties. He adduces evidence to show that Christianity embraced greater numbers, and covered a wider societal spectrum, than has sometimes been allowed; and that the penetration of paganism by Christian ideas was considerable. The very fact that apologies were needed is evidence that to some, at least, Christianity was a force to be reckoned with; Gnosticism was not uninfluenced by Christian concepts;[34] and the moral homilies of such second century writers as Epectetus, formally contemptuous of Christianity though he was, owed something to current Christian ethics. As for Neo-platonism, its founder, Ammonius Saccas, was born of Christian parents, and was for a time a Christian himself; and his precursor, Numenius, was also influenced by Jewish and Christian thought-forms. After producing his evidence, Orr expressed the hope that he had 'done something to intensify our sense of the mighty power which, as the Divine Leaven introduced into humanity, Christianity from its first entrance into the world exercized on everything it touched'.[35] This is by no means to say,

however, that Christianity simply offered to the world into which it came
more *of the same kind* than it had before:

> Christianity won the day because . . . it met the deepest necessity of
> the age into which it had come. It met the monotheistic tendency of
> the age; it met the universalistic tendency of the age; it met the deeper
> and stronger ethical tendency represented by Stoicism. Above all, it
> met the deep craving of the age for spiritual peace and rest, its need of
> certainty, its longing for redemption, and for direct communion with
> God. To these wants it brought a satisfaction which no other religion
> of the time could pretend to offer. It did not meet them by teaching
> merely—as if Christ were only a new Socrates—but it met them by the
> positive exhibition of the redeeming love of God in Christ, by the
> setting forth of the personal Jesus in His life, death and resurrection,
> by the proclamation of forgiveness of sins through Him, by the
> bestowal of the power of the Holy Spirit. It was not a doctrinal religion
> merely, but a religion of *dynamic*—of power. It did not only *tell* men
> what to do, but gave them power to do it. [36]

In a word, there is an ineradicable supernaturalism inherent in
Christianity: and it is Harnack's denial of this which, according to Orr, is
the presupposition of his emaciated Christianity, which will not allow (in
any full-blooded sense) that Christianity is a religion of redemption.
Harnack 'places the essence of Christianity in the three great ideas of the
Kingdom of God and its coming; of God the Father, and the infinite value
of the human soul; of the higher righteousness, and the commandment of
love. There is indeed more than this in Christianity—much more: the idea of
redemption in particular is conspicuously absent'. [37] Biblical criticism had
done its work; the doctrines of revelation and inspiration had been
damaged; the progress of science encouraged many to rule out any
possibility of the supernatural. As far as Orr was concerned, 'if God, in
truth, has not entered by word and deed into history, and given to man
sure and reliable knowledge regarding Himself, and His character and
purpose; if the Son has not truly come as the Saviour of the world, and the
promise of the Spirit to guide into all truth has not actually been fulfilled;
then, beyond doubt, the legitimacy, and even the possibility of dogma
. . . fall to the ground. But with this also falls the entire Christian
faith'. [38]

We shall have more to say concerning the supernatural when we come
to Orr's apologetics. Meanwhile we revert to his conviction that doctrinal
theology cannot be expunged from Christianity. The fact is that 'there is a
truth, or sum of truths, involved in the Biblical revelation, for [*sic*] which
it is the duty of the Church to bear witness; that Christianity is not

something utterly formless and vague, but has an ascertainable, statable content, which it is the business of the Church to find out, to declare, to defend, and ever more perfectly to seek to unfold in the connection of its parts, and in relation to advancing knowledge; that this content of truth is not something that can be manipulated into any shape men's fancies please, but something in regard to which we should not despair of being able to arrive at a large measure of agreement . . .'[39] When he adds the comment, 'I venture to say that what the Church suffers from to-day is not, as so many think, too much theology, but too little theology, of an earnest kind',[40] it is difficult not to apply his words directly to our own time.

Orr defines 'doctrine' as 'the direct, often naïve, expression by Christian faith of the knowledge it possesses, or the convictions it holds, regarding God and divine things'. 'Theology' is the 'reflective exercise of mind upon the doctrines of faith.' 'Dogma' stands for 'those formulations of Christian doctrine which have obtained authoritative recognition in wide sections of the Church, and are embodied in historical creeds'.[41] Although the ultimate test of dogma is Scripture, Orr would have us remember that 'We are more dependent on the past than we think even in our interpretation of Scripture . . .'[42] Other tests include the inner coherence of the dogmatic system, and its correlation with the vital experience, not of the individual, but of the Church as a whole; there is the appeal to the practical results which have followed the upholding of dogma; and—what particularly concerns Orr—there is the 'practically unerring verdict of *history* . . . the history of dogma is the judgement of dogma'.[43] There is a process of accretion and criticism; there is an organic evolution of dogma, which does not entail the jettisoning of the past, but the fulfilling of it. The law or reason underlying this development emerges when we notice the remarkable parallel between the historical course of dogma on the one hand, and the scientific order of systematic theology text books on the other. God, man, objective and subjective soteriology, eschatology— these are the successive divisions of the books, and this is the order in which, in history, the dogmas have been defined.

What shall we make of Orr's schematization? There is something to be said for it, provided that we do not press it too far. Subjectivity must, however, be guarded against. Thus, having proceeded through the centuries, allotting the several doctrines to their successive ages, Orr is left with the nineteenth century, and with eschatology. He finds that 'the modern mind has given itself with special earnestness to eschatological questions, moved thereto, perhaps, by the solemn impression that on it the ends of the world have come, and that some great crisis in the history of human affairs is approaching'.[44] We do not deny that with Brethrenism and other millenarian and dispensational movements, Orr was not altogether unjustified in his claim. But two things need to be said. First, the eschatological debate of the late nineteenth century hardly has the weight that Orr's other 'moments' have: we can perhaps see this from our vantage point more clearly than he could from his. Secondly, what has happened to that 'department' of systematic theology entitled 'Ecclesiology'? Orr has to treat of the Church and the sacraments *en passant*; the apparent logicality of his scheme seems to go awry here. If we were to try to complete Orr's picture there might be something to be said for calling *our* century, with its considerable inconclusive ecumenical concerns, the age of Ecclesiology. This would then leave the next century for Eschatology—a possibility which, from their own point of view, some of our gloomier ecologists might be inclined to endorse! The ease with which we can juggle with our themes and centuries should caution us against undue schematic arbitrariness. To this extent a criticism of Orr by A. E. Garvie is just; but when Garvie goes on to say that since 'historical conditions so fully explain why certain questions emerged for discussion at a particular time' it 'appears even a little audacious to assume a special providential guidance of the order',[45] he surely goes too far. Indeed, he is at this point an incipient deist. May we not assume that the providence of God extends over the course of dogmatic history, even if we are cautious of making too neatly thematic bundles out of that history?

We cannot here recount Orr's findings across the entire field of dogmatic history, but it will not be inappropriate if we select for consideration his treatment of Calvinism; for he has wise things to say concerning this much-maligned system and, furthermore, this is the tradition to which all eight of our divines, to a greater or lesser extent, adhered. Orr maintains that the creeds of the Reformation offer, practically for the first time, full, biblically-based statements of the great articles of Christian doctrine. Of Calvinism he writes,

> Calvin's system is the reflection of his mind—severe, grand, logical, daring in the heights to which it ascends, yet humble in its constant reversion to Scripture as its basis. Mounting to the throne of God, Calvin reads everything in the light of the eternal divine decree. Man in his state of sin has lost his spiritual freedom, and the power to do anything truly good, though Calvin freely admits the existence of natural virtue, and attributes it to a working of divine grace even in the unregenerate. God's providence is all-governing . . . Whoever is brought into the kingdom of God is brought there by a free act of grace, and even the passing by of the unsaved, however mysterious,

must be traced to an origin in the eternal divine will . . . It is not an arbitrary, but a holy and good will, though the reasons for what actually takes place in the government of the world are to us inscrutable . . .[46]

Orr goes on to speak of the ecclesiology and of the spread of Calvinism; but in the sentences just quoted we have the seeds of the battles which were to rage around Calvin's head. Orr recognizes that the rock offence in Calvin's system is his doctrine of predestination. He points out that Calvin's supreme concern is to exalt God's sovereignty; all things, in nature and grace, depend upon God. He is the sovereign Lord. Orr further reminds us that the doctrine of the divine decrees, far from standing at the head of Calvin's system, is not introduced until the work of the Holy Spirit in regeneration and sanctification is under consideration. Even so, he grants that there is an aspect of Calvin's doctrine which prompts disquiet. Calvin is right to exalt the sovereignty of God, but 'he errs in placing his root-idea of God in sovereign will rather than in love . . . God's will, certainly, is not with Calvin an arbitrary will . . . It is a holy, wise, and good will . . . even a loving will [cf. *Institutes* I,v]; but love, in this more special sense, takes the direction which sovereignty gives it—it does not regulate the sovereignty'.[47] Thus, God decrees to save some, and to pass others by—'Now this, I think I may safely say, is not a conception in which the Christian mind can permanently rest . . . I do not . . . abate one whit from the sovereignty of God in the election, calling, and salvation of such as are saved; but I do feel strongly that this election of God must not be disjoined from the context in which it is set in God's historical purpose, which, grounded in His love, embraces the widest possible ultimate blessing for the whole world.'[48] No doubt Kennedy of Dingwall would have detected incipient universalism here, and would have retorted that since all men are sinners, the wonder is not that some are passed by, but that any are saved.

In further elucidation of his point[49] Orr makes plain the distinction between Calvin's view of predestination and Augustine's. For Calvin, regeneration is effected via God's word and Spirit; for Augustine it is effected via baptism—hence the inconsistency between the ecclesiastical and the evangelical aspects of Augustine's thought. Calvin purged sacramentarianism from his doctrine of predestination. On the other hand, Augustine rightly speaks only of predestination *to life*. Calvin speaks, albeit cautiously, of a predestination to salvation and a predestination to destruction [*Institutes* III,xxi,5, etc.] There is, however, this difference between the two varieties of predestination: whereas men are saved by the sheer, unmerited grace of God, no man is damned except on the ground of his own sin. In his discussion of Augustine's thought, Orr helpfully underlines the *religious* interest which is conserved by the doctrine of predestination to life:

> it is simply the expression of an experience which lies at the root of all genuine Christian consciousness, viz., that in this matter of personal salvation, the last word is always grace, not nature; that it is not *our* willing and running which has brought us into the kingdom of God, but *His* mercy . . . and that all this was no *afterthought* of God, but an eternal counsel of His love which has now effectuated itself in our salvation. This is the *religious* interest in the doctrine of predestination which gives it its abiding value.[50]

Dr. Kennedy would have demanded more; but that he would have agreed so far is clear from his sermon on 'The Father's Drawing'.

Orr offers help in the understanding of Calvinism at a number of other points. Thus, he makes plain Calvin's assertion of free will. Man is responsible for his voluntary actions and, as the Westminster Confession declares, far from being denied, the liberty of second causes is established by the doctrine of God's sovereignty. How can this be? Orr explains that man's freedom is one factor only in life. There are factors which are given in any situation, over which man has no control. Secondly, apart from the divine sovereignty, human volitions are only, to the divine prescience, possibilities. Such possibilities are infinite, and God alone can determine which shall be actualized. Apart from God's sovereignty man could not freely do what he actually does at all. Again, Orr shows how the doctrine of regeneration is the correlate or predestination to life; for if man is wholly disabled by sin so that he can will no spiritual good, only regenerating grace can rescue him. Orr is anxious that this grace, sometimes called irresistible, shall not be misunderstood: 'Grace is certainly not "irresistible" in the sense that the natural will cannot resist grace; for that is what, in the Calvinistic view, it is constantly doing . . . When Calvin, with Augustine, speaks of efficacious grace, what he has in view is not a grace which overpowers the will, or puts any foreign force or pressure upon it, but a grace which *renews* the will, and restores it to its true freedom—which so acts upon it that it *freely* chooses the good . . . As little does "efficacious grace" mean that God can or does override the laws of human nature which He has Himself ordained . . . What is meant is that God can use *such* means, can *so* deal with the individual in Providence and grace, can bring him under *such* outer and inner discipline, as, in harmony with, nay, through the laws of human freedom, to overcome his resistance. If it be asserted that, even when grace has done its utmost for the soul, there is still a possibility of resisting it, Calvin, with Augustine, would reply that there is a higher freedom still—that in which even the desire to resist the good is overcome, and which therefore *certainly*, but none the less freely, chooses God'.[51]

Finally, and with reference to our earlier discussion of the free offer of the gospel,[52] Orr shows that with slight exceptions (e.g. in his Commentary on John 3:16) Calvin did not subscribe to the view that Christ died for the elect alone. Dr. Cunningham agrees, while pointing out that the issue was not a live one in Calvin's day.[53] Orr's own view is that the discussion has passed into a phase in which there is little disposition 'shown on any side to deny the love of God to the whole world in the gift of His Son for its salvation'[54]—and he cites recent Declaratory Acts in evidence. Here, once more, Dr. Kennedy would out-conservative the conservative Orr. Orr was glad that the 'offensive harshness' of Calvinism was being modified, but he concluded that 'The perennial elements of truth in Calvinism will no doubt survive'.[55]

Towards the end of his account of the progress of dogma, Orr said that 'the outlook in theology, if not all bright, is assuredly not all dark'.[56] He does not manifest that wistful yearning for the old paths which was so prominent a feature of Kennedy's writings. He looked to the future, he drew upon the past. He opined that the forthcoming battle would be round 'the fortress of the worth and authority of Holy Scripture.'[57] As we look back we can see that there have been skirmishes over this issue from time to time. But there is no real consensus, and the liveliest current debate seems to be that *between* conservatives over the necessity or otherwise of maintaining belief in the inerrancy of the original biblical autographs.[58] For the rest, there is a polarization of attitudes, and little cross-frontier debate. Again, as Orr peered into the future he expected the twentieth century 'to be an era of Christian Ethic even more than of Christian Theology'.[59] There has undoubtedly been much work in the former field, and both individuals and such corporate bodies as Councils of Churches have shared in it. But what is noticeable is that those who have been most conservatively sure of the authority of the Bible have—at least until fairly recently—done least in this field.[60]

Orr made a further prediction, which leads us directly into our next section: 'A constructive period may confidently be expected to follow the present season of criticism and testing of foundations, and then will be witnessed the rearing of a grander and stronger edifice of theology than the ages have yet seen'.[61] As events have turned out, the situation has been mixed, and we can only speculate upon what Orr's reactions might be were he alive today. We cannot imagine that he would altogether have approved of some of the systems we have been offered, such as Barth's,

which threatens to imprison Christian thinking within the circle of
revelation, or Tillich's, which would doubtless seem to Orr to be doing
less-than-healthy commerce with the idealism of Orr's own day. As for
those who, under the impact of linguistic analysis, have declared that the
time is not ripe for system-building, and that all we may properly
undertake is preliminary ground-clearing, Orr would probably interpret
this as failure of nerve. Although, as he showed, there has been a
development of dogma, he was as acutely aware that old heresies
continually reappear: that there was more than a little of Celsus in the
Deists, Voltaire and Strauss;[62] that Basilides was the Hegel, Valentinus
the Schelling, and Marcion the Ritschl of Gnosticism;[63] and that in
christology there is a line from Paul of Samosata to the modern
Unitarians.[64] We may well suspect, therefore, that Orr redivivus would
find, thinly disguised, any number of heresies which he thought he had
vanquished long ago.

II

One of Orr's more popular apologetic works—indeed, he describes it as
his personal testimony—is entitled, *The Faith of a Modern Christian*. In the
preface he explains that the writer is modern 'in the sense only that he
lives in a modern time, and can claim a fairly adequate acquaintance with
modern ideas. He is not "modern" in the sense of the "modernists", who
grant no place for the supernatural interposition of God for man's
redemption in human history'.[65] In another preface he writes, 'in a multitude of respects, the Christian view of the world is *not* the so-called modern
view; in principle, in fact, is irreconcilable with it; and we ought to have
the courage to avow this, and take the consequences'.[66] Here we have the
clue to Orr's apologetic intentions. He wishes to defend the faith against
attack, and to him in his day this means the reasoned assertion of supernaturalism and the vanquishing of naturalism. The anti-supernaturalistic
attack was being launched against all the crucial facts of the faith, from
the Virgin Birth to the Resurrection, and as he voices his protest Orr's
fundamental presupposition comes into view, namely 'that Christian
truth forms an *organism*—has a unity and coherence which cannot be
arbitrarily disturbed in any of its parts without the whole undergoing
injury. Conversely, the proof that any doctrine fits in essentially to that
organism—is an integral part of it—is one of the strongest evidences we
can have of its correctness'.[67] While every part of the organism is sensitive

to change in any other, the pivotal truth is that concerning God: 'As a man thinks God to be, so will his theology be'.[68]

We would next draw attention to the word 'thinks' in the quotation just given. Orr was utterly convinced of the need to hold reason and faith together: 'Reason and faith are two sides of our nature, which only the unwise will seek to separate from one another'.[69] While welcoming Kant's emphasis upon a moral teleology, and upon the practical reason, Orr regretted the theoretical agnosticism which accompanied it. Hegel rightly saw that it is only as a thinking spirit that man has the capacity for religion. Accordingly, the apologist who would refute materialistic, pantheistic and monistic theories must meet them on their own ground, and show that 'the Christian theistic view is that most in harmony with right reason, as well as best established by the facts of religion'.[70]

Four very important matters arise from the preceding paragraph, and we must draw out each in turn. The first is Orr's claim that there *is* a Christian view of the world, and his associated claim that it differs from all others:

> He who with his whole heart believes in Jesus as the Son of God is thereby committed to much else besides. He is committed to a view of God, to a view of man, to a view of sin, to a view of Redemption, to a view of the purpose of God in creation and history, to a view of human destiny, found only in Christianity. This forms a 'Weltanschauung', or 'Christian view of the world' which stands in marked contrast with theories wrought out from a purely philosophical or scientific standpoint.[71]

Although Christianity is not in competition with science, its results must be reconcilable with the established findings of science, and must harmonize with 'the conclusions at which sound reason, attacking its own problems, independently arrives'.[72]

Secondly, what of reason's activities in the realm of natural theology? How does Orr stand in relation to the older theism? He stands broadly in the tradition of Flint (who, incidentally, thought highly of *The Christian View of God and the World*), though he makes stronger statements of the distinctive Christian starting-point than Flint, and pays less overt attention to Butler. Thus, he can say that 'Christian apologetic can never be satisfactorily separated from the positive exhibition of the Christian system . . . Christianity in short, is its own best apology'.[73] That he was well aware of the limits of natural theology is clear from the following passage:

> The time is past when men's minds were captivated by the idea of a

'Natural Religion' consisting of a few simple articles drawn from, and
capable of proof by, reason apart from supernatural revelation—that
favourite dream of the Deists and eighteenth-century illuminists; and
while the 'speculative' theory which would render theology independent of history by resolving its essential doctrines into metaphysical
ideas has still its advocates, its sceptre is long broken in the domain of
really serious theology. There remains as a source of theological
knowledge the positive revealing and redeeming acts and words of God
which constitute the subject-matter of historical revelation, though it
may be contended that these stand in no antagonism to the conclusions
of sound reason reflecting on the structure of the universe, or pondering
the deeper questions of origin and destiny, but rather are in truest
consonance with the latter, and furnish reason with a light to help it on
its way.[74]

What, then, of the possibility or otherwise of 'proving' God's existence?
Orr pointedly recalls Jacobi's saying that a God capable of proof would be
no God at all,[75] since a God so 'proved' would have had his existence
deduced from something higher; he avers that this restriction applied only
to 'the ordinary reasoning of deductive logic' and not to the 'higher kind
of proof which may be said to consist in the mind being guided back to
the clear recognition of its own pre-suppositions'; and he declares that
'Proof in Theism certainly does not consist in deducing God's existence as
a lower from a higher; but rather in showing that God's existence is itself
the last postulate of reason—the ultimate basis on which all other
knowledge, all other belief rests'.[76] Consistently with this he welcomes
T. H. Green's rational realism for its assertion that thought is necessary
prior to all else that is, and he does not find this position open to the
objection brought against the ontological argument in the form in which
Anselm put it—namely, that it involves an illicit inference from mere
idea to existence. Green's view has this in common with Anselm's,
however, 'that the existence of an Eternal Reason is shown to be involved
in the very thinking of this, or indeed of any thought . . . I cannot but
maintain, therefore, that the ontological argument, in the kernel and
essence of it, is a sound one, and that in it the existence of God is really
seen to be the first, the most certain, and the most indisputable of all
truths'.[77] Here we have it clearly laid down that God is the postulate of all
other knowledge and belief. But then, almost in the same breath, Orr can
say 'What we mean by proof of God's existence is simply that there are
necessary acts of thought by which we rise from the finite to the infinite,
from the caused to the uncaused, from the contingent to the necessary,
from the reason involved in the structure of the universe to a universal and

eternal Reason, which is the ground of all, from morality in conscience to a moral Lawgiver and Judge'.[78]

The term 'proof' is notoriously ambiguous—mathematical 'proof', scientific 'proof' and legal 'proof' are all different from each other in important ways. It seems that what Orr calls 'proof' in the sentence just quoted is really 'orderly testimony'. He well knows that 'To say that faith has reasonable grounds, or is rationally justified, is very different from saying that in every case it rests on *reasoned* grounds'.[79] The situation therefore seems to be that Orr sets out to uphold the God-postulate on the one hand, but that he also hankers after the older natural theology on the other. He grants that there can be no logically coercive demonstration of the existence of God; that God's existence must be *the* postulate of thought, and that all other knowledge and belief rest upon it; that the Christian world view is distinct from all others, and that it is not irrational. He declares, 'If I undertake to defend Theism, it is not Theism in dissociation from Revelation, but Theism as completed in the entire Christian view'.[80] At the same time, in a number of places he speaks as if there is common ground between believing and unbelieving rational beings, such that the commendation of the faith can proceed on *mutually shared* presuppositions. Thus he can say that no theory which has found wide acceptance is ever wholly false, and that the apologist's task is that of showing Christianity to be that synthesis within which the aspects of truth which are yielded by other systems find their rightful home.[81] Now we are not deists, and we do not wish to exclude the omnipresent God from any part of his universe! There *are*, precisely because of God's sovereignty, glimpses of truth and worthy moral actions in areas where he is not acknowledged. But if God is not a system's postulate, can that system be other than fundamentally faulty—given that God is who Christians say he is? And if that is so, is it not better to attack the unbeliever's presuppositions rather than to agree with him that he has x, y and z truths which need Christianity for their completion? Ought not the apologist to consider whether or not it is his duty to show the unbeliever that he cannot consistently maintain his truths apart from the postulation of him who is the truth? On Orr's own principles we might have expected some such procedure, but in practice he is content with the less radical synthesizing position.[82] It is, moreover, a position which does not take account of the noetic effects of sin—yet in connection with those who stand by the sufficiency of natural revelation he says, 'The pure mind which the hypothesis postulates is not there'.[83] This insight does not seem to be carried forward with sufficient determination into his apologetic methodology.

Why should this be? The only conclusion seems to be that when Orr (and Flint) wrote, it was much more possible than it is now to take theism, the God postulate, for granted, and to move on from there. Thus Orr can say, 'Atheism—blank atheism—is a very uncommon frame of mind at any time'; and he can assume that most unbelievers will acknowledge a Supreme Power.[84] But the real question, of course, is not how many or how few are either atheists or believers in a (non-Christian) Supreme Power. The question is one of apologetic method. If we nowadays find it necessary to advocate a more radical approach in apologetic *practice*—though one in accord with Orr's *principle*—it is because we live in the aftermath of logical positivism; it is because we are confronted by an unbelieving, articulate humanism; it is, in short, because we have had borne in upon us the need to take the most serious account of the presuppositional *disharmonies* which separate system from system. Orr knew as well as any that we know God because he graciously makes himself known, and that supremely in Christ. He knew that Christian apologists cannot satisfactorily proceed as if that were not the case. Perhaps we have needed militant atheism to prompt us once and for all to complete the Reformation on its philosophical side by dispensing with scholasticism in both theory and practice. To repeat, we are not deists; we do not say that there is no knowledge of God apart from his revelation in Christ; the firmament *does* show his handiwork. But we cannot argue thence to God, and there are both logical and moral reasons why that is so. Hence the practical question is not 'Is God to be seen in the things he has made?' but rather 'How are we to approach those who do not, and will not, see him anywhere?' What is required is testimony (not more evidence) on the one hand, and the renewing of the mind on the other. Homiletics is much closer to the philosophy of religion than some preachers would believe, or than some philosophers would think decent! As Orr himself realized (and few did so more clearly), 'There is only one way of bridging that gulf between God and man; and that is that God Himself should speak . . . Whoever has been satisfied with what we sometimes call natural revelation, it has not been those who have been left to it'.[85]

Thirdly, if right reason harmonizes with faith, as Orr maintains, there can be no necessary conflict between science and religion. On this point Orr is very much in accord with Iverach. He is in no way nonplussed by evolutionary theory. He tackles it in both its Darwinian-naturalistic form, and in its Hegelian-immanentist variety. As to the former, he notes the many modifications of Darwin's theory which have been offered since the theory was first propounded. This suggests to him that all is not settled—

that we have an hypothesis only, and not a copper-bottomed fact. He more than once reiterates the point that Darwinism cannot explain origins,[86]and his supreme objection to it is that 'it asks from unintelligent, unguided, forces work that can only be accomplished by mind.'[87] Orr was quite happy to regard evolution as the method of God's working in nature,[88] though he viewed the immanentist-evolutionary philosophy of Hegel and his successors with disfavour. The idea of immanent spirit could, he was sure, lead to wholly unacceptable attenuations of the faith (as was the case with Strauss). Again, in the hands of Bousset, the evolutionary-immanentist theory did not so much universalize revelation as exclude it, because Bousset sought to make good the case—strictly impossible of proof—that the higher religions were evolved out of the lower.[89] Moreover, the evolutionary-immanentist theory threatens the Christian doctrine of sin by making sin a necessity of man's life, even a necessary stage, on the way to good.[90] Finally, it threatens the doctrine of the Incarnation by facilitating a degree-christology: 'The real incarnation', according to this view, 'is, first, in the universe, then in humanity. Christ is but the topmost twig of the tree'.[91]

Fourthly, Orr must challenge those whose scepticism causes them to devalue reason, and those whose theological presuppositions prompt them to advocate the divorce of reason from faith. Here Orr's major campaigns are against Hume and Ritschl respectively. Hume sought to explain the origin of human knowledge, and he is represented as using a singularly blunt instrument. Orr quotes his own words thus: 'If we take in our hand any volume, of school divinity, or metaphysics, for instance; let us ask, *Does it contain any abstract reasoning concerning quantity or number?* No. *Does it contain any experimental reasoning concerning matter of fact and existence?* No. Commit it then to the flames; for it can contain nothing but sophistry and illusion'.[92] In the light of this policy, Hume endeavours to show that whereas we may in practice believe in the external world, in the soul, or in necessary cause-effect connections, we can have no theoretical or rational ground for so doing. Thus reason and ordinary belief are left by Hume in irreconcilable opposition.[93] Orr will not allow Hume to rest his case. He shows that Hume has to presuppose the very reason for which his system has no room: 'Affecting to ignore the rational nature of man, and seeking to get along without it, he yet is compelled continually to presuppose its existence, and avail himself of its help, in his reasonings and language'.[94] In his theory Hume overlooks the fact that 'the mind that can deny rationality in the universe, in the very act of its doing so proclaims itself rational, and the universe as well'.[95] But in his practice Hume constantly assumes 'mind' or 'soul' as the seat of (though not the origin of) impressions. He cannot, in short, manage without the terminology of personal consciousness. What is it that holds together Hume's 'train of impressions and ideas', or *knows* it as a train? Orr, indebted to Kant at this point, denies the possibility of knowledge unless we may posit a unifying conscious thinking principle. Kant, however, did not go far enough. He did not regard the principles of knowledge as constitutive of the world, but only of thought. Orr favours no such limitation. Again, Hume inconsistently introduces seven varieties of relations—resemblance, identity, space-time, quantity and number, degree, contrareity, cause and effect—from which his undue subjectivism, the function of his view that the object is a mere datum of sense, ought to have precluded him. As far as Orr can see, Hume's dilemma is twofold: '(1) Either the object is something truly external to the mind, in which case the mind cannot know it, or even obtain a clue to the fact of its existence, since mind cannot in the nature of things overleap its own consciousness—get outside its own ideas; or (2) the object is an idea of the mind— or "bundle of perceptions" (which is his own hypothesis)—in which case there is no external world to know, and our knowledge of it is illusion'.[96] All of which leads Orr to his conclusion that the following three propositions can never finally be extruded from philosophy: that the universe is an intelligible system (the truth of idealism); that the universe is actual, and independent of man's individual consciousness (the truth of realism); and that the universe is known to us under the conditions and limitations attaching to human consciousness (the truth of relativity).[97] So much for Orr's defence of rationality against Humean scepticism.

Orr did more than most to introduce Ritschl (1822–1889) to English readers, and though he was as concerned to warn as to expound, he was characteristically quick not only to indicate the deficiencies, but also to measure the strengths of Ritschlianism. The following is his most concise statement on the matter:

> I do not think that as a system [Ritschlianism] will admit to be brought to the test of Scripture . . . I cannot accept its non-mystical view of religion; I cannot accept its divorce of faith and reason; I cannot accept its restriction of religious truths to value-judgements; I cannot accept its agnostic denial of the right of natural theology; I cannot accept Ritschl's practically humanitarian Christology; I cannot accept its denial of hereditary or original sin—for this this is another tenet of the Ritschlian faith; I cannot accept its view of the divine righteousness, which with Ritschl is only another name for God's consistency in carrying out His ends, and does not denote anything judicial; I cannot accept as adequate its doctrine of reconciliation; I cannot accept its

ignoring of Christ's heavenly reign, and living action by His Spirit in the souls of men. The elements of value which I recognize in it are its fresh, full insistence on the self-evidencing nature and exhaustless spiritual potency of the revelation of God in Christ; its recognition of the uniqueness of Christ as the One in whose Person and work God's purpose has come fully to light, and through whom it has obtained historical realization; the prominence it gives to the great Gospel idea of the kingdom of God; and, together with these merits, the protest it maintains against a one-sided intellectualism, and its constant reversion to the fact of a positive revelation.[98]

We shall note some of the doctrinal attenuations of Ritschlianism in our final section; for the moment we fasten upon the faith-reason dichotomy advocated by Ritschl and his successors. In Orr's opinion, 'The highest principle of the Ritschlian theology . . . is . . . the sole Revelation-value of Christ, in contrast with all commingling of Christian faith with philosophy or nature-knowledge, and under the condition that the theologian has his standing within the Christian community as one who shares its faith and experience'.[99] Orr is convinced that the contrast here posited cannot but land Ritschl in subjectivism. It is not the Person of the Redeemer who is the objective source of theology; rather the source is held to be the subjective apprehension-in-faith of the church. Further, the attempt to drive a wedge between faith and metaphysics does not succeed. Ritschl himself vacillates in practice, and says, 'It is an unthinking and incredible contention that I exclude all metaphysics from theology'.[100] Nevertheless, the metaphysic he seeks is one which would exclude metaphysics from theology. Having followed Kant in affirming that human knowledge is of phenomena only, he thinks the way is clear for the rejection of all 'mysticism' in religion. Orr complains that this goes counter to a fundamental and proper part of the Christian's claim—that of having an immediate and essential conscious relation with God. For Ritschl, however, 'Religious knowledge moves in the sphere of independent judgements of value'.[101] He does not deny the reality to the mind of the objects it entertains, but holds that the conviction of their reality is not reached theoretically, but evaluatively. Orr is happy to agree that value-judging is an inescapable element in religion; but he protests against Ritschl's Kantian-based idea that religious knowledge consists only in judgements of value, and that religious truths form an entirely separate class from all other truths. He views with dismay the re-emergence of the hoary distinction between 'truths of faith' and 'truths of reason'. And he cannot conceive of a value judgement which does not have either tacit or explicit reference to an actual object. Far from there being any opposition between judgements of value and judgements of existence, the former depend upon the latter. Hence, in relation to Christian faith, 'Before we can state anything in terms of religious value about God, we must have some means of assuring ourselves that God *is* . . . If we *know* this, then our statements have an objective as well as a subjective validity—they represent reality, and are not "judgements of value" only'.[102]

Ritschlianism errs in beginning from man's need to relate himself to the world, and in denying the original, immediate bond between God and the soul. 'This is fatally to invert the true idea',[103] and it is compatible with Ritschl's rejection, under the inspiration of Kantian phenomenalism, of any natural revelation. Orr holds that 'Faith in Christ . . . has its grounds in the immediate appeal which the objective revelation in Christ and His Gospel make to the soul—it has its central point in the self-certitude of the consciousness of reconciliation with God through Jesus Christ, and of the new life which springs from this . . .'[104] But here we are in the realm of the supernatural—and Orr, for one, would not dream of denying it. Indeed, such are the attenuations of Ritschlianism that he suggests that 'It would not be an unfair description of the Ritschlian theology to say that it is an attempt to show how much of positive Christianity can be retained, compatibly with the acceptance of the modern non-miraculous theory of the world. This is not to keep Christianity separate from modern thought, but to make a surrender to it'.[105] We shall now see how Orr makes good this contention in a wider context, following his conviction that 'to tear asunder faith and reason is to render no service to religion, but is to pave the way for theoretical scepticism'.[106]

III

We have already seen something of Orr's overriding concern to combat all who sought to eradicate the supernatural from Christianity. This concern governs his attitude towards biblical criticism, his view of miracle, and his treatment of the central doctrines of the Christian faith. It is a concern to which we consider the theology of the last quarter of the twentieth century, with its radical immanentism, its covert naturalism, and its transcendence from below, would do well to pay heed.[107]

Orr is quick to realize that the situation which confronts him is more complicated than the naturalistic-supernaturalistic distinction might at first suggest. For characteristic of many 'moderns' is their claim that far from denying the supernatural, they affirm it—but 'it is a supernatural which is not distinct from nature, but which expresses itself *in* nature's own forces and laws, and in the orderly course of nature's events'.[108] Orr's response to this is to ask whether immanence is *all*; and his answer is that to the 'moderns' it is, whereas to orthodox Christianity it is not. What he finds particularly incongruous is the position of those critics whose approach to the Bible owes everything to naturalism, while they claim to be upholding traditional Christian supernaturalism. Thus, for example, in an article review of W. E. Addis's *Hebrew Religion to the Establishment of Judaism under Ezra* (1906) he expresses surprise that the author can profess his unswerving belief in the Incarnation of Christ, and in the supernatural revelation to be witnessed in Israel's history, while taking a naturalistic stance *vis-à-vis* the origins and early stages of Israel's religion.[109]

Orr was under no illusions concerning the logical outcome of naturalism, and he quoted Bavinck's view of the Dutch situation as a warning:

It is a slow process of dissolution that meets our view. It began with setting aside the Confession. Scripture alone was to be heard. Next, Scripture also is dismissed, and the Person of Christ is fallen back on. Of this Person, however, first His Divinity, next His pre-existence, finally His sinlessness, are surrendered, and nothing remains but a pious man, a religious genius, revealing to us the love of God. But even the existence and love of God are not able to withstand criticism. Thus the moral element in man becomes the last basis from which the battle against Materialism is conducted. But this basis will appear to be as unstable and unreliable as the others.[110]

Orr's standing objection to naturalism is that it does not fit the facts. In particular, its picture of an obedient martyr-Jesus fails lamentably. The naturalist's presuppositions alone enable him to overlook the self-consciousness of Jesus as the Son of God, his sinlessness, his unique relation to the Father, his supernatural power, and his claims.[111] Again we underline Orr's perplexity that some, having wielded so many of naturalism's weapons, should still wish to declare for Christian supernaturalism.

Among the most glaring examples of this was the German liberal theologian Otto Pfleiderer (1839–1908). Like Addis, Pfleiderer maintains the supernatural, but it is a supernatural which can express itself only in the natural. Miracles in the strict sense cannot occur. Orr can readily understand the position of the supernaturalist and the position of the agnostic, but is puzzled by the combination of these normally opposed views. On the one hand, Pfleiderer's God is said to be a God of love who is not to be identified with the natural order; on the other hand, the possibility of miracle is denied on metaphysical grounds. This, thinks Orr, is 'plainly incompetent. Not less illegitimate is the assertion of the *a priori* scientific impossibility of miracle'.[112] Again, Pfleiderer wishes to affirm the actuality of the communion between divine and human spirits, whilst at the same time endorsing a naturalistic-immanentist metaphysic which would not consistently permit the transcendence of the natural: 'Once grant, what lies in Professor Pfleiderer's own philosophy, that spirit is higher than nature, consciousness than unconsciousness, personality than impersonality, and that the goal of all God's workings and leadings alike in nature and history is the realization in humanity of a kingdom of love . . . and some direct, immediate, articulate word of God to man is the most natural and probable thing imaginable'.[113] Further, if (as Pfleiderer contends) the goal is the kingdom of God realized in nature and history, we need, for the attainment of that goal, a better knowledge of God than is open to us on the hypothesis of immanent development. Orr observes that absolutist philosophers tend to shy away from personality and, more importantly, he shows that Pfleiderer's metaphysical presuppositions cause him to impose restrictions upon our understanding of the development of God-consciousness. Pfleiderer explains this development in terms of the evolution of man's innate religious endowment; Orr explains it by reference to the response of men to God's supernatural revelation. Israel did not derive its idea of God either from nature or from history.

A number of doctrinal attenuations flow from Pfleiderer's position. Sin becomes part of man's original constitution, and a necessary stage in his development; Jesus is our motive, but the true Saviour is the ideal man within ourselves. Indeed, Jesus is 'so far as historical reality is concerned, little else than a figure to hang [Pfleiderer's] idealizations upon'.[114] Pfleiderer's Jesus was not sinless, and if there are no miracles, *a fortiori* there was no Resurrection—the apostles had visions. Pfleiderer is happy to retain the 'picture language' of the church, and he criticizes the Ritschlians for their violations of it. Orr was never more ironical: 'Let all be carefully preserved. Let the Church be maintained, with its institutions, its sacraments, its festivals . . . let the old prayers be recited, the old hymns be sung, the old Scripture lessons be read, the old service be gone through. The philosopher knows its meaning, and it edifies the people'.[115] The trouble is that the sceptic knows its meaning too, and he is not satisfied. Orr's investigation of the evidence leads him to say,

I read these Gospels, and find in them the most wonderful impress of historical reality. But if the Christ of these Gospels was an historical Person, He made claims, He did works, He spoke from a consciousness of unity with God, He asserted an authority, He wielded prerogatives, which you cannot fit into a merely human—least of all naturalistic— frame. To the life and death of such a One as Jesus Himself claimed to be, the Resurrection was a natural sequel . . . And it is faith in such a Divine Christ . . . which is the victory that overcomes the world.[116]

We should seriously mistake Orr's position if we were hastily to assume that, as a conservative supernaturalist, he was opposed in principle to biblical criticism. On the contrary, he did not shirk his duty of writing in *The Fundamentals* (even!), 'By all means, let criticism have its rights. Let purely literary questions about the Bible receive full and fair discussion. Let the structure of books be impartially examined . . . No fright . . . need be taken at the mere word, "Criticism".'[117] While not overawed by rash claims made on the basis of the 'settled results' of criticism,[118] Orr argued in many writings for a responsible criticism which would read narrative as narrative, poetry as poetry—he was no literalist. He is quite ready to deny that the Christian doctrine of redemption turns upon Genesis 3: 'It would be truer to say that I believe in the third chapter of Genesis, or in the essential truth which it contains, because I believe in sin and Redemption, than to say that I believe in sin and Redemption because of the story of the Fall'.[119] But what he does most strongly object to is the application to the Bible of a priori naturalistic principles, notably that which denies 'that God ever has entered into human history, in word and deed, in any supernatural way'.[120] He declares that 'The one thing criticism can never expunge from this book, the Bible, is what we speak of as the *Gospel*—its continuous, coherent, self-attesting discovery to man of the mind of God regarding man himself, his sin, the guilt and ruin into which sin has plunged him, and over against that the method of a divine salvation, the outcome of a purpose of eternal love, wrought out in ages of progressive revelation, and culminating in the mission, life, death, atoning work, and resurrection of His Son Jesus Christ, and in the gift of His Spirit to the Church and believers'.[121] Orr advocated a more positive view of the structure of the Bible than many held, the acknowledgement of a supernatural revelation of God, and the recognition of 'a true supernatural inspiration in the record of that revelation'.[122] This last point merits further examination.

Our way in to Orr's understanding of inspiration must be via his view of revelation. Revelation is distinctively historical— indeed, it is one of the gains of modern scholarship, he thinks, to have made this plain. God acts in history; but there is always an interpretative word, apart from which the meaning of the revelation would not be intelligible. Again, an internal element is always connected with the external, objective element,[123] for 'No revelation from without, however strongly attested, could produce faith of a vital kind, unless at the same time there were this inward susceptibility to appeal to: it is the meeting of the outward and the inward which engenders faith'.[124] Given the fact of revelation, 'it is reasonable to expect that provision will be made for *the preservation* of the knowledge of the revelation *in some permanent and authoritative form*'.[125] The Bible suffices as such a record in that 'beyond it we do not need to travel to find *God's whole will* for our salvation'.[126] Certainly Scripture is 'God-inspired', but Orr points out that the inspiration refers primarily to the individual writer, and only to the book as the product of the inspired person. Moreover, due account must be taken of the limitations of inspiration, occasioned by the progressiveness of the revelation itself. As for the preservation through the ages of the materials of the record, this is a matter not of inspiration, but of the general workings of providence. Hence, 'Where sources of information fail, or where . . . there are *lacunae* . . . or errors of transcription . . . it is not to be supposed that supernatural information is granted to supply the lack. Where this is frankly acknowledged, inspiration is cleared from a great many of the difficulties which misapprehension has attached to it'.[127] Nevertheless, and notwithstanding the fact that 'No claim to inspiration made in the Bible . . . can be regarded as covering the whole of Scripture as we have it', he insists that 'the inspired record must be, and is, sufficient to convey to us, in purity and faithfulness, the whole will of God for our salvation and guidance'.[128]

Orr is by no means an upholder of mechanical, 'dictation' views of inspiration. For him, 'inspiration does not annul any power or faculty of the human soul, but raises all powers to their highest activity, and stimulates them to their freest exercize'.[129] He does not find the term 'verbal inspiration' altogether helpful. It has its use as a testimony against the notion that revelation is 'all in the mind', whereas the language in which it is conveyed is entirely in the hands of the penman; but it is apt to suggest the dictation theory of inspiration, and to imply 'a *literality* in narratives, quotations, or reports of discourses, which the facts, as we know them, do not warrant'.[130] As for the doctrine of inerrancy, Orr thinks that the attempt to demonstrate the reliability of biblical minutiae is, on the face of it, 'a most suicidal position for any defender of revelation to take up'.[131] At the same time, Orr finds himself 'in substantial harmony with the defenders of this view in affirming that *the sweeping assertions* of error and discrepancy in the Bible often made cannot be substantiated'.[132]

Although revelation precedes inspiration, they are 'closely and inseparably united', since inspiration is a condition of the apprehension by the individual of the revelation. This leads to the doctrine, beloved of the Reformers, of the *testimonium Spiritus Sancti*. But though valuable, this principle can be pressed too far, as when unwarrantable interpretations are 'justified', or when unappealing portions of Scripture are discarded. The truth is that 'Many evidences converge to sustain inspiration—internal witness, testimony of the books, use by other Scriptures, witness of Christ and His apostles, effects and fruits in experience and history—and all are to be welcomed'.[133] Orr's conclusion is that 'the proof of the inspiration of the Bible—not, indeed, in every particular, but in its essential message—is to be found in the life-giving effects which that message has produced, wherever its word of truth has gone'.[134]

Now to revert to Orr's supernaturalistic campaign: from the 'essential message' of the Bible, the miraculous cannot be extruded. We have seen how he countered the naturalistic Pfleiderer, and we shall not be surprised to learn that on the question of miracle Hume and Ritschl pleased him no better. To Hume, 'A miracle is a violation of the laws of nature, and as a firm and unalterable experience has established these laws, the proof against a miracle, from the nature of the fact, is as entire as any argument from experience can possibly be imagined'.[135] Orr cannot see, in the first place, how a belief in the uniformity of nature, which on Hume's own principles is simply a product of custom—of the subjective association of our ideas—can be invoked to preclude the miraculous. He would need to show that such 'violations' are not believable by us; but this would conflict with his admission that 'accounts of miracles and prodigies' are found in all history. Further, in declaring that a firm and unalterable experience has established these laws, Hume begs the question, 'For such a universal induction is, in strictness, impossible.'[136] Hume really rests his case upon the conviction that it is more probable that deviations from the known course of nature do not occur, than that fallible human testimony to the contrary is credible. As Orr bluntly puts it: 'Hume *assumes* in his general proposition that no one has ever had experience of a miracle, then adduces this as *proof* that miracles have never happened!'[137] If, however, we have a presumption in the nature of the case *for* miracle rather than *against* it, and if we have the testimony of reliable and competent witnesses, the evidence for miracle may be very strong. This does not mean that miracle will have any evidential value to a sceptic, but rather that there are no rational grounds for the absolute exclusion of miracle. Those who *do* exclude miracle are working with faulty presuppositions, which will not permit them to take adequate account of all the facts in the case.

This is supremely true of the Ritschlians, to whom miracle is a 'religious', not a 'scientific' notion. This accords with their theoretic-religious dichotomy, to which we referred earlier. It makes the pronouncement of miracle a matter of value-judgement, without entailing supernatural intervention. Thus for example Harnack will not allow any place to real (as distinct from seeming) miracles.[138] Against this, Orr protests that 'The gulf cannot be concealed between the Christian view of the world, and a view which refuses to accept the presence and working in history of a supernatural Power';[139] and he avers that 'the one thing that may be held certain *a priori* of the Almighty Author of the universe, assuming Him to be personal, free, and loving, is that He will not bind His hands by natural ordinances in any such way as will preclude His effective interposition for the help of His moral creatures, when they need and seek His help'.[140] Conversely,

> if miracles do not happen, it is plain enough what becomes of the Bible and its history. The Bible is the history of a *supernatural revelation*, or it is nothing . . . The Gospel itself, centring in Jesus Christ, is a supernatural interposition of God in human history for the ends of redemption. Purge out everything of the nature of miracle from the Bible, and the bottom is taken from its whole message. Its credit is destroyed.[141]

If we approach the Bible with presuppositions which preclude such an interposition of God, the reverberations will be felt throughout Christian doctrine; and moreover, since (as Orr insists) Christian doctrine is an organism, the application of anti-supernaturalistic presuppositions to any part of it will adversely affect the whole. We are now in a position to see how Orr makes good this claim.

Orr can certainly not be accused of shirking the contentious issues. He wrote on *God's Image in Man and Its Defacement in the Light of Modern Denials* (1907), *The Virgin Birth of Christ* (1907), *The Resurrection of Jesus* (1908) and *Sin as a Problem of Today* (1910). It will be convenient (and he would doubtless have approved the order) if we group our remarks under the headings of God, man and sin, the person and work of Christ, and eschatology.

The God of the Bible is a personal, ethical, self-revealing being.[142] He is also self-contained. Against pantheistic immanentism (and not altogether without implications for more recent process theologies), Orr argues that

A God in process is of necessity an incomplete God—can never be a true personal God. His being is merged in that of the universe; sin, even, is an element of His life. I hold it to be indubitable that God, in order truly to be God, must possess Himself in the eternal fulness and completeness of His own personal life; must possess Himself for Himself, and be raised entirely above the transiency, the incompleteness, and the contingency of the world-process. We are then enabled to think of the world and history, not as the necessary unfolding of a logical process, but as the revelation of a free and holy purpose; and inconsistency is no longer felt in the idea of an action of God along supernatural lines—above the plane of mere nature, as wisdom and love may dictate—for the benefit of His creature man. [143]

Man is indeed God's creature; but he is a rebellious creature. In Christ, however, he may become a son. Rebels by nature, men may become sons by grace. Such a status results from 'a divine adoption' and 'the impartation of a new supernatural life'. [144] But this is the work of God the Holy Spirit. So it transpires that 'Our salvation, as the New Testament exhibits it, has not one, but three Divine fountain-heads—God the Father, God the Son, and God the Holy Ghost'. [145] Orr is an unashamed trinitarian, recognizing as he does that the Trinity is an *'induction* from the facts of the Christian revelation'. [146] The true God is one in three persons—and at this point Orr cautions against tritheism, and explains that in the doctrinal affirmation a person is not a separate individual. What has to be maintained is the existence 'in the Divine nature of three mutually related yet distinct centres of knowledge, love, and will, not existing apart as human individualities do, but in and through each other as moments in one Divine self-conscious life'. [147] Orr's God is immanent, yet transcendent. He is righteous holy love, and he redeems his rebel children by a supernatural miracle of grace.

With further reference to rebel man, we would reiterate Orr's objection to any immanentist view which would make sin in some way part of the natural order. As far as he is concerned, 'Sin is that which ought not to be *at all*. It has throughout the Bible a volitional and *catastrophic* character'. [148] At the root of sin is egoism: the refusal to have God to reign over us. [149] Sin is not simply a moral matter, it is religious: 'Sin is transgression *against God*'. [150] The consequence is total depravity, not in the sense that man is as bad as he can be, but in the sense that there is nothing about him which is unaffected by the pollution of sin. Further, although sin is voluntary and individual in origin, its results are racial in their scope. [151] Orr goes so far as to defend stoutly the view that sin is the cause of physical death: 'Death , as I understand it, is not a necessary part of man's lot at all. Had man not sinned, he would never have died.

Death—the separation of soul and body, the two integral parts of his nature—is something for him abnormal, unnatural'.[152] Again, 'It was no part of the Creator's design in his ideal constitution that body and soul should ever be separated'.[153] Consequently, man, apart from sin, would have enjoyed immortality just as he was. Orr's successor D. W. Forrest argued cogently against this position, holding Orr's view to be tantamount to the assertion, not that man was fundamentally spiritual, but that he was not at all natural. Orr's view 'postulates a permanence and continuity of life which the material world in every part of it denies. "The things which are seen are temporal"; and a human body is none the less temporal that it is united to a spirit charged with immortality'.[154] We cannot resist the conclusion that the nature of the biblical evidence is such that absolute assurance on either side of the argument may not be claimed. Nor is it necessary, at least from the point of view of man's practical situation now.

What then of the person and work of the Redeemer? Orr's contention is that given man's plight, a gracious, free, unmerited, supernatural act of God alone will save him. Christ's person, ministry, atoning work and victory all partake of the requisite character. Christ cannot be accounted for along either naturalistic of Ritschlian lines. Orr has four crucially important things to say about the Incarnation. Firstly, Christ's personality is fundamentally divine. He is the eternal Son of God. His Godhead is not, with Ritschl, to be resolved into a value judgement: 'Here Ritschlianism is guilty of more than an abuse of language. It asks us to value as God one who is not God in fact. It will not allow us even to inquire into what or who Christ really is, on the ground that this would involve "metaphysics".'[155] The truth is that we are *not* reduced to silence. We are able to make true statements about Christ, and these affirmations are factually grounded. Thus the Virgin Birth is a witness of Christ's divinity; and if he *is* who he claims to be, what more natural than that the pre-existent Son should be miraculously born of a virgin? Orr cannot understand why it is that some, who wish to maintain belief in Christ's pre-existence, his Incarnation, and his Resurrection, should stumble at the Virgin birth: 'To me . . . it is no way *a priori* incredible that God should make a new supernatural beginning in the entrance of His Son into humanity'.[156] Conversely, he was sure that the perils of a humanitarian christology loomed large before those who too easily rejected the Virgin Birth; and, bearing his view of the organism of Christian truth in mind, we can see why he quoted his predecessor A. B. Bruce with approval: 'With belief in the Virgin Birth is apt to go belief in the Virgin Life, as not less than the other a part of that veil that must be taken away that the true Jesus may be seen as he was—a morally defective man, better than most, but not perfectly good'.[157] Finally, to those who declare in favour of the physical impossibility of the Virgin Birth, Orr (again following Bruce) retorts that a sinless man in the moral world is as much a miracle as a Virgin Birth in the physical world.[158] In any case, 'To me the stupendous miracle is always the Incarnation itself, and any lesser miracle which is involved in that loses its power to offend'.[159]

Secondly, Christ humbled himself by a voluntary act and became man. There *is* a true kenosis. Christ grew, developed, and even—as Calvin admitted—confessed ignorance (though not error);[160] but he did not sin. As for kenoticism, however, Orr shares Bruce's hesitations, and agrees in particular that the kenotic theories 'involve an impossibility, inasmuch as they ask us to believe in the temporary suspension of the consciousness, and the cessation from all Divine functions, of one of the Persons of the Godhead! . . . The sense of the apostle's words seems sufficiently met by the lowly form of Christ's earthly manifestation—"despised and rejected of men, a man of sorrows, and acquaintedwith grief".'[161] We shall have more to say concerning kenoticism when we come to examine the thought of D. W. Forrest. We might however bear in mind the question, 'For all his *prima facie* approval of kenoticism, how much more does Forrest actually believe than Orr and Bruce concerning Christ's humiliation?'

Thirdly, 'In this superhuman Person. . .*perfect humanity is united with full divinity*. The Divine is manifested in and through the human, yet without impairing the integrity of the latter. Humanity is recipient of the Godhead, yet the Divine in union with the human loses none of its essential attributes, nor, in a cosmical relation, ceases to exercise them'.[162] This is Orr's testimony to a popular audience. Now it must be granted that at times in his more technical discussions, he lends hostages to fortune. Thus for example in his eagerness to draw an analogy between the person of Christ and the immanence-transcendence of God, he is quoted by W. L. Walker as saying, 'So the Divine Son took upon Him our nature with its human limits, but above and beyond that, if we may so express it, was the vast over-soul of His Divine consciousness'.[163] This, as Walker rightly points out, would still leave us with two centres of consciousness in Christ, of which the Jesus of the New Testament gives no inkling; and it would threaten his *real* humanity. But elsewhere, Orr maintains 'You cannot have two Egos in Christ's one Divine-human Person . . . If the human Ego retains in any measure its distinction from the Divine, then we have not an Incarnation, but a Nestorian relation of persons'.[164] Nowhere does Orr make his position clearer than in relation to the Chalcedonian Formula, and it will be instructive to compare what he says about the Formula with some views expressed in our own time by John Hick.

Of the Formula's treatment of Christ's humanity and divinity Orr writes that 'It puts the predicates alongside of each other, but does nothing to show their compatibility and mutual relationship. If I may say so, the formula resembles the statement of the terms in a proportion sum: it gives the ratios, but does not work out the sum'. [165] Professor Hick agrees: 'The Chalcedonian formula . . . merely reiterated that Jesus was both God and man, but made no attempt to interpret the formula'. [166] But then Professor Hick draws his conclusion: 'The doctrine of the incarnation is not a theory which ought to be able to be spelled out but . . . a mystery. I suggest that its character is best expressed by saying that the idea of divine incarnation is a mythological idea . . . a myth is a story which is told but which is not literally true, or an idea or image which is applied to someone or something but which does not literally apply, but which invites a particular attitude in its hearers. Thus the truth of a myth is a kind of practical truth consisting in the appropriateness of the attitude to its object. That Jesus was God the Son incarnate is not literally true, since it has no literal meaning, but it is an application to Jesus of a mythical concept whose function is analogous to that of the notion of divine sonship ascribed in the ancient world to a king'. [167] Orr would in no way dissent from the view that the Incarnation is a mystery; but on many other counts he would be highly suspicious of Professor Hick's conclusion. We suspect that he would detect more than a little of the value judgement about it, and well as the naturalistically-inspired refusal to look the facts (as Orr sees them) in the face. He would conclude that Chalcedon did not take a sufficiently 'penetrative' view of the human-divine union, and that therefore Christ's humanity was, in subsequent debate, well nigh annulled. The truth is, 'as a deeper psychology shows, that it is only as the human takes up the divine into itself, and assimilates it, that it realizes the true and complete ideal of humanity'. [168] Finally, when Professor Hick goes on to say of Christ that 'he is so far above us in the "direction" of God that he stands between ourselves and the Ultimate as a mediator of salvation', [169] Orr (no doubt suspecting the 'first-among-equals Jesus') would presumably deny that such a one is the Son of God, and that the employment of Son-of-God language about such a one would be not so much mythological as utterly misplaced. He might also be inclined to think that the exalted evaluation which Professor Hick does place on Jesus requires a nobler theory than the one he propounds.

Fourthly, the end of the Incarnation is redemption. Orr is at pains to point out that redemption means more than atonement, crucial though the latter is. Christ is prophet and king, as well as priest. Indeed, 'even creation itself is built up on Redemption lines'.[170] Denney queried whether such a statement might not adversely affect the doctrine of the atonement by blurring the nature-grace distinction, and making our understanding of Christ's work less definite than it might otherwise be.[171] But Orr viewed the Incarnation as 'a pledge and anticipation of reconciliation',[172] and moreover, the Christo-centrism which flavours his work as much as the older federalism flavoured that of Kennedy hardly allows him to divorce Incarnation from atonement. W. L. Walker brought a further objection in connection with Orr's view of the God-man kinship, and his view of the immanent God working out his purpose in the world: 'why should it be deemed necessary to go outside the world to bring into it, at some moment of time, the Son of God to be incarnate, He who has already been acknowledged as the immanent cause of the whole development?'[173] Orr would doubtless reply that God is transcendent as well as immanent; that the creator/creature distinction must be maintained; and that, above all, man's moral and filial relations with God have been disrupted by man's sin. *That* is why a supernatural miracle of grace is required. And that is why the Christ of reductionist views is grossly inadequate to the task which needs to be done.[174]

What has Christ done? Orr stands broadly within the Reformed tradition. Christ's death was expiatory in character; by it satisfaction was rendered to God's holy law, which had been violated by sin:

> 'God's love, and even Fatherhood, do not divest Him of those fundamental attributes which constitute Him the Upholder and Vindicator of moral law in the universe; and if redemption reveals an infinite and all-compassionating love for the world, it does not detract from this love that it manifests itself towards sinners in "reigning through righteousness" unto life, not in annulling righteousness.'[175]

Orr cannot therefore be satisfied with such views as those of Schleiermacher, Erskine of Linlathen, Bushnell or McLeod Campbell, which sought to minimize the so-called forensic aspect of the atonement. As for the view that the Fatherhood of God excluded the forensic, 'This I believe to be a profound mistake, carrying with it the overthrow of much else than a doctrine of atonement—even of those pillars of righteousness on which the stability of the moral universe depends'.[176] In Orr's view, as we might by now expect, none sailed closer to the wind than Ritschl: 'God in the Ritschlian theology . . . is purely and solely love; of the awful holiness which abhors, and cannot but react against, and punish sin, there is no adequate recognition'.[177] Sin is natural; it is due to ignorance; there is no objective condemnation of the race which requires to be removed; sin is an individual matter; guilt is less than disturbing. With such an inadequate view of man's plight, it is not to be wondered that, in Orr's view, the Ritschlian understanding of the remedy leaves a lot to be desired; nor is it surprising that Ritschlians cannot, on the whole, find adequate room in their systems for the regenerating work of the Holy Spirit. For all its benefits, which he generously appreciated, Orr's final verdict upon Ritschlianism was sepulchral indeed: 'For the purposes of the Evangelical Church . . . Ritschl's theology is *impossible*'.[178]

The Resurrection is the great confirmation of the claims of Christ, and the supreme vindication of his work. As with the Virgin Birth, so with the Resurrection: it is entirely compatible with reality, given that Christ is the Son of God, and that the supernatural is not to be proscribed: 'It is granted, then, that, in the Resurrection of Jesus Christ from the dead, we are in presence of a miracle—a miracle, however, congruous with the character, personal dignity, and claims of Him whose triumph over death is asserted—and there is no evading the issue with which this confronts us, of an actual, miraculous economy of revelation in history'.[179] The Resurrection marks the completion of Christ's redemptive work; it is the Father's seal upon, and public declaration of acceptance of, that work; and it signals the entrance of Christ upon his exalted and universal reign. Its implications for man are highly significant too. We have to do not with the emancipation of surviving spirits, but with the resurrection of the personality in its wholeness. On the details of the after-life we must maintain a reverent agnosticism. Crass literalism is as out of place as Ritschl's classification of 'eschatology' under the rubric of 'mythology'. For Ritschl, the idea of the kingdom is that of the ideal human society, motivated by love. The Bible's idea is infinitely richer:

> the kingdom of God is that new, spiritual, invisible, order of things introduced into the world by Christ, which is, on the one hand, the reign of God in His Fatherly love and grace in hearts trustfully submitted to Him through His Son, and, on the other, the union of those thus saved and blessed for the doing of God's will, and the realization of righteousness, which is but another name for the divine supremacy, in all the spheres and departments of their earthly existence, yet with the hope of a longer and fuller existence in eternity, when God shall be truly "all in all".'[180]

Such a picture carried with it implications of judgement, and Orr would by no means avoid these. But God is holy love, and while we have no ground for subscribing to universalism, 'We may be absolutely certain that the mercy of God will reach as far as ever it is possible for it to reach'.[181]

As far as Orr was concerned, the organism of Christian truth was intact. The naturalistic challenge 'is only to be met by the firm reassertion of the whole truth regarding the Christ of the New Testament Gospel—a Christ supernatural in origin, nature, works, claims, mission, and destiny; the divine Son, incarnate for the salvation of the world, pure from sin, crucified and risen, ever-living to carry on to its consummation the work of the Kingdom He founded while on earth'.[182] Naturalistic challenges not only fail, they cannot but fail for, as Celsus found long ago, 'It is not enough that Christianity be refuted: it must be explained, and Celsus had no satisfactory explanation to offer'.[183]

IV

James Orr was biblically more conservative than any other of our divines, with the single exception of Kennedy. His apologetic was more Bible-based than that of Flint, and more dogmatically and historically competent than that of Bruce. He was not uninfluenced by the older theism, and at times he conceded too much to the newer evolutionism, but at his best he made it abundantly clear that the Christian world view could be founded only upon Christian postulates. Nor were these postulates theoretical only. If God comes first in our thinking it is because he has made himself known. What is more, he makes himself known to, and redeems, sinners. The supernatural cannot be avoided. Philosophically, Orr was nearer to Iverach than to Caird; he was at one with Bruce in his concern for the historicity of the gospel; he was as christocentric as we shall see that Forrest and Denney were. He stimulates us in our methodological quest, and by his supernaturalism he prompts us to investigate a good deal of present-day theology with a view to seeing whether, for all its professed breadth and ecumenism, it does not proceed upon narrowly naturalistic presuppositions. Above all, Orr's objective was practical. He sought to clarify the gospel which had to be proclaimed. Kennedy, Orr and Denney could each have said the following words—and they would have meant something rather different by them! But Orr holds the middle ground with vast learning, and with great charity: 'The teachers of our new theologies are never under a greater mistake than when they imagine that it is the preaching of this old Gospel of the grace of God—old, yet ever new—which is alienating the modern world from the Churches. It is not the preaching of this Gospel which is emptying the churches, but the want of it'.[184]

CHAPTER EIGHT

David William Forrest (1856–1918): The Centrality of Christ

If blood has been spilled in religious crusades, ink has been spilled in theological crusades. In recent years advocates of the death of God, of situation ethics, of liberation theology—to name but a few causes—have sallied, sometimes sensationally, into print. The old soldiers of these movements tend to fade away, but christological warriors march on. What is especially interesting about the latter is the way in which they have not resorted to new-fangled explosives, but have returned to such tried and trusted weapons as the Chalcedonian Formula and the idea of kenosis. Thus George S. Hendry, while recognizing all the difficulties which kenoticism poses, yet declares that 'The incarnation unquestionably involves an element of *kenosis*, and christological thought must continue to strive after its meaning.'[1] B. L. Hebblethwaite concurs;[2] and D. M. Mackinnon has averred that 'it is the notion of *kenosis* which more than any other single notion points to the deepest sense of the mystery of the incarnation'.[3]

What is particularly striking is the way in which so many of our contemporary writers pay little heed to their British forebears. We attribute this state of affairs not so much to arrogance on the part of the scholars in question, as to the 'instant' nature of much present-day theological writing, and to the short (or, at any rate selective—some of them are accomplished Patristics scholars) memories of some of the writers. As we have seen, A. B. Bruce pioneered the consideration of kenoticism in this country. Further, P. T. Forsyth was brilliantly suggestive in this field; H. R. Mackintosh wrote with great insight upon the theme; and D. W. Forrest wrote two major works in which kenotic thought was treated, *The Christ of History and of Experience* (1897) and *The Authority of Christ* (1906). Seven editions of the former and four of the latter appeared. In these books Forrest propounded a subtle kenoticism which held firmly both to the historical Jesus and to the reality of the Christian believer's experience. Can this voice from the not very distant

172

past aid current Christological endeavours? We shall see; but first, who was David Forrest?[4]

I

Born at Glasgow on 16th May 1856, David William Forrest was a son of the United Presbyterian manse. His father, also David, had previously ministered at Troon, but was now in charge of St. Rollox Church, whose industrial and working-class environment, with its considerable Roman Catholic population, demanded all his patience, resourcefulness and tact. As he lay dying, Forrest senior called his son and daughter to his bedside and charged them to 'Love one another'. The father died in 1877; the son and daughter lived together until the former died on 3rd March 1918.

Forrest was a pupil at Glasgow High School, where he earned many prizes and won the Paul and Ewing gold medals for proficiency in Greek. At the age of fourteen he told his Mother of his determination to be a minister, and in 1872 he entered the University of Glasgow. Here he won the Buchanan Prize in Professor John Nichol's English Literature class, but none of his teachers made a greater impression upon him than Edward Caird, Professor of Moral Philosophy, to whom he later referred as 'The Dead Master' in a memorial tribute in *The Scotsman*.

To study was Forrest's delight, and his successes were many: medals in Greek, Logic and English; the first prize in Latin and Moral Philosophy; a prize in Mathematics; the Cowan Gold Medal in Latin, and an Honours M.A. in Philosophy. Forrest was in his element in the Dialectic Society, as his friend Dr. A. B. D. Alexander recalled: 'when it got abroad that "wee Forrest" was going to reply or lead off in some debate everyone was on the alert and full of expectation'.[5] Sir Henry Jones had a similar recollection of him: 'I remember soon after I came to Glasgow, a lonely student from Wales, hearing him speak at a great political meeting, and marvelling at his power and eloquence and gifts'.[6] In view of his debating skills, some envisaged Forrest as a barrister, while Caird urged him to apply for the Snell Exhibition at Oxford. But the sense of call to the ministry persisted, and Forrest proceeded to the United Presbyterian Theological Hall at Edinburgh, where his teachers were John Cairns (Principal), John Ker (Practical Theology), Robert Johnstone (New Testament), J. A. Paterson (Old Testament), and David Duff (Church History).

On leaving Edinburgh, Forrest studied at Leipzig, under Delitzsch, Kahnis and Luthardt, and when he returned home he was licensed as a probationer minister in October 1880. Many churches sought his services, but not until June 1882 was he ordained, at Saffronhall, Hamilton. There he remained until May 1887, when he moved to Moffat. He declined a call to Dr. Joseph Leckie's old charge, Ibrox, Glasgow, but in 1894 went as colleague to Dr. James Black of Wellington Church, Glasgow. Never robust, the strain of working in this large church began to tell, and this, together with the strain imposed by his appointment as Kerr Lecturer in 1894, prompted his removal to Skelmorlie United Free Church in 1899. His Kerr Lectures, *The Christ of History and of Experience*, were published in 1897, and in the following year Glasgow University conferred its D.D. upon him. The Anglicans Boyd Carpenter and the brothers Caird, and the nonconformists Alexander Maclaren, Hugh Price Hughes and Joseph Parker, gave the book a cordial welcome. In the preface to his first edition, Forrest thanked James Orr, whom he was later to succeed at the Glasgow United Free Church College, 'for valuable counsel and suggestion'.

Forrest's fame spread, and in 1900 he was offered the Chair of Apologetics at Knox College, Toronto. Despite the imploring of the Professor of Theology there, Dr. Kilpatrick, Forrest declined the invitation. But if he would not leave his homeland for a long period, he had no objection to a brief excursion to America. Thus in 1901 we find him lecturing at Hartford Divinity School, Union Theological Seminary, New York, and the Universities of Princeton, Montreal, Chicago and Cleveland. While in America he served as Glasgow University's delegate at the Bicentenary celebrations at Yale, and delivered the Carew Lectures in Theology there.

Meanwhile, in 1900, Forrest had been chosen to move the resolution in the United Presbyterian Assembly which committed the Church to union with the Free Church of Scotland. This task was thoroughly congenial to Forrest's ecumenical temperament, as the following extract from the Assembly speech he delivered on 30th October 1900 shows:

> Nothing has tended more to bring [the union] about than what may be termed the *centripetal movement of Christian thought* in these days of scientific method and critical enquiry, the growing and indisputable conviction that the essentials of faith are few, and that apart from these the widest range and diversity of view does not constitute the weakness but the strength of the Church . . . And, believing as we do that Christ's ideal of His Church is not only a unity, but a manifested unity, we rejoice to be permitted to labour in any measure for the realisation of that end by the creation of a Church, free, large, comprehensive, inclusive of many divergent types of Christian thought and life, but loyal in its every part to its one Lord and Head.[7]

Forrest enjoyed still wider ecclesiastical discussions through the Unity Association, where he ably argued the subordinate importance of questions of church government, and gracefully declined to accept the historic episcopate as a *sine qua non* of the church. He was also very alive to the possibility that ecclesiastical and especially sacerdotal pressures could smother the vitality of the gospel.[8]

As convener of its Education Committee, Forrest led his Church in support of the continuance of religious instruction in the teachers' training colleges, which were in the process of passing from ecclesiastical to state control. Some, including Dr. George C. Hutton, the Moderator of the 1906 Assembly at which the debate on the question took place, held this to be an inconsistent stance for a voluntary church to adopt, but Forrest won the day.[9]

By now Forrest was in what was to be his last pastorate. In 1903 he had gone to North Morningside, Edinburgh, as colleague to Dr. Mair. He had been there for about one year only when, on the death of Dr. John Laidlaw, he was invited to allow his name to go forward for consideration by the committee charged with appointing the next Professor of Systematic Theology at New College, Edinburgh. In view of his recent assumption of new duties, he declined, and in the event H. R. Mackintosh was voted to the Chair over John Oman.[10] In 1906 an invitation to become Principal of the United College, Bradford, was likewise declined, and in the same year his *The Authority of Christ* appeared. His editorial collaboration with the son of Dr. John Brown resulted in the publication of the latter's *Letters* in 1907.

Visits to the Highlands, and foreign travel—especially to Italy—delighted Forrest, but such excursions were curtailed when in the spring of 1914 the United Free Church Assembly appointed him to the Chair of Systematic Theology in the Glasgow College in succession to James Orr. It is an indication of the theological vitality of the United Free Church at that time that the Assembly received no fewer than five nominations for the vacant Chair. The names of A. B. D. Alexander, A. B. Macaulay and W. R. Thompson were eliminated by a show of hands, and in the final result Forrest gained a slender majority over Daniel Lamont.[11]

To his students Forrest was an approachable man and, in private, a merciful man. From the rostrum, however, he promulgated the need of regular attendance at classes, and would admonish by name any student not taking notes. His own standards were high, and he expected much of others. For all his interest in, and work for, organizations devoted to the social betterment of the people, 'he thought that the primary concern of every man was to know his own business, and that ministers of the Gospel should aim first of all at being professional theologians rather than amateur sociologists'.[12]

In addition to his college duties, Forrest served as Moderator of the Glasgow Presbytery. He preached regularly, and he followed the fortunes of his friends with genuine pastoral concern.[13] As J. H. Leckie rightly said, 'He was not only a theologian; he was eminently a preacher and a pastor'.[14] His preaching was solid, yet popular; his thoughts sublime, yet earthed. He emphasized the need of obedience to the law of righteousness, but never overlooked the love of the One who is touched with a feeling for our infirmities. Above all, his preaching and his personal faith were rooted in the assurance of the heavenly inheritance. Tributes to Forrest's ministry were paid at his ministerial semi-jubilee, on which occasion Henry Jones both spoke for himself and conveyed the greetings of Edward Caird.

Forrest was a slight man, agile of mind and swift of speech. He loved poetry, he served people. He was a 'bonnie fighter' for worthy causes, and prone to private flashes of temperament. He needed a reason for his hope, and was fully alive to the intellectual difficulties which the Christian faith faced. Indeed, at the age of nineteen he had composed a sonnet which ended,

> This is our highest knowledge while below
> To feel devoutly that we nothing know.[15]

No man should be held to his adolescent positions, but we can see already in those words a questing, tentative mind to which the methodology of Butler was to make a profound appeal: 'Multitudes . . . of sincere Christians, either because of a deficient spiritual experience or of a peculiar mental characteristic, will always find in such a method as Butler's the strongest support of a faith that often tends to waver'.[16]

Before the war was over and student classes returned to a more normal size, Forrest died, on 3rd March, 1918. He had been nominated to succeed James Denney as Principal of the Glasgow College. In his nursing home he asked his friend W. R. Thompson to take charge of his classes and from under his pillow he drew out the manuscript of his lecture notes. 'It was the thing', said Thompson, 'apart from his home, that he cared for most, for it was the symbol of what was the main interest in his life'.[17] To his sister Forrest said, 'Well, if this is the end, my work is over; and sometimes it has been pretty hard'. On the other hand he had earlier said to another friend, 'Whatever I have been able to do has been fully recognized. This cannot be said of every man'.[18] We need not doubt that Forrest would have endorsed his own words in a characteristic sermon on immortality: 'If we grow in love to God and in loyalty to Him by daily self-denials, then it matters not when or where the summons to depart shall sound, for it can usher us into no world where we shall not find ourselves at home in Him who is not the God of the dead, but of the living, unto whom all live for evermore'. [19] The churches to which Forrest had ministered provided a memorial stone to him in the Western Necropolis, Glasgow, and a window to his memory was erected in North Morningside Church.

II

We come now to a consideration of the general cast of Forrest's thought, and of his approach to a variety of theological questions, which will lead us on to examine his Christology.

Butler's methodology, which made such a great appeal to Forrest, was but one of the philosophical influences upon him. He never completely turned his back upon the idealism of his teacher Edward Caird. He maintained the reasonableness of faith, and he sought to harmonize apparently conflicting views wherever possible. His feeling for the wholeness of experience, as against a crippling atomism, was also part of his legacy from idealism, as was his confidence in the possibility of articulating a *system* of thought. Again, in a discussion of miracles he understands such occurrences as showing that 'nature exists for the sake of spirit', and he refers *inter alia* to John Caird with approval at this point. [20] While willing to acknowledge the force of the evolutionary motif, and ready to take the consequences as far as confessional interpretation was concerned, he could not accept the naturalism of many evolutionary thinkers; and he could never agree with those idealists who supposed that evil was merely a stage on the way to good. Echoing Orr, he maintained that to Christ, evil 'was essentially the thing which *ought not to be*'. [21] Again, Forrest was highly suspicious of the pantheizing tendency within Hegelian and post-Hegelian idealism, and he wrote his Kerr Lectures with a view to making plain faith's anchorage in historical facts and in the believer's own experience. He complained that the new Hegelianism of T. H. Green and Edward Caird

> has less and less tended to commend itself as a fair or satisfactory interpretation of the historical personality of Jesus. Fundamentally, it conceives Him merely as the symbol of a Divine humanity, of an Ideal which may never have been realized; not as the Lord, who by a unique Divine achievement in His own person guarantees to us a spiritual victory. Thus it attempts to secure Christian experience, while

D.D.F.—L

undermining the foundation on which as a matter of fact that experience has always rested.[22]

Forrest takes exception to Green's view that 'There is an inner contradiction in that conception of faith which makes it a state of mind involving peace with God and love towards all men, and at the same time makes its object that historical work of Christ of which our knowledge depends on evidence of uncertain origin and value'.[23] To Forrest there is no such absolute contradiction, and he sets out to show that the historical and the moral, far from being incompatible, are 'inseparably fused together in human life'.[24] When Green grants that the idea of self-sacrifice, though not confined to any nation or age, is most fully recognized as the power of a present and spiritual resurrection, Forrest observes that this construction involves at least the purity of Christ's life and his actual resurrection, and 'in affirming these we are already in the historical sphere'.[25] Again, when Caird and Green offer their account of Christ, they are found wanting. To Caird, 'the pure idea of a divine humanity was apprehended by Jesus and made into the great principle of life.' But to Forrest this means that our religious emotion reads deity and sinlessness into Christ; and this will not do.[26] Here we are a long way from the facts of Christ's life, and it is not at all surprising that the neo-Hegelians cannot give an adequate account of Christ's work. To them 'it is only the supreme revelation of that law of dying to self which applies both to Him and to us . . . But what Christ reveals to us is not simply that self-sacrifice is the principle of all spiritual life, and therefore common to Him and to us, but that *He* realized it, and that *we* do not . . . As a mere example, He is no encouragement to us, for His moral experience has different conditions from ours'.[27]

So it becomes apparent that the idealistic approach, which sets out to bring Christ close, and to protect him from the ravages of historical criticism, inevitably reduces him and idealizes him away.[28] Forrest realizes that *his* task is to show that a faith which rests upon historical facts is not inherently contradictory. His method is to argue that Christianity does not rest upon external evidence alone. The outward testimony receives inward corroboration. So we move to religious experience, to the self-verifying power of truth, and to the believer's understanding of the authority of Christ. Here we are dealing not with literal facts alone, but with moral facts. Certainly we may not dispense with the historical events of Christ's life, rely upon the experience of the Christian ages, and still expect to maintain a lively faith. Even R. W. Dale erred in supposing the contrary, for 'that experience of the centuries was what it was, because it had in the heart of it the indisputable conviction, conveyed by the records, of Christ's reality as a unique person in history . . . If the knowledge of the human life of Jesus was necessary for the first disciples, it could never be a matter of indifference to the faith of any subsequent generation . . . To declare to those who assail the genuineness of the Gospels, that our faith would remain substantially unchanged even if they succeeded in discrediting them, is to play into their hands . . . *It is exactly this direct touch with the historical Jesus* which the simplest Christian knows to lie at the root of his confidence'.[29] Forrest would have us be warned that 'Whenever the Church has treated the historic record with indifference, it has invariably fallen either into scholasticism or mysticism'.[30]

In the light of what we have seen so far, Forrest's specification of the dogmatic task comes as no surprise: 'Dogmatic has for one of its functions continually to reinterpret the symbolic language of religion in the light of actual Christian experience . . . while Dogmatic ought never to be subjected to the specific categories of any philosophic system, it is futile to imagine that it can remain uninfluenced by the intellectual atmosphere and attitude characteristic of the age'.[31] There must be constant commerce between the intellectual environment and the corporate Christian experience, and the latter is an intensely down-to-earth matter: 'The Church's spiritual vision in the future will depend on its practical fidelity; and as the vision is, so will the Dogmatic be'.[32] That vision must be open; Forrest could not sanction the confessionalism of the closed mind. He had been in favour of the Declaratory Acts, and while accepting the value of Confessions as bonds of union between believers, and as witnesses to the faith commonly held among them,[33] he regarded it as a 'great danger' that 'the Church may pronounce a judgement which the future will reverse: may declare a doctrine to be false which subsequent generations will hail as important truth'.[34]

It is essential that we appreciate the balance of Forrest's thought. He attaches great importance to the historical, while recognizing that bare history does not provide the deliverances of faith. He endorses Schleiermacher's view that the characteristic mark of religion—a primary instinct in man—is 'the sense of dependence on a Being or Beings who are to us invisible'[35] while denouncing attempts to idealize the historical record away. He regards Butler's method as appropriate, not least for those whose faith, though real, is assailed by doubt; yet at the same time he acknowledges the final inadequacy of the theistic proofs as rational demonstrations of God's existence. To the unsympathetic Forrest may thus appear to be a 'Mr Facing-All-Ways', but he no doubt would have replied that such a posture was justifiable if the facts supported it, and if Christian experience demanded it; and that in any case it made a refreshing change from the polarities represented by neo-Hegelianism on the one hand and the older confessional Calvinism on the other. Let us then examine the ingredients which go to make up Forrest's methodology one by one.

Forrest is for the historical, and against psychologism: 'Seeing that historical affirmations are inherently involved in Christian faith, it is a grave mistake so to put the emphasis on the proofs derivable from the Christian consciousness of salvation as to disparage the element of historical evidence'.[36] Equally, he is for the historical and against gnosticism, ancient or modern: hence, for example, his understanding of John's Gospel not as 'a philosophical treatize on the dogma of the Logos, in which the Gnostic antithesis of the principles of light and darkness is worked out in the form of an idealised picture of Christ's life', but as 'emphatically a historical document, grounded on a minute knowledge of facts'.[37] It is precisely the weight he attaches to the historical which inclines Forrest towards Butler, and opposes him at this point to John Caird (and, as we have seen, to T. H. Green and Edward Caird).

To Butler the demand for a demonstrative proof of God's existence was out of the question. True, he was replying to the Deists, and he could assume a shared theism in a way in which those who confront latter-day positivism and agnosticism may not. Nevertheless, in Forrest's opinion his assertion of the apologetic utility of probability was of great importance. John Caird, however, finds it contradictory to 'believe with a mind half-convinced . . . to let probability have the force of certainty is not only an irrational but an immoral act'.[38] Forrest grants that Caird here describes 'with vivid eloquence the inward assurance that belongs to highest religious faith',[39] but he cannot resist the conclusion that Caird is dealing with an abstraction. Butler has a more careful eye to the facts on which faith rests, and as soon as history is involved, we are in the realm of probabilities. It is all very well for Caird to speak 'vaguely of Christianity as the revelation of that "infinite righteousness, goodness, love, which found its highest human expression in the life of Christ",'[40] but on what grounds do we make such a claim? We advert to the historical. And how would we seek to controvert one who denied the claim? By weighing the evidence, Butler-style.

Moreover, the believer is often conscious of a debate within his own soul. The doctrine of prayer and the problem of undeserved suffering raise intractable problems to the honest *believer*:

In this stress of faith, then, what is the course which an honest mind pursues? It is compelled to confess that even its fundamental affirmations regarding the being and character of God are attended by grave perplexities springing from two sources; on the speculative side, it is involved in antinomies which it cannot reconcile, and on the practical side it has to acknowledge facts which it cannot explain or vindicate. Inevitably, therefore, it is driven to the very attitude which Principal Caird repudiates; it has to strike a balance of arguments. . .'[41]

Forrest is at one with the neo-Hegelians to the extent that they obliterate the distinction between natural and revealed theology. It is of no practical use

to speak of such doctrines as those of God, Duty and Immortality as belonging to the 'natural' order, meaning thereby that they can be investigated and established by human reason, in contrast with other doctrines such as the Incarnation, the Trinity, and the Atonement, revealed to us by the act of God. For not one of the truths of what is called 'natural' religion remains unchanged when incorporated into the Christian system. Our conception of God, of Duty, of Immortality, if we have one at all, is essentially Christ's conception.[42]

He goes so far as to say that 'Few will deny that it is the thinkers who have laid no claim to producing an irresistible demonstration of Christian faith who have done most for that faith's vitality'.[43]

At this point we are conscious of a certain uneasiness. It concerns Forrest's opposition to a priori ideas on the one hand, and his view of faith as a hypothesis on the other. First, Butler appealed to Forrest in part because his methodology constituted a bulwark against a priori notions: 'The Jews missed the vision of the Messiah when He appeared, because they were certain they knew "by what methods" God would interpose for their deliverance . . .'[44] Both Roman Catholicism and Protestantism have similarly been subject to misapprehensions because of their entertaining a priori ideas. In opposition to this illicit procedure, history must be attended to. Again, when examining the biblical narratives 'we are, of course, not entitled to presuppose the inspiration of the four Gospels.[45] Nor does Forrest take his stand on Christ's divinity 'and of what as Divine He must have known . . . The *a priori* method is utterly illegitimate, and issues in a perverted exegesis'.[46] More generally, 'To set up an *a priori* test, and rule out whatever seems exceptional, is the surest way, whether in the natural or the spiritual sphere, to miss the truth we seek'.[47] Finally, he has little patience with exponents 'of what is called "modern thought"' who *rule out* the deliverances of faith on a priori grounds:

Their doubt or denial of God's existence is invalidated for this reason, that even if He did exist and could be known by man, it would be impossible for them to find Him on their lines of inquiry. And as Professor William James says, 'a rule of thinking which would absolutely prevent me from acknowledging certain kinds of truth, if those kinds of truth were really there, would be an irrational rule.'[48]

Thus, on the one hand Forrest can declare that 'to realize the inner life of Jesus as a veritable attestation of the presence of a redeeming God involves a special experience wrought by the Spirit';[49] and on the other, the manward side, he can say 'We are sure of Him because of what He is to us, because of the place he has in our life, ruling, rebuking, uplifting'.[50] We agree with both sides of this equation. But why then should Forrest make so much of faith as a hypothesis? How can he say that 'He who begins with what seems to him only probable evidence may end, and justly, in assured and indisputable conviction.'[51] He may, of course; but as the quotation from Forrest previously given makes plain, it will not be just because of the strength of the evidence, or because of the individual's power to analyse it. It will be because of the agency of God the Holy Spirit. We have here to do with more than reason. As Forrest elsewhere grants, faith involves the will, and Christ himself 'begins with the moral and so explicates it that it ends in the affirmation of the spiritual; and then He shows how the spiritual as centre radiates out into the fullness of moral obligation'.[52] Christ necessarily begins in this way, for 'The sin which impairs man's personal communion with God has, as a necessary result, blinded him to the signs of God's presence in the universe'.[53]

But if it be true that apart from the de-scaling of our eyes and the renewing of our will by God the Holy Spirit we do not see things aright, is there not a long existential leap from the last piece of 'evidence' to the 'assured and indisputable conclusion'? And if this is so, how much common ground is there between believers and unbelievers? Forrest says that we have to supply the latter 'with reasons which will carry force from their point of view'. But this begs the question of the warped point of view of natural man. The weighing of evidence may reassure the doubting Christian; cogent testimony may, *under the Spirit*, awaken the unbeliever, but nobody ever came to faith merely by following the steps of a logical argument. At one level Forrest knows this well; indeed, he says that 'In the end, the Christian believer, just in so far as he shows "the mind of Christ", will transcend the sphere where the law of probability rules' (though, presumably, having dismissed the Cairds and Green on this matter, he would not intend us here to understand that he is smuggling them back in again). But he does not always carry this thought sufficiently far into his argument.

Forrest was ever, and rightly, on guard against humanistic attenuations of the Faith. Thus, for example, he recalls George Eliot's reported comment upon God, immortality and duty: 'how inconceivable was the *first*, how unbelievable the *second*, and yet how peremptory and absolute the *third*.'[54] As far as Forrest was concerned, Eliot was living on borrowed capital, and unless the inter-relationships of the three concepts were appreciated, duty became an oppressive weight, and life a charade. Similarly, Forrest charged Martineau with evacuating the concept 'Son of Man' of all references to the coming glory. Martineau understood it as referring exclusively to Christ's lowliness. Now the lowliness of Christ weighed heavily with the kenoticist Forrest, but so also did Christ's fulfilling of the Mosaic Law, his demand of obedience and, his forgiving of sins.[55] In a word, Forrest's down-to-earthness was not of the kind which rules out the supernatural. Far from it: 'The whole Christian revelation is penetrated with the supernatural, and the repudiation or surrender of it in the sphere of nature will not lessen by an iota the antagonism of unbelief to it in the spiritual sphere of Christ's person and man's regeneration'.[56] In any case, 'the miracles of Christ's ministry are not isolated marvels, hanging in air, but hold an inseparable relation to One who has already proved Himself an exception to the continuity of nature'.[57] The 'most mysterious of all supernatural manifestations'[58] is the resurrection of Jesus; and it is certain that 'Until we have received the impression from the Gospels of Christ's moral supremacy, of the unshared relation to the Father to which His inmost consciousness testified, and of the correspondence between His unique personal experience and His unique claim to be the mediator of a new life of sonship to others, the resurrection will seem but an idle tale'.[59] Thus, 'the miraculous is not a mere addition to the Christian revelation; it is an integral part of it . . . With the surrender of the belief in a definite historical intervention of the Divine in humanity, we do not simply lose one of the strongest buttresses to Christian faith: the faith itself has ceased to be specifically Christian'.[60]

Our references to the Resurrection now bring us face to face with what is to be our main question: what is Forrest's understanding of the person and work of Christ?

III

Forrest sought to drive to the heart of things. He wished to distil the essence of the gospel, to free it from the confessional fetters of a bygone age. He wished too to take due account of the distinction between the essentials of the gospel, and its culturally-conditioned modes of expression. This emerged in his address to the final Assembly of the United Presbyterian Church.[61] But the essentials of the Faith *were* essentials: Christianity is not something vague and indefinite. There can be no going back on the following convictions, namely that

> Jesus holds a unique place as the Revealer of the Father, and the Redeemer of men: that it is through Him alone that men can truly know God or be reconciled to Him: that the Spirit of God who illumines, renews and sanctifies men, is the Spirit not only of God but of Christ, and has for His supreme function the interpretation of Christ in human experience; and that the life thus originated by the historic revelation of God in Christ, and mediated by the Spirit, is essentially ethical, means personal appropriation of the mind of Christ, and consecration in His name to the service of the Kingdom of God.[62]

To this confession we are brought by the illumination of the Spirit on the one hand, and by the examination of the facts on the other. Our faith is rooted in history in two ways: first, we advert to the life and work of the historical Jesus; second, 'He Himself possesses His present power to deliver and renew us only because He was once a sharer in the moral struggle of our race, and came forth from it victorious'.[63] Forrest goes so far as to say that 'Our entire conception of Him must be construed, and if necessary reconstructed, in the light of the *data*.'[64] What did Forrest himself find as he examined the data?

It is interesting on the way into our theme to observe that in the course of a critique of John Robinson's christology, Robert Butterworth complains that those who have concerned themselves with the person of Christ have made but scant reference to Jesus's faith.[65] Fr. Butterworth has recent scholars in mind; certainly the charge could not be levelled at Forrest. He made much of Christ's devotional life and personal experience of his Father, and at the same time he stoutly affirmed Christ's moral uniqueness. In a nutshell, to Forrest, Christ is distinguished from all others by reason of his sinlessness and his mediatorship or Lordship.[66] In fact, 'The unique character of Christ's moral self-consciousness is the fundamental fact regarding Him'.[67] According to the gospels he confesses ignorance, is overwhelmed by grief, and wrestles in prayer. But he is never contrite or repentant.[68] Nor is his sinlessness to be regarded negatively. It is not the mere absence of defect, but 'the presence of an active and pervading holiness.'[69] If Forrest were given the advice which Fr. Butterworth has lately offered, namely, that we should say nothing of Jesus 'that indicates or implies that he is any less human than we ourselves are—except that he is not a sinner, as we are.'[70] we fancy that he would retort: 'But by virtue of his sinlessness Christ is *more* human than we are.'

Indeed, having argued that Christ differs from all others not only in degree but in kind, Forrest concludes, 'Christ's freedom from stain or shortcoming is not the destruction of His humanity, but its completion'.[71] To him 'sin is not an inherent characteristic of human nature; it is an intrusion'.[72] In all this, Luther's description of Christ as the 'proper man' comes to mind; and we cannot resist the feeling that those who in our time advocate a mythological understanding of the Incarnation are to some extent prompted by their acceptance of the presupposition that empirical humanity is normal humanity, and consequently, that there *cannot* really be a God-man. This, presumably, will be the conclusion of supposedly autonomous 'Enlightenment' men of every age.

Forrest finds weighty evidence for Christ's sinlessness in the fact that Jesus is never represented as praying *with* his disciples; and on this topic he found himself opposed by A. B. Bruce. Forrest's point was that since prayer includes confession, prayers with the disciples which include confession of sin would have given them a false impression of Jesus's character; whereas any such times of prayer from which confession were excluded, would have given them a false impression of their own characters.[73] Bruce replied that on more than one occasion Jesus's conduct was misunderstood, and that the refusal on his part to pray with his disciples would have 'doomed Him to an aloofness which meant death to fraternity'.[74] Forrest's rejoinder included the following points: (a) Jesus's conduct, however it might be misinterpreted, must be the faithful expression of his character. He often had to correct mistaken notions of his person and purpose, but he could not confess to sin and then later retract such a confession, since this would be to mislead, and to cast doubt upon his veracity; (b) when Bruce asks, 'In what other instance did Jesus follow this imaginary principle of aloofness with a view to prevent a false impression of His character?' Forrest replies that he never, in addressing the disciples, referred to God as *our* Father; (c) if, in Patristic fashion, we suppose that in confessing sin Jesus was speaking not as an individual, but as a representative of the sinful race, we make genuine understanding of our Lord's experience impossible. We cannot so divide Christ, as Bruce himself elsewhere affirmed;[75] (d) The records nowhere show Jesus as engaging in corporate prayer, and we may not proceed on the basis of a priori ideas as to what he *must* have done;[76] (e) Bruce's laudable desire to exalt the attractiveness and sympathetic nature of Christ's humanity has led him to overlook or minimize other aspects of his character. To some of these aspects we now turn.

Christ is distinguished from all other men in that he alone has fulfilled the Law. He pronounces on the characters of individuals.[77] He forgives sins, and in no way (*pace* Bruce[78]) suggests that all who share his spirit may share his title to pronounce forgiveness.[79] He makes attachment to himself an essential condition of the receipt of spiritual blessings now and hereafter.[80] In all these ways his authority emerges. Moreover, he was conscious of his Messiahship even before his baptism in the Jordan,[81] and his training of his disciples was such that after the Resurrection they would interpret him aright.[82] That he succeeded in this latter objective is shown by the fact that the earliest form of the apostles' thought was determined by the fact that he who was now Lord of all had been their companion, and that his work of redemption was to be construed under the category of Messiahship.[83] We cannot reproduce Forrest's supportive arguments here, but what is plain is that he is convinced that our understanding of Christ's person is all of a piece with our understanding of his work. Christ does what he does because he is who he is; we learn who he is by seeing what he does. Forrest would have agreed with Professor Macquarrie that 'it is when the doctrine of Christ's Person has been separated from the doctrine of His work that Christology wanders off into speculation, Christ comes to be regarded as a metaphysical mystery rather than as the One who brings wholeness to men, and we end up in the unrealities and irrelevances of docetism'.[84]

In no sense then does Christ's death stand apart from the rest of his ministry. On the contrary, it marks the culmination of his obedience to his Father.[85] Furthermore, 'the Incarnation *without the Cross* would lack precisely that revelation of God's love which is to us the most immediately impressive and soul-subduing—His yearning compassion for the un-worthy'.[86] Christ does not pity only; he redeems, and in order to redeem he endures the Cross. 'Mere compassion working by gentleness would not have redeemed. Compassion had to be governed by moral intensity and to reveal itself in severity and judgement, in national sorrow and catastrophe, before it could achieve salvation for Israel.'[87] On the other hand, while declaring that Christ's ministry and death are all of a piece, Forrest by no means subscribes to the view of such Ritschlians as Herrmann who work in a priori fashion by ruling miracles and, *a fortiori*, a real resurrection out of court) that redemption has *as much* to do with the life as with the death of Jesus. To Forrest, as to the New Testament writers, sin is a 'desperate and dissolvent reality in God's world, requiring a supreme mysterious sacrifice for its removal'.[88] Understandably, 'What Herrmann calls the self-attesting power of the inner life of Jesus is [to agnostics] the product of mingled emotion and imagination'.[89] By a sure instinct the Church at large has held that 'the impression upon us of Christ's personality which declares the sinlessness includes the resurrection, and that the disbelief of the latter leads by no uncertain path to the denial of the former'.[90]

Does Christ's work avail for all men? Is Forrest an universalist? Certainly he is not an exponent of double predestination, and he does not think that quasi-quantitative talk about a 'limited atonement' is to the point. But he nowhere asserts that all will be saved. Since Christ's atonement is to the *race* it provides the possibility of pardon for all, but we must never forget the 'universal principle, that all spiritual service, human or divine, is conditioned in its effect by the receptivity of the person to whom it is rendered, and thus so far may be spent in vain'.[91] We can well imagine what John Kennedy's reaction would have been to this latter aside—has Forrest not forgotten the activity of the Holy Spirit who makes us receptive, and does not leave us with a God who is pitiable rather than pitiful, since He desires earnestly to save us, but we will not let him? Forrest's more general habit is not to forget the work of the Holy Spirit, but rather to emphasize the fact that only by the Spirit's inner testimony do we come to see who Christ is.

Consistently with his entire methodological approach, Forrest is emphatic upon the humanity of Christ. Christ's revelation 'is a revelation *in* humanity; not partly in it and partly out of it'.[92] This might appear to be a Christology 'from below', to use contemporary jargon, though we should be cautioned that, as we have seen, Forrest will not tolerate any humanistic attenuations of the Faith. On the contrary, if we properly attend to the fact of the resurrection we find that 'it constitutes the great point of transition in the Christian faith, at which He who appeared as a single figure in history is recognized as in reality above historical limitations, the abiding Lord and life of souls'.[93] Forrest is no adoptionist, and he would undoubtedly have endorsed this recently expressed view: 'the approach to Christology from below up is not merely a good apologetic device in a secular age but is a recapitulation of the way taken by the first disciples. They knew first the human Jesus; but somewhere along the way they discerned in him a depth that led them to confess his Godhood'.[94] Or, in the words of Professor Sykes, 'I can see no *a priori* reason for supposing that the humanity of Christ may not itself contain genuine elements of novelty; and it is these novel elements which provide us with the factual reasons for embarking upon Christology at all'.[95] Professor Sykes goes on to admit the difficulty that when we begin to specify in what respects Jesus is remarkable we are in danger of removing him from empirical humanity. But Forrest might suggest (and we certainly should) that to the extent that empirical humanity is not the genuine article, this is no bad thing; and, furthermore, those sceptics and humanistic Christian theologians who emphasize Christ's kinship with us often seem to posit *such* a good man as to be in danger of a kind of docetism by inversion: their 'Elder Brother' is just too good to be true: in fact he bears a suspicious likeness to an Arian demi-god. For his part, Forrest is quite clear that 'if the personality of Christ alone attests and conveys to us the Father's life as a redeeming power, if through it alone we truly know and possess God, the noumenal and finally real, then it is impossible to treat that personality as itself a mere historical phenomenon'.[96]

So we proceed to the question of Christ's divinity, and with Forrest as our guide we need not fear Apollinariansim. Far from the divine Logos's replacing the human *nous*, humanity is a fit vehicle, as inanimate nature and the animal world are not, for the expression of the Logos, for man's nature is revelatory of character. If we say that Christ is the Son of God, or if we speak of his eternal generation, we are, of course, using metaphors. But we are not making purely subjective judgements; rather they are judgements which 'have a real, though not perfect, correspondence to *objective* truth'.[97] Apart from eternal generation, there is no kenosis—and in the Incarnation there *is* a kenosis. Consistently with this Forrest defends the Nicene Creed thus:

> The Nicene Creed in declaring that Jesus Christ as the Son is 'of one substance with the Father' is simply asserting a doctrine from which the Church is never likely to recede. It expresses it, indeed, in metaphysical terms which may not seem to some of us the most suitable. The word 'substance' (οὐσία) has often been criticized on the ground that it is not appropriate as applied to God who is a spirit; that we can attach no definite meaning to it when so applied; that it is not sufficiently spiritual; that the inmost secret of personality, either in God or man, is not to be conceived as substance, but as will. This, it seems to me, is hyper-criticism and rather misses the mark. What the Nicene fathers meant to affirm was that Christ belonged to the essence of Godhead: that in whatever sense we ascribe being or substance to God, in the same sense we ascribe it to Christ. Nor would the substitution of 'will' for 'substance' bring out the idea any better. It would rather tend to confuse it, for unless we employ 'will' as including thought and feeling, it does not adequately represent the being of God; and that is exactly what 'substance' is intended to signify: that Christ belongs to the sphere of Reality which we call the Divine.[98]

It is Forrest's very balance in regard to the Church's traditional affirmations of faith which renders his kenoticism sensitive and restrained: he is no kenoticist of the wilder kind. As he said,

If it should prove, as is likely, that Christian thought will always feel impelled, both by the declarations of the New Testament and by the witness of religious experience, to adhere to the historic designation of Jesus Christ as 'true God of true God' and as 'the everlasting Son of the Father,' it will also be forced, in loyalty to the facts of the Gospels, to recognize that the Divine in Him underwent a real 'self-emptying' during the period of His earthly Incarnation.[99]

We find it difficult to conceive how kenoticism of the kind Forrest proposes can be left out of any satisfactory christology, though there are varieties of kenoticism which we should do well to avoid. Thus, on the one side, there have been theories of a highly speculative, quasi-quantitative kind which have sought to determine of which aspects of his divinity Christ must be stripped—or, less radically, which divine attributes must be held in abeyance—if Christ is to become man. So, with Thomasius, we have the distinction drawn between the immanent and the relative attributes of God. On the other side we find adoptionism: Jesus the man empties himself on behalf of others, and is thereupon exalted to Christhood. Forrest prefers what he takes to be the facts: his examination of the life of Jesus, and of apostolic testimony concerning him, prompt him to the conviction that in Christ we have a real limitation of the divine, in order that the Logos might appear under the conditions of space and time. It could not be otherwise, given Christ's pre-existence.

We see, then, that Forrest's kenoticism is broadly and historically based. He denies that it turns upon the exegesis of Philippians 2:6 or 2 Corinthians 8:9, for these verses 'only emphasize what the narratives of Christ's life suggest, and their elimination would leave the problem as presented in the Gospels precisely where it was'.[100] The fact that Christ came at all is evidence of his self-renunciation.[101] In practical terms this means that 'just as His thought was not the omniscience proper to Deity, so His miracles were not the outcome of the omnipotence proper to Deity. Neither His words nor His acts were those of the Eternal Son in His absolute being, but of the Son speaking and acting under human conditions as Son of Man.'[102]

At one point in particular we find a real difficulty in Forrest's earlier kenotic thought. He writes, 'That this unimaginable surrender of divine prerogatives was a part of the essential plan of God's revelation of Himself, appears to me wholly improbable, and only to *become* probable through the arising of a dire and exceptional problem, which love for its own sake had to solve'.[103] What does this imply concerning God's omniscience? Was God taken by surprise by man's sin? Forrest himself supplies the answer in his later work:

That sin exists through the perversity of man's will, that it is in no sense attributable to the action of God but is a direct defiance of His purpose, is a fundamental affirmation of the Christian consciousness. But while it has thus entered as an intrusion into a world where from the divine standpoint it had no right to be, yet its appearance was no surprise to God . . . From the first He knew that He would have to deal with it. His redemptive thought was as original as His creative. [104]

Forrest does not deny that kenoticism, especially in some of its forms, presents real difficulties to the understanding. There is the problem of the alleged temporary loss by Christ of his divine consciousness. In this connection Forrest found some of the suggested 'solutions' incredible. Christ's humanity is not the 'outer mask of His plenary Deity'; nor do a human and a divine mind lie in juxtaposition within his consciousness. [105] Again, there is the difficulty of reconciling 'the cessation of the Son's cosmic function during the period of His humiliation with what Christ reveals of Fatherhood and Sonship in the Godhead'. [106] Here Forrest will not speculate beyond the biblical evidence, and accordingly, the criticism levelled against kenoticisms which do so speculate—by A. B. Bruce before Forrest and by D. M. Baillie after him[107]—pass Forrest by. Notwithstanding all the difficulties, kenoticism renders a twofold service:

(1) It represents an advance on the Chalcedon symbol, in that it gives a truer impression of the New Testament facts and teaching as to the divine *sacrifice* involved in the Incarnation, and thus emphasizes the very quality that endues the Incarnation with its power of moral appeal. (2) By insisting that the elements in Christ's character which verify His Deity are not metaphysical, but ethical and spiritual, it reminds us that the deepest qualities in God and man are akin, and that humanity is grounded in and reproduces the eternal sonship in God. [108]

Such a statement stands as a bulwark against a purely human Christ—a Christ of Martineau, with whom Forrest was familiar, or a Christ of some recent theologians, whom he was spared. Such a Christ cannot effect the redemption we need, or justify the claims Christian experience (and Christ himself) makes. [109] No one else has (or could) go through Christ's self-renunciation; no one else, having done what he did, was raised on the third day. In Forrest we see kenoticism at its least speculative and most empirical.

We also see further evidence of the profound difference in spirit between Forrest and John Caird. Caird reviews kenotic theories and says, for example, that 'the self-renunciation of omniscience, the self-reduction of infinite to finite knowledge, is . . . a contradiction in terms'. [110] He notes that some, in the face of such difficulties as this, have spoken of a *'veiling or concealment*, of the divine presence and power under the form of humanity';[111] but this makes Christ a concealment of God, and 'makes Him to be, not God manifest in the flesh, but God disguised and hidden under the illusory form of the flesh'.[112] We cannot agree. It is part of the Lord's condescension to make himself known as we can know him; and this entails his willing curtailment of certain aspects of his divinity—ubiquity, for example. Forrest concurs; indeed, beginning as he does from history, he cannot see how it could be otherwise. Caird, beginning as he does from the principle of continuity, regards kenoticism as requiring the *laying aside*, rather than the willing *curtailment* of Christ's attributes. To Caird, 'God must be seen not to shroud His divine essence in the one perfect human life, but to shine forth there in the full effulgence of His glory'.[113] But apart from the difficulty of our being able to comprehend any such revelation, or even to bear it, and apart from the implicit docetism here there is an exegetical point on which we would do well to heed a New Testament scholar, T. A. Thomas:

> When the apostle says that Christ exchanged the 'form of God' for the 'form of a servant', he is saying that in His condescension to take upon Himself humanity that effulgence of the divine glory which was the visible expression of his deity was veiled or hidden . . . But in no sense were His deity or any attributes surrendered.[114]

Forrest, as we saw, did not hold that kenoticism depends upon Philippians 2 alone, but that passage as here interpreted becomes an excellent summary of it. Caird, on other occasions, speaks so movingly of Christ's condescension, that he seems to grant all that Forrest (though not other kenoticists necessarily) requires. Thus in a sermon he says, 'Surely the trembling heart may cease to despair of itself, or regard the past with hopeless despondency, when that very Being, in whom all law and right are centred, who is Himself essential Holiness, identified in His very being with absolute Good, condescends to wed the nature of man, guilty and fallen though he be, into closest affinity with Himself'.[115] Caird, we said, *seems* to grant what Forrest requires; and certainly the idea of condescension is here. But still Caird's emphasis upon the divine-human continuity obscures the fact that it is only redeemed man who can be said to be in 'closest affinity' with God through Christ. Elsewhere Caird even uses the words we have just seen him criticize: he speaks of 'the world's great Creator' as 'concealed' in the 'humble guise' of the 'gentle-hearted and pitying Man of Nazareth'.[116] In the nature of the case, and given the mystery which we can never fully plumb, there can be no absolute 'knockouts' here. But we cannot resist the feeling that Forrest, taking account of the facts as he does, wins on points. We may also feel that what Forrest affirms as kenoticism would also be affirmed by Orr, and perhaps even by Bruce, so moderate was Forrest's kenoticism, and so biblical his understanding of kenosis.

One summary of Forrest's position on the person of Christ is as follows: 'The person was divine, but self-restrained within the limits of humanity; His thoughts *typically* those of a human mind, His resolves those of a human will. The Incarnate retained indeed His consciousness of Deity, knew Himself to be the Eternal Son, but never broke through the restrictions of human nature which He had voluntarily assumed'.[117] In this way Forrest attempts to avoid the substance-staticism and incipient dualism of Chalcedon, and to maintain the unity of Christ's consciousness.[118]

In the wake of fresh impetus towards the understanding of personality provided by Schleiermacher, and developed by later psychologists, B. B. Warfield protested, 'No Two Natures, no Incarnation; no Incarnation, no Christianity in any distinctive sense',[119] on which statement Sydney Cave remarked, 'That statement simply is not true. It is possible to believe in the Incarnation, and yet reject the explanation of it which the two-nature theory affords'.[120] We find ourselves occupying a position between these two worthies. Warfield seems to err in not allowing sufficiently for the dualistic pitfalls in the old terminology, and for the *unity* which Chalcedon sought to posit. Cave is mistaken in thinking that the two-nature theory is an explanation of anything. As Orr said, the terms of the sum are set down, but nothing is worked out. As we read Chalcedon we receive the overwhelming impression that we are in the realm of witness-bearing rather than of psychosomatic theory, or even of systematic theology. From another point of view, H. M. Relton sought to avoid the dualism of Chalcedon by going beyond Schleiermacher to the Greek emphasis upon the 'essential affinity between the Divine and the human natures'.[121] He recognizes the danger of blurring the creator/creature distinction, and might have mentioned the *imago dei* in support of his contention. But any approach of this kind needs to guard against the possibility of attenuating the doctrine of the atonement in such a way that deification, rather than redemption, becomes the matter in hand. When that happens we so often find that sin is something less than radical, and that Christ need not be much more than a teacher.[122]

Forrest is not always as careful as we should like him to be. On occasion (shades of neo-Hegelianism!) he comes near to blurring the creator–creation distinction: 'God and the soul are not merely related, they are one', he declares.[123] Again, when he says that we call God Father on the ground of our spiritual kinship with him.[124] we would more cautiously say that by virtue of our creation in his image we are aware of his claim upon us; but by virtue of his revelation in Christ we call him Father. Once again, we detect a neo-Hegelian reversion when Forrest writes of the corporate body of believers that 'In a true sense we may call the Church of the Extension of the Incarnation, not only because it is the human body in which the divine manifests itself, but because it is the true Christopher, the bearer through the Spirit of the incarnate risen One'.[125] We are by no means persuaded of the desirability of calling the Church the extension of the Incarnation, and this precisely because of the uniqueness of Christ (which Forrest elsewhere staunchly maintains) and because of the sinfulness of the Church. We do not deny that the risen Lord is present through the Spirit with his people. But to employ the category of Incarnation to make this point obscures more than it reveals, and can work towards the neglect of the doctrine of the atonement—and this in defiance of Forrest's own recommendation, that Christ's life and work are to be seen as all of a piece.

Of all the reviews of Forrest's work, Warfield's must surely be the most tendentious. Warfield classes Forrest with those who 'set their hearts on a merely human Christ'.[126] But this, as we have repeatedly seen, is precisely what Forrest does not do. Few emphasized more than he the difference between Christ and other men; to him Christ was the *real* man. Negatively, Forrest never hesitated to criticize adversely those who found in Jesus nothing more than an example: 'The peculiarity of His attitude', he said, 'is that it *cannot be imitated.* Here is a note we cannot sound. It is as if He said, I am first: there is no second'.[127] This emphasis upon Christ's uniqueness appears in many contexts in Forrest's work. He invokes it when countering that rather sentimental liberalism in theology whose ethical prescription consists in the address to oneself of the question, 'What would Jesus do?' It is not only, said Forrest, that times and circumstances have changed, with the result that we may not universalize from Jesus's own actions; it is that Jesus came to fulfil a unique mission, in regard to which we cannot even begin to emulate him.[128] We may distil *principles* of action from the Bible, and we have the guidance of the Spirit; and this suffices.

As for man's moral accountability before God, this was a theme to which Forrest continually returned. It was, he thought, 'the glory and mystery of human life; the deepest fact in it, which makes all men equal, prince and peasant, the most brilliant genius and the humblest labourer. Each of them has been put in charge of himself, and he has to answer for himself in the end'.[129] What is more, none may hide behind high-sounding talk of heredity in the attempt to evade such personal responsibility.[130] Forrest was in no way blind to the need to work out this responsibility socially, though he did not fall headlong for the Social Gospel. Indeed, he warned that 'We have a lively conviction of the duty we owe to our brother, but not such a clear perception of the duty we owe to God'.[131] Again, in a perceptive reading of The *Imitation of Christ* he criticized Thomas à Kempis for his preoccupation with the individual soul, and his neglect of social considerations;[132] and his long chapter on 'Christ's Authority on Corporate Duty; or Christianity and the State' in *The Authority of Christ* constitutes his attempt to achieve a proper balance between individual and corporate concerns.

Finally, to recall a point made in our biographical section, all Forrest's ethical teaching was given under the influence of a strong grasp of immortality. He makes much of the probationary character of this life. To think of life as merely educative is not enough: 'Are we not led often to treat this earthly life merely as an education, not as a probation at all—to lose the sense of the awful issues with which it is weighted?'[133] Of two things Forrest was absolutely certain: first, that although the conditions of life after death are not those of this present life, the life itself is continuous;[134] and secondly, that the final destinies of men will be determined along the lines of perfect justice and infinite mercy.[135] He does not go as far as the late John Baillie in speaking of those who believe in the bottom of their hearts if not with the top of their heads,[136] thereby seeming to make unbelief an impossibility. But he feels that the morality of the matter requires that the question of the destiny of unbelievers be left open in view of the universality of Christ's redeeming work for humanity, and the non-culpability of those who have not heard of Christ (however culpable the Church may be for not having told them!). Forrest was prepared to leave the issue in a tentative and hypothetical state: 'if any who hold other religious opinions are saved, it is not on the ground of these opinions or of their own good works, but solely because, as seen by God, they possess something of the same receptivity to the Spirit who proceedeth from the Father through the Son'.[137] What other position could be taken by one who held so firmly to the centrality of Christ?

CHAPTER NINE

James Denney (1856–1917):
A Preachable Theology

'Though it is my business to teach', wrote James Denney to his great friend William Robertson Nicoll, 'the one thing I covet is to be able to do the work of an evangelist, and that at all events is the work that needs to be done.'[1] A similar remark of Denney's was recalled by his colleague James Moffatt: 'I haven't the faintest interest in any theology which doesn't help us to evangelize'.[2] Certainly no theologian ever delighted to rehearse the gospel of the atoning death of Christ more than Denney. It occupied his major works; it runs through his sermons; it recurs time and again in his letters. Like John Caird, Denney was a man of one theme, and the two men are interesting because of the *difference* in their themes. Denney takes his stand on the atoning work of Christ as *the* answer to man's radically tragic condition, and views everything else from the perspective thus gained. Caird, as we saw, made the divine-human continuity his starting-point, with all that that entailed concerning the muffling of his deepest religious convictions.

Denney was born at Paisley on 5th February 1856, and spent his childhood at Greenock, to which town his parents moved when he was four months old. His father John Denney was a joiner by trade and a Reformed Presbyterian by conviction, and served as a deacon in his church. In 1876 parents and son, together with the majority of their co-religionists, united with the Free Church of Scotland. Denney was educated at the Highlanders' Academy, Greenock, under the disciplinarian William Bowie, and in the company of John Davidson the poet. In November 1874, after experience as a Sunday School teacher and as a clerk in Liddell and Brown's tug boat office, Denney proceeded to Glasgow University, where he excelled in classics under Professor (later Sir) Richard C. Jebb, of whom he wrote to J. P. Struthers 'If there is the faintest whiff of Christianity about the creature, he neutralizes it somehow or other with absolute success'.[3] He later contributed an appreciation to Jebb's biography. Denney's philosophical prowess was demonstrated when he won the Gold Medal in Edward Caird's class (while refusing to adopt the Master's philosophy) and in his assistance of the Professor of Logic, John Veitch. In 1897 Denney graduated with first class honours in Classics and Philosophy, and went on to the Glasgow Free Church College for his theological education and ministerial training. Here his teachers were James S. Candlish, A. B. Bruce and Thomas M. Lindsay.[4]

Nicoll suggests that Denney was most influenced by Bruce, and doubtless this is true. On 13th July 1915 he wrote to Mrs. H. M. Fellows: 'I too remember [Bruce] vividly, both as my teacher long ago and as a colleague for three years at a later date . . . if you spoke to him, he always answered as one who had put his mind to what he was talking about . . .'[5] At the same time, Denney's relentless honesty required him to say that 'Bruce's hatred of legalism is unmistakable, but though his moral sense is the very strength of him, I don't think he appreciates sufficiently the need in his theology of this safeguard against ἀνομία'.[6] In a letter to Struthers, his opinion of Bruce—not to mention the Gifford Trust—is further clarified: 'The Gifford Trust is really a gigantic abuse, and ought to be suppressed; but I hope Bruce will make something effective out of his two years. Bruce is not a philosopher, and he is not a scholar, but there is one thing he can do thoroughly well, and that is to speak about the beginnings of the Christian religion. It is the only subject on which he is an authority at first hand'.[7]

Denney completed his training in 1883, and sought appointment to the Free Church College, Calcutta. He failed in this, and became a Home Missionary in the east end of Glasgow under the auspices of Free St. John's whose minister was John Carroll. Two years later he published, anonymously, his first work. It was a critique of Henry Drummond's *Natural Law in the Spiritual World* by 'a brother of the natural man';—'not the character in which we knew him best', opined Robert Mackintosh.[8] Denney objected to Drummond's treatment of natural man, contending that wherever light and truth, love and righteousness were to be found, there was Christ, life, grace, and God. Drummond's book, he thought, was one 'that no lover of men will call religious and no student of theology scientific'. Two comments require to be made upon this early work. First, here we have Denney at his most 'liberal'. We shall have more to say on this point later; but for the present we must note that in 1886, the year of his ordination to Broughty Ferry as successor to Bruce, he married Mary Carmichael, daughter of John Brown of Glasgow. There appears to be some substance in the suggestion that it was she who drew Denney back to the older evangel. Among other things, she enticed him to read the sermons of C. H. Spurgeon, for which he developed a growing appreciation. Nicoll goes so far as to say that 'It was Spurgeon perhaps as much as anyone who led him to the great decision of his life—the decision to preach the Atoning Death of the Lord Jesus Christ'.[9] Secóndly, we should note that Denney's attitude towards Drummond subsequently mellowed as his appreciation of the importance of scientific enquiry increased. When his colleague J. Y. Simpson sent him a biography of Drummond he confessed in his letter of thanks that 'You make one who somehow never appreciated him fell how much he lost—I don't know how it was, but he and I seemed always to look at things through the opposite ends of the telescope, but I always *did* admire the *Ascent of Man* . . .'[10]

While at Broughty Ferry, Denney published the works which were to make his name as a scholar. Consistently with his quest of a preachable theology, these included commentaries which grew directly out of his pulpit work: *Thessalonians* (1892) and *II Corinthians* (1894). In 1891 his translation of Delitzsch's commentary on Isaiah appeared, and in 1894 his *Studies in Theology*. The *Studies* were based upon lectures delivered in April 1894 at Chicago Theological Seminary, on which occasion Denney was accompanied by his wife. As ever, his comments are revealing. He was struck by the 'total want of a natural connection between the Churches and the public life of the country . . . Here they are too Pietistic, or too Plymouthistic in spirit, though what *we* call Plymouthism is hardly known. There are many things strong which I dislike—Baptist principles, belief in the millenium, premillenial notions, and in general the fads of the uneducated and half-educated man'.[11] Denney felt, for all that, that he could do no other than allow himself to become the sixth man only to be awarded Chicago's D.D., and in the following year Glasgow University similarly honoured him,[12] Aberdeen subsequently following suit. In 1896 Denney published a more popular work, *Gospel Questions and Answers*, and soon he was found contributing articles and reviews to The *British Weekly* (edited by Nicoll), The *Expositor*, and The *Expository Times*.

Though happy in his pastorate, Denney answered the call of his Church to succeed Candlish as Professor of Systematic Theology at the Glasgow Free Church College. The election took place on 25th May 1897 during the General Assembly. Denney received 456 votes to John Macpherson's 76, and became the first alumnus of the College to be appointed to a Chair there.[13] Denney's quiet sternness was well known to lazy students, and his zeal for teaching was apparent to all. On his own testimony, 'whenever one is learning enough to be interested himself, he need have no anxiety about interesting his students'.[14] After Bruce's death, Denney moved to the Chair of New Testament Exegesis and Theology in 1899 and there he remained, despite a suggestion that on the reorganization of the College at the union of 1900 he should return to Systematic Theology. The year 1905 saw a further visit to America, and in 1909 he delivered a course of lectures at the Presbyterian College, Vancouver. In 1915 Denney was the sole nominee for the Principalship of the College in succession to Lindsay. Denney had thought highly of Lindsay as scholar, churchman and man,[15] and he had cordial relations with his other colleagues too. If he found Orr's *Sin as a Problem of Today* 'rather like the extempore speech of a well-equipped Parliamentary candidate who interrupts every sentence to give a slap . . . to some audacious person who has interrupted *him*';[16] he was under special obligation to Orr's *The Christian View of God and the World*.[17] We recall Denney's words when that doughty warrior died, 'he was a big man by the grace of nature and of the Gospel too, and his removal makes a great void'.[18] Of Moffatt, Denney said that 'I seem to have more interests in common with him than with any of my other colleagues';[19] and he spoke of Forrest (who, like Orr, had been an United Presbyterian) as 'my warm-hearted colleague, to whom I have become much attached'.[20]

On the question of theological education, Denney was anxious that the Church should retain control of its colleges,[21] and that those colleges should place ministerial training above academic education for its own sake.[22] He feared that much of the training given was 'doubly irrelevant: it is unsuitable for the men we get, and it is no preparation for their work'.[23] Although a considerable exegete himself, he was prepared to curtail, for some men, the linguistic aspects of the course—to the disapproval of James Iverach, who good-humouredly compared Denney's Aberdeen address on ministerial training 'to Chamberlain's fiscal speeches—the work of a person who is quite clear, quite sure that he is right, very plausible, but entirely, hopelessly, and, if he cannot be suppressed, fatally wrong'.[24]

Denney was in no doubt, however, that all ordinands should give thought to sermon construction: 'Gentlemen, the first thing in a sermon is lucidity; the second is lucidity; and the third is lucidity'.[25] He certainly took his own advice, and his sermons are models of expository preaching: 'I am very much dependent on my text, as a rule, and have spent much pains in trying to get students to treat their texts with proper respect, and to give them an innings in their sermons somewhere'.[26] Above all, the sermon should be 'not an exhibition of the preacher but of Jesus',[27] in which connection Moffatt recalled Denney's epigram: 'You can't, in preaching, produce at the same time the impression that you are clever and that Christ is wonderful'.[28]

Denney made his major contributions to scholarship while in Glasgow. In 1900 there appeared his *Romans* in *The Expositor's Greek Testament* series. In Nicoll's opinion this was perhaps the best piece of work he ever did.[29] Equally careful exegesis underlay his works on the person and work of Christ: *The Death of Christ* (1902); its sequel, *The Atonement and the Modern Mind* (1903), a series of lectures given at a summer school for the alumni of his College at Aberdeen; *Jesus and the Gospel* (1908); and the more historical (undelivered) Cunningham Lectures, *The Christian Doctrine of Reconciliation* (1917). A collection of Denney's sermons appeared in 1911 under the title, *The Way Everlasting*; his Drew Lecture on Immortality, *Factors of Faith in Immortality*, was published in the same year, and also in two parts in The *Expositor*; and his horror of war and his anti-pacifist stance found expression in *War and the Fear of God* (1916). *The Church and the Kingdom* (1910) was among his more popular works, and he contributed articles to Hastings's *Encyclopaedia of Religion and Ethics*, *Dictionary of the Bible*, and *Dictionary of Christ and the Gospels*.

There can be no doubt that the event which marked Denney more deeply than any other was the death of his wife in 1907. 'We had been married for more than twenty-one years', he wrote to Nicoll, 'and in all that time I hardly ever had a thought of which my wife was not part'.[30] He threw himself into his work, and in later years became increasingly known as a trusted ecclesiastical administrator. From 1901–6[31] he and Orr edited the *Union Magazine* (the successor of Orr's United Presbyterian magazine) of the United Free Church, but not even the transfer of its business affairs to Messrs. Hodder & Stoughton (at Nicoll's suggestion) and the articles of its editors could keep it in being.

More lastingly productive was Denney's growing zeal for church union. Not indeed that he loved largeness and legal corporations for their own sakes. On the contrary, on more than one occasion he expressed sympathy with the Congregational way: the Church, he held, is a spiritual fellowship.[32] As for the Establishment principle, in his earlier days he had vehemently attacked it. To his friend Struthers he wrote, 'I could be a Papist (provided I were Pope) or a Quaker, but not a nationalist in religion'.[33] J. A. Robertson recalls that at a conference at Inverness in 1904, following the decision by the House of Lords in the Free Church Case, Denney blamed '"establishment" for nearly all the worst troubles in the history of the Church'.[34] No doubt he never departed from his view that 'It is always dangerous when we call in the law . . . to defend the gospel',[35] but he could appreciate the importance of a change in the spiritual climate. Thus, he later wrote more sympathetically about union in an article entitled, 'The Constructive Task of Protestantism';[36] and at the same time he wrote to Nicoll 'That union with the Church of Scotland, though it seems to me a clear duty to attempt it, will strengthen the Church in the country, I do not see: what it needs is to be spiritually strengthened, not politically or financially, and meanwhile we seem to have lost contact with the source of power'.[37] True to his word, Denney spoke in favour of continued discussions with the Church of Scotland at the General Assembly of the United Free Church in 1914: 'He was sorry that, after all the years they had spent on that subject, there should still be some who apparently had not got beyond the barren logomachy of talking about establishment and disestablishment, who thought that by manipulating such abstract nouns they would be able to adjust a complicated historical question. . . . The main question before them was: How were two Churches such as theirs in the modern State, such as it was, to secure at once spiritual freedom and the national recognition of religion without prejudice to the interest or conscience of anyone?'[38]

By far the most outstanding piece of ecclesiastical service rendered by Denney was that as convener of his Church's Central Fund Committee, whose major responsibility was the collection of dues from which ministerial stipends were paid. He assumed his duties in 1913 and when, during the following year, Alexander Whyte expressed the hope that a book on Paul would be forthcoming from his pen, Denney replied, 'If I were free, I might try a chapter or two, but in the meantime I have left the Word of God to serve tables'.[39] On 10th March 1917 Nicoll wrote in some alarm to H. R. Mackintosh, 'We cannot afford to lose Denney. These next ten years should be his best. But I knew he was doing far too much in connection with the Central Fund'.[40] On 25th March Denney wrote what was to be his last letter to Nicoll. 'I have been a little astonished', said he, 'at the people who condoled with me on having to postpone the Cunningham Lectures. The things I *am* sore at being unable to help at are the Temperance Cause and the Central Fund.'[41] Two days later he wrote to his sister, informing her how relieved the Committee had been that he had agreed to accept the convenership for a further two years. 'But', he continued, 'unless there is a great and decisive change for the better in my health soon, I fear the "relief" will be a delusion.'[42] So, sadly, it proved to be. James Denney died on 11th June 1917 at the age of sixty-one. It was said that had he lived he would almost certainly have been called to his Church's highest office, that of Moderator of the General Assembly; and, with pardonable exaggeration, it was said that if Denney had lived to vote in his Assembly for union with the Church of Scotland, union would automatically have ensued. The funeral took place on Friday

15th June. The Reverend G. A. F. Knight, minister of the Kelvingrove Church, in which Denney had held office, conducted a service in the home; a public service in the College was conducted by D. W. Forrest, with Principal Iverach, Professors H. A. A. Kennedy and George Milligan, and Dr George Reith participating; and the burial service in Glasgow's Western Necropolis was conducted by Dr John S. Carroll and Professor H. R. Mackintosh. On the tombstone of Dr and Mrs Denney were inscribed the words, 'Because I live, ye shall live also'. The Minute of the College Committee includes the following words:

> The Committee feels that it is impossible to express adequately what the loss of Principal Denney means to our Church and Colleges, to the cause of theological learning, and to the life of our country. The withdrawal of a personality of such rich and gracious endowment, of a mind of such vigour and compass, and of a moral force of such mass and intensity, is an impoverishment that must fill every heart with mourning and dismay.[43]

It is unnecessary to catalogue all of Denney's many comments on the men and affairs of his day, but a random sample may help to further our understanding of him. A liberal in politics, he yet lamented Nicoll's advocacy of votes for women. 'I admit', he wrote, 'this is a subject on which I can get few to agree with me, and that my dear wife was, as her sister is, altogether on the wrong side'.[44] On the basis of a wide, non-sacerdotal understanding of ordination he was prepared to advocate the ordination of women to those duties within the Church to which they might be called; he did not, however, specify in detail what those duties might be, though he did suggest that Sunday School teachers, whether men or women, might well be ordained to their important function.[45] Denney was particularly exercized by the paucity of candidates for the ministry, even before the war. The three United Free Church Colleges received only thirty-seven new men in 1913, and 'the glaring reason which no one refers to—is that [men] are not becoming members of the Church at all'.[46]

Among the most memorable phrases of Denney are those concerning men, places and books. Thus, of the writings of Kierkegaard, a specimen of which he had contemplated translating (from the German), he said that 'with sober minds a little paradox goes a long way'.[47] On the eminent Principal Rainy's work on *The Ancient Catholic Church* he commented, 'He could not be uninteresting as long as he was actually awake. But occasionally, like Homer, he nods'.[48] As for J. G. Frazer, he wrote in disbelief to Nicoll: 'Do you expect me to read Frazer's book *through* before

I review it? I sympathize with Johnson: "One set of savages is very like another"'; and of the man he remarked, 'Surely no man ever had a mind so full of facts and so void of ideas'.[49] Denney's travels in America interested him, though he was not altogether at ease there. There is some reason to think that he would have been even less at home in Australia: 'By all one can hear of it, Australia seems to be about the most godless place under heaven'.[50] Any desire he might have had to visit the Holy Land was somewhat less than compelling: 'rightly or wrongly', he wrote, 'I have no interest in Palestine, and feel much more inclined to go to sleep for six weeks than to go anywhere'.[51] Finally, we may observe that it took more than a name to impress James Denney: 'The Cambridge History is a terrible book. It is like being shown through the Co-operative Stores. There is everything in it you want, and everything you don't want, and an impression from which you cannot get away that the whole thing comes short somehow of being first class'.[52]

Denney lived to serve and to proclaim the gospel. With his scholar's stoop, his close-fitting spectacles, his close-cropped hair and beard, and his reedy, high-pitched voice, he was not a commanding presence in the pulpit. Nor was he adept at those illustrations which are alleged to hold the attention of the flock—indeed, he confessed that his difficulty was that he could always see where illustrations broke down.[53] But if he lacked the more popular gifts, this only served to throw into relief the gospel—and that he had. He preached with passion. He was a modest man, who did not find it easy to reach common ground with his students, though their interests were very close to his heart. He did try to be approachable, however, even to the extent of making ungainly attempts to smoke cigarettes with his men. He revelled in Shakespeare; he loved the eighteenth-century wits; his enthusiasm for Burke and Johnson was unbounded. Traces of the style of the last named were in evidence in more than one Assembly speech which Denney delivered. But there was one area from which all levity had to be excluded. As he wrote to Struthers, 'if I had to lecture on the humour of the Bible I should soon be at my wits' end . . . Everything draws in it to Mount Sinai or Mount Calvary, and these are not places to be funny at'.[54] The Cross was his theme, and because of that many would have echoed the high praise of Alexander Whyte: 'I can honestly say that the writings of no living man restore me and reassure me more than yours nor so much'.[55] To these writings we now turn.

I

Denney confounds any who would too quickly label him. Was he a

conservative or a liberal in theology? The fact that from some points of
view each label aptly describes him is a witness to the slipperiness of the
matter.[56] What could sound more liberal than Denney's 1890 Assembly
intervention during the Dods-Bruce Case? He was reported as saying that
'for verbal inerrancy he cared not one straw, for it would be worth nothing
if it were there and it was not'.[57] During the 1891 Assembly he declared
that

> The Word of God infallibly carries God's power to save men's souls.
> That is the only kind of infallibility I believe in. Authority is not
> authorship. God attests what is in this book as His own, but God is not
> the author of it, in the sense in which a man is the author of the book
> he writes. To say so is meaningless.[58]

It is interesting in this connection to note that Denney re-wrote his
Chicago lecture on 'Holy Scripture' prior to publication, 'not with the
view of retracting or qualifying anything, but in order, as far as possible,
to obviate misconception, and secure a readier acceptance for what the
writer thinks true ideas on the authority of Scripture'.[59] His positive point
was that

> The Bible is, in the first instance, a means of grace; it is *the* means
> through which God communicates with man, making him known
> what is in His heart towards him . . . We cannot *first* define its
> qualities and *then* use it accordingly; we cannot start with its
> inspiration, and then discover its use for faith or practice. It is through
> an experience of its power that words like inspiration come to have any
> meaning.[60]

Certainly the Bible is not just like any other book. Indeed, 'When the
Bible is just another book, Christ is just another man'.[61] Once this is
admitted, responsible criticism can proceed, and to such criticism Denney
had no objection at all; but he had little patience with naturalistically-
inspired criticism, and in his crusade against such work the figure of
Schmiedel constantly loomed before him. Of his efforts Denney
expostulated, 'It is just Strauss over again, but without a spark of the wit
or genius'.[62] Nor did critics nearer to home escape unscathed. Of those
Anglicans who wrote *Essays and Reviews* he declared, 'It is too ridiculous
for men to write about the Christian religion from a great University,
when they really could not pass a good examination on the apostolic
texts'.[63]

Denney set out to help Christians 'face the kind of questions criticism
raises, and to *meet* them with the composure of intelligence, as well as the
assurance of faith'.[64] When he did this himself he concluded, 'liberally'

enough, that Genesis 1 is not science, and that Genesis 3 is not history;[65] but he 'conservatively' found the substitutionary theory of the atonement in the Bible (and, moreover, found it to be the basis of the unity of the New Testament to a degree that some scholars, then as now, would dispute) when many liberals were rejoicing that they had heard the last from responsible scholars of such an immoral notion. Denney sought to show that the authority of the Bible rested upon that to which it supremely testified: 'God's judgement and mercy to penitent souls. There can be no authority higher than that';[66] and he wished to defend the Bible from those who would make a Sadducean straitjacket out of it. Thus, for example, of the Sermon on the Mount he said that 'It would be a great point gained if people would only consider that it *was* a sermon, and was *preached*, not an *act* which was *passed*'.[67]

If the Bible could not be regarded as a straitjacket, nor *a fortiori* could creeds and confessions. In the preface to *Jesus and the Gospel*, Denney declared his hand: 'The Church must bind its members to the Christian attitude to Christ, but it has no right to bind them to anything besides'.[68] He was quite convinced that 'No person of ordinary intelligence and education could possibly accept in the twentieth century the intellectual statement of religion which suited the sixteenth or seventeenth'; and he welcomed the fact that 'our Church expressly gives those who sign its confession liberty to dissent from it on matters not entering into the substance of the Reformed faith'.[69] We know how treacherous John Kennedy thought *that* kind of attitude was; but Denney was unrepentant, and was prepared to take the consequence that the answers given in any age to the great questions can be provisional only. Further, the answers may be revised, 'not because He changes . . . but because men change in their apprehension of Him'.[70] There is, moreover, a proper place for agnosticism in religion. Mansel rightly appreciated this, though he erred in giving the impression that agnosticism was the principle of religion;[71] and as he began to prepare for his professorial work, Denney wrote to Struthers, 'Dogmatic seems to be a fine thing for producing dubiety: I mean to leave plenty of room in my "course" for agnosticism. "Canst *thou* by searching find out God?" It is too ridiculous'.[72]

Although Denney could not but think that the requirement of credal subscription was prejudicial to the creeds themselves, he was not averse to devising a formula on the basis of which he thought all Christians could unite. He felt strongly that the metaphysical and doctrinal interests underlying older creeds and confessions (not excluding the Westminster Confession) militated against their usefulness in the sphere of present *religion*. They seemed to operate at one remove from the believer's faith.

Hence, 'What we want as a basis of union is not something simpler, of the same kind as the creeds and confessions in our hands; it is something of a radically different kind'.[73] Of course, our attitude to Christ is related to certain convictions about him, but faith comes first, and 'though there is one faith there is not one Christology'.[74] Jesus's vitally important question was 'Who say ye that I am? not, How think ye that I came to be? No doubt the two questions must be related somehow, but happily it is possible to answer the first, by assuming the Christian attitude to Christ, while the other remains in abeyance; and all that is urged here is that this ought to be recognized in the confession of the Church'.[75]

Denney's own suggestion for a symbol of the Church's unity was, 'I believe in God through Jesus Christ His only Son, our Lord and Saviour'.[76] To the objection that there is no reference here to the Holy Spirit, Denney replied that the New Testament nowhere speaks of the believer as having faith in the Holy Spirit; and he noted that the historic creeds betray 'a certain degree of embarrassment' in their treatment of the Holy Spirit.[77] Even granting the latter point, however, we feel that Denney could have devised a more satisfactory statement. As for the New Testament, it undoubtedly teaches that it is *by* the Holy Spirit that our Christian experience comes, and our desire to make any kind of Christian testimony arises. The truth seems to be that it is *Denney* who is a little embarrassed by the Holy Spirit (to whom he consistently refers as 'it'); and there is some justice in the charge that in his last book he so identified the Spirit with the risen and present Christ as to land in binitarianism.[78] On the other hand, Denney could offer a perfectly proper exposition of Romans 8:15f., which includes the claim that 'The Spirit beareth witness with our spirit, that we are the children of God'. Said Denney, 'Our own spirit tells us we are God's children, but the voice with which it speaks is, as we know, prompted and inspired by the Divine Spirit itself'.[79] All the more strange therefore that Denney did not begin his symbol of unity with the words, 'By the Holy Spirit I believe . . .'

To any who might complain of the indefiniteness of his symbol, and say that Arian and Athanasian alike might adopt it, Denney replied, 'The differences which we associate with the names Arian and Athanasian are differences which emerge in another region than that in which we confess our faith in Christ . . . and *all* such differences, where the Christian attitude to Christ is maintained . . . must be dealt with by other means than excommunication. Arianism and Athanasianism both give answers to a question which multitudes of genuine Christians never ask'.[80] Finally, if any found the resurrection and the atonement conspicuous by their absence from his suggested affirmation, Denney would reply that the former is accounted for in the term 'Lord', the latter in 'Saviour'. His attitude may be summed up by a saying of his recalled by Moffatt: 'The Church's Confession of faith should be sung, not signed'.[81]

For all his 'liberalism' Denney was determined to adhere to the central realities ('real' was a favourite word of his). This entailed focussing upon Christ and defending the reliability of the biblical witness to him. The religion, as ever, preceded the scholarship. This order of priorities determined his methodology, and made him suspicious of idealism and ambivalent towards Ritschlianism.

Christ is central: 'Christianity may exist without any speculative Christology, but it never has existed and never can exist without faith in a living Saviour'.[82] The burden of *Jesus and the Gospel* is that the New Testament writers are unanimous in this testimony, and that they took their cue from Jesus himself. Jesus

> stands over-against the world, and He knows that He has what all men need, and has it in such fulness that all men can obtain it from Him. This is the ultimate proof of his divinity, this is the infallible sign that He is Saviour: He can do for men, and for all men, what all men need to have done, He can give to men, and to all men, what all men need to receive; in His company, misgivings die, for He is the Author of perfection, of eternal life, to those who receive Him. There were men present when Jesus spoke who could certify that that was so.[83]

It follows that 'Faith is not the acceptance of a legal arrangement; it is the abandonment of the soul, which has no hope but in the Saviour, to the Saviour who has taken its responsibilities on Himself, and is able to bear it through'.[84] In a word, 'The final faith in God owes its *differentia* . . . to Him. The God in whom the Christian believes is the God who is Father of our Lord Jesus Christ, the God who gave Him up for us all, who raised Him from the dead and gave Him glory, and who has called us to this eternal glory in Him'.[85] Jesus was not, then, given his unique place by the New Testament writers; it *was* his place, and then they wrote about it. Indeed, 'To be a Christian means, in one aspect of it, to take Christ at His own estimate',[86] and he was more than satisfied, after the most careful enquiry, that we have a reliable account of what that estimate was. It is not enough to be able to satisfy ourselves that this event and that actually took place. The *meanings* of Jesus and of the New Testament writers are part of the case. Nor should we ever forget that 'The primary testimony of the disciples to Jesus was their testimony to His resurrection: except as Risen and Exalted they never preached Jesus at all. It was His Resurrection and Exaltation which made Him Lord and Christ . . . The real historical evidence for the resurrection is the fact that it was believed, preached, propagated, and produced its fruit and effect in the new phenomenon of the Christian Church, long before any of our gospels was written . . . Not one of them would ever have been written but for that faith'.[87] Christ did not (*pace* some of Denney's liberal contemporaries) simply rise in the hearts of his disciples; the Cross *per se* gave no grounds for any such resurrection. The resurrection was preached as a *gospel*, and it had real moral power issuing in exuberant, corporate Christian life. Hence, 'The resurrection is not attested in the gospels by outside witnesses who had inquired into it as the Psychical Research Society inquires into ghost stories; it is attested—in the only way in which it can be attested at all—by people who are within the circle of realities to which it belongs . . .'[88] All of which can only mean that 'the historical Christ is more than historical: it is as present and eternal that He invokes repentance and faith in the soul, and asserts His abiding and essential place in the spiritual life. This . . . is the *datum* of Christianity; and the man who disregards it is really not speaking of Christianity, but of something quite different'.[89]

Denney viewed all else from the vantage-point of God's revelation in Christ and far from being averse to the quest of a coherent world view, he maintained that '*All* that man knows—of God and of the world—must be capable of being constructed into one coherent intellectual whole'.[90] In fact, 'if [the theologian] is not to stultify his reason by living two or three separate lives, he must combine and harmonize in his theology all his knowledge and experience, physical, metaphysical, historical, and religious'.[91] Yet some of the greatest Christian thinkers have failed methodologically. Thus, for example, whereas Denney can say that Anselm's *Cur Deus Homo?* is 'the truest and greatest book on the Atonement that has ever been written' because it portrays so vividly the difference sin makes to *God*, concerning Anselm's method as a whole he had grave reservations:

For him, as for all Christians in his time, there was only one dogma, that of the incarnation of the God-man . . . The title of his famous work, *Cur Deus Homo?* . . . intimates that what he is in quest of is the rationale of Christianity itself. If he can answer his question, he has rationalized the Christian religion and raised to the level of science the dogma which was accepted by faith on the authority of the Church . . . The argument that he is going to conduct, though it is all about Christ, does not owe anything to Christ. It is to be as convincing to Jews and pagans as to Christians . . . This is not attractive or convincing to the modern reader. We are not interested in what can be said in defence of Christianity *remoto Christo* or *quasi nihil sciatur de*

Christo; we do not believe that Christ and all that the Church believes about Him . . . can be deduced by a necessary process of reasoning from any premises whatsoever, just as we do not believe that history is a subject for deductive reasoning at all. History is a datum . . . Nevertheless, Anselm was a great Christian, and in answering the question *Cur Deus Homo?* he wrote a great book. Put briefly, the answer to the question is that God became man because only thus could sin be dealt with for man's salvation, and God's end in the creation of man secured. In other words, the rationale of the incarnation is in the atonement.[92]

To repeat, 'it is the historical Christ to whom we have to go back as the true fountain of our theology'.[93] If our opponents cannot find the historical Christ, still less the supra-historical Christ, this is because their presuppositions will not permit them to do so. In that event, 'though it is vain to controvert such a dogma by argument, it may be demolished by collision with facts'.[94] In other words, 'Without professing or feeling any undue sympathy with the Paley or Old Bailey school of apologetics, we may surely have our doubts as to whether the testimony of the first witnesses can be so easily disposed of'.[95]

The reference to Paley prompts us to note Denney's opinion of traditional theistic reasoning. He is quite clear that 'No religion ever took its origin in such reasoning . . . The being and the personality of God, so far as there is any religious interest in them, are not to be *proved* by arguments, they are to be *experienced* . . .'[96] This is not to say that the theistic arguments are valueless, for 'they do interpret, more or less adequately, impressions made on the human mind by God and His works . . . To pooh-pooh them because they never made anybody religious is unintelligent; what is really claimed for them is that there is a truth of God *in* them, especially in their combination . . .'[97] (The last phrase is reminiscent of Flint). This concession notwithstanding, Denney is much more in the tradition of Bruce-like Bible-based apologetics than he is in the line of eighteenth-century theists.

Nor, again, is he in much danger of succumbing to the allurements of post-Kantian, and especially of neo-Hegelian, idealism. His emphasis upon the historical saves him here: 'Our sound course is, not to say no matter what come of the facts the Christian faith is secure, but to point out the entire security of the facts on which that faith reposes'.[98] Hence his alarm at Schmiedel's position: 'What do you think of this from Schmiedel? "The inmost religious good which I possess would not be injured at all if I had to admit the conviction today that Jesus never lived . . ." . . . How it is to be cured I do not see, but the number of people who are on the slope that ends here, and who suppose that they are Christians while it is all the same to them if Christ had never lived, is appalling'.[99] The underlying difficulty posed by idealism is that 'it assumes certain relations between the human and the divine, relations which foreclose the very questions which the Atonement compels us to raise. To be brief, it teaches the essential unity of God and man . . . On such a system there is no room for atonement in the sense of the mediation of God's forgiveness through Jesus Christ. We may consistently speak in it of a man being reconciled to himself, or even reconciled to his sins, but not, so far as I can understand, of his being reconciled to God, and still less, reconciled to God through the death of His Son'.[100] Denney appreciated the motive of those who wished to spare faith from the hostilities of historical criticism, but the remedy was worse than the disease; 'we must take care that the desire to put Christianity on a basis independent of history, a basis beyond the reach of historical doubt, does not lead us to withdraw from under it the only basis on which it has ever been sustained'.[101] Again, Denney did not deny that there was a sense of the ultimate unity of the natural and the spiritual running through the Bible itself;[102] but it was not a unity bought at the price of the historical. On the contrary, the unity of the historical and the eternal 'is the very stamp and seal of the Christian religion'.[103] He could even appreciate pantheism's grain of truth concerning the fundamental dependence of all things on God.[104] But there was one point at which he called 'Halt!' Pantheizing philosophies all too easily blurred the distinction between right and wrong, and the assertion of this distinction is quite as important as the assertion of underlying unity.[105] J. A. Robertson recalled Denney as saying that 'The difference between right and wrong is real and ultimate: Christ *died* for the difference between right and wrong'.[106] Denney went so far as to think that the idealism of Henry Jones, his friend of college days, was a potent factor in diverting some men from both Church and gospel.[107] This comment should, however, be read in the light of Denney's fluctuating attitude towards philosophy. On one occasion he could say. 'Philosophers used to be our botheration, now it is economists, but they all have souls above parsing.'[108]

As we have seen, Denney did not emphasize the historical in isolation. Indeed, 'The only thing to be trusted is experience', he said.[109] God speaks through the Word *to us*; he acts in Christ *for us*. Thus far, and also in his belief that the paramount blessing of the gospel is reconciliation, he is at one with Ritschl.[110] The Ritschlians valuably send us back to Christ as our starting-point, and their ethico-historical emphasis is to be applauded and welcomed. But Denney could not swallow Ritschl whole.

Nor need we; but it must be confessed that some of Denney's early criticisms of the German were violently expressed and unsupported.[111] Accordingly, and in order to avoid the tedium of raking over dead ashes, we shall select Denney's criticisms which seem to have more permanent validity.

Consistent with his attitude towards the theistic proofs is Denney's complaint that Ritschl unduly pressed the distinction between religion and metaphysics. However convenient it may appear to be to say that the theologian examines religion, and the scientist nature, and that since they never meet they can never collide, 'it is a superficial platitude all the same. The theologian cannot think of God and leave out of sight the fact that the nature with which the scientific man is busy is constituted by God and dependent on Him; and one would hope that the scientific man also, living not only in nature but above it, and as its interpreter, would feel the need of defining the relation of nature as a whole to the spiritual power which can be recognized both in it and in himself'.[112]

Further, Denney regretted the Ritschlian tendency to sit lightly to the transcendent and the supernatural. He found Harnack, for example, quite inconsistent in that having confined miracles to the realm of faith, he sought to erect Christianity on assured historical facts—most of which he found permanently dubious![113] In Denney's opinion, 'When we define the supernatural only in a religious way, and refuse to form a conception of it in relation to nature or history, the practical result is that we surrender it altogether'.[114]

With more zeal than charity (or even accuracy) Denney rather indiscriminately trounced Ritschl and his disciples for having eliminated the Resurrection, and therefore for having no room for the exalted Christ or for eschatology.[115] He did, however, find value in Ritschl's understanding of Christ as the fulfiller of a vocation, though he felt that Ritschl had an inadequate understanding of the nature of that vocation. Ritschl's Christ is too much one who, in fulfilling his own destiny, fulfils ours also. Denney would, with Forrest, emphasize that which Christ had to do, but which we could never do precisely because his needs were *not* ours: 'Christ bears our sins; *that* is the very soul of His vocation . . . Unto Him be glory for ever.'[116] But with the mention of Christ's work we come to the heart of Denney's theology.

II

Christ is like no other religious leader. He makes claims for himself which no other makes; he requires obedience; he fulfils, and where necessary abrogates, the old Law. He was not *a* son of the Father, but *the* Son, who 'intimated to those who were able to understand it His consciousness of being head of a new, universal, and everlasting kingdom, in which all that was truly and characteristically human should have authority'.[117] Negatively 'He was *not* one thing which we all are; He was *not* a sinner'.[118] Far from being implicated in sin, he is the Judge of sinners—and their Saviour too.[119] Here, once more, is the point which idealism cannot allow for. If we see Christ in the light of his own self-consciousness, the 'speculative theorem' concerning 'the essential unity of the human and the divine' may be seen as 'a formal and delusive platitude'.[120]

Like Forrest, Denney held that 'The formula of two natures in one person does not adequately reproduce the impression which He makes. He is all one—that is the very strongest conviction we have . . .'[121] But unlike Forrest, Denney was not favourably disposed towards kenoticism: 'This idea impresses the imagination and touches the heart rather than aids the intelligence'.[122] At the heart of Denney's christology, and against that of Harnack *et al.*, is the claim that 'The Christ of faith was the Jesus of history'.[123] With Orr he insists that the supernatural cannot be expunged. Rather, it is supremely fitting. 'It is in harmony with that unique relation to God and man which is of the essence of His consciousness, that there should be something unique in the mode of His entrance into the world as well as in that of His leaving it.'[124] In no sense, then, do we share the faith *of* Jesus; rather, with the apostles,[125] we believe in God *through* him. With Paul behind him, Denney proclaims that 'Christ is the whole of Christianity—Christ crucified and risen'.[126]

Like Paul, Denney had no time for speculation for its own sake. Paul met God in Christ, and even in Colossians 'He is not directly deifying Christ, he is Christianizing the universe'.[127] Similarly, in the prologue to John's Gospel 'There is not . . . a single word which betrays a purely speculative interest, such as we find, for example, in Philo'.[128] But was Denney perhaps *too* unspeculative? In a letter to Denney, Nicoll said that he had searched *Jesus and the Gospel* in vain for an unequivocal statement to the effect that Jesus is God.[129] Denney replied:

> I feel inclined to say that such a statement seems unattractive to me just because it is impossible to make it unequivocal. It is not the true way to say a true thing. I think I have made it plain that for me to worship Jesus as God is worshipped, to trust Him as God is trusted, to owe to Him what we can owe to God alone, is the essence of Christianity . . . Jesus is man as well as God, in some way therefore both less and more than God.[130]

However the question as to Christ's nature is to be settled, we know him through what he does. It is, in fact, 'the doctrine of the Atonement which secures for Christ His place in the gospel, and which makes it inevitable that we should have a Christology.'[131] Christ bestows eternal life upon us—life which depends upon the propitiation for our sins which he alone could make, and has done once for all. The very unity of the New Testament consists in its consistent witness to the revelation of God's redeeming love to men in Christ. Central to this revelation is the death of him who is yet alive for evermore. The death of Christ was by no means an isolated event: however allusively, it was part and parcel of his earthly ministry from his baptism onwards: 'from the very beginning of His public work the sense of something tragic in His destiny . . . was present to the mind of Jesus'.[132] After Peter's confession at Caesarea Philippi, Jesus began to refer explicitly to his death, thereby acquainting his disciples with the unfamiliar idea of a *suffering* Messiah. When, after the resurrection, the full import of his words came home to them, 'The centre of gravity in their world changed . . . Their inspiration came from what had once alarmed, grieved, discomfited them. The word they preached was the very thing which had once made them afraid to speak'.[133] They came to see that the life of Christ had been sacrificially and victoriously laid down; and they came to experience the reality of life under the new covenant, a life entered by baptism, and of which the Lord's Supper was the sign and seal: 'The sacraments, but especially the sacrament of the Supper, are the stronghold of the New Testament doctrine concerning the death of Christ'.[134]

Christ is the propitiation for our sins; and to any who would cavil at the word, Denney replies that 'propitiation is merely a mode of mediation, a mode of it no doubt which brings home to us acutely what we owe to the Mediator, and makes us feel that though forgiveness is free to us it does not cost nothing to Him . . . The Christian faith is a specific form of dependence on God, and to cavil at the atonement is to begin the process of giving it away in bits.'[135] In any case, 'His death, and His bearing of our sins, are not two things, but one'.[136] Nor can the word 'substitution' be avoided. There is 'an incalculable motive power' in the fact of the obligation under which we stand to Christ.[137] *God* does *this* for *us*—and in the process he absorbs and vanquishes sin's cosmic consequences. This is an objective, finished work; and if any should baulk at the cost of redemption, or think it immoral of God to require the death of his sinless Son, we must remind them that 'There can be no gospel unless there is such a thing as a righteousness of God for the ungodly. But just as little can there be any gospel unless the integrity of God's character be maintained'.[138] The Son is not divorced from the Father at the Cross. Rather, atonement 'is the Father's way of making it possible for the sinful to have fellowship with Him . . . The words of the revival hymn, "Jesus paid it all, All to Him I owe", have the root of the matter in them'.[139] When we are claimed by God's righteous love we die to sin and to the flesh, and we are no longer under the curse of the Law. This is the testimony supremely of Paul and John; and it is all the result of the death of Christ.

So much for a summary statement of Denney's position. It will help to make it clearer if we further elucidate the terms 'sin', 'forgiveness', and 'repentance'. Of all the biblical writers it was Paul who exercized the greatest influence upon Denney's understanding of sin. To appreciate Paul fully, said Denney, we require not historical scholarship, or the insight of genius, but despair.[140] 'What is the serious element in sin?' he asks:

> Is it man's distrust of God? man's dislike, suspicion, alienation? Is it the special direction of vice in human nature, or its debilitating corrupting effects? It is none of these things, nor is it all of them together. What makes the situation serious, what necessitates a gospel, is that the world, in virtue of its sin, lies under the condemnation of God . . . The thing that has to be dealt with, that has to be overcome, in the work of reconciliation, is not man's distrust of God, but God's condemnation of man.[141]

It cannot be otherwise, for 'sin, as a disturbance of the personal relations between God and man, is a violence done to the constitution under which God and man form one moral community . . .'[142] This disturbance calls forth, or rather (since God is righteous) it requires, the revelation of God's wrath. The reality of the sinner's plight is that he is under that wrath.[143] Any other conclusion is 'practical atheism', for it is to deny that whereas 'Our responsibility *is* our own . . . it is a responsibility *to God*'.[144] God can, however, initiate remedial action, and he has done so in Christ. He gives his Son as the propitiation for our sins, and thereby 'justice is done not only to the grace of God but to His wrath—to that solemn reaction of God against all ungodliness and unrighteousness of men from which the apostle sets out in the exposition of his gospel (Romans 1:18).'[145] Denney underlines the contrast between this teaching and that of Socinianisers: 'God is love' say Socinianisers in every age, 'and therefore He dispenses with propitiation; God is love, say the apostles, for He provides a propitiation.'[146]

Against this background we can see why Denney, with the fourth evangelist, emphasizes the fact that at the heart of the gospel is forgiveness;[147] but we must always remember that 'Forgiveness is not impossible, nor is it a matter of course; it is a miracle'.[148] Furthermore, it is costly, and it is inextricably linked with the death of Christ:

> it is possible for God to forgive, but possible for God only through a supreme revelation of His love, made at infinite cost, and doing justice to the uttermost to those inviolable relations in which alone . . . man can participate in eternal life, the life of God Himself—doing justice to them as relations in which there is an inexorable divine reaction against sin, finally expressing itself in death. It is possible on these terms, and it becomes actual as sinful men open their hearts in penitence and faith to this marvellous revelation, and abandon their sinful life unreservedly to the love of God in Christ who died for them.[149]

This abandonment is of the essence of repentance. Denney put his point well in a letter to P. Carnegie Simpson:

> Except as an element in the whole process of 'turning to God,' sorrow for sin—or even change of mind, one might add—does not amount to repentance. We do not get the chance of being sorry or not being sorry—we are made sorry for our sins without being consulted; but we do get the chance of returning, or refusing to return, to God. I remember a saying of Mrs. Booth's apropos of the Prodigal Son, to this effect: 'It was not repentance when he grew hungry, nor when he remembered his father's house, nor even when he said, 'I will arise and go to my father'; you see repentance where it is said, 'he arose and came to his father'.[150]

We must never be trapped into thinking that repentance is our work; nor must we deny the gracious, unconditional freedom of the gospel by suggesting that the propitiation is for those who are sufficiently penitent.[151]

We come now to three matters concerning which questions have been raised by Denney's critics. Some have been exercized by his emphasis upon the death of Christ. This concern has taken a number of forms: First, there are those who argue that Denney too closely associates the ideas of sin and death. Thus for example T. H. Hughes remarks that, as Paul put it, 'God passed over and winked at' the death originally predicted in Genesis;[152] and Robert Mackintosh draws attention to the *other* things Paul says about death—above all, that the 'last enemy' is vanquished, and that death is gain.[153] Concerning the former point Denney would probably reply that it is not his intention to take Genesis 3 as literal history, and to Mackintosh he might reply that Paul's words in context have to do with *believers*, and that this makes all the difference. Certainly, and contrary to what Mackintosh seems to imply,[154] Denney does not take sin to be the cause of physical death. This is clear in all three of his books on the atonement. His positive point is that biological death is a (legitimate) abstraction, useful for certain purposes, but that 'when we come to speak of man, who is a spiritual being, there is no such thing as merely physical death'.[155]

Secondly, some have objected that Denney reverts to a forensic doctrine of penal substitution. It cannot be denied that Denney's mature statement on this matter is ambivalent:

> while the agony and the Passion were not penal in the sense of coming upon Jesus through a bad conscience, or making Him the personal object of divine wrath, they were penal in the sense that in that dark hour He had to realize to the full the divine reaction against sin in the race in which He was incorporated, and that without doing so to the uttermost He could not have been the Redeemer of that race from sin, or the Reconciler of sinful men to God.[156]

It is difficult to see how the last part of this statement has any penal reference at all unless, against Denney's intention, we introduce such quasi-quantitative notions as imputation—more than once Denney protested against such 'bookkeeping' as was involved in the notion of the transfer of merit.[157] Professor Paterson came nearest the mark when he said,

> The truth is that Dr Denney, while refusing to admit the distinction between the fact and the theory of the Atonement, made a laborious search for a satisfactory theory of the *modus operandi* of Christ's sacrifice in procuring the boon of reconciliation, found none which he could adopt in its entirety, and ended by proclaiming that no theory showed so deep spiritual insight as that of MacLeod Campbell, which even Prof. A. B. Bruce had spoken of most disrespectfully, and which had been combated by Crawford and Hodge as a fantastic and pernicious novelty.[158]

Justice demands the qualification, however, that what Denney found helpful in Campbell was his grasp of the fact that atonement mattered from the point of view of God's holiness, as well as of man's need; he did not endorse the idea of vicarious repentance on the part of the sinless Son of God.[159]

A further motive behind Denney's substitutionary theory of the atonement was his conviction that subjectivist, Abelardian theories will not suffice. Thus, for example, he asks,

Who is Rashdall, who gives the Ritschlian appreciation of Anselm and
Abelard in the shape of a Univ. Serm. in *Expositor*? I think that *line* of
interpretation has been taken as far as it will go now . . . and that it is
time to rediscover the fact that the Apostles in their doctrine of
atonement were dealing with something which never comes within
Rashdall's (nor Ritschl's) view—namely, God's condemnation of sin as
a terrifically real and serious thing . . . A martyrdom in plain English,
no matter how holy and loving the martyr, is an irrelevance . . . There
is a fascinating way of presenting Abelardism, but as a fisher-
evangelist, a friend of mine, once said to me, to preach it is like fishing
with a barbless hook: your bait is taken, but you don't catch men.[160]

Such strictures notwithstanding, Denney did, as Robert Mackintosh
realized, come dangerously near to 'moral influence' psychologism when
referring to the realization of reconciliation in human life:[161] 'The new life
springs out of the sense of debt to Christ. The regenerating power of
forgiveness depends upon its cost: it is the knowledge that we have been
bought *with a price* which makes us cease to be our own, and live for Him
who so dearly bought us.'[162] Elsewhere, in connection with worship, he
says, 'what our circumstances require is not a prophetic, but an evangelic
criticism of the prevalent worship . . . a manifestation of what God has
done for us in Christ, so true and appealing that souls will kindle under it
to adoring reverence and love'.[163] What is missing here is a reference to
the work of God the Holy Spirit.[164]

Thirdly, some have complained that Denney emphasized the atonement
at the expense of the incarnation and the resurrection. J. K. Mozley, for
example, was of this opinion.[165] Now Denney in no way wished to deny
that throughout his earthly ministry Jesus was about the business of
reconciliation;[166] he affirmed the absolute necessity of the resurrection;[167]
but he insisted on the centrality of Christ's death: otherwise, he thought,
we land via neo-Hegelian immanentism in a mystico-metaphysical rather
than a moral union of God with sinful men. There must be 'no
sublimation of Christianity into "ethical" or "spiritual principles", or into
"eternal facts", which absolve us from all obligation to a Saviour who came
in blood. Except through the historical, there is no Christianity at all, but
neither is there any Christianity till the historical has been spiritually
comprehended'.[168] Any other position, he was convinced, entailed the
shifting of the centre of gravity of the New Testament. By the same
token, as we saw earlier, he objected to James Orr's assertion that creation
is built on redemption lines, as blurring the distinction between nature
and grace, and hence as making our understanding of Christ's work
vaguer than it need be.[169] Some, including H. R. Mackintosh, felt that

Denney had found greater unanimity in the New Testament writers than was actually there;[170] but Denney never modified his view, supported by exegesis of a high order, that however many differences of emphasis there might be between the writers of the New Testament (and he *did* allow for such differences), it remained true that 'In regarding Jesus as Redeemer at the cost of His life, as well as Revealer of God, the consciousness of the New Testament Christian corresponds to the consciousness of the Christ Himself'.[171]

So much for Denney's emphasis upon the death of Christ *per se*. Some of his critics have objected that even if what he says about the death of Christ is true, he externalizes the doctrine to such an extent that he cannot give due place to Paul's doctrine of the mystical union of the believer with Christ. In a nutshell, Denney's reply is (as we might expect) that we must not assert the mystical union in any way which would make that relation seem inevitable, and the cross redundant; and further, that any true union with Christ is a union of *believers* with him. And believers stand where they do only by reason of the atonement wrought at Calvary. He is anxious to guard against the inversion of the gospel, and in particular wishes to make plain the pitfall into which those tumble who think of Christ more as a representative than as a substitute. Christ is *not* put forward by man on man's behalf; he is given by God to do that for man which man could never do for himself. Paul's Adam, indeed, is a 'hypothetical abstraction', and Paul knew Christ and what he was able to do for men independently of speculations concerning Adam: 'Paul's Adam is simply the abstraction of human nature, personified and placed with a determining power at the beginning of human history. Such a figure has no reality for our minds, and I own it seems to me a hopeless task to seek the key to the work of Christ in the assumed "racial" action of this hypothetical entity.'[172]

This last remark was made in the course of a controversy with the Primitive Methodist scholar A. S. Peake, who contended that 'if we place ourselves at Paul's point of view, we shall see that to the eye of God the death of Christ presents itself less as an act which Christ does for the race than as an act which the race does in Christ.'[173] Denney pulls no punches:

This is presented to us as something profound, a recognition of the mystical depths in Paul's teaching: I own I can see nothing profound in it except a profound misapprehension of the apostle . . . the fundamental fact of the situation is that . . . Christ is *not* ours, and we are *not* one with Him . . . To speak of Christ as our representative, in the sense that His death is to God less an act which He does for the race than an act which the race does in Him, is in principle to deny the whole grace of the gospel, and to rob it of every particle of its motive power.[174]

Denney later came to tone down his statements on this matter, as when he interpreted Paul as teaching that Christ the Second Adam absorbs and sums up the mass of humanity.[175] 'That', commented the Anglican scholar Sanday, 'is not mysticism, but it shows the approach made towards mysticism by a mind to which it is not naturally congenial'.[176] Denney did deny that the New Testament speaks of union with Christ; but this union 'is not a presupposition of Christ's work, which enables us to escape all the moral problems raised by the idea of a substitutionary atonement; it is not a presupposition of Christ's work, it is its fruit'.[177] But still not all of Denney's friends could understand him at this point. Nicoll remained convinced that Denney laid insufficient emphasis upon the notion of union, and Denney explained that the union which really mattered was moral rather than mystical, though for the believer he thought the two kinds of union were identical.[178] 'I cannot understand', said Denney, 'the man who thinks it more profound to identify himself with Christ and share in the work of redeeming the world, than to abandon himself to Christ and share in the world's experience of being redeemed. And I am very sure that in the New Testament the last is first and fundamental'.[179]

Our final question is, 'Did Denney's position change radically with the passage of the years; if so, in what respects—and were any changes there may have been for the better or the worse?' C. Wistar Hodge, of Princeton, was more certain than any other critic we have read that Denney's position did undergo radical and damaging modifications.[180] Hodge finds a progressive watering-down of the satisfaction doctrine of the atonement, and a slackening of grip upon such ideas as wrath and imputation, coupled with slighting comments upon the terms 'forensic' and 'legal'. The upshot is that Christ can only make salvation possible, he cannot actually save sinners. In a word, Denney combines the positions of Grotius and McLeod Campbell. All Christ had to do was to *understand* in sympathetic fashion the plight of sinners, and to realize what sin means to God. This reduction of the truth, says Hodge, results from the fact that Denney has no adequate conception of God's justice as a divine attribute; and this deficiency is the consequence of Denney's undermining of the authority of scripture. He approaches the Bible with premises analogous to those of dogmatic rationalism, except that he sets out from Christian experience rather than from the principles of reason.

For our part we do not find that Denney ever departed from the idea of satisfaction, though we have earlier expressed concurrence with Professor

Paterson that his position on the *penal* question was never entirely satisfactory. But the question arises, 'Can the human mind ever produce an entirely satisfactory statement regarding the atonement?' With commendable reticence, those who framed the ancient creeds never attempted to do so. But more important than any hesitation of Denney's on this point is his repudiation of those 'bookkeeping' theories of the atonement which suggested that God could not be loving and merciful *until* the price was paid.

We cannot here pursue Hodge's criticism of Denney's doctrine of scripture, though we find ourselves more in sympathy with the latter's position (as earlier stated) than with the former.[181] But we cannot pass over Hodge's complaint that Denney held an inadequate view of the justice of God, or that he underemphasized the wrath of God in his later years. It is true, as more than one critic has observed, that Denney gives greater place to love in his later, mellower writings, but this is a gain. For example, in his posthumously-published work he writes, 'The last reality is . . . a love which submits to all that sin can do, yet does not deny itself, but loves the sinful through it all'.[182] But in the same volume he holds love and justice very closely together: 'In the divine nature justice and mercy do not need to be composed, they have never fallen out'.[183]

For ourselves, we detect a greater emphasis upon the resurrection and upon the exalted Christ in works from *The Atonement and the Modern Mind* (1903) and this is welcome. We remain uneasy, however, about the less-than-generous attention paid by Denney at crucial points to the Holy Spirit of God. On the main issue, though, we are persuaded that Denney had the pearl of price, and as far as we can see he had it at least from the time of his marriage. Unlike some writers, Denney's doctrine of the atonement was nicely balanced between the objective and subjective aspects of Christ's work (not indeed that Denney liked those adjectives).[184] The atonement has a value for God in that it satisfies his just wrath; and its value for man is clearly that it is the means of his salvation.

It is the satisfaction of divine necessities, and it has value not only for us, but for God . . . It is because divine necessities have had homage done to them by Christ, that the way is open for sinners to return to God through Him. When they are forgiven, it is *propter Christum* as well as *gratuito*: it is not by unconditional love—an expression to which no meaning can be attached which does not obliterate the distinction between right and wrong—but a love the very nature of which is that it does absolute homage to the whole being and self-revelation of God, and especially to the inexorable reactions of the divine nature against sin'.[185]

So it comes about that 'To an unsophisticated Christian, to talk of a redemption to which the death of Christ is not essential is to talk about nothing at all. The simplest evangelist here will always confound the subtlest theologian: the foolishness of God is wiser than men'.[186] Of course it is a *living* Lord in whom the Christian believes, 'but he believes in a living Lord who died an atoning death, for no other can hold the faith of a soul under the doom of sin'.[187]

Of Denney's last book, Alexander Whyte wrote that 'No old book, however true and powerful, will speak to preacher and hearer in our days as Dr Denney's *Reconciliation* will speak'.[188] We may well imagine that Denney would have welcomed that comment; for though he lived by teaching, he lived to preach:

> The proclamation of the finished work of Christ is not good advice, it is good news: good news that means immeasurable joy for those who welcome it, irreparable loss for those who reject it, infinite and urgent responsibility for all.[189]

CHAPTER TEN

Epilogue

Of John Caird, Professor John Dickie wrote, 'I am too firmly convinced that "it has not pleased God to effect the salvation of His people by dialectics" to discuss him profitably'.[1] It is not for us to say that we have discussed any of our eight divines *profitably*; but we have found it interesting to study those who bolster our own convictions, and exciting to probe the presuppositions of those from whose views we dissent. We have sought in the first place to *listen* to our selected thinkers, and as far as possible, we have allowed them to speak for themselves. (This is not only right in principle but useful, given that some of the works in question are becoming increasingly scarce.) Having listened, we have challenged when we could no longer keep silent.

On occasion our divines have exasperated us; sometimes they have puzzled us; quite frequently they have fed us; but they have always stimulated us. This last point is underlined by the fact that they all raise questions which are, or ought to be, on theology's current agenda.

Thus, Kennedy invites us to consider the question, 'How plastic may theology be, and what is it that must be conserved if the gospel is faithfully to be proclaimed from age to age?' That there is something to be conserved would seem to be beyond doubt. Kennedy is right to emphasize both the continuity of need between sinners of one generation and another, and the constancy and 'once-for-allness' of God's gracious provision to meet that need. But then further questions are raised: 'How are we to distinguish between new interpretations of the "faith once delivered to the saints" and the peddling of "other gospels"?' On the one hand, to rule out the possibility of new interpretations would seem to imply a defective understanding of the work of God the Holy Spirit, who guides the people of God into ever fresh realizations of the truth of the gospel. On the other hand, as P. T. Forsyth wrote, 'There must surely be in every positive religion some point where it may so change as to lose its identity and become another religion'.[2] Could it be, for example, that what Forsyth warned against has happened in some modern Anglo-Saxon theology which, setting out from the incarnation conceived in immanentist terms as making for continuity with the teachings of other faiths (and this at the expense of atonement doctrine), have arrived at gnosticism which has cut Christianity loose from history and turned Christ into an idea?[3] This, we suggested, was the direction in which John Caird's methodology, though not his actual Christian convictions, led him.

As we face such issues, we cannot escape the ecumenical ramifications of the discussion. In this connection the issue may be encapsulated thus: 'What is tradition, and what are we to make of it?' Roman Catholics, as is well known, have a view on this, together with a supportive understanding of doctrinal development (variously construed). What is quite clear is that latter-day Kennedys can no longer suppose that the appeal to 'scripture alone' is altogether 'un-traditional', or that in paying deference to specific confessional statements they are acting in an ahistorical void. Indeed, when Kennedy complained that 'not a few of the latest accessions to the ministry' were showing more respect for the 'errant Germans' than for 'the doctrines of the Confession of Faith, and for the accredited systems of Calvinist theology' he was clearly making an appeal to tradition—the tradition of which he happened to approve. We might even note in his remark a tendency to elevate a subordinate standard above the gospel—to do which is, on his own terms, surely verging on the blasphemous.

A further question posed by Kennedy is that concerning the establishment of religion. He articulated a traditional, anti-voluntary view at a time when the debate was raging. By no stretch of the imagination can the establishment question be said to be a live issue at present. It may, however, be suggested that it is a matter to which ecumenical theologians might well pay some attention. It is not simply that the ecclesiastical world gives evidence of different varieties of establishment (Anglican in England, Presbyterian in Scotland, Lutheran in Scandinavia, Reformed in some, but not all, of the Swiss cantons), it is that establishment raises a fundamental ecclesiological question: 'How is Christ's lordship over the Church to be given full sway?', and question basic to the faith: 'Who is a Christian? Does one become a Christian by being born in a parish, by being baptized as an infant, by being born again, by making a profession of faith and becoming an enrolled saint? What are we to make of folk religion on the one side and Christian exclusivism on the other?' That such questions cannot be answered without reference to pastoral considerations is abundantly clear.[4]

The question of a viable natural theology, which the study of Flint's work raises, has been very much on the philosophico-theological agenda during the years which separate us from him. It would not be untrue to say that this question has inspired a philosophical cottage industry! But the particular issue which both Flint and Orr bequeath us is, 'Which philosophico-theological method will adequately meet a situation in which a generally subscribed theism can no longer be assumed?' Again, in somewhat different ways, both Flint and Orr prompt us to reflect on the nature and extent of common ground between believer and unbeliever.[5] What are the epistemological implications of revelation? Is it permissible, for example, to claim to know that x is true in the absence of the only kind of demonstration which would satisfy an out-and-out empiricist (let us hope so!)?

Forsyth's fear that a religion may so change as to become a different religion leads us to the perennial question raised by the work of John Caird: 'How far ought a philosophical ism, however enticing, to influence our presentation of the Christian faith?' Our shorthand answer to this question[6] is that while encounter with the thought-forms of the day is an inescapable obligation upon the theologian if he is, positively, to communicate his insights and, negatively, to shun the security of the theological ghetto (and even the ecumenical ghetto—a sublime contradiction in terms!), everything turns upon the manner in which he proceeds; for it is possible so to attenuate the gospel by subjecting it to 'alien' categories as to distort it. Caird is one among many who illustrate the truth that unless the thought of the age is viewed in the light of the gospel viewed as historically rooted in a gracious, redemptive act, 'ideas' can all too easily take over, to the detriment of Christian proclamation. The immanentist tendency was peculiarly attractive to many theologians in the heyday of philosophical idealism, for it provided, as they thought, a bridge of continuity on which Christian truth could be traded. Of all the writers we have considered, none was more patient in exposing the pitfalls of this approach than Iverach, none more insistent than Forrest, and none blunter than Denney. On the same point Forsyth was his usual pungent self: 'Christianity is what it is in the spiritual region by its *peculium* and not by its *continuum*, by confronting other creeds not prolonging them, by the distinctive thing in it and not by what it shares supremely with other beliefs'.[7] From the fact that 'confronting' is not a 'good word' in contemporary inter-faith dialogue we may not necessarily conclude that there is nothing worthy of discussion in the position of our elders.

Turning now to our trio of apologists, Bruce, Iverach and Orr, we find that they exhibit procedural and temperamental similarities and contrasts; and that each leaves us with still more questions for theology's present-day agenda.

While Bruce's manner was anti-oracular (and *therefore*, some said, unduly hesitant), Iverach had no inhibitions about taking his opponents by the scruff of the neck—'pulverizing' was his word. If Bruce declared that to do battle against dogmatic unbelief was futile, Iverach never ceased to urge upon opponents the consideration that in rejecting Christianity they were behaving *irrationally*. Bruce made more than the other two of the fact that there are babes in the faith who are not yet adapted to strong dogmatic meat, while Orr insisted that Christianity had a *content* which can and must be discerned and given systematic expression. Whereas, to Bruce, the scriptures were witnesses rather than authorities, to Orr the Bible was more authoritative in the broadly conservative sense than it was to any other of our divines except Kennedy. This, no doubt, explains the fact that Orr has (in some circles at least) worn better than any of the others. In the middle years of this century, before the considerable resurgence of conservative biblical and theological scholarship which more recent decades have witnessed, Orr was for many an anchor in the storm. Indeed his name still receives honourable mention—and that not only in footnotes, and despite the fact that some modern exponents of biblical inerrancy have found him unduly concessive on that issue, as we saw.

Bruce would have us consider, 'How far is it necessary, possible, desirable, to perpetuate the distinction between natural and revealed theology?', a distinction which he, like Forrest, was concerned to obliterate. Again, now that Bruce's view that 'Patripassianism is not wholly a heresy' has gained currency in some contemporary quarters, we may ask afresh how adequate is his christological starting-point in the humiliation of Christ? Yet again, how do Bruce's strictures against Lutheran christology appear after the passage of a hundred years of water under both Lutheran and Reformed bridges; and how useful is the idea of kenosis in healing any remaining breach? Finally, may not Bruce's insistence that 'Orthodoxy will not save the Church' bear examination in relation to those faith-and-order documents which insist variously that bishops, synods, creeds and confessions guard, defend, or preserve the Church? Do they do this? Can they do this? And where in all of this is God the Holy Spirit?

In pointing out that 'the concern of science is with the force itself and its way of working, and not with the origin and cause of it', Iverach helped to establish an approach in the debate on the relations between science and Christianity which remains viable to this day. He valuably distinguished between evolution conceived as a way of accounting for change, and evolution (wrongly) construed as a theory of origins. This distinction is by no means irrelevant to the arguments over creation which still rumble—and on occasion even rage—in some (mostly American) quarters.

Iverach was pre-eminently the frontiersman among our divines. His calling and talent was to stand at the frontier between science and faith. Where are the analogous frontiers in our time? Are they between faith and political theory, social theory, economic theory, counselling theory? All of these come to mind. What are the untoward, tacitly held or even unrecognized presuppositions which need to be exposed? Is there any 'pulverizing' to be done?

Orr engaged with the thought of his day on a broader front than did either Bruce or Iverach. He continues to challenge us to discern and state Christianity's content, and to face the question, 'Is it true that apart from the supernatural there is no gospel and hence no Christianity?' Orr's answer to this question was an unqualified affirmative, as was P. T. Forsyth's. As we have elsewhere said, 'the gospel is and must be supernatural in at least two ways. First, its provision is not from nature, and least of all from man. Secondly, it has to restore nature—especially man's'.[8] Again, as our 'James Orr meets John Hick' paragraph demonstrated, Orr has a contribution to make to the continuing discussion of the worth of the Chalcedonian Formula.

D. W. Forrest poses two challenges to contemporary theology, in the first of which he is joined by Denney. First, he is opposed to gnosticisms ancient and modern which would idealize Christ off the stage of history. He stands by the essential accuracy of the gospel records, declaring (in the line of Butler) that the evidence must properly be weighed. It is no secret that both before and since Forrest's day, some New Testament scholars have cast grave doubts upon the historicity of the gospel records; further, some systematic theologians have erected theological edifices on shaky exegetical foundations, thereby scandalizing those of their biblical colleagues who are given to reading systematic treatises. Clearly there is still important work to be done here, and this is not the place to do it. Suffice it to record our own conviction concerning the heart of the faith (which was first Paul's) that if Christ be not raised our faith is vain. This is not perversely to say that since it is a requirement of faith that Christ be raised he must have been raised! It is not to reduce the *meaning* of the resurrection to the statement 'On such and such a day x, who was dead, came to life and left the tomb'. It is, however, to claim that without the basis of an actual historical event we are reduced to appealing to 'the intuitions of the disciples of all ages' or to some sort of existential encounter *now*, and that neither of these by themselves will suffice.

Secondly, Forrest's restrained and non-speculative kenoticism, when viewed in relation to his suggestive defence of the Nicene Creed, may well have a contribution to make to those theological conversations in which ecumenical theologians—especially those engaged in dialogue with Orthodox churchmen—are currently engaged.

Both Forrest and still more Denney challenge modern theology to hold the incarnation and the atonement together. Against theologians (especially idealistic ones) who would begin elsewhere, Denney declares that it is 'the doctrine of the Atonement which secures for Christ His place in the gospel, and which makes it inevitable that we should have a Christology or a doctrine of His Person'. With this we profoundly agree. For while it is true that Christ can do what he does because he is who he is, it is nevertheless true that 'The doctrine of the Incarnation grew upon the Church out of its experience of Atonement'.[9]

'How are the churches to confess the gospel today? How far and along what lines may a satisfactory Christian world view be articulated?' These are among other questions which Denney poses to contemporary Christian thought. The former is receiving considerable attention in ecumenical circles, and Denney's views deserve consideration in this context. The latter is not perhaps receiving sufficient attention from Christian philosophers of religion. For too long many have persuaded themselves (following, consciously or otherwise, C. D. Broad in 1924[10]) that the time is not ripe for synthesis. Accordingly they have assumed the 'humbler' analytical role of ground-clearing. We may be forgiven for suspecting that by now some of the ground has been cleared so many times that erosion has set in.

Both because of the questions they press upon us, and because of the guidance we have found them to offer at a number of crucial points, we may justifiably conclude that while our eight divines have been neglected, they have not altogether been outgrown.

Notes

CHAPTER ONE:
INTRODUCTION

1. For further brief elucidation see A. P. F. Sell, *The Great Debate: Calvinism, Arminianism and Salvation*, Worthing: H. E. Walter 1982 and Grand Rapids: Baker Book House 1983, pp. 91–93. For more detailed discussion of Erskine and Campbell see John B. Logan, 'Thomas Erskine of Linlathan, lay theologian of the "inner light"', *The Scottish Journal of Theology* XXXVII 1984, pp. 23–40; Donald Campbell (ed.), *Memorials of John McLeod Campbell*, London: Macmillan 1877; John Macquarrie, 'John McLeod Campbell,' *The Expository Times* LXXIII 1972, pp. 236–238; J. B. Torrance, 'The contribution of McLeod Campbell to Scottish theology,' *The Scottish Journal of Theology* XXVI, 1973, pp. 295–311. Erskine and Campbell are in *DNB*.
2. For the biblical scholars A. B. Davidson, William Robertson Smith and George Adam Smith see Richard Allan Riesen, *Criticism and Faith in Late Victorian Scotland*, Lanham, MD: University Press of America 1985. For our study of 'The rise and reception of modern biblical criticism' see A. P. F. Sell, *Theology in Turmoil: The roots, course and significance of the conservative-liberal debate in modern theology*, Grand Rapids: Baker Book House 1986, ch. II.
3. For Fairbairn see W. B. Selbie, *The Life of Andrew Martin Fairbairn*, London: Hodder & Stoughton 1914; A. P. F. Sell, 'An Englishman, an Irishman and a Scotsman . . .' (i.e. W. B. Pope, Robert Watts and A. M. Fairbairn), *The Scottish Journal of Theology* XXXVIII 1985, pp. 41–83. For 'Writings related to P. T. Forsyth' see Donald G. Miller, Browne Barr and Robert S. Paul, *P. T. Forsyth, The Man, The Preacher's Theologian, Prophet for the Twentieth Century*, Pittsburgh: The Pickwick Press 1981, pp. 93–106. Charles S. Duthie (1911–1981), to whom the book just mentioned is dedicated, was a more recent 'exile'. Fairbairn is in *DNB*.
4. For Simon see F. J. Powicke, *David Worthington Simon*, London: Hodder & Stoughton 1912. Simon was Principal of the Congregational Theological Hall, Edinburgh, 1884–1893. He was succeeded there by J. M. Hodgson, who served from 1894–1917, and he by A. J. Grieve, who served from 1917–21. For Grieve see C. E. Surman, *Alexander James Grieve*, Manchester: Lancashire Independent College 1953. More recent temporary sojourners from England have included Harry Francis Lovell Cocks (1894–1983), Principal of the Scottish Congregational College, 1937–1941.
5. See further A. P. F. Sell, 'The peril of reductionism in Christian thought,' *The Scottish Journal of Theology* XXVII 1974, pp. 48–64.

CHAPTER TWO:
JOHN KENNEDY OF DINGWALL (1819–1884):
THE OLD PATHS

1. J. Kennedy, *The Present Cast and Tendency of Religious Thought and Feeling in Scotland* (Edinburgh: Hunter 1902), 18. This volume comprises eight articles contributed to the *Perthshire Courier*, 4.2.1879 to 1.4.1879.
2. John Noble, 'Memoir of the Rev. John Kennedy, D.D.', prefixed to the latter's *The Days of the Fathers in Ross-shire* (5th edn. Inverness: *Northern Chronicle* Office 1897) cxlix; (reprinted by Christian Focus Publications, Inverness, 1979).
3. John Macleod, *Scottish Theology in Relation to Church History since the Reformation* (Edinburgh: Free Church of Scotland 1943) 327; (repr. Banner of Truth, Edinburgh 1974).
4. Kennedy wrote a sketch of his father entitled, 'The Minister of Killearnan'. See *The Days of the Fathers in Ross-shire*, 165–267. For Kennedy himself see *DNB*; Alexander Auld, *Life of John Kennedy* (London: Nelson, 1887); *In Memoriam Rev. John Kennedy, D.D., of Dingwall*, Inverness: *Northern Chronicle* Office, 1884; J. Noble, *op.cit.*, xxix– clxi. *The Days of the Fathers*, 5th edn. also includes a memoir of Mrs. Kennedy by John Kennedy of Caticol. Auld's *Life* is interspersed with extracts from Kennedy's diary entitled 'Annotationes Quotidiandae'; it includes tributes to his usefulness; a number of his letters; and to it are appended notes of some of his sermons and addresses. For a sketch of the history of Killearn Free Church see *The Monthly Record of the Free Church of Scotland*, November 1969, 219–220. A full account of Kennedy's funeral is given in *In Memoriam*. We are informed, *inter alia*, that a special train brought mourners from Inverness, and that on the day of the funeral the boats in Inverness harbour flew their flags at half mast. The volume also contains a sketch of Kennedy's life, a list of his publications, twenty pulpit tributes, the memorial minute of the Dingwall Free Church Presbytery, eight press opinions, and an elegy. See further the centenary reappraisals of John Kennedy: Hugh Cartwright, 'Dr. John Kennedy,' *The Monthly Record of the Free Church of Scotland,* October 1983, 210–12; ibid., 'Our fathers, where are they?' (editorial), May 1984, 99–101; and G. N. M. Collins, *An Orchard of Pomegranates* (London: Pickering & Inglis, n.d.), 159–167.
5. While at Assynt Kennedy senior encountered Norman Macleod, who is charged by John Kennedy with separatist tendencies and sundry extravagances. See *The Days of the Fathers*, 200–201, and John Macleod, *By-Paths of Highland Church History* (Edinburgh: Knox Press, 1965), ch. xii. For N. Macleod's lively riposte see the latter, ch. xiii.
6. For a sketch of the history of Dingwall Free Church see the F.C. *Monthly Record*, March 1970, 47–48.
7. Though such was the esteem in which Kennedy was held by the directors of the railway company that they would reserve a coach for his use.
8. For Ferintosh Free Church see the F.C. *Monthly Record*, December 1970, 244. Macdonald (12.2.1779–18.4.1849) is in *DNB*. Therein his predecessor at Ferintosh is given as 'Caldwell'. He was, in fact, Charles Calder.
9. Kennedy, *The Present Cast and Tendency*, 9, 10.
10. For Robert Mackintosh see A. P. F. Sell, *Robert Mackintosh: Theologian of Integrity* (Bern: Peter Lang 1977).
11. So J. Noble, 'Memoir', cxxxi.
12. Kennedy, *The Days of the Fathers*, 110. The first class of unworthy 'professors'

indicates an important distinction which may be drawn between the best of the Men and the North Country separatists, of whom the best known was Alexander Gair. For separatism see J. Macleod, op. cit., chs viii–xiii. See also Alexander Auld, *Ministers and Men in the Far North* (1869; 2nd edn. Edinburgh: Menzies 1891).

13. *The Days of the Fathers*, 37.For Fraser see A. P. F. Sell, 'John Locke's Highland critic,' *Records of Scottish Church History Society*, forthcoming.

14. Ibid. 52–53. Charles Calder was one of three brothers, all of whom became ministers. The diary of his father, James Calder of Croy, was republished as no. 130 of *The Banner of Truth*, July–August 1974. Robert Mackintosh (see n. 10 above) was among his descendants.

15. Ibid. 77.

16. Ibid. 84. In the preface to the first edition of this work, Kennedy said of the Ross-Shire fathers that he could not 'refrain from an effort, such as I could make, to revive their memory, and to turn the eye of a backsliding generation to their good old ways'. We may note two further biographies by Kennedy: those of the Rev. Dr Mackintosh McKay, Dunoon, and the Rev. Donald Sage, Resolis. These were contributed to Wylie's *Disruption Worthies of the Highlands* (ed. J. B. Gillies) Edinburgh, (Edinburgh: Jack, 1881).

17. In this section a mere Englishman has the feeling of walking through a minefield. The fact that Kennedy had his views on English cricket does not entirely justify our bravado! But something must be said if Kennedy's stand, and the ecclesiastical background of all our divines, are to be understood. The following are among the standard works on the subject: William Mackelvie, *Annals and Statistics of the United Presbyterian Church* (Edinburgh: Oliphant, 1873); Andrew Thomson, *Historical Sketch of the Origin of the Secession Church*, and Gavin Struthers, *History of the Rise of the Relief Church* (Edinburgh: Fullarton, 1848); Peter Bayne, *The Free Church of Scotland* (2nd edn. Edinburgh, 1894); G. N. M. Collins, *The Heritage of Our Fathers* (Edinburgh: Knox Press, 1974); Thomas Brown *Annals of the Disruption* (Edinburgh: Macniven and Wallace, 1893); A. McPherson (ed.), *History of the Free Presbyterian Church of Scotland, 1893–1970*, F. P. Church, 1974; James Barr, *The United Free Church of Scotland* (London: Allenson, 1934).

18. The word *some* is important in two ways. Not only were some Free Church ministers, Kennedy among them, untouched by such fellowship on principle; but in many areas, notably in the highlands, Free Church and United Presbyterian ministers were not geographically close enough to have made fellowship possible even if it were desired.

19. J. Kennedy, *Unionism and the Union* (Dingwall: Ross 1870, 1900), 21. The reprinting of this tract was occasioned by the impending union with the United Presbyterians. Cf. a speech by Kennedy on 'The Union Question', delivered at Inverness, and reprinted from the *Inverness Courier* as Free Church Tract No. 3.

20. J. Kennedy, *Unionism and its Last Phase* (Edinburgh: Grant, 1873), 5. Hugh Martin was another prominent opponent of mutual eligibility. See his *Mutual Eligibility. Two Letters to Robert Buchanan, D.D., and Sir Henry W. Moncrieff, D.D., Bart.* (Edinburgh: Edmonston & Douglas, 1872). Buchanan's speech to the Presbytery of Glasgow was published: *The Mutual Eligibility Overture Shown to be in Full Agreement with the Laws and Constitution of The Free Church of Scotland* (Edinburgh: Greig, 1872). Kennedy declined to agree, as his *Reply to the Ten* (Free Church Tract, New Series, no. 6) shows: 'We love our Church, because we believe her constitution was moulded according to the will of Christ. We believe that He so formed it as to exclude from her communion all who are avowed Voluntaries, all whose views indicate a deviation from the

Calvinistic doctrine of the Atonement, and all who would impair the simplicity of Presbyterian worship' (4, 5).

21. Ibid.
22. P. Carnegie Simpson took the contrary view. See his *The Life of Principal Rainy* (London: Hodder & Stoughton, popular edn., n.d.) I, 159–161. In Free Church Tract no. 9 on *The Union Question*, n.d., Kennedy wrote, 'We did not expect, before 1863, that some of the leaders in the Union movement would have declared in our Assembly that the doctrine of Establishments was outside of the Confession . . .' (4).
23. *Unionism and its Last Phase*, 10. Not a type of argument that Kennedy would approve of in relation to the Bible!
24. *The Present Cast and Tendency*, 21.
25. Ibid. 35.
26. Quoted by P. Carnegie Simpson, op. cit. i, 258.
27. D. Ogilvy, *The Present Importance of Free Church Principles; or, Disestablishment the Necessary Sequel of the Disruption* (Edinburgh. Maclaren & Macniven, 1875) 31. On 8 December 1874 Rainy addressed a public meeting in Edinburgh and his speech was immediately published: *Disestablishment in Scotland, considered from the Point of View of the Free Church*.
28. See John Adam, *Shall we Return to the Establishment? A Question for Free Churchmen* (Glasgow: Bryce, 1874).
29. See R. Buchanan, *The Established Church and the Free: In What do they Differ?* This drew an anonymous reply: *An Answer to Dr. Buchanan's Speech in Moving his Overture in the Free Church Presbytery of Glasgow, on 1st April 1874, on The Principles and Position of the Free Church* (Glasgow: Maclehose, 1874).
30. J. Kennedy, *The Distinctive Principles and Present Position and Duty of the Free Church* (Edinburgh: Grant, 1875), 27.
31. J. Kennedy, *The Establishment Principle and the Disestablishment Movement* (Edinburgh: Gemmell, n.d.), 32.
32. Ibid. 57.
33. J. Kennedy, *The Disestablishment Movement in the Free Church* (Edinburgh: Gemmell, 1882), 28. This pamphlet was quoted in translation from its Gaelic version in support of the Free Presbyterian case that *they* truly continue the witness of the Disruption Church. See the *Free Presbyterian Magazine*, vi (1901), 158. Kennedy enumerated the advantages of an Established Church in *The Present Cast and Tendency*, 47–48.
34. *The Present Cast and Tendency*, 46.
35. For James Begg (1808–1883) see *DNB*. P. Carnegie Simpson traced one letter only (in fact addressed to himself), in which Rainy was severe against an opponent. That opponent was Begg: 'Begg was the evil genius of the Free Church. He introduced a policy of conspiracy and of attempting to carry points by threatening us with law. No man did more to lower the tone of the Church and to secularize it', *op. cit.* ii, 50. Kennedy conducted Begg's memorial service on 7th October 1883. His sermon on Isaiah 52:1, afterwards printed, was entitled 'The Death of the Righteous, as a Gain, and as a Warning'. The sermon includes a tribute to Begg; but for a more homely description by 'Wan o' the Hielan' Host' (i.e. Kennedy) see *A Purteeklar Acoont o' the Last Assembly* (Edinburgh, 1881), 13: 'Then there wus oor ould freend Dr Beg, an when he rose he planted himsel so staidy on his ouwn two feets, wi' a hed acordin' to his name, an' his hair like Samson's afore that Phullusteen jade got ut kut off. Och, but ye can understan him, an' ye can hear him murover wi'oot pittin ye hans ahint yer lugs . . .'

36. J. Kennedy, *Hyper-Evangelism 'Another Gospel', Though a Mighty Power* (Edinburgh: Grant, 1874), 26. That issues of this kind are still alive to Free Churchmen may be seen e.g. from an article by Angus Smith on 'Evangelism' in the *Monthly Record of the Free Church of Scotland*, Jan. 1979, 16–17. Mr. Smith argues that 'It would be most foolish of us as a church to forget what it cost us before we were able, at last, to throw off the shackles of instrumental music and uninspired hymns'.

37. *The Present Cast and Tendency*, 57. Cf. his *Expository Lectures*, ed. J. K. Cameron (Inverness: Northern Counties Newspaper Co., 1911), 193–9.

38. *Unionism and its Last Phase*, 18.

39. *The Present Cast and Tendency*, 51.

40. Ibid. 53.

41. Quoted by A. Auld, *Life* of Kennedy, 175. For the wider context of this debate see A. P. F. Sell, *Theology in Turmoil. The roots, course and significance of the conservative-liberal debate in modern theology* (Grand Rapids: Baker Book House, 1986), ch. II. See also H. F. Henderson, *The Religious Controversies of Scotland* (Edinburgh: T. & T. Clark, 1905), ch. ix. Smith is in *DNB*.

42. It should be pointed out that although Smith could not identify the *words* of the Bible with the Word of God, he was not an anti-supernaturalist.

43. Quoted by J. Macleod, *Scottish Theology*, 310.

44. *The Present Cast and Tendency*, 39.

45. Ibid. 39–40.

46. Ibid, 44.

47. J. Kennedy, *The Doctrine of Inspiration in the Confession of Faith* (Edinburgh: Free Church Publications, n.d.), 11, 23.

48. Quoted in Auld, op. cit. 121; cf. 323–7.

49. See H. Bonar, *The Old Gospel: Not 'Another Gospel', but The Power of God unto Salvation* (Edinburgh: Elliot, 1874). Kennedy countered these charges in his *Reply* published in the following year. Bonar had sided with Kennedy in opposition to union with the United Presbyterian Church. It is worthy of note that Kennedy's father 'did not regard with much hopefulness or pleasure' the religious awakening which came about shortly before his death in 1841: 'He expected but little permanent fruit as its result, and was much pained by the countenance given, in the excitement of that time, to manifest delusions!' See *The Days of the Fathers*, 254.

50. See *Hyper-Evangelism*, 8.

51. Ibid. 20.

52. Ibid. 22.

53. *The Present Cast and Tendency*, 12; cf. *Expository Lectures*, 156.

54. J. Noble, 'Memoir', *op. cit.* clii n. Noble incorrectly gives the text as Isaiah xlii. Cf. *Expository Lectures*, 91.

55. J. Kennedy, *The Apostle of the North* (London: Nelson, 1866) 331. Principal Macleod's edn. of this book has been republished by Free Presbyterian Publications, Glasgow, 1978.

56. The practice of labelling theologians is fraught with peril. Thus in half a sentence Professor John Kent places Kennedy as 'a hyper-Calvinist leader in the Highlands, who disputed Moody's offer of free salvation as obstinately as a minority English Calvinist like J. K. Popham of Liverpool was to do a little later.' See his *Holding the Fort. Studies in Victorian Revivalism* (London: Epworth, 1978), 137. In the absence of a definition of 'hyper-Calvinism' Professor Kent's point remains unclear. We would make three points in reply. (1) Kennedy was *not* inhibited in offering the gospel. In

his *Reply* to Bonar he wrote (p. 38): 'Because I will not ignore the sovereignty of God, and the necesity of conviction of sin through the law, in order to shut sinners up to the faith of the gospel, and of spiritual illumination and renewal in order to the reception of Christ, it is imagined that the gospel which I preach cannot be free. These are the things on which I have insisted, and on the ground of which I am called a Hyper-Calvinist . . . the task is easy, to show that I could not adhere to the Westminster Confession if these were not my views'. So much for theory. Of Kennedy's practice the Rev. Archibald Beaton, Urray, wrote, 'His moving appeals to the unconverted were often overpowering . . . Often in the midst, or at the close, of his discourse he would suddenly swoop down upon them, and in a few well chosen and weighty sentences he would utterly demolish the excuses men make for not accepting the great salvation'. See *In Memoriam*, 54–55. (2) Kennedy's complaint against (the unnamed) Moody was that the latter's 'free' gospel was one which suited the sinner's disposition only, and not his state: in particular, 'law work' was neglected. In similar vein he charged Bonar with anomianism. Bonar denied the charge. (3) On the other hand, as we shall see, Kennedy did refrain from announcing that God loves *sinners*, and that he is Father of all. At this point he seems to be in opposition to Romans 5:8, etc., and we might say that he is 'hyper-ish'! He is also at his most tortuous: 'is the call of the gospel an expression of love to each individual to whom it is addressed? True, the doctrine of the gospel is a revelation of God's love to sinners; and the embrace of divine love is assured to all who close with the call of the gospel. But is not this something very different from the call being an expression of love to all to whom it is addressed?' *Man's Relations to God Traced in the Light of 'The Present Truth'* (Edinburgh: Maclaren, 1869), 87–88. But still he offered the gospel, and we cannot therefore readily place him in the line of e.g. Hussey, Skepp, Gill, Brine, Wayman—or of William J. Styles and others, who denied that faith was a duty incumbent upon unbelievers. Further, in denying that the gospel was to be offered to 'sensible sinners' only, Kennedy was consistent in being wary of that undue introspection which was designed to satisfy the individual that he, being a 'sensible sinner', had a warrant to believe. Thus he writes, 'There is a danger, too, of substituting feeling for faith, and of resting on a certain experience, instead of on what is objectively presented in the Word, as a ground of hope. All earnest souls are apt, at a certain stage, to search for the warrant of faith in their own state of feeling, rather than in the written Word. True, reception of Christ is the immediate duty of all who hear the gospel; and nought can excuse their not doing so. But is it not extremely dangerous even to appear to say that faith is the opposite of feeling?' (*Hyper-Evangelism*, 12). Our conclusion is that Kennedy was not always consistent; but that if by 'hyper-Calvinist' is meant one who refuses to offer the gospel, denies that faith is the duty of the unbeliever, encourages undue introspection in quest of warrants to believe—even more, if by 'hyper-Calvinist' is meant 'antinomian'—then Kennedy was not a hyper-Calvinist, and any blemishes in his theory were more than compensated for by his pulpit practice. For an account of the history of the issues raised here see A. P. F. Sell, *The Great Debate: Calvinism, Arminianism and Salvation* (Worthing: H. E. Walter 1982; Grand Rapids: Baker Book House, 1983).

57. *The Present Cast and Tendency*, 17.
58. The pages quoted in our summary of *Man's Relations to God* are: 6, 18, 25, 30, 42, 56, 94, 95, 111, 112, 113, 118, 123, 131, 149, 175.
59. Our sympathies here are with two other of our divines: Bruce and Orr. Bruce informs us that in Paul's mind, 'the antithesis was between a son *indeed*, and a son who is

nothing better than a servant; in the mind of the systematic theologian it becomes sonship *of a sort* versus creaturehood, or subjecthood, the original relation of man to God as Creator and Sovereign. We are in a wholly different world of thought, while using the same phrases'. See *St. Paul's Conception of Christianity* (Edinburgh: T. & T. Clark, 1896), 191. Elsewhere Bruce claims that 'The Divine Father regards all men as His children, and by means of sun and rain confers on them in every clime food and raiment—all things needful for temporal well-being. Nor does He provide for their bodily life alone; He remembers that they are men made in His image, and that their spiritual nature needs food convenient . . . He is the Father, not of the few but of the many, not of the privileged cultured class, but of the uncultured, unsanctified mass of mankind . . .' *The Moral Order of the World* (London: Hodder & Stoughton, 1899), 252–3; cf. p. 268. For Orr's position see his *The Christian View of God and the World* (Edinburgh: Elliot, 1893), 120, 275. Orr was later to write 'Is God universally Father? Is man, by creation, a son? In one sense . . . when God created man, it was to a destiny of *sonship* . . . So far the advocates of universal Fatherhood are right . . . But man by sin turned his back on that destiny . . . If his destiny of sonship was to be realized, it could no longer be on the basis of creation, but only on the basis of *redemption*'. See his *Side-Lights on Christian Doctrine* (London: Marshall, 1909), 17. As Orr says, the prodigal does return to his *Father's* house.

60. See *Expository Lectures*, 101.
61. *The Present Cast and Tendency*, 21–36; cf. *Unionism and its Last Phase*, 17.
62. Ibid. 26.
63. Romans 5:8.
64. *Expository Lectures*, 76.
65. See e.g. ibid. 54.
66. Ibid. 5.
67. Quoted by J. Noble, 'Memoir', op. cit. cxxii–cxxiii.
68. In *The Present Cast and Tendency*, 20, he verges upon a concession; 'The only respect in which the present seems favourably to compare with the past, is in the extent to which missionary enterprises are now prosecuted'. But he warned that 'it would be rash to judge that such zeal, as may be expressed in missionary efforts, is always an indication of a Church being in a healthy spiritual condition'. Kennedy was not an ecclesiastical administrator by nature, and he was sure that ministers ought to occupy themselves in their proper calling, and not seek membership of this and that socio-religious agency. He was for a time Chairman of the School Board at Dingwall, feeling as he did that the minister ought to have a concern for the education of the young. But he opposed (for example) the organized temperance movement, and published two pamphlets upon it, *Total Abstinence Schemes Examined* (Edinburgh: Grant, 1879), and *A Reply to Some Recent Defences of Total Abstinence Schemes* (Edinburgh: Grant, 1879). He subsequently took a more lenient view of the aims of the movement. Among his other writings, to which we have not so far alluded, we note *An Address to Volunteers* (Edinburgh: Gibson, 1886), in which he praised those who had joined the Volunteer movement, argued that a free Britain was worth defending, and reminded them of *the* Captain, Christ, and of the assured victory in him; and an allegory, *A Visit to Leper Isle; and the voyage thence to 'The Land that is very far off'* (2nd ed., Glasgow: Bible Warehouse, 1892).
69. J. Kennedy, *The Father's Drawing* (Gisborne, NZ, n.d.), 8.

CHAPTER THREE:
ROBERT FLINT (1838–1910):
THEISM AND THEOLOGY IN TENSION

1. F. D. Maurice, *Moral and Metaphysical Philosophy* (London: Macmillan, 1882), ii, 219.
2. For Flint see Donald Macmillan, *The Life of Robert Flint* (London: Hodder & Stoughton, 1914); *DNB* 1901–11, 35–6, *Who Was Who* i, 1897–1915, 248. *Life and Work*, Jan. 1911, 18–19; S. R. Obitts, *The Thought of Robert Flint*, unpublished doctoral thesis, Univ. Edinburgh, 1962. *Contra DNB*, Flint prepared, but was prevented by ill health from delivering, the Gifford Lectures for 1908–9.
3. See *Mind* iii (1878), 150.
4. Macmillan, op. cit. 333.
5. Cf. R. Flint, *Theism* (11th ed., Edinburgh and London: Blackwood, 1905), 1.
6. Ibid. 6.
7. Ibid. 18.
8. Ibid. 21.
9. Cited ibid. 29.
10. Ibid. 32.
11. Ibid. 38.
12. Ibid. 60.
13. Ibid. 71.
14. Ibid. 74.
15. This view is diametrically opposed to that of Cook Wilson, for example, who protested vigorously that 'we don't want merely inferred friends. Could we possibly be satisfied with an inferred God?' See his *Statement and Inference* (ed. A. S. L. Farquharson, Oxford, 1926), ii paras. 565 ff.
16. *Theism*, 78.
17. Ibid. 79.
18. Ibid. 81.
19. Ibid. 95.
20. The title of Lecture IV.
21. Ibid. 107.
22. Ibid. 119.
23. Ibid. 130.
24. Ibid. 148.
25. Ibid. 150–151. We cannot resist the temptation of setting over against this lyricism the comment of the (unnamed) historian quoted by Bernard Lord Manning: 'When I hear a man say "All history teaches" . . . I prepare to hear some thundering lie.' See his *Essays in Orthodox Dissent* (London: Independent Press 1939, 1953), 97.
26. *Theism*, 180.
27. Ibid. 186–7.
28. Ibid. 216–7.
29. Ibid. 231.
30. Ibid. 264.
31. Ibid.
32. Ibid. 265.
33. Ibid. 267.
34. Ibid. 291.

35. Ibid. 301.
36. Ibid. 302.
37. Ibid. 305, 307–8.
38. Ibid. 321.
39. D. Macmillan, op. cit. 37.
40. J. Lindsay in D. Macmillan, op. cit. 359. Lindsay contributed chap. xii, 'His Contribution to Theism', to this work; Professor W. P. Paterson contributed chap. x, 'Flint's Doctrinal System'; Professor R. M. Wenley wrote chap. vii, 'His Philosophical Teaching'. Flint's works on the history of philosophy should be noted as highly esteemed examples of his great erudition. They are *The Philosophy of History in Europe* (1874) and *History of the Philosophy of History* (1893), both published by Blackwood.
41. *Philosophy as Scientia Scientiarum* (Edinburgh and London (Blackwood, 1904), 24.
42. J. K. Mozley, *Some Tendencies in British Theology* (London: SPCK, 1957), 114.
43. J. Lindsay, in D. Macmillan, op. cit. 350–351.
44. A. S. Pringle-Pattison, *The Idea of God in the Light of Recent Philosophy* (2nd rev. edn., New York: OUP, 1920), 300. Pringle-Pattison further notes an oscillation in Flint's use of 'first' in 'first cause' between 'temporally first cause' and 'true and only cause' (301).
45. Quoted by A. G. N. Flew, *God and Philosophy* (London: Hutchinson, 1966), 74. Cf. D. M. Emmet, 'The Choice of a World Outlook', *Philosophy* xxiii (1948), 213.
46. A BBC debate, 1948, reprinted in ed. J. H. Hick, *The Existence of God* (New York: Macmillan, 1964), 175.
47. See J. Caird, *Spinoza* (Edinburgh: Blackwood), 167–8.
48. F. C. Copleston, *A History of Philosophy* (New York: Doubleday, Image Books), vi, 207. Some conservative Christians continue to find Paley's approach useful. See e.g. R. E. D. Clark, *The Universe—Plan or Accident?* (3rd edn., London: Paternoster Press, 1961).
49. *Theism*, 397.
50. Ibid. 181–2
51. A. Caldecott, *The Philosophy of Religion in England and America* (London: Methuen, 1901), 124.
52. L. Stephen, *History of English Thought in the Eighteenth Century* (New York: Harcourt Brace, 1962), i, 347.
53. *Theism*, 390, n. xxii. Cf. ibid. 208.
54. V. Phelips (i.e. Philip Vivian), *The Churches and Modern Thought* (London: Watts, 1931), 158.
55. F. D. Maurice, op. cit. 601.
56. R. Flint, 'Theism' in *Ency. Brit.* 9th edn. (1888), xxiii, 247.
57. See J. Lindsay in Macmillan, op. cit. 350, and A. Caldecott, op. cit. 125.
58. See R. M. Wenley in Macmillan, op. cit. 241. Flint never married; his sister Janet, with whom he lived, survived him and greatly assisted Macmillan in his biographical labours. The biography is dedicated to her.
59. Willis B. Glover, 'Christian Origins of Modern Secular Culture', *Religion in Life* xxxii (1963), 447.
60. J. Baillie, *The Sense of the Presence of God* (London: OUP, 1962), 19.
61. F. C. S. Schiller, 'On Preserving Appearances', *Mind* xii (1903), 346. For further contemporary estimates of and reactions to idealism see A. P. F. Sell, 'Christian and Secular Philosophy in Britain at the Beginning of the Twentieth Century', *The*

Downside Review, xciii (1975), 122–143; and id., *The Philosophy of Religion 1875–1980* (London: Croom Helm, forthcoming, 1988).
62. A. Caldecott, op. cit. 126.
63. Dedication to *Meditations*.
64. Flint quoting Chalmers in *Theism*, 335–6, n. iii.
65. Ibid. 337.
66. Ibid. 351, n. ix, citing an article by G. T. Ladd in *Bibliotheca Sacra* xxxiv.
67. Ibid. 352.
68. Ibid. 353, citing *Ad Autolycum* i.c. 2.
69. *Westminster Confession* Ii. (Our italics)
70. *Theism*, 398–9, n. xxv.
71. Ibid. 401, n. xxvii.
72. J. Lindsay in D. Macmillan, op. cit. 353.
73. 'Theism', *Ency. Brit.* xxiii, 247–8.
74. *Theism*, 354, n. ix.
75. Ibid. 271.
76. Ibid. 279.
77. Ibid. 289.
78. Ibid. 268.
79. A. Caldecott, op. cit. 125.
80. But sometimes the absolute prompted rather than prevented reductionism in Christian thought. See A. P. F. Sell, 'The Peril of Reductionism in Christian Thought', *Scottish Journal of Theology*, xxvii (1974), 48–64.
81. *Theism*, 79.
82. J. Dickie, *Fifty Years of British Theology* (Edinburgh: T. & T. Clark, 1937), 63.
83. Sermon, 'The earth is the Lord's, preached in the East Church, Aberdeen, 18th September 1859; reprinted in *Christ's Kingdom upon Earth, A Series of Discourses* (Edinburgh and London: Blackwood, 1865), 7; revised and reprinted in *Sermons and Addresses* (Edinburgh and London: Blackwood, 1899), 56–66.
84. J. Dickie, op. cit. 66.
85. Theism, *Ency. Brit.* xxiii, 249.
86. *Theism* 74–5; cf. his *Agnosticism* (Edinburgh and London: Blackwood, 1903), 589.
87. A. Caldecott, op. cit. 123.
88. In *Theism*, 449, n. xli, Flint refers us to his *Anti-Theistic Theories* (Edinburgh and London: Blackwood, 1879), 405 ff., and to his sermon, 'The Good and Perfect Gift of Art', preached in St. Giles's Church Edinburgh on 27th October 1889 before the National Association for the Advancement of Art, and reprinted in *Sermons and Addresses*, 28–38. Caldecott's most serious mistake was in supposing that the reading of Flint's *Theism* had led G. J. Romanes into atheism. In fact this was not so, and when the error was pointed out to Caldecott he apologized in the *Spectator* of 2nd September 1902. See A. Caldecott, op. cit. 126; Flint, *Theism*, 451–4, n. xli; D. Macmillan, op. cit. 328–331.
89. *Theism* 447, n. xl; Cf. *Agnosticism*, 578–602.
90. In addition to *Christ's Kingdom upon Earth* and *Sermons and Addresses* see e.g. his *On Theological, Biblical, and Other Subjects* (Edinburgh and London: Blackwood, 1905).
91. Macmillan, op. cit. 228.
92. Quoted by Macmillan, op. cit. 332.
93. For the Scottish school see James McCosh, *The Scottish Philosophy* (London: Macmillan, 1875); for Reid see Sir W. Hamilton *Works* (2 vols. Edinburgh 1846–

63); A. C. Fraser, *Thomas Reid* (Edinburgh 1898); S. A. Grave, *The Scottish Philosophy of Common Sense* (Oxford, 1960).

94. R. Flint, *Vico* (Edinburgh and London: Blackwood, 1884). This work earned the high praise of J. H. Stirling, who considerd that it was 'the fullest and most original' of all the books in the series in which it appeared. See Macmillan, op. cit. 422.

95. See T. Reid, *An Inquiry into the Human Mind on the Principles of Common Sense* (1819 ed.), 394–5.

96. Wenley, quoting H. G. Graham, *The Social Life of Scotland in the Eighteenth Century*, 358, in Macmillan, op. cit. 222. It is interesting to note that Hume and Reid were on friendly terms.

97. Wenley in Macmillan, op. cit. 54.

98. In a prize essay on 'General and Professional Education', quoted in Macmillan, op. cit. 56–7.

99. So Wenley in Macmillan, op. cit. 239.

100. R. Mackintosh, 'Theism', *Ency. Brit.* (11th ed.) xxvi, 754.

101. Cf. G. F. Woods, *Theological Explanation* (London: Nisbet, 1958) 20–21: 'Many of the deistic criticisms of orthodoxy were, in fact, not so much "rational" criticisms as objections raised on the basis of historical and scientific investigations'.

102. *Theism*, 208. Dr. W. T. Pennar Davies suggests that Butler may have acquired his main argument against the deists from the 'fertile and penetrating' mind of Samuel Jones, tutor at the dissenting academy at Tewkesbury where Butler, originally a Presbyterian, was educated. See 'Episodes in the History of Brecknockshire Dissent', *Brycheiniog* iii (1957), 33.

103. B. Ramm, *Varieties of Christian Apologetics* (Grand Rapids: Baker Book House, 1973), 109.

104. *Agnosticism*, 425.

105. J. Lindsay in Macmillan, op. cit. 356, citing Flint's *Agnosticism*, 425, (though the reference in Macmillan is incorrectly given as p. 245).

106. J. Caird, *University Addresses* (Glasgow: Maclehose, 1899), 221. Caird goes further in suggesting that to allow probability the force of certainty is not only irrational, it is immoral (219).

107. Ibid. 221.

108. Ed. W. Knight, *Colloquia Peripatetica . . . Being notes of conversations with the late John Duncan* (Edinburgh and London: Oliphant, 1907), 1,3.

109. *Theism*, 438–9, n. xl.

110. J. M. Frame in J. W. Montgomery (ed.), *God's Inerrant Word* (Minneapolis: Bethany Fellowship, 1974), 170. Cf. C. F. H. Henry, *Remaking the Modern Mind* (Grand Rapids: Eerdmans, 1946), 225.

111. C. Van Til in E. R. Geehan (ed.), *Jerusalem and Athens* (Grand Rapids: Baker Book House, 1971), 426. Van Til had doggedly maintained this position (little discussed in Britain) over many years, in such works as *The Defense of the Faith* (1955) and *A Christian Theory of Knowledge* (1969). Flint can write (*Theism*, 78) that 'Clear and conspicuous as [the facts which prove that there is a God] are, worldliness and prejudice and sin may blind the soul to their significance'.

112. *Theism*, 253–8. Flint anticipates in this section the question which has been repeated in our own time by J. L. Mackie, 'Evil and Omnipotence', *Mind* N.S. xliv (1955), 206–212; and A. G. N. Flew, 'Divine Omnipotence and Human Freedom' in A. G. N. Flew and A. C. Macintyre (eds.) *New Essays in Philosophical Theology* (London: SCM Press, 1955), 144–169. Flint writes, "But, it will be objected, could not God

have made moral creatures who would be certain always to choose what is right, always to acquiesce in His own holy will? and if He could do this, why did He not?" (pp. 255–6). He provides the legitimate reply, "It seems to me that when you have resolved the problem of the origin of moral evil into the question, Why has God not originated a moral universe in which the lowest moral being would be as excellent as the archangels are? you have at once shown it to be speculatively incapable of solution and practically without importance . . . A merely imaginary universe is one on which we have no data to reason. We who are so incompetent judges of the actual universe, notwithstanding the various opportunities which we possess of studying it . . . can have no right to affirm its inferiority to any universe which we can imagine as possible". (Pp. 256–7).

113. See his preface to Butler's *Three Sermons on Human Nature* (1848), x, xi.

114. J. Butler, *The Analogy of Religion* (ed. W. E. Gladstone, Oxford: Clarendon Press, 1896), 10.

115. W. Paley, *Natural Theology* (2nd ed. Oxford, 1828), ii, 220.

116. V. Phelips, op. cit. 127–33.

117. F. D. Maurice, op. cit. 450. Cf. A. B. Bruce, *Apologetics; or Christianity Defensively Stated*, (Edinburgh: T. & T. Clark, 1892), 126, for the view that compared with the deists and their 'honey-pots of optimism', Butler errs on the side of gloom.

118. *Theism*, 258–9.

119. J. Hick, *Evil and the God of Love* (London: Collins Fontana, 1968), 244. We should not forget, however, that Flint's early experience as a city missionary brought him face to face with the societal ills perpetrated against the working classes, and that his *Socialism*, (London: Ibister 1894), though not uncritical either of conservative complacency or of certain aspects of socialist theory, is permeated by a passion for social righteousness. D. Macmillan quotes a reviewer of the book who said that it was "a work written with the ink of human love by the right hand of good fellowship". *Op. cit.*, p. 433. Flint answered the kind of charge levelled by Professor Hick with a *tu quoque:* his critics, he said, (*Theism*, note xl, pp. 439–40) had produced no better answer than he. Perhaps they hadn't—then.

120. T. Chalmers, *On Natural Theology*, 1835, ii, 380. Professor Daniel F. Rice's article, 'Natural Theology and the Scottish Philosophy in the Thought of Thomas Chalmers', *Scottish Journal of Theology* xxiv (1971), 23–46, is particularly illuminating on the Chalmers side of the Chalmers-Flint comparison. We should note that in his later work Flint welcomed the revival of interest in the concept of God's holy love, attributing it to the influence of a number of German scholars, but omitting any reference to Chalmers. See *Agnosticism*, 594.

121. *Christ's Kingdom upon Earth*, 6. Cf. the revised version of the sermon in *Sermons and Addresses*, 60.

122. *On Theological, Biblical, and Other Subjects*, 74.

123. *Theism*, 326, n.i. Cf. 351, n. ix, where he quotes G. T. Ladd with approval: 'The truth becomes ours only as a gift from without. All truth is of the nature of a revelation . . .'

124. H. F. Lovell Cocks, *By Faith Alone* (London: James Clarke, 1943), 68.

CHAPTER FOUR:
JOHN CAIRD (1820–1898):
APOSTLE OF CONTINUITY

1. Edward Caird, 'Memoir of Principal Caird', prefixed to J. Caird, *The Fundamental Ideas of Christianity* (Glasgow: Maclehose, 1900), i, xxix.
2. E. Caird (op. cit. xxxii) states that this was his brother's first publication. But on 15th March 1855, John Caird wrote to thank Bishop Wordsworth for his kind remarks upon a Good Friday sermon preached by him in London and published in *The Penny Pulpit*. See Charles L. Warr, *Principal Caird* (Edinburgh: T. & T. Clark, 1926), 138.
3. J. Caird, 'General and Professional Education', in *University Addresses* (Glasgow: Maclehose, 1899), 373–383.
4. H. Jones, *Principal Caird. An Address Delivered to the Students of the Moral Philosophy Class on the Opening Day of the Session 1898–99* (Glasgow: Maclehose, 1898), 29.
5. John Macleod, *Scottish Theology in Relation to Church History since the Reformation* (Edinburgh: Free Church of Scotland 1943; reprinted Edinburgh: Banner of Truth 1974), 300.
6. For John Caird see *DNB*; *Who Was Who*, 1897–1916, 111; J.C., 'The Very Reverend John Caird, D.D., Ll.D., Principal of the University of Glasgow', *Home and Foreign Missionary Record of the Church of Scotland*, Sept. 1898, 272–3; E. Caird, *op. cit.*; C.L. Warr, *op. cit.*; Donald Macleod, 'John Caird, D.D. An Appreciation' prefixed to Caird's posthumous *Essays for Sunday Reading* (London: Pitman, 1906), vii–xxi; H. M. B. Reid, *The Divinity Professors in the University of Glasgow, 1640–1903* (Glasgow: Maclehose, 1923), chap. xv.
7. We designate the Church thus by way of reminding ourselves (a) that the Disruption men regarded themselves as being the *true* Church of Scotland; and (b) that they upheld the Establishment principle.
8. See his memorial tribute in the *Scotsman*, 1st August 1898.
9. Edward Caird's comment (op. cit. xli) to the effect that this union 'added greatly to the happiness of his after life' is delightfully ambiguous!
10. E. Caird, op. cit. lxx.
11. Ibid. lxxiii.
12. On 13th April 1895 E. Caird wrote thus to Miss Mary Sarah Talbot: 'It is the worst side of the Oxford change that it separates me from him [i.e. J. Caird] in his old days (he is fifteen years older than me). I am afraid he feels it a good deal when University troubles harass him'. See H. Jones and J. H. Muirhead, *The Life and Philosophy of Edward Caird* (Glasgow: Maclehose, 1921), 206.
13. Caird preached before the University on the occasion of Barclay's death. His text was 2 Tim. 4:7. The sermon was published, Glasgow: Maclehose, 1873).
14. H. Jones, *Principal Caird*, 12.
15. So Warr, op. cit. 171.
16. J. Caird, *Sermons* (Edinburgh: Blackwood, 1858), 134.
17. J. Caird, *Essays for Sunday Reading*, 147–8.
18. C. L. Warr, op. cit. 44–5. Cf. E. Caird (op. cit. cxl): 'As a thinker, he had not perhaps the highest kind of originality, but he never simply repeated the ideas of others, or uttered anything that he had not made his own'.
19. C. L. Warr, op. cit. 164.

20. Deas Cromarty, *Scottish Ministerial Miniatures* (London: Hodder & Stoughton, 1892), 9.
21. C. L. Warr., op. cit. 135.
22. Ed. J. H. Leckie, *David W. Forrest, D.D.* (London: Hodder & Stoughton, 1919), 124.
23. Quoted by E. Caird, op. cit. xxii.
24. J. Caird, *University Addresses* (Glasgow: Maclehose, 1898), 79.
25. E. Caird, op. cit. xvii.
26. D. Cromarty, op. cit. 11–13.
27. J. H. Leckie, *Secession Memories* (Edinburgh: T. & T. Clark, 1926), 235 n.
28. *DNB Supp.*, 368 incorrectly gives Dr Robert Wallace as editor of this volume. For the *Scotch Sermons* controversy see H. F. Henderson, *The Religious Controversies of Scotland* (Edinburgh: T. & T. Clark, 1905), chap. x. Cf. Donald Macmillan, *The Life of Robert Flint* (London: Hodder & Stoughton, 1914), 371–2.
29. Quoted by E. Caird, op. cit. li.
30. *University Addresses*, 60–61.
31. J. Caird, *University Sermons* (Glasgow: Maclehose, 1898), 4, 22, 160, 205–6, 236.
32. *University Addresses*, 180.
33. Quoted by E. Caird, op. cit. xxxix.
34. *Essays for Sunday Reading*, 129, 133, 244–5. These sentiments were echoed by Bruce and Denney, as we shall see.
35. *University Addresses*, 85.
36. *University Sermons*, 85.
37. *Essays for Sunday Reading*, 105.
38. Ibid. 162.
39. J. Caird, *Christian Manliness. A Sermon preached before the University of Glasgow on the first Sunday of Session 1871–2*, (Glasgow: Maclehose, 1871), 23, 29–30.
40. *University Sermons*, 46.
41. Ibid. 100.
42. *Sermons*, 33.
43. *Essays for Sunday Reading*, 54; cf. *The Fundamental Ideas of Christianity* ii, chap. xix.
44. *University Sermons*, 399.
45. *Sermons*, 62; cf. also pp. 133, 164, 217.
46. Ibid. 29.
47. *An Introduction to the Philosophy of Religion* (2nd ed. Glasgow: Maclehose, 1904), 1.
48. Ibid. 2.
49. Ibid. 3.
50. Ibid. 58.
51. *The Fundamental Ideas of Christianity*, i, 140.
52. *An Introduction to the Philosophy of Religion*, 9.
53. Ibid. 10.
54. Ibid. 57.
55. Ibid. 60.
56. Ibid. 62.
57. Ibid. 64.
58. Ibid. 69.
59. Ibid. 73.
60. Ibid.
61. Ibid. 79.

62. Ibid.
63. Ibid. 87.
64. Ibid. 111.
65. Ibid. 121.
66. Ibid. 125.
67. Ibid. 140.
68. Ibid. 150.
69. Ibid. 177–8.
70. Ibid. 179.
71. Ibid. 193.
72. Ibid. 195.
73. Ibid. 203.
74. Ibid. 218.
75. Ibid. 221.
76. Ibid. 236.
77. Ibid. 242.
78. Ibid. 283.
79. Ibid. 284.
80. Ibid. 334.
81. Ibid. 343.
82. Ibid. 290.
83. H. Jones, *Principal Caird*, 11.
84. Ibid. 22–3.
85. Quoted by E. Caird, op. cit. lix.
86. *University Addresses*, 187.
87. Ibid. 15. Cf. Caird's sermon, *Mind and Matter*, preached before the British Medical Association on Tuesday 7th August 1888, and published in the same year by Maclehose of Glasgow.
88. J. Caird's preface to *An Introduction to the Philosophy of Religion*, p. vi.
89. *The Fundamental Ideas of Christianity*, i, 15—16.
90. *University Addresses*, 19.
91. See A. P. F. Sell, *Theology in Turmoil. The roots, course, and significance of the conservative-liberal debate in modern theology* (Grand Rapids: Baker Book House, 1986), ch. iii.
92. E. Caird, op. cit. cxli.
93. Quoted ibid. cxxxi.
94. *The Fundamental Ideas of Christianity*, i, 49.
95. Cf. e.g. *Sermons*, 36–7.
96. Quoted by E. Caird, op. cit. lvii; cf. *The Fundamental Ideas of Christianity*, i, 74.
97. H. Jones, *Principal Caird*, 17.
98. J. Caird, *The Universal Religion. A Lecture delivered in Westminster Abbey on the Day of Intercession for Missions, November 30th 1874* (Glasgow: Maclehose, 1874), 11.
99. Ibid. 29.
100. *The Fundamental Ideas of Christianity*, i, 19.
101. A. Seth, *Scottish Philosophy* (Edinburgh: Blackwood, 1890), 209.
102. One of the fascinating theological questions of our time is whether such theologians as Pannenberg can at one and the same time rescue theology from positivistic hands, and make genuine room for the individual in their eschatologically construed history in a way that Hegel did not.

103. H. Jones, *Principal Caird*, 19–20.

104. *The Fundamental Ideas of Christianity*, i, 46.

105. *Essays for Sunday Reading*, 243, 244.

106. *University Addresses*, 54. Cf. *Essays for Sunday Reading*, 229.

107. See further, A. P. F. Sell, *Theology in Turmoil*, ch. 1.

108. *Quoted by J. Passmore, A Hundred Years of Philosophy* (London: Duckworth, 1957), 49.

109. J. Caird, *Spinoza* (Edinburgh: Blackwood, 1888), 89; cf. *The Fundamental Ideas of Christianity*, i, 107.

110. *University Sermons*, 311.

111. *The Fundamental Ideas of Christianity*, i, 87–8.

112. Ibid. 104–5.

113. Ibid. 84; our italics.

114. Ibid. 113.

115. See A. Seth. *Hegelianism and Personality* (Edinburgh: Blackwood, 1887), 189–192. In this connection it is interesting to note that at the beginning of a sermon on the idea that God's thoughts and ways are not like ours (Isaiah 55:7,8) Caird says that 'there is a point of view from which we must hold the very opposite of this proposition to be the truth'. See *University Sermons*, 27.

116. J. Caird, 'Union with God', in W. A. Knight (ed.), *Scotch Sermons* (London: Macmillan, 1880), 24.

117. Ibid. 34.

118. H. M. B. Reid, op. cit. 329.

119. E. Caird, op. cit. lxvii, lxxvi.

120. Letter to the Rev. J. P. Struthers dated 15.2.1893, in J. Moffatt (ed.) *Letters of Principal James Denney to his Family and Friends* (London: Hodder & Stoughton, 1920), 49.

121. *Sermons*, 193.

122. H. R. Mackintosh, *Types of Modern Theology* (London: Nisbet, 1937), 105.

123. *The Fundamental Ideas of Christianity*, i, 58.

124. C. L. Warr, op. cit. 184.

125. W. P. Paterson, *The Rule of Faith* (London: Hodder & Stoughton, 1912), 33.

126. *An Introduction to the Philosophy of Religion*, 244–5.

127. *Sermons*, 44, 216.

128. Cf. A Campbell Fraser's verdict on Hegelianism in this connection: 'We ask for intellectual relief for moral difficulties, and we are offered "the organisation of thought". We look for bread and we find a stone'. See his *Berkeley* (Edinburgh: Blackwood, 1881), 229.

129. *The Fundamental Ideas of Christianity*, i, 172.

130. Ibid. in 172–3 (our italics).

131. Ibid. ii, 227.

132. Ibid. ii, 20.

133. *The Universal Religion*, 7.

134. Ibid. 30–31.

135. *The Fundamental Ideas of Christianity*, ii, 218–220, quoting J. Orr, *The Christian View of God and the World* (Edinburgh: Elliot, 1893), 362. We shall have more to say of Caird's account of the person of Christ in our chapter on D. W. Forrest below.

CHAPTER FIVE:
ALEXANDER BALMAIN BRUCE (1831–1899):
SEEING AND SHOWING JESUS

1. A. B. Bruce, *With Open Face, or Jesus Mirrored in Matthew, Mark, and Luke* (London: Hodder & Stoughton, 1896), 24.
2. For Bruce see *DNB* Supp.; *Who Was Who, 1897–1916*, 96; W. M. Clow, 'Alexander Balmain Bruce', *Expository Times* xi (1899–1900), 8–11; George Reith, 'Professor A. B. Bruce, D.D.', *Free Church of Scotland Monthly*, October 1899, 229–230; W. M. Macgregor, *Persons and Ideals* (Edinburgh: T. & T. Clark, 1939), chap. I.
3. See P. Carnegie Simpson, *The Life of Principal Rainy* (London: Hodder & Stoughton, popular edn., n.d.), ii, 117 n.
4. A. B. Bruce, *The Moral Order of the World in Ancient and Modern Thought* (London: Hodder & Stoughton, 1899), 309.
5. A. B. Bruce, *Apologetics; or, Christianity Defensively Stated* (Edinburgh: T. & T. Clark, 1892), 42.
6. H. F. Henderson, *The Religious Controversies of Scotland* (Edinburgh: T. & T. Clark, 1905), 251–2, quoting *Memorials of a Ministry on the Clyde*, with a memoir of Macellar by Bruce, 1876.
7. Ibid. 267, quoting Assembly *Proceedings* 1890, 175.
8. *Apologetics*, 503.
9. A. B. Bruce, *The Training of the Twelve* (Edinburgh: T. & T. Clark, 1871), vi.
10. *The Free Church Hymn Book* (Paisley: Parlane, 1882). v.
11. W. M. Clow, op. cit. 11. Bruce himself wrote that when reading the Bible 'The risk of miscarriage somehow is so great that we do well to read with the prayer in our heart—"Send forth Thy light and Thy truth."' See his *The Chief End of Revelation* (London: Hodder & Stoughton, 2nd end., 1890), 286. P. Carnegie Simpson published a letter written by Rainy to Mrs. Bruce during her husband's last illness. See Carnegie Simpson, op. cit. ii, 293–4.
12. A. B. Bruce, *The Providential Order of the World* (London: Hodder & Stoughton, 1897) 3.
13. A. B. Bruce, *St. Paul's Conception of Christianity* (Edinburgh: T. & T. Clark, 1896), 395.
14. A. B. Bruce, *The Parabolic Teaching of Christ* (London: Hodder & Stoughton, 8th edn. 1891), 321.
15. *The Training of the Twelve*, 172; cf. A. B. Bruce, *The Kingdom of God: Christ's Teaching according to the Synoptical Gospels* (Edinburgh: T. & T. Clark, 4th edn. 1891), chap. viii.
16. *The Providential Order of the World*, 4.
17. *The Training of the Twelve*, 78.
18. Ibid. 315. In this connection his observation concerning Rainy is interesting: 'I have no objection to people's treating Rainy as Caesar, if they choose; but when they treat him as a god and infallible, then I do protest.' So W. M. Macgregor, op. cit. 3.
19. Ibid. 7–8.
20. *The Kingdom of God*, 204–5; cf. ibid. 229: 'Who would not rather ascend the high hills of God in the kingdom of heaven than walk the treadmill in the prison-house of Rabbinism!'

21. *The Chief End of Revelation*, 306, 310; cf. *The Kingdom of God*, 353–7.

22. Ibid. 304–5.

23. *With Open Face* (london: Hodder & Stoughton, 1896), 308. The Primer, comprising 122 catechetical questions based upon the biblical text, comprises the bulk of chap. xiii. Cf. *The Kingdom of God*, 351: 'What is wanted is not a dogmatic catechism, or commentaries on it written in a Rabbinical spirit, but a *Christian* Catechism or Primer, framed on a historical method . . .' He contemplated writing a larger catechism if the Primer found favour, but did not in fact produce such a work.

24. *The Parabolic Teaching of Christ*, 248–9, cf. 290, 292 etc.

25. *The Kingdom of God*, 144.

26. Ibid. 146.

27. *St. Paul's Conception of Christianity*, 155–6; cf. 182.

28. *The Kingdom of God*, 245.

29. *Ibid*. 322–3.

30. *Assembly Proceedings*, 176, quoted by H. F. Henderson, op. cit. 267–8. See also *The Case Stated. Statement by Ministers and Other Office-Bearers of the Free Church in Regard to the Decision of last General assembly in the Case of Drs. Dod and Bruce*, 1890. For an example of criticism directed at Bruce's *The Kingdom of God* see Peter Richardson, *Dr. Bruce on 'The Kingdom of God'* (Glasgow: Bryce, 1890). He finds that Bruce takes too much notice of German theologians; that he is too naturalistically sceptical; and that his manner leaves much to be desired. He speaks of 'the vehemence with which Dr. Bruce champions charity and deals hard blows as the Hammerer of modern Rabbinism . . . I wish there had been more . . . profound and loyal worshipfulness in this book' (p. 19). As far as Bruce's students are concerned, Richardson recognizes (p. 21) that 'Bravery, especially when in divergence, and so in defensive battle, will always win youthful admiration'. But he fears for them. For an account of the Dods-Bruce Case by a present-day Free Church scholar, see G. N. M. Collins, *The Heritage of Our Fathers* (Edinburgh: Knox Press, 1974), 77. His verdict is, 'Gradually, "the way of the transgressor" was being made smooth'.

31. *The Kingdom of God*, 89.

32. Ibid. 92.

33. Ibid. 95.

34. Ibid. 100–101. Elsewhere Bruce emphasizes the rationality of prayer: see, e.g. *The Training of the Twelve*, 68, 290.

35. A. B. Bruce, 'The gracious Invitation', *The Expositor* (1st series) vi (1885), 152.

36. *The Training of the Twelve*, 331.

37. Ibid. 317.

38. Ibid. 392.

39. Ibid. 454. Erasmus fails to measure up: 'One rash, blundering, but heroic Luther, is worth a thousand men of the Erasmus type, unspeakably wise, but cold, passionless, timid, and time-serving'. (Ibid. 312). Bruce's soft spot for the Stoics is also apparent: 'The ethical temper of Stoicism is not faultless. It is too self-reliant, too proud, too austere. Nevertheless it is the temper of the hero, whose nature it is to despise happiness so-called, to curb passion, and to make duty his chief end and chief good'. See *The Moral Order of the World*, 138–9.

40. Ibid. 258; cf. *The Parabolic Teaching of Christ*, 174; *Apologetics*, 238.

41. *The Providential Order of the World*, 147. Bruce regards Schopenhauer's pessimistic philosophy as the new asceticism: 'Goodness, said the old ascetic, is not compatible

with remaining in the world. Goodness, teaches Schopenhauer, is not compatible with retention of *personality*'. Ibid. 148–9.

42. *The Parabolic Teaching of Christ*, 48. For his strictures against High Churchmanship see *The Training of the Twelve*, 234–5.
43. *St. Paul's Conception of Christianity*, 377.
44. Ibid. 183.
45. See e.g. *The Training of the Twelve*, 106–7.
46. *The Parabolic Teaching of Christ*, 28.
47. *The Kingdom of God*, 270.
48. Ibid. 272.
49. *The Training of the Twelve*, 238, 466.
50. Ibid. 215.
51. *With Open Face*, 155.
52. *Apologetics*, 354.
53. Ibid. 359.
54. On occasion Bruce overplayed his hand, as when he said of forgiveness that Christ 'is willing that it should be exercized by all on earth in whom dwells His own spirit'. See *The Kingdom of God*, 174. This indiscretion did not go unnoticed by D. W. Forrest: See his *The Christ of History and of Experience* (Edinburgh: T. & T. Clark, 1914), 51.
55. *The Kingdom of God*, 177.
56. Ibid. 180.
57. *Apologetics*, 398.
58. *The Humiliation of Christ*, 2nd edn. 1881, 3.
59. Ibid. 6–7.
60. Ibid. 13–14.
61. Ibid. 14.
62. *With Open Face*, 205.
63. *The Humiliation of Christ*, 22.
64. Ibid. 30; cf. 34. Though on p. 31 he notes that in the history of interpretation most have felt it necessary to apologize for the insight given by Hebrews, and to restrict Christ's glorification to his state of exaltation. See further his *The Epistle to the Hebrews. The First Apology for Christianity* (Edinburgh: T. & T. Clark, 1899). Bruce contributed the article on 'Hebrews' to James Hastings (ed.), *A Dictionary of the Bible* (Edinburgh: T. & T. Clark, 1899). The reviewer in the *Church Quarterly Review* xlix (Jan. 1900, 506–7) found Bruce on occasion 'needlessly offensive in language' in his article, notably in his thrice-repeated description of the Levitical priest as a 'sacerdotal drudge'. Was Bruce being provocative? Did the reviewer find the cap fitting?
65. Ibid. 72.
66. Ibid. 101–2. Present-day scholars would wish to modify Bruce's judgment on Zwingli.
67. Ibid. 105.
68. Ibid. 107.
69. Ibid. 114.
70. Ibid. 115.
71. Ibid. 134–5.
72. We shall have cause to refer to kenoticism again in our chapter on D. W. Forrest.

73. *The Humiliation of Christ*, 167.
74. Ibid. 171.
75. Ibid. 191.
76. Ibid. 206. The question 'How far was Schleiermacher a pantheist?' is a vexed one indeed. For our own position, namely, that there are pantheizing tendencies if not pantheizing intentions in Schleiermacher, see A. P. F. Sell, *Theology in Turmoil. The roots, course and significance of the conservative-liberal debate in modern theology* (Grand Rapids: Baker Book House, 1986), ch. i.
77. Ibid. 234. Surely we are right to read 'precludes' for 'includes' in this paragraph?
78. Ibid. 279.
79. *Church Quarterly Review* xlv (Jan. 1898), 497.
80. *Expository Times* viii (1896–7), 113–114.
81. See T. H. Darlow, *William Robertson Nicoll, Life and Letters* (London: Hodder & Stoughton, 1925), 133: letter dated [Sept.] 1896, referring to Bruce's treatment of 'The Synoptic Gospels' in *The Expositor's Greek Testament*, i (London: Hodder & Stoughton, 1897)—a series edited by Nicoll himself. Similarly, in his *Persons and Ideals*, W. M. Macgregor, while recognizing that Bruce and A. B. Davidson had exercized a greater influence for good on their students than any man since Chalmers, nevertheless opined that Bruce 'had little of the technical equipment of the scholar'. (pp. 1–2).
82. *Apologetics*, 404–5.
83. T. H. Darlow, op. cit. 350. Letter to James Denney dated 24.2.1901.
84. Though as early as 1889 Bruce had spoken of Jesus's 'high doctrine concerning the dignity of man'. See *The Kingdom of God*, 128.
85. We were interested to discover A. E. Garvie's similar comment on Bruce's *Apologetics*: 'If Dr. Bruce had acquired more of the Hegelian faculty (some, perhaps, will prefer to say caught the Hegelian trick) of "thinking things together", he would have given to the "Christian Theory of the Universe", as he conceives it, a rational unity that would have been more satisfying to some minds. That Dr. Bruce is doubtful of the possibility, and does not recognize the necessity of such a complete synthesis, there are some indications in this work . . ." See his 'Professor Bruce's "Apologetics,"' *Expository Times* iv (1892–3), 158. That Bruce was not unduly inclined to be helped by Hegel we shall shortly see.
86. Mt.26:6–13; Mk.14:3–9; Jn.12:1–8.
87. *The Training of the Twelve*, 308–9.
88. *The Kingdom of God*, 231.
89. Ibid. 232.
90. *The Training of the Twelve*, 361.
91. Ibid. 363.
92. Ibid. 365.
93. Ibid. 369; and *The Kingdom of God*, 250–251.
94. *St. Paul's Conception of Christianity*, 166–7, referring to Romans 3:25, Galatians 3:13 and 2 Corinthians 5:21 respectively.
95. Ibid. 171.
96. *The Epistle to the Hebrews* (Edinburgh: T. & T. Clark, 1899), 428. Thus, the fact that Cerisier could say in a review of *Apologetics*, 'Is not Jesus above all the *Saviour* who delivers man from the power of evil? To say that He is the Supreme *Revealer* is well, but it is not enough, 'suggests that the Frenchman was misled by Bruce's tendency, to which we earlier referred, to say one thing at a time, and to be somewhat sparing

in his provision of qualifying comments. Cerisier's review in *Revue de Théologie* is quoted in *Expository Times* vii (1895–6), 549–560.

97. Ibid. 436–7.
98. Ibid. 450–1.
99. *Apologetics*, 2.
100. *The Humiliation of Christ*, 307.
101. Ibid. 309.
102. Ibid. 311.
103. Ibid. 313. For an illuminating treatment of redemption by sample, see Robert Mackintosh, *Historic Theories of Atonement* (London: Hodder & Stoughton, 1920), chap. xiii.
104. *St. Paul's Conception of Christianity*, 292.
105. *The Humiliation of Christ*, 318.
106. Ibid. 351.
107. Ibid. 352.
108. A. B. Bruce, *The Chief End of Revelation* (London: Hodder & Stoughton, 2nd edn. 1890), xi–xii.
109. Ibid. vi.
110. Ibid. vii.
111. *Apologetics*, 37.
112. Ibid.
113. *The Providential Order of the World*, 16.
114. Ibid. 5.
115. Garvie, found this 'candid and cordial acceptance of critical results' to be 'an unexpected feature in apologetic literature' (op. cit. 159).
116. *The Providential Order of the World*, 10.
117. *The Kingdom of God*, 348. The remedy is to magnify the importance of the gospels as historically reliable documents (340).
118. *The Chief End of Revelation*, 60.
119. Ibid. 58.
120. Ibid. 56. It is conceivable, he thinks, that an exclusively oral revelation of God might be given in history (ibid. ix).
121. It would be a gross libel to say, as some of the oponents of of biblical criticism did say, that those who favoured criticism were all alike inspired by naturalistic philosophy. This was true of some, but not of all; and it was not true of Bruce. See A. P. F. Sell, *Theology in Turmoil*, ch. ii. Statements such as the following antagonized some conservative believers: 'The errorless autograph for which some zealously contend is a theological figment'; 'Faith could live and even thrive with a very reduced New Testament: the Synoptical Gospels and Paul's four all but universally recognized Epistles might suffice to start with'. (*Apologetics*, 303, 513). On the other hand, Bruce gave no support at all to the ultra-liberal notion that Christianity is not creed, but life. He certainly regarded the ethical teaching of Jesus as being very important, but to him the function of Christ as Redeemer was even more important. This emerges plainly in his most adversely criticized book, *The Kingdom of God*; see e.g. p. 40. Elsewhere he faults Matthew Arnold for saying that 'the Bible was not intended to teach, and does not in fact teach, any definite doctrines concerning God, man, or the world, but has for its sole object to promote the practice of piety, justice, and charity' (*Apologetics*, 31; cf. *The Chief End of Revelation*, 42–9). At this point R. B. Braithwaite's *An Empiricist's View of the Nature*

of Religious Belief, reprinted in I. T. Ramsey (ed.), *Christian Ethics and Moral Philosophy* (London: SCM Press, 1966), comes to mind. Indeed, Braithwaite (p.69) claims Arnold as 'the patron saint whom I claim for my way of thinking'.

122. See further A. P. F. Sell, *Theology in Turmoil*, ch. iii.
123. See e.g. *The Chief End of Revelation*, chap. iii.
124. *The Moral Order of the World*, 409.
125. *Apologetics*, 343.
126. *The Providential Order of the World*, 47–8. A fine example of late Victorian rhetoric!
127. Ibid. 136.
128. Ibid. 374. And cf. his criticisms of eighteenth, and some nineteenth century optimism, in *The Moral Order of the World*, 280–2. He much prefers Browning to Theodore Parker and Emerson, as taking more account of the facts. Walt Whitman is the acme of 'optimistic audacity'.
129. Ibid., Lecture iv.
130. *The Moral Order of the World*, 368, quoting B. Kidd, *Social Evolution*, 28.
131. *The Moral Order of the World*, 370.
132. Of Jesus he writes, 'He did not regard faith as an isolated faculty separate from reason, and still less as opposed to reason, but rather as a function of the whole mind exercized on religion' (*The Kingdom of God*, 100–1).
133. *The Moral Order of the World*, 351.
134. *The Chief End of Revelation*, 61.
135. *The Moral Order of the World*, 352. Cf. *The Training of the Twelve*, 400–1, where the reference is to the Westminster Confession.
136. *Apologetics*, 40.
137. Ibid. 20.
138. Ibid. 21, quoting Mark Pattinson, 'Tendencies of Religious Thought in England, 1688–1750', *Essays and Reviews* (London: Parker, 1860), 297.
139. *Apologetics*, 157. The last part of this sentence reminds us of Professor Norman Malcolm's apposite observation to the effect that he could 'imagine an atheist going through [Anselm's ontological argument] 'becoming convinced of its validity, acutely defending it against objections' yet remaining an atheist'. See his 'Anselm's Ontological Arguments', reprinted in J. H. Hick (ed.), *The Existence of God* (New York: Macmillan, 1964), 67.
140. *Apologetics*, 158. He can thus confess 'considerable sympathy with the religious attitude' (though not necessarily with the philosophical presuppositions) of such a Ritschlian as Herrmann. See *Apologetics*, 502. Garvie deems him to fail in not 'showing how the evidences of the existence of God and the conception of the nature of God mutually imply each other'. See art. cit. p. 159.
141. See the general outline of Bruce's theory in *The Providential Order of the World*, Lecture i.
142. *Apologetics*, 148.
143. Ibid. It should be noted that Bruce does not say that religious faith is an hypothesis.
144. Ibid. 114.
145. *The Providential Order of the World*, 55–6.
146. See especially A. B. Bruce, *Ferdinand Christian Baur* (London: Religious Tract Society, 1885).
147. Cf. *The Chief End of Revelation*, 168: miracles are to be regarded 'not as mere signs annexed to revelation for evidential purposes, but as constitutive elements of revelation, as forming in fact the very essence of the revelation'. On the whole

question of miracle see A. B. Bruce, *The Miraculous Element in the Gospels* (London: Hodder & Stoughton, 1886).

148. See *The Moral Order of the World*, Lectures ii, x, xi.
149. See *Apologetics*, 115–131; cf. *The Training of the Twelve*, 349; *The Providential Order of the World*, 60. Butler is charged with holding a deistic view of transcendence in *The Providential Order*, 171.
150. *The Providential Order of the World*, 26; cf. 57, 62, etc.
151. Ibid. 59.
152. Ibid. 369.
153. See *The Kingdom of God*, 332–3.
154. See *Ferdinand Christian Baur* for further charges against Strauss and Hegel, and also *Apologetics*, 132–146, on speculative theism.
155. *The Humiliation of Christ*, 12.
156. Ibid. 171.
157. *The Providential Order of the World*, 167.
158. Ibid. 84.
159. *The Chief End of Revelation*, 296.
160. Ibid. 303.
161. See n. 22 above.
162. *Apologetics*, 494.
163. *Expository Times*, xi (1899–1900), 113.
164. In this repsect he was like his contemporary Henry Rogers, on whom see A. P. F. Sell, 'Henry Rogers and the Eclipse of Faith', *Journal of the United Reformed Church History Society*, ii, (May 1980), 128–143.
165. B. B. Warfield, in the *Bible Student*, June 1899, quoted in *Expository Times* xi (1899–1900), 568.
166. What is required is what the late Alan Richardson called apologetics *as distinct from* apology. Using Bruce as an example, and while sympathizing with the need for apology in every age, Richardson understood apologetics to be that stock-taking exercize undertaken by Christian thinkers *vis-à-vis* contemporary philosophy and science, which ought properly to precede apology. See his *Christian Apologetics* (London: SCM Press, 1949), 20 and n. Still, it might not come amiss to observe that in these latter days many have preferred the comparatively secure, if important, task of ground-clearing to that of carrying the banner into alien territory: indeed, some now wonder whether the banner *ought* ever to be so carried. To such as these Bruce's swashbuckling style will appear as foolhardy as to us it appears rather refreshing. On the main point we note Professor Caldecott's opinion that Bruce 'had not cleared his mind as to the methods of Theism'. See A. Caldecott, *The Philosophy of Religion* (London: Methuen, 1901), 411.
167. J. K. Mozley, *Some Tendencies in British Theology* (London: SPCK, 1951), 108.
168. *The Epistle to the Hebrews*, 430.
169. Quoted by W. M. Macgregor, op. cit. 2.
170. *The Training of the Twelve*, 14.
171. Quoted by W. M. Macgregor, op.cit. 8.

CHAPTER SIX:
JAMES IVERACH (1839–1922):
THEOLOGIAN AT THE FRONTIER

1. Donald Mackenzie, 'James Iverach', *Expository Times* xxxii (1920–21), 55. For Iverach see further *Who Was Who, 1916–1928*, 544; J. A. Selbie, 'The Late Principal James Iverach, D.D.', *Monthly Record of the United Free Church of Scotland*, September 1922, 283–4; Deas Cromarty, *Scottish Ministerial Miniatures* (London: Hodder & Stoughton, 1892), 46–9.

2. George M. Reith, *Reminiscences of The United Free Church General Assembly (1900–1929)* (Edinburgh: Moray Press, 1933), 138.

3. J. Iverach, *The Christian Message and Other Lectures* (London: Hodder & Stoughton, 1920), 310. On the other hand, he elsewhere spoke of the 'touching metaphysical simplicity' with which Tait 'speaks of a conception reaching us through the senses and through subjective impressions, never thinking of the work done by the mind ere impressions can reach the standard of conceptions', *Descartes, Spinoza and the New Philosophy* (Edinburgh: T. & T. Clark, 1904), 115–6.

4. *The Christian Message*, 311.

5. See P. Carnegie Simpson, *The Life of Principal Rainy* (London: Hodder & Stoughton, popular edn., n.d.), ii, 165.

6. G. M. Reith, op. cit. 67; cf. 82–5.

7. See G. F. Barbour, *The Life of Alexander Whyte, D.D.* (London: Hodder & Stoughton, 1924), 522.

8. G. M. Reith, op. cit. 234.

9. George M. Duncan, *The Philosophical Review* xiv (1905), 95.

10. See our chapters on Kennedy, Bruce and Orr for further references to Robertson Smith.

11. *The Christian Message*, 56–7.

12. G. M. Reith, op. cit. 138–9. That Iverach in no way favoured extreme criticism appears in a number of his reviews. Thus he can write, 'It is well that in Germany, the home of so much irresponsible criticism, there should be such workers as Professor Kähler'! See *Expository Times* xviii (1906–7), 357. Earlier in the same volume (p.67), having reviewed a clutch of books on Jesus, he complained that 'the theologians of Germany, who seem to live in an unreal world . . . breathe an academic atmosphere, and they seem to dwell remote from the world in which real men live'.

13. J. Iverach, *The Other Side of Greatness* (London: Hodder & Stoughton, 1906), 53.

14. *The Christian Message*, 57.

15. Ibid. 136.

16. Ibid. 25.

17. Ibid. 54.

18. D. Cromarty, *Scottish Ministerial Miniatures*, 47.

19. *Expository Times*, vi (1894–5), 412.

20. J. Iverach, *Christianity and Evolution* (London: Hodder & Stoughton, 1894), 1. For our own account of the prevailing climate of thought see A. P. F. Sell, *Theology in Turmoil. The roots, course and significance of the conservative-liberal debate in modern theology* (Grand Rapids: Baker Book House, 1986), ch. iii.

21. J. Iverach, *The Philosophy of Mr. Herbert Spencer Examined* (London: Religious Tract Society, 1884), 35.

22. *Christianity and Evolution*, 108–9.
23. J. Iverach, *Theism in the light of Present Science and Philosophy* (London: Hodder & Stoughton, 1900), 89, 91; cf. *Christianity and Evolution*, 86. Iverach's *Theism* was enthusiastically reviewed in *Expository Times* xi (1899–1900), 370, while H. N. Gardiner was somewhat cooler in *Philosophical Review* ix (1900), 672–3.
24. J. Iverach, *Is God Knowable?* (London: Hodder & Stoughton, 1884), 193.
25. *Theism*, 41.
26. *Christianity and Evolution*, 8.
27. Ibid. 118; cf. *Theism*, 74.
28. *Christianity and Evolution*, 95.
29. *Is God Knowable?*, 51.
30. *Christianity and Evolution*, 174–5. The reference is to A. R. Wallace, *Natural Selection*, 240.
31. Ibid. 175–6. (Though he also holds that 'a postulate of religion is the transcendence of God', *Theism*, 287.)
32. *The Philosophy of Mr. Herbert Spencer Examined*, 35.
33. *Christianity and Evolution*, 10.
34. *The Philosophy of Mr. Herbert Spencer Examined*, 43, 38.
35. *Theism*, 94–5.
36. Ibid. 274–5.
37. *Christianity and Evolution*, 208.
38. *Theism*, 52.
39. *Christianity and Evolution*, 12.
40. Ibid. 26, 130; cf. 'Authority', in J. Hastings (ed.) *Encyclopaedia of Religion and Ethics*, ii, 250; *Theism*, 3, 18 etc.
41. See *Theism*, chap. iv; *Christianity and Evolution*, chap. viii.
42. *Theism*, 277. In this connection he remarks that in many of the current philosophies of religion the philosophy remains, but the religion escapes; ibid. 231–2.
43. Ibid. 237.
44. See the *Expositor*, 7th series, iii (1907), 493–507; iv (1907), 20–35, 152–168.
45. Ibid. iii, 502–3.
46. Ibid. 506.
47. Quoted by Iverach, *Is God Knowable?*, 214.
48. *Theism*, 292. See further, A. P. F. Sell, 'Christian and Secular Philosophy in Britain at the Beginning of the Twentieth Century: A Study of Approaches and Relationships', *The Downside Review*, xciii (April 1975), 122–143; and id., *The Philosophy of Religion 1875–1980* (London: Croom Helm, forthcoming, 1988).
49. J. Iverach, 'Edward Caird', *Expository Times* v (1893–4), 205.
50. The *Expositor*, 7th series, iv, 33.
51. 'Edward Caird', op. cit. 209; cf. J. Iverach, 'Thomas Hill Green', *Expository Times* iv (1892–3), 167: 'for Green the historical Christ has vanished, and has been succeeded by the idea'.
52. *Is God Knowable?*, 151.
53. The *Expositor*, 7th series, iv, 156. Cf. Orr's view in the next chapter.
54. Ibid. 163, 164. Cf. his review of J. Watson, *The Interpretation of Religious Experience* in the *Expository Times*, xxiv (1912–13), 295–300. Iverach found F. H. Bradley's logic rigorous against Appearances and slack in respect of the Absolute. See his 'Consciousness', *ERE* iv, 58.
55. *Is God Knowable?*, 49. For a delightful philosophical example of the pot calling the

kettle black consider Spencer's verdict upon Plato: 'Time after time I have attempted to read, now this dialogue and now that, and have put it down in a state of impatience with . . . the mistaking of words for things . . .' See his *Autobiography*, iii, 442.

56. *Theism*, 142. Cf. *Descartes, Spinoza and the New Philosophy* (Edinburgh: T. & T. Clark, 1904), *passim*.

57. *The Christian Message*, 75.

58. *Christianity and Evolution*, 207.

59. *Is God Knowable?* 56.

60. Ibid. 110.

61. J. Iverach, 'The Foundations of Belief', *Expository Times* vi (1894–5), 503.

62. See especially, J. Iverach, *The Ethics of Evolution Examined* (London: Religious Tract Society, 1886).

63. 'Consciousness', op. cit. 52.

64. *Christianity and Evolution*, 186, 188. Cf. A. G. N. Flew, *Evolutionary Ethics* (London: Macmillan, 1967), 43–4.

65. Ibid. 191.

66. Ibid. 200.

67. 'Professor Thomas Hill Green', op. cit. 165. cf. J. Iverach, 'Desire', in J. Hastings (ed.) *Dictionary of Christ and the Gospels* i, 451–2.

68. Ibid. 166.

69. J. Iverach, *Jonathan Edwards* (Edinburgh: Macniven & Wallace, 1884), 129. Cf. *The Christian Message*, 160. For a classic discussion of 'freedom' in Reformed theology, and one to which Iverach alludes (*J. Edwards*, 127) see William Cunningham, *The Reformers and the Theology of the Reformation* ((1862) London: Banner of Truth, 1967), Essay ix.

70. Elsewhere Iverach criticizes Balfour for having failed to take account of the new context in which freedom is now to be discussed. See 'Foundations of Belief', op. cit. 452; Cf. *The Christian Message*, 115–6.

71. 'Professor Thomas Hill Green', 166.

72. J. Royce, *The World and the Individual*, ii, 385, quoted by Iverach, the *Expositor*, 7th series, iv, 165.

73. Quoted ibid.

74. Ibid.

75. *Theism*, 112.

76. Ibid. 216.

77. D. Mackenzie, op. cit. 60.

78. J. Iverach, 'Belief', *Dictionary of Christ and the Gospels* i, 188.

79. *Theism*, 226.

80. *Christianity and Evolution*, 69.

81. *Descartes, Spinoza and the New Philosophy*, 88, 232.

82. *Theism*, 174.

83. *The Ethics of Evolution Examined*, 64; cf. *The Christian Message*, 166–7, 258–9.

84. D. Cromarty, op. cit. 48–9.

85. J. Iverach, *The Truth of Christianity*, 56.

86. *The Christian Message*, 8.

87. Ibid. 15, 105–6.

88. Ibid. 62, 76–77.

89. Ibid. 38.

90. Ibid. 58; cf. 233–4. Iverach did not write extensively on ecclesiology. However, his

opposition to sacerdotalism emerges clearly in his 'Mr. Gore on the Incarnation', *Expository Times* iii (1891–2), 302–7.
91. Ibid. 66.
92. Ibid. 69–70.
93. Ibid. 115.
94. *The Other Side of Greatness*, 71.
95. *The Christian Message*, 184.
96. Mackenzie, op. cit. 56.
97. For a discussion of these matters see Ian G. Barbour, *Issues in Science and Religion* (London: SCM Press, 1966).
98. *Church Quarterly Review* xxxii (1891), 550.

CHAPTER SEVEN:
JAMES ORR (1844–1913):
THE INERADICABILITY OF THE SUPERNATURAL

1. J. Orr, 'The Contribution of the United Presbyterian Church to Religious Thought and Life', in *Memorial of the Jubilee Synod of the United Presbyterian Church* (Edinburgh: U.P. Publications Office, 1897), 88–89. For Orr see *Who Was Who, 1897–1916*, 540; E. Russell, 'The Late Professor Orr—An Appreciation', *The Missionary Record of the United Free Church of Scotland*, November 1913, 552–3; Deas Cromarty, *Scottish Ecclesiastical Miniatures* (London: Hodder & Stoughton, 1892), 50–53; and other refs. below.
2. *Letters of Principal James Denney to W. Robertson Nicoll, 1893–1917* (London: Hodder & Stoughton, 1920), 219; dated 7.9.1913.
3. J. H. Leckie, *Secession Memories* (Edinburgh: T. & T. Clark, 1926), 237.
4. The other so to distinguish himself was Dr M'Kichan, of the Free Church Mission, Bombay. The D.D. regulations were altered at the suggestion of Principal Caird, who 'felt strongly the evils incident to the earlier mode of bestowing it as a matter of favour on private or personal grounds'. It thus became possible to secure the degree either by passing a higher examination, or by submitting a thesis of the required standard. The arrangements did not prove entirely satisfactory, and they were subsequently further modified. See E. Caird's 'Memoir' of John Caird, prefixed to the latter's *The Fundamental Ideas of Christianity* (Glasgow, Maclehose, 1899) I, xciii.
5. See Hugh Watt, *New College Edinburgh. A Centenary History* (Edinburgh: Oliver & Boyd, 1946), 93.
6. For the issues between conservative and liberal Christians see A. P. F. Sell, *Theology in Turmoil. The roots, course and significance of the conservative-liberal debate in modern theology* (Grand Rapids: Baker Book House, 1986), ch. v, vi.
7. See Joseph H. Leckie, *Fergus Ferguson, D.D.: His Theology and Heresy Trial* (Edinburgh: T. & T. Clark, 1923).
8. For this case see H. F. Henderson, *The Religious Controversies of Scotland* (Edinburgh: T. & T. Clark, 1905), ch. xi.
9. So P. Carnegie Simpson, *The Life of Principal Rainy* (London: Hodder & Stoughton, popular edn., n.d.), ii, 273.
10. J. H. Leckie, op. cit. 238.
11. See our chapter on Denney below, and Denney's letters to Nicoll, op. cit. *passim*.

12. The others were the Assembly Clerk, Dr Thomas Kennedy, and Drs. John Young and A. R. MacEwan.
13. P. Carnegie Simpson, op. cit. ii, 196.
14. See ibid. 218–221.
15. See George M. Reith, *Reminiscences of the United Free Church General Assembly (1900–1929)* (Edinburgh: Moray Press, 1933), 40. For an account of the entire course of the union debate see Rolf Sjölinder, *Presbyterian Reunion in Scotland, 1907–1921* (Edinburgh: T. & T. Clark, 1964).
16. See Sjölinder, op. cit. 231.
17. Quoted ibid.; cf. Denney's *Letters* to Nicoll, 207–8, 203.
18. G. M. Reith, op. cit. 153.
19. Op. cit. 91.
20. Ibid., pp. 97–98.
21. Ed. J. H. Leckie, *David W. Forrest, D.D. . . . Memoir, Tributes, etc* (London: Hodder & Stoughton, 1919), 300.
22. J. H. Leckie, *Secession Memories*, 238.
23. J. Orr, *The Progress of Dogma* (London: James Clarke, [1901]), 4.
24. Ibid. 5–6; cf. his *The Christian View of God and the World* (Edinburgh: Elliot, 34d edn., 1893), 16–26.
25. *The Progress of Dogma*, 13.
26. Ibid. 50.
27. Ibid. 51, his italics. We shall later note Orr's criticisms of Ritschl and Ritschlianism concerning the divorce of faith from reason.
28. Cf. A. P. F. Sell, 'Theology and the Philosophical Environment: Some Illustrations and Lessons from the Second Century AD', *Vox Evangelica* xiii, 1983, 41–65, and xiv, 1984, 53–64.
29. *The Progress of Dogma*, 53 (our italics).
30. Ibid. 53–4.
31. Ibid. 55.
32. Ibid. 60.
33. Ibid. 64.
34. Some have suggested that Orr thought of Gnosticism as being more of a movement *within* the Church than it was in its totality. If they are correct, we shall have to say that *some* varieties of Gnosticism were not uninfluenced by Christian concepts.
35. J. Orr, *Neglected Factors in the Study of the Early Progress of Christianity* (London: Hodder & Stoughton, 1899), 226. It is an interesting indication of Orr's catholicity and accuracy to note that both this book and *The Progress of Dogma* were praised by the reviewer in the *Church Quarterly Review*. See l (April 1900), 244–5, and lv (Oct. 1902), 212–216. For the early period see also Orr's *History and Literature of the Early Church* (London: Hodder & Stoughton, 1913) which remains a clear and concise text book.
36. J. Orr, 'The Factors in the Expansion of the Christian Church', in J. B. Paton *et al. Christ and Civilization* (London: National Council of Evangelical Free Churches, 1910), 218–9.
37. J. Orr, *God's Image in Man* (London: Hodder & Stoughton, 1907), 27.
38. *The Progress of Dogma*, 8.
39. Ibid. 8–9.
40. Ibid. 9 n.
41. Ibid. 12–13.

42. Ibid. 15.
43. Ibid. 17. Not indeed that final verdicts are ever passed. As we shall see by the end of this section, the ghosts of 'vanquished' heresies quite often visit later centuries.
44. Ibid. 29–30.
45. A. E. Garvie, *The Christian Doctrine of the Godhead* (London: Hodder & Stoughton, 1925), 23.
46. *The Progress of Dogma*, 291.
47. Ibid. 292–3.
48. Ibid. 293, 294–5. This is consistent with his preference for sublapsarianism as against supralapsarianism. See his articles on these in J. Hastings (ed.) *Encyclopaedia of Religion and Ethics*, xi, 909–910, and xii, 123. Cf. his 'Calvinism', in *ERE* iii, 152–3, and *The Progress of Dogma*, 296.
49. J. Orr, 'Calvinism', *ERE* iii, 150–151.
50. *The Progress of Dogma*, 152–3.
51. 'Calvinism', 151–2. Cf. *The Progress of Dogma*, 247 for Orr's view that 'the Church, from a very early period, went seriously astray in its doctrinal and practical apprehension of the divine method of the sinner's salvation'.
52. See chap. II, above.
53. See W. Cunningham, *The Reformers and the Theology of the Reformation* ([1862], Edinburgh: Banner of Truth, 1967), 396–7.
54. 'Calvinism', 153.
55. Ibid. 155.
56. *The Progress of Dogma*, 352.
57. Ibid.
58. A. P. F. Sell, *Theology in Turmoil*, chs. v, vi.
59. *The Progress of Dogma*, 353.
60. See A. P. F. Sell, *Theology in Turmoil*, ch. vi.
61. *The Progress of Dogma*, 353.
62. Ibid. 41.
63. J. Orr, 'The Old Testament Question in the Early Church,' the *Expositor*, 5th series, i (1895), 359.
64. *The Progress of Dogma*, 101–2.
65. J. Orr, *The Faith of a Modern Christian* (London: Hodder & Stoughton, 1910), vi.
66. *God's Image in Man*, vi.
67. Ibid. 260–1.
68. Ibid. 7. Coleridge's words, 'In no case can true Reason and a right Faith oppose each other' are prefixed to the first of Orr's *Kerr Lectures*. See *The Christian View of God and the World*, 2.
69. J. Orr, 'What is God?' in *Questions of Faith. A Series of Lectures on the Creed* (London: Hodder & Stoughton, 1904), 6.
70. *The Progress of Dogma*, 321.
71. *The Christian View of God and the World*, 4. On p. 32–34, Orr provides a sketch of the Christian world view and on p. 7 he writes: 'It is a singular circumstance that, with all the distaste of the age for metaphysics, the tendency to the formation of world-systems, or general theories of the universe, was never more powerful than at the present day'. Those of us who learned our philosophy during the hey-day of linguistic analysis tended to be taught that, no matter how hard it might be to understand, everybody in Orr's day actually *liked* metaphysics! Orr redresses the balance somewhat.

72. Ibid. 8.
73. *The Progress of Dogma*, 322.
74. Ibid. 359–60.
75. Cf. Tillich's assertion that it is as atheistic to affirm the existence of God as to deny it: *Systematic Theology*, (Chicago: University of Chicago Press, 1951) I, 237.
76. *The Christian View of God and the World*, 94.
77. Ibid. 105–6; cf. p. 150. Orr was not unaware, however, of the dangers to which even the most exalted idealism could lead. He also notes a downgrade from Green's 'Eternal Self-Consciousness' to 'an Absolute—the Ground or Reality of the universe—for which good and evil, in the ordinary sense of the terms, no longer exist'. Bradley and McTaggart are adduced as examples of this unwholesome tendency. See *Sin as a Problem of Today* (London: Hodder & Stoughton, 1910). 40–41.
78. *The Christian View of God and the World*, 94–5.
79. J. Orr, *Ritschlianism, Expository and Critical Essays* (London: Hodder & Stoughton, 1903), 255.
80. *The Christian View of God and the World*, 77.
81. See Ibid. 11.
82. See Ibid. 11, 12.
83. J. Orr, *Revelation and Inspiration* (London: Duckworth, 1910), 47; cf. 27–31.
84. 'What is God?' op. cit. 6–7.
85. Ibid. 20.
86. See e.g. *The Progress of Dogma*, 329; *The Faith of a Modern Christian*, 216. Cf. his 'Science and Christian Faith' in *The Fundamentals* iv (Chicago: Testimony Publishing Co., n.d.), 91–104; *God's Image in Man*, 89–108, 154.
87. *Sin as a Problem of Today* (London: Hodder & Stoughton, 1910), 160. We should note that although opposed, supremely on the ground here stated, to material*ism* (cf. *The Christian View of God and the World*, 142–150), Orr was no less opposed to 'The abstract spirituality of a Plotinus, or of a hyper-refined idealism, which regards the body as a mere envelope of the soul . . .' (*The Christian View of God and the World*, 136). Certainly the Bible gives the material its rights, ibid. 136–7. Orr found the newer naturalistic monism of Haeckel *et al.* indistinguishable from the older naturalism in procedure and results. See *God's Image in Man*, 68–78.
88. *God's Image in Man*, 87–88. His general verdict was, 'On the general hypothesis of evolution, as applied to the organic world, I have nothing to say, except that, within certain limits, it seems to me extremely probable, and supported by a large body of evidence'. (*The Christian View of God and the World*, 99).
89. *Revelation and Inspiration*, 38.
90. *Sin as a Problem of Today*, 22; cf. 109, and *God's Image in Man*, 19–23.
91. *The Faith of a Modern Christian*, 92. Cf. *Sidelights on Christian Doctrine* (London,: Marshall, 1909) 86. For the general background to the points just made see A. P. F. Sell, *Theology in Turmoil,* ch. iv.
92. J. Orr, *David Hume and his Influence on Philosophy and Theology* (Edinburgh: T. & T. Clark, 1903), 46 (quoting Hume's *Works*, iv, 187).
93. Ibid. 101, 11.
94. Ibid. 12.
95. Ibid. 103.
96. Ibid. 155.
97. Ibid. 164–5.

98. J. Orr, *Ritschlianism* 29–30. For the context of the Ritschlian debate and for our own reflections upon it see A. P. F. Sell, *Theology in Turmoil*, ch. iv.
99. J. Orr, *The Ritschlian Theology and the Evangelical Faith* (London: Hodder & Stoughton, 2nd edn. 1898), 49.
100. Ibid. 60, quoting *Theol. und Met.*, 40.
101. Ibid. 67.
102. Ibid. 247.
103. Ibid. 250.
104. *Ritschlianism*, 260.
105. *The Ritschlian Theology*, 236.
106. *The Christian View of God and the World*, 29.
107. See A. P. F. Sell, 'Transcendence, Immanence and the Supernatural', *The Journal of Theology for Southern Africa* (March, 1979), 56–66 and 'Transcendence, Immanence and the Loss of Authority', *Churchman*, xcvi (1982), 123–141.
108. *Revelation and Inspiration*, 7.
109. J. Orr, 'Professor W. E. Addis on Hebrew Religion', *Expository Times*, xviii (1906–7), 119–125.
110. *The Christian View of God and the World*, 399. Cf. Warren C. Young, *A Christian Approach to Philosophy* (Grand Rapids: Backer Book House, 1973), 21.
111. *Revelation and Inspiration*, 131–9.
112. J. Orr, 'Can Professor Pfleiderer's View Justify Itself?' in R. Rainy *et al.*, *The Supernatural in Christianity* (Edinburgh: T. & T. Clark, 1894), 46.
113. Ibid. 52; and cf. this powerful statement in *The Christian View of God and the World*, 76: 'If God is a reality, the whole universe rests on a supernatural basis. A supernatural presence pervades it; a supernatural power sustains it; a supernatural will operates in its forces; a supernatural wisdom appoints its ends.'
114. Ibid. 63.
115. Ibid. 65.
116. Ibid. 66–67.
117. J. Orr, 'Holy Scripture and Modern Negations', *The Fundamentals*, ix, 33.
118. See e.g. his *The Problem of the Old Testament* (London: Nisbet, 1906), and his more popular work, *The Bible on Trial* (London: Marshall, 1907).
119. *The Christian View of God and the World*, 182; cf. 'The Early Narratives in Genesis', *The Fundamentals*, vi, 86. He does not, however, regard the story of the Fall as a myth. Rather, it 'enshrines the shuddering memory of an actual moral catastrophe in the beginning of our race, which brought death into the world and all our woe' (p. 89); similarly with the creation and flood narratives (p. 97).
120. 'Holy Scripture and Modern Negations', op. cit. 34.
121. *Revelation and Inspiration*, 18–19.
122. 'Holy Scripture and Modern Negations', 37–8; cf. *The Faith of a Modern Christian*, chap. i.
123. *Revelation and Inspiration*, 67.
124. *Ritschlianism*, 249.
125. *Revelation and Inspiration*, 155.
126. Ibid. 159.
127. Ibid. 165.
128. Ibid. 181, 175.
129. Ibid. 169.
130. Ibid. 210.

131. Ibid. 198.
132. Ibid. 215. It is a tribute to Orr's generosity of spirit that he invited B. B. Warfield to contribute the article on 'Inspiration' to the *International Standard Bible Encyclopaedia*, although he did not agree at all points with Warfield. A reviewer in the *Expository Times*, xviii (1906–7), 517, praises Orr thus: 'Professor Orr is the great God—send of the modern believer in the verbal inspiration of the Bible. He does not believe in verbal inspiration himself. He is as far removed from that fetish as Professor Cheyne. But he finds so very little to alter in the Bible, that the believer in verbal inspiration can in these dire times accept him as a brother and be thankful'. Some latter-day conservative scholars have found Orr unduly concessive. Cf. e.g. E. J. Young, *Thy Word is Truth* (London: Banner of Truth, 1963), 141; Roger Nicole, 'Theology', in C. F. H. Henry (ed.) *Contemporary Evangelical Thought* (Grand Rapids: Baker Book House, 1968), 81.
133. Ibid. 204.
134. Ibid. 217. Note, again, the unanalyzed term 'proof'. Here it is like 'proof' in 'the proof of the pudding is in the eating'.
135. *David Hume*, 210, quoting *Works*, iv, 130.
136. *Revelation and Inspiration*, 115.
137. Ibid.
138. On which Orr comments, 'He calls a halt only when the view of the world becomes monistic . . . This, all the same, is a rather important qualification of the position that Christianity has nothing to do with philosophy or theories of nature'. See *Ritschlianism*, 119.
139. Ibid. 147.
140. *Revelation and Inspiration*, 51.
141. *The Faith of a Modern Christian*, 62.
142. 'What is God?', op. cit. 9.
143. *The Progress of Dogma*, 323–4 n.
144. Ibid. 326.
145. 'What is God?' op. cit. 25.
146. *Sidelights on Christian Doctrine*, 38.
147. *The Christian View of God and the World*, 268; cf. *Sidelights on Christian Doctrine*, 47.
148. *Sidelights on Christian Doctrine*, 94; cf. *The Christian View of God and the World*, 171.
149. See *God's Image in Man*, 216–17.
150. *Sin as a Problem of Today*, 7.
151. See e.g. *God's Image in Man*, 228.
152. J. Orr, 'The Early Narratives of Genesis', *The Fundamentals*, vi, 96.
153. *The Christian View of God and the World*, 198; cf. *God's Image in Man*, 252, 258; *Sin as a Problem of Today*, 277ff., etc.
154. D. W. Forrest, *The Christ of History and of Experience* (Edinburgh: T. & T. Clark 7th edn., 1914), 430. B. B. Warfield, on the other hand, said with respect to Orr's assertion of the connection between sin and death: 'A firm grasp upon this element of the Biblical doctrine notably clears the air'. See his *Critical Reviews* (New York: OUP, 1932), 138.
155. *The Ritschlian Theology*, 263.
156. J. Orr, *The Virgin Birth of Christ* (London: Hodder & Stoughton, 1908), 14; cf. *The Faith of a Modern Christian*, 97–8; 'The Virgin Birth of Christ', *The Fundamentals*, i, 7–20, etc.
157. *Sin as a Problem of Today*, 294, n. 2.

158. *Ritschlianism*, 224.
159. *The Virgin Birth*, 221.
160. *Revelation and Inspiration*, 150–2.
161. *The Christian View of God and the World*, 243.
162. *The Faith of a Modern Christian*, 96.
163. W. L. Walker, *The Spirit and the Incarnation* (Edinburgh: T. & T. Clark, 1899), 257.
164. *The Christian View of God and the World*, 245.
165. *The Progress of Dogma*, 193.
166. In J. H. Hick (ed.), *The Myth of God Incarnate* (London: SCM Press, 1977), 178.
167. Ibid.
168. *The Progress of Dogma*, 194; cf. 332–3.
169. J. Hick, op. cit. 179.
170. *The Christian View of God and the World*, 280.
171. J. Denney, *Studies in Theology* (London: Hodder & Stoughton 1902), 100, 101.
172. *The Christian View of God and the World*, 296.
173. W. L. Walker, op. cit. 275.
174. See e.g. *The Christian View of God and the World*, 171.
175. *The Progress of Dogma*, 239.
176. Ibid. 342.
177. *The Ritschlian Theology*, 266.
178. *Ritschlianism*, 92.
179. *The Resurrection of Jesus* (London: Hodder & Stoughton, 1908), 53.
180. J. Orr, 'The Kingdom of God', *The Expository Times*, iv, 1892–3, 466. Orr contributed the article on 'Kingdom of God' to J. Hastings (ed.), *Dictionary of the Bible*, ii, 844–56.
181. *Sidelights on Christian Doctrine*, 179.
182. *The Resurrection of Jesus*, 266.
183. *The Progress of Dogma*, 43.
184. *The Faith of a Modern Christian*, 234.

CHAPTER EIGHT:
DAVID WILLIAM FORREST (1856–1918):
THE CENTRALITY OF CHRIST

1. G. S. Hendry, 'Christology', in A. Richarson (ed.) *A Dictionary of Christian Theology* (London: SCM Press, 1969), 61.
2. B. L. Hebblethwaite, 'The Appeal to Experience in Christology', in S. W. Sykes and J. P. Clayton (eds.) *Christ, Faith and History* (Cambridge: CUP, 1972), 274.
3. D. M. Mackinnon, '"Substance" in Christology—A Cross-Bench View', in Sykes and Clayton, op. cit. 297.
4. For the sketch which follows we are largely indebted to J. H. Leckie's 'Memoir' in J. H. Leckie (ed.) *David W. Forrest, D.D., . . . Memoir, Tributes, Sermons and Theological Lectures* (London: Hodder & Stoughton, 1919), 5–112. See also *Who Was Who, 1916–1928*, 368; W. M. Clow's appreciation in *The Record of the Home and Foreign Misson Work of the United Free Church of Scotland*, April 1918, 73–4.
5. Quoted by J. H. Leckie, op. cit. 13.

6. Ibid.
7. Ibid. 29–30.
8. Ibid. 116.
9. See George M. Reith, *Reminiscences of The United Free Church General Assembly (1900–1929)* (Edinburgh: Moray Press, 1933), 74–5.
10. Ibid. 47 and n.
11. Ibid. 153–4.
12. So J. H. Leckie, op. cit. 85.
13. Elsewhere J. H. Leckie wrote: 'Forrest was more faithful in visiting my father [Joseph Leckie of Ibrox Church, Glasgow] than any other clergyman, and the older man rejoiced wholeheartedly in his conversation, so agile, so free, and so generous. Nor did Forrest ever abate this loyal friendship, which was continued to Dr. Leckie's children for the father's sake'. See his *Secession Memories* (Edinburgh: T. & T. Clark, 1928), 238.
14. *D. W. Forrest*, 4.
15. Quoted ibid. 43.
16. Ibid. 293.
17. Quoted ibid. 91.
18. Quoted ibid. 92, 65.
19. Ibid. 138.
20. D. W. Forrest, *The Christ of History and of Experience* (hereinafter *CHE*) (Edinburgh: T. & T. Clark, 7th edn., 1914), 120–121.
21. D. W. Forrest, *The Authority of Christ* (hereinafter *AC*), (Edinburgh: T. & T. Clark, 4th edn., 1914), 300, 303; cf. *CHE*, 264.
22. *CHE*, v.
23. Ibid. 301–2.
24. Ibid. 302.
25. Ibid. 304.
26. Ibid. 305 and n.
27. Ibid. 307–8.
28. *D. W. Forrest*, 294.
29. *CHE.*, 325, 329, 330; cf. n. 37, 463–468, on 'Fact and Ideal'. The reference is to R. W. Dale, *The Living Christ and the Four Gospels* (London: Hodder & Stoughton, 1890), 39–41. It is interesting to compare Forrest's response here with that of such an anti-Bultmannite as Dr. William Neil: 'Many of us may find it impossible tt see how Bultmann and his disciples can combine such a sceptical view of the historical value of the gospel with a full-blooded acceptance of the traditional Christian faith. This has always been a tight-rope act which the Germans seem to be able to accomplish very successfully but it is a journey which less adventurous Anglo-Saxons find hazardous in the extreme'. See his 'Second Thoughts V. The Jesus of History', *Expository Times*, lxxv (June 1964), 262.
30. Ibid. 335.
31. *D. W. Forrest*, 309; from Forrest's Inaugural Lecture as Professor of Dogmatic Theology and Apologetics at Glasgow United Free Church College, 'Christian Faith and its Intellectual Expression'.
32. Ibid. 314.
33. Ibid. 307.
34. Ibid. 316.
35. Ibid. 279.

36. *AC*, 27.
37. *CHE*, 79.
38. In our account of Forrest on Butler and Caird we largely follow his Inaugural Lecture, in which the references are to Caird's article on Butler in *University Addresses* (Glasgow: Maclehose, 1898), 191–222.
39. *D. W. Forrest*, 276.
40. Ibid. 293.
41. Ibid. 283.
42. Ibid. 279. The last sentence here is a clear echo of John Caird: 'There is not a single doctrine of natural religion which, when it enters into the context of the Christian faith, remains what it was outside of Christianity'. See his *The Fundamental Ideas of Christianity* (Glasgow: Maclehose, 1899), i, 22.
43. Ibid. 298.
44. *AC*, 56.
45. *CHE*, 17. B. B. Warfield took great exception to this point: see his *Critical Reviews* (New York: OUP, 1932), 154–172.
46. Ibid. 104.
47. Ibid. 205.
48. *AC*, 132–3.
49. *CHE*, 166.
50. *AC*, 107.
51. *D. W. Forrest*, 291; cf. 288. With Forrest's approach may be contrasted the statement, 'Properly speaking, we cannot say that God is known when there is no religion or piety', (Calvin, *Institutes*, I.ii.1); and, more recently, 'We have even preachers telling the public, with an incredible stupidity, that to prove Christianity to yourself you must try it, and find how well it goes. As a matter of fact, you cannot try it till you believe it!' (P. T. Forsyth, *The Justification of God* ([1917], London: Independent Press, 1948), 93.
52. *AC*, 154.
53. *CHE*, 123.
54. Ibid. 15–16.
55. Ibid. 60–62.
56. Ibid. 125.
57. Ibid. 120.
58. Ibid. 157.
59. Ibid. 158.
60. *D. W. Forrest*, 295.
61. See above, n. 7.
62. *D. W. Forrest*, 301–2.
63. *CHE*, 4.
64. D. W. Forrest, 'Did Jesus Pray with His Disciples?', *Expository Times* xl (1899–1900), 357. This article is substantially reprinted as an appendix to *CHE* (7th edn.) 472–481.
65. Robert Butterworth, 'Bishop Robinson and Christology', *Religious Studies* xi (1975), 81–2.
66. *AC*, 10.
67. *CHE*, 43.
68. Ibid. 19.
69. Ibid. 27.

70. R. Butterworth, 'Has Chalcedon a Future?' *The Month* x (April 1977), 116. John 'Rabbi' Duncan averred that the confession that all are sinners is 'the hypocrite's *pillow* . . . the believer's *bed of thorns*'. See his *Pulpit and Communion Table* (Inverness: Free Presbyterian Publications, 1969), 38.

71. *CHE* 40; cf. 34., and P. T. Forsyth, *The Person and Place of Jesus Christ*([1909], London: Independent Press, 1961), 302: 'the incarnation was a moral act so supreme and complete as to be possible only to a conscience at the pitch of the perfectly holy . . . Sin is no factor of the true humanity, but only a feature of empirical humanity which is absolutely fatal to the true'.

72. Ibid. 38.

73. See ibid. 22–27; 385–6; and 472–481 for this and the following points.

74. A. B. Bruce, 'The Baptism of Jesus', The *Expositor*, March 1898, 196–7.

75. See A. B. Bruce, *The Humiliation of Christ* (Edinburgh: T. & T. Clark, 2nd rev. edn. 1881), 366–372; cf. AC, 54–5.
    AC, 54–5.

76. Cf. *AC* 19. A. Stewart entered the debate to suggest that Jesus may well have confessed sins on behalf of his disciples, without implying that he was himself a sinner. See *Expository Times* xi (1899–1900), 477–8. But this is an argument from silence.

77. *CHE*, 47.

78. See A. B. Bruce, *The Kingdom of God* (Edinburgh: T. & T. Clark, 1889), 17.

79. *CHE*, 51.

80. *AC*, 33.

81. *CHE*, 96–8.

82. Ibid. 133–4. Forrest would have been in accord with Professor S. W. Sykes in the latter's implied criticism of some of our contemporary christological writers: 'Christology cannot in the end avoid the significance of the *difference* between the story of Jesus and the lives of other men'. See Sykes and Clayton, op. cit. 64.

83. *CHE*, 173.

84. J. Macquarrie, 'A Dilemma in Christology', *Expository Times*, lxxvi (April 1965), 210.

85. *AC*, 334.

86. *CHE*, 189.

87. *D. W. Forrest*, 143.

88. *CHE*, 161.

89. Ibid. 164.

90. Ibid. 165. Forrest further remarks that when Herrmann talks of the inner life of Jesus 'as a present fact in our own life . . . he conveys suggestions of the transcendence of Christ's person which his entire theory repudiates . . . It is time to protest against this abuse of language, which ascribes to a theory fatal to the historic faith the intimate and continuous fellowship with Christ which that faith alone makes possible'. Ibid. 167.

91. Ibid. 247n.

92. *AC*, 92.

93. *CHE*, 158.

94. J. Macquarrie, 'The Humanity of Christ', *Theology* lxxiv (1971), 249.

95. In Sykes and Clayton, op. cit. 65.

96. *AC*, 37.

97. Ibid. 46.

98. *D. W. Forrest*, 71–2.
99. *CHE*, vi.
100. *AC*, 98.
101. Cf. ibid. 41.
102. Ibid. 82.
103. *CHE*, 191.
104. *AC*, 341.
105. Ibid. 100.
106. *CHE*, 201; cf. *AC*, 95–6.
107. See D. M. Baillie, *God Was in Christ* (London: Faber, 1961), 94–8.
108. *CHE*, 203–4.
109. Cf. e.g. B. L. Hebblethwaite in Sykes and Clayton, op. cit. 264.
110. J. Caird, *The Fundamental Ideas of Christianity*, ii, 129.
111. Ibid. 132; italics his.
112. Ibid. 133.
113. Ibid. 137.
114. T. A. Thomas, 'The Kenosis Question', *Evangelical Quarterly*, xlii (1970), 151.
115. J. Caird, *Sermons* (Edinburgh: Blackwood, 1858), 27.
116. Ibid. 153–4.
117. *AC*, 90; cf. 91.
118. We may here note that the term 'nature' posed problems in the Chalcedonian age too. According to the then-prevailing Aristotelianism, 'nature' is universal, 'person' is individual. Hence 'two natures in one person' appears as logically contradictory. For this reason Leontius of Byzantium proposed the view that the human nature of Christ had *no* personal centre of its own, but achieved personality in the Logos. The Second Council of Constantinople (553) endorsed this view.
119. B. B. Warfield, 'Christology and Criticism', reprinted in his *The Person and Work of Christ* (Philadelphia: Presbyterian and Reformed, 1950), 211.
120. S. Cave, *The Doctrines of the Christian Faith* (London: Independent Press, 1952), 209.
121. H. M. Relton, *A Study in Christology* (London: SPCK, 1922), 122ff.
122. See further A. P. F. Sell, 'Platonists (Ancient and Modern) and the Gospel', *Irish Theological Quarterly* xliv (1977), 153–174.
123. *D. W. Forrest*, 136.
124. *AC*, 117.
125. *CHE*, 287.
126. B. B. Warfield, *Critical Reviews*, 168.
127. *CHE*, 59.
128. *AC*, 189–203.
129. *D. W. Forrest*, 170.
130. Ibid. 124. On occasion Forrest speaks of our acknowledgement of obligation to God in a somewhat misleading way, e.g. 'In yielding the heart to God, we enrich Him; we give Him that which He has not already, and which He could not have but by our willing consent'. (*CHE*, 277). Lower down the same page Forrest redeems himself to some extent by remarking that whatever God gains is gained only as his Spirit works within us.
131. Ibid. 122.
132. Ibid. 190.
133. Ibid. 126.
134. Ibid. 138.

135. *AC*, 326.
136. See John Baillie's *Our Knowledge of God* (London: OUP, 1939) 52; cf. and *The Sense of the Presence of God* (London: OUP, 1962); and the criticisms of H. D. Lewis in his *Philosophy of Religion* (London: The English Universities Press, 1965), chap. xi.
137. *CHE*, 369; and see the entire chapter.

CHAPTER NINE:
JAMES DENNEY (1856–1917):
A PREACHABLE THEOLOGY

1. *Letters of Principal James Denney to W. Robertson Nicoll, 1893–1917*, (hereinafter *LN*) (London: Hodder & Stoughton, 1920), 176, dated 5.11.1911.
2. *Letters of Principal James Denney to His Family and Friends* (hereinafter *LFF*), ed. James Moffatt (London: Hodder & Stoughton, 1922), xii–xiii. Cf. Denney's article, 'Preaching Christ', *Dictionary of Christ and the Gospels* in J. Hastings (ed.), ii, 393–403. For Denney see, in addition to *LN* and *LFF*, *DNB* 1912–21, 153–4; *Who Was Who, 1916–1928*, 280; Alexander Gammie, *Preachers I Have Heard* (London: Pickering & Inglis, n.d.), 161–3; George Johnstone Jeffrey, 'James Denney, 1856–1917', in R. Selby Wright (ed.), *Fathers of the Kirk* (London: OUP, 1960), 252–261; W. M. Macgregor, *Persons and Ideals* (Edinburgh: T. & T. Clark, 1939), Samuel J. Mikolaski, 'The Theology of Principal James Denney', *Evangelical Quarterly* (1963), xxxv, 89–96, 144–8, 209–22; Principal Denney: Some Tributes, '*The Record of the Home and Foreign Mission Work of the United Free Church of Scotland*, August 1917, 160–164; and the comments upon his theology by C. Wistar Hodge, H. R. Mackintosh and W. P. Paterson to be noted below. See further, B. G. Worrall, 'Substitutionary atonement in the theology of James Denny, *Scottish Journal of Theology* (1975) xxviii, 341–57; and two unpublished theses: J. R. Taylor, *Principal James Denney: A Survey of his Life and Work* (Aberdeen, 1956), and S. J. Mikolaski, *The Nature of Human Response to the Work of Christ in the Objective Theories of the Atonement advanced in Recent British Theology by R. W. Dale, James Denney and P. T. Forsyth* (Oxford, 1958).
3. *LFF*, 52, dated 17.7.1893.
4. *LN*, xv.
5. *LFF*, 182.
6. *LN*, 6, dated 10.12.1894.
7. *LFF*, 70, dated 18.5.1896.
8. Robert Mackintosh, *Historic Theories of Atonement* (London: Hodder & Stoughton, 1920), 284.
9. *LN*, xvi.
10. *LFF*, 109–110, dated 15.11.1901.
11. *LFF*, 56, dated 3.5.1894.
12. Though his friend, J. P. Struthers, who was to have been honoured with him, declined.
13. So W. R. Nicoll,*LN*, 10. Strangely, Nicoll here refers to the General Assembly of the *United* Free Church. But it was not until 1900 that the United Presbyterians joined with the Free Church majority to constitute that body.
14. *LFF*, 175; to P. Carnegie Simpson, dated 13.12.1914.

15. See e.g. *LN*, 64, 77; *LFF*, 91, 178.

16. *LN*, 168, dated 23.12.1910.

17. James Denney, *Studies in Theology* (London: Hodder & Stoughton, 1894), 258.

18. *LN*, 219, dated 7.9.1913.

19. Ibid. 253, dated 1.10.1915; cf. 248, dated 27.5.1915.

20. Ibid. 257, dated 16.12.1916.

21. Ibid. 88–89, dated 7.4.1907.

22. Ibid. 206, dated 9.9.1912. He had thought that a second class degree in Philosophy was the very worst preparation for theological education!

23. Ibid. 221, dated 18.9.1913. Cf. J. Denney, *The Second Epistle to the Corinthians* (London: Hodder & Stoughton, 1916), 107. 'A distinguished career at the University, or in the Divinity Schools, proves that a man can write with ink, under favourable circumstances; it does not prove more than that; it does not prove that he will be spiritually effective, and everything else is irrelevant.' Cf. a letter of Denney to Nicoll, dated 18.4.1908, in T. H. Darlow, *William Robertson Nicoll: Life and Letters* (London: Hodder & Stoughton, 1925), 371.

24. Ibid. 35, dated 28.11.1903.

25. Quoted by A. Gammie, op. cit. 162.

26. *LN*, 173, dated 3.2.1911. It is interesting to note that both Denney and John Caird published a sermon on Mark 14:3, and that whereas Caird fastens upon the fact that actions of the type performed by the woman in anointing Jesus have immortal honour, symbolic power, and non-utilitarian criteria, Denney emphasizes the idea of Christ's *being anointed* before his death and burial. See J. Caird, *Essays for Sunday Reading* (London: Pitman, 1906), 59–88; J. Denney, *The Way Everlasting* (London: Hodder & Stoughton, 1911) 282–93.

27. *The Way Everlasting*, 104. Denney was overwhelmed by Nicoll's generous comments on this collection of sermons, himself feeling that they were unduly repetitious. See *LN*, 187, dated 8.12.1911, and 190, dated 16.12.1911. For further remarks of Denney on preaching see his *The Epistles to the Thessalonians* (London: Hodder & Stoughton, 1892), 48–9.

28. *LFF*, ix.

29. *LN*, xvii.

30. Ibid. 104, dated 13.1.1908. A number of letters in both collections refer to Mrs. Denney, and to Denney's sense of loss after her death. They had no children.

31. Moffatt gives 1904, *LFF*, 116; but cf. *LN*, 70–71, dated 7.8.1906.

32. See e.g. *LN*, 66, dated 6.6.1906; 94, dated 10.5.1907.

33. *LFF*, 69, dated 18.5.1896. In the same letter he remarks of the Cameronians (his own stock) that 'To abjure·both Church and State . . . was to proceed upon an impossible theory'.

34. *LN*, xl. Of the continuing Free Churchmen he wrote, 'It really looks as if they thought the highness of their creed could cover any depth of lowness in their conduct. (Ibid. 41, dated 5.1.1904).

35. *Studies in Theology*, 195.

36. See the *Constructive Quarterly*, June 1913.

37. *LN*, 220–221, dated 18.9.1913.

38. G. M. Reith, *Reminiscences of the United Free Church General Assembly (1900–1929)* (Edinburgh: Moray Press, 1933), 155.

39. Quoted by G. F. Barbour, *The Life of Alexander Whyte* (London: Hodder & Stoughton, 1924), 508. For an appreciation of his service as convener, see 'Principal

Denney: Some Tributes', op. cit. 162. The same journal includes appreciations by his minister, George Reith, and by a former student, James A. Robertson.

40. T. H. Darlow, op. cit. 260.

41. *LN*, 263, dated 25.3.1917. Denney was an earnest writer and speaker on behalf of prohibition, and was highly suspicious of the suspected financial link between brewers and politicians. For an appreciation of his work in this connection see 'Principal Denney: Some Tributes', op. cit. 162–3. *Who Was Who* gives the date of Denney's death as 12th June; *DNB* gives 15th June.

42. *LFF*, 215, dated 27.5.1917.

43. Extracts from the College Committee's Minute, see 'Principal Denney: Some Tributes', op. cit. 160.

44. *LN*, 187, dated 15.11.1911.

45. *LFF*, 191–3, being a quotation from the Report of the Committee on the Recognition of the Place of Women in the Church's Life and Work, submitted to the United Free Church General Assembly of 1916.

46. *LN*, 224, dated 4.10.1913.

47. Ibid. 55, dated 11.4.1905.

48. *LFF*, 113, dated 5.2.1902.

49. *LN*, 155, dated 27.5.1910 and 232, dated 19.1.1914.

50. Ibid. 87, dated 1.4. 1907.

51. *LFF*, 117, dated 2.3.1904.

52. *LN*, 228, dated 31.10.1913.

53. *LFF*, 36, dated 17.1.1890.

54. Ibid. 79–80, dated 2.11.1903.

55. Quoted by G. F. Barbour, op. cit. 507.

56. For a fuller and wider-ranging discussion see A. P. F. Sell, *Theology in Turmoil. The roots, course and significance of the conservative-liberal debate in modern theology* (Grand Rapids: Baker Book House, 1986), chs. v, vi.

57. Quoted by P. Carnegie Simpson, *The Life of Principal Rainy*, ii (London: Hodder & Stoughton, popular edn., n.d.), 115.

58. Quoted by J. Moffatt in *LFF*, 23.

59. *Studies in Theology*, pref.

60. Ibid, 202–3; cf. J. Denney, *The Atonement and the Modern Mind* (London: Hodder & Stoughton, 1903), 4–5, 9.

61. *The Way Everlasting*, 211.

62. *LN*,22, dated 1.3.1901. J. A. Robertson recalled Denney's classroom onslaught upon Schmiedel and others: 'And so this evangelist has gone on deceiving the world all these centuries—*till Schmiedel found him out!*' See *LN*, xxxiv.

63. Ibid. 214, dated 19.12.1912.

64. Ibid. 24, dated 9.1.1902.

65. *Studies in Theology*, 219; cf. 'Fall (Biblical)', in *ERE* v. No doubt some conservatives were on the watch for such phrases as the last in the following quotation: 'Now what is true of . . . all, of us, . . . may be true of the race, or of the first man, if there was a first man'. See *The Atonement and the Modern Mind*, 56.

66. Ibid. 223.

67. *LN*, 71, dated 7.8.1906.

68. J. Denney, *Jesus and the Gospel* (London: Hodder & Stoughton, 2nd edn. 1909), viii.

69. *The Way Everlasting*, 69. In a letter to P. Carnegie Simpson he said that the difficult

question of credal revision 'makes one wish sometimes he were a Quaker or a Congregationalist, and had only to believe in the gospel, not in a creed at all'. (*LFF*, 119, dated Nov. 1904).

70. *Jesus and the Gospel*, 395.
71. *LN*, 17, dated 4.1.1901.
72. *LFF*, 73, dated 20.8.1897.
73. *Jesus and the Gospel*, 391.
74. Ibid. 395.
75. Ibid. 405.
76. Ibid. 398.
77. Ibid. 401.
78. See J. Denney, *The Christian Doctrine of Reconciliation* (London: Hodder & Stoughton, 1917), 311. For A. E. Garvie's criticism of Denney in this connection see his *The Christian Doctrine of the Godhead* (London: Hodder & Stoughton, 1925), 360–1. Denney had earlier been more traditionally disposed: 'The distinction of Father and Son was the most obvious, and it was enriched, on the basis of Christ's own teaching, and of the actual experience of the Church, by the further distinction of the Holy Spirit'. See *Studies in Theology*, 70. Similarly, he did not in his later works repeat so definite a Trinitarianism as this: 'That doctrine (i.e. the Trinity) . . . is nothing if not historical and Christian'. (Ibid. 71). He never recanted his Trinitarianism, but it was not a central theme with him.
79. J. Denney, '*Romans*' in *The Expositor's Greek Testament*, ad loc. Nb '*itself*'.
80. *Jesus and the Gospel*, 403.
81. See *LFF*, ix.
82. *Jesus and the Gospel*, 30; cf. 58.
83. J. Denney, *Gospel Questions and Answers* (London: Hodder & Stoughton, 1896), 7–8.
84. *Studies in Theology*, 155.
85. *Jesus and the Gospel*, 48–9.
86. Ibid. ix.
87. Ibid. 107, 111.
88. Ibid. 157.
89. J. Denney, 'Christianity and the Historical Christ', the *Expositor* (8th series, v, 1913), 20.
90. *Studies in Theology*, 4.
91. Ibid. 17. Of Christ, Denney elsewhere wrote 'He is a Person so great that St. Paul is obliged to reconstruct His (*sic*) whole world around Him'. (*The Death of Christ*, London, 1902, 199).
92. *The Christian Doctrine of Reconciliation*, 64–5; cf. 75, 185–6; *The Atonement and the Modern Mind*, 84.
93. *Studies in Theology*, 44.
94. *Jesus and the Gospel*, 108; cf. 164 and *Studies in Theology*, 207–8.
95. Ibid. 120.
96. *The Way Everlasting*, 3.
97. *Studies in Theology*, 7.
98. *The Way Everlasting*, 147.
99. *LN*, 99–100, dated 7.11.1907. In fairness it should be added that Schmiedel did not think it could be shown that Jesus never lived. We may also note Denney's evident distate for R. J. Campbell's 'New Theology', See *LN*, 79, 85–6, 87, 107,

148. Campbell later retracted. See further, A. P. F. Sell, 'Platonists (Ancient and Modern) and the Gospel'. *The Irish Theological Quarterly* xliv (1977), 153–174.
100. *The Atonement and the Modern Mind*, 27–8.
101. *Jesus and the Gospel*, 132–3, cf. 85, 102, 375–6. In this last reference he counters Lessing's view that 'accidental truths of history can never become the proof of necessary truths of reason'. 'Christianity', he declares, 'does not mean the recognition of necessary truths of reason, but an attitude of the soul to God, determined by Christ; and history is not to the religious man a chapter of accidents, but the stage on which a Divine purpose is achieved which could not be more ineptly described than by calling it accidental. Religion can no more be simplified by making it independent of history than respiration would be simplified by soaring beyond the atmosphere'.
102. *The Atonement and the Modern Mind*, 62.
103. *Jesus and the Gospel*, 86; cf. 6.
104. *LN*, 81, dated 29.1.1907; cf. *The Christian Doctrine of Reconciliation*, 4.
105. *The Way Everlasting*, 10.
106. *LN*, xxxv.
107. Ibid. 148–9, dated 12.11.1909. But Jones's biographer is at pains to point out that this estimate, though just, should not be read as indicating that Jones 'turned the interest of any of his students away from religion, or gave them anything but a profoundly reverent interpretation of Christianity'. See H. J. W. Hetherington, *The Life and Letters of Sir Henry Jones* (London: Hodder & Stoughton, 1924), 82.
108. *LN*, 167–8, dated 14.12.1910.
109. *The Way Everlasting*, 275.
110. J. Denney, 'Ritschl in English', *Expository Times*, xii (1900–01), 139. For our broader reflections on Ritschl see A. P. F. Sell, *Theology in Turmoil*, ch. iv.
111. A. E. Garvie (among others) certainly thought that Denney had experienced an excess of adversely critical zeal. See his *The Ritschlian Theology* (Edinburgh: T. & T. Clark, 1899), 187, 222, 286–95. On the other hand James Orr wrote of the 'uncalled-for severity' of Garvie's strictures upon Denney. See his *The Ritschlian Theology and the Evangelical Faith* (London: Hodder & Stoughton, 1898), 78. Garvie was later to write enthusiastically of Denney's *The Christian Doctrine of Reconciliation*, though he did observe the weakness on the Spirit and the Trinity to which we have already adverted. See his '"Christ Crucified" for the Thought and Life of Today', *Expository Times*, xxx (1918–19), 83–5.
112. *Studies in Theology*, 3.
113. Ibid. 12. Cf. Denney's 'Harnack and Loisy on the Essence of Christianity', *Expositor* (6th series, xi, 1905), 103–123. For a consideration of these issues as they affect present-day theology see A. P. F. Sell, 'Transcendence, Immanence and the Supernatural,' *Journal of Theology for Southern Africa* (March, 1979), 56–66.
114. Ibid. 13.
115. e.g. *Studies in Theology*, 14, 49, etc.
116. Ibid. 145; cf. *The Death of Christ*, 132.
117. Ibid. 37; cf. *Jesus and the Gospel*, 80.
118. Ibid. 40.
119. Ibid. 42.
120. *The Atonement and the Modern Mind*, 31.
121. *Studies in Theology*, 69.

122. Ibid. 57. Though, as we have seen, Forrest's was such a modified kenoticism that the difference between the two colleagues was probably little more than verbal.

123. *Jesus and the Gospel*, 15.

124. Quoted by H. R. Mackintosh in *The Doctrine of the Person of Jesus Christ* (Edinburgh: T. & T. Clark, 1956), 531.

125. *Jesus and the Gospel*, 20; cf. 25–6.

126. Ibid. 28.

127. Ibid. 37.

128. Ibid. 89; cf. *Studies in Theology*, 59–61.

129. T. H. Darlow, op. cit. 360, dated 4.12.1908.

130. *LN*, 121, 125, dated 7.12.1908 and 12.12.1908.

131. *The Death of Christ*, 318.

132. Ibid. 15.

133. Ibid. 36.

134. Ibid. 278; cf. 134ff.

135. Ibid. 58–9.

136. Ibid. 98.

137. Ibid. 100.

138. Ibid. 166; cf. *The Christian Doctrine of Reconciliation*, 24.

139. Ibid. 213, 286, etc; and especially *The Atonement and the Modern Mind*, 85: 'God, no doubt, would not do justice to Himself if He did not show His compassion for sinners; but, on the other hand . . . He would not do justice to Himself if He displayed His compassion for sinners in a way which made light of sin, which ignored its tragic reality, or took it for less than it is'. Denney does not award many trophies to the Socinians, but he does grant that they were right in denying that there could be a justice-mercy schism in God. See *The Christian Doctrine of Reconciliation*, 104.

140. *The Christian Doctrine of Reconciliation*, 180.

141. *Studies in Theology*, 102–3.

142. *The Atonement and the Modern Mind*, 54–55.

143. *The Christian Doctrine of Reconciliation*, 142ff.

144. J. Denney, 'Can Sin be Forgiven?' in J. Denney *et al.*, *Questions of Faith* (London: Hodder & Stoughton, 1904), 160.

145. *The Christian Doctrine of Reconciliation*, 157; cf. *Studies in Theology*, 103–4.

146. *Studies in Theology*, 131.

147. See *Jesus and the Gospel*, 96.

148. *The Way Everlasting*, 301.

149. *The Atonement and the Modern Mind*, 81.

150. *LFF*, 17; cf. *The Christian Doctrine of Reconciliaton*, 16, and *The Atonement and the Modern Mind*, 90: 'All true penitents are children of the Cross'.

151. See *The Death of Christ*, 291. We are reminded of those extremer Calvinists who have gone so far as to say that the gospel may be preached only to 'sensible sinners'. No doctrine is more calculated to distract the gaze from Christ, and to lead to an introspection which can become almost morbid.

152. T. H. Hughes, *The Atonement* (London: Allen & Unwin, 1949), 88.

153. Robert Mackintosh, *Historic Theories of Atonement*, 292, 294.

154. Ibid. 292. J. K. Mozley incorrectly takes Denney as holding that death 'was not a natural event so far as man is concerned'. See his *Some Tendencies in British Theology* (London: SPCK, 1951), 132.

155. *The Christian Doctrine of Reconciliation*, 211; cf. ibid. 280; *The Death of Christ*, 127, 229; *The Atonement and the Modern Mind*, 63–69.
156. Ibid. 273.
157. See e.g. *The Atonement and the Modern Mind*, 95.
158. W. P. Paterson, 'Dr. Denney's Theology', *Constructive Quarterly*, March 1919, 84–5.
159. *The Christian Doctrine of Reconciliation*, 259. See the illuminating article by J. B. Torrance, 'The Contribution of McLeod Campbell to Scottish Theology', *Scottish Journal of Theology*, xxvi (1973), 295–311.
160. *LN*, 1, 2; cf. *The Death of Christ* 233; *The Atonement and the Modern Mind*, 110. H. Rashdall's reply is in his *The Idea of Atonement in Christian Theology* (London: Macmillan, 1920), 440–443.
161. For this theme see e.g. *The Death of Christ*, 93, 332; *The Atonement and the Modern Mind*, 40; *The Christian Doctrine of Reconciliation*, 12, 329. For R. Mackintosh's comment see his *Christianity and Sin* (London: Duckworth, 1913), 196: 'It will not do to teach or even to suggest that mankind are renewed and sanctified exclusively by the consciousness of being forgiven'. Cf. his *Historic Theories of Atonement*, 5, 6.
162. *The Death of Christ*, 286.
163. J. Denney, *The Church and the Kingdom* (London: Hodder & Stoughton, 1910), 15.
164. Though Denney did write on 'The Spirit and the New Life' in the *Expositor*, Dec. 1901.
165. See J. K. Mozley, *The Doctrine of the Atonement* (London: Duckworth, 1915), 212 n.
166. A point not taken e.g. by W. Morgan, 'The Death of Christ', the *Expository Times*, xiv (1902–1903), 171–2.
167. Though Denney would not go as far as W. Lofthouse, *Ethics and the Atonement* (London: Methuen, 1906), 191, in saying that 'the value of the death is that it made possible the resurrection'. See *The Christian Doctrine of Reconciliation*, 287 and n.
168. *The Death of Christ*, 280. Cf. *The Christian Doctrine of Reconciliation* 183: 'the real objection to the speculative theories of an incarnation independent of sin is that they assume us to know, in independence of the Saviour and of His sin-bearing work, what incarnation means'. See also 37, 59, 181, 182; *The Death of Christ*, 211, 322–7. He points out that Socinianism began with the denial not of the incarnation, but of the atonement.
169. *Studies in Theology*, 100, 101, citing J. Orr, *The Christian View of God and the World* (Edinburgh: Elliot, 3rd edn., 1893), 319ff.
170. H. R. Mackintosh, 'Principal Denney as a Theologian', *Expository Times*, xxviii (1916–17), 491.
171. *Jesus and the Gospel*, 346.
172. J. Denney, 'Adam and Christ in St. Paul', the *Expositor* (6th series, ix, 1904), 148n. Peake replied in *The Primitive Methodist Quarterly* to Denney's view as first set forth in *Studies in Theology*, and reaffirmed his own position in his *Guide to Bible Study*. Denney's *The Death of Christ* brought further comment from Peake in *PMQ*, and Denney responded in *The Atonement and the Modern Mind*. Peake's final retort was in the *Expositor* for Jan. 1904, and Denney's was the article referred to here. See J. T. Wilkinson, *Arthur Samuel Peake* (London: Epworth, 1971), 119, 120.
173. Quoted by Denney, *The Atonement and the Modern Mind*, 97–8.
174. Ibid. 98–99. He was, be it noted, happy to interpret Paul as teaching that Christ takes the death of the sinful race to himself; but the fact remains that 'Christ does not commit sin, and we do not make atonement'. See *The Death of Christ*, 147, 237.
175. *Jesus and the Gospel*, 33–4.

176. William Sanday, *Christologies Ancient and Modern* (Oxford: Clarendon Press, 1910), 126.

177. *The Atonement and the Modern Mind*, 102; cf. *The Death of Christ*, 106, 185; 'Adam and Christ in St. Paul', op. cit. 152.

178. *LN*, 37, dated 28.11.1903. For Nicoll's letter, dated 21.11.1903, see T. H. Darlow, op. cit. 352–3. On 24.10.1903 Nicoll had written to Peake: 'I have grave difficulty in understanding [Denney's] position, but he seems to me to have an intense dislike of all mysticism, and this is a serious disqualification in writing of St. Paul.' Denney's final and characteristic remark on the subject to Nicoll was: 'In spite of Peake and Stevens and many more—perhaps even in spite of you—I consider myself a mystic; just as Dr. Johnson considerd himself a very polite man'. See T. H. Darlow, op. cit. 401. H. R. Mackintosh (art. cit. 492) said that Denney 'did not really ignore the truth of Union with Christ'; but H. W. Robinson misunderstood Denney's point concerning the transcendence of the mystical by the moral, in so far as he did not realize that according to Denney, for the *believer*, the two are one. See his *The Christian Experience of the Holy Spirit* (London: Collins Fontana, 1962), 180. It is thus not correct to say, as *DNB* does, that Denney 'did not shrink from denying that St. Paul taught a mystical union of the believer with Christ'. The *DNB* article was written by Peake, who also comments, with rather more justification, 'What [Denney] could see he saw with exceptional lucidity. What he could not see, had for him no existence and no right to exist'. Robert Mackintosh wrote of Denney, 'That imperious theologian reminds a reader constantly of the Gladstonian temperament and temper—preternaturally clear in seeing what it sees; so impatiently contemptuous of those who dare to observe anything which the Master-mind had not detected'. He further wryly remarked, 'One was inclined to think that his transference from a chair of Dogmatic to a chair of New Testament was extremely wholesome for such a mind'. See *Historic Theories of Atonement*, 6, 284, and 'Adam and Christ in St. Paul', art. cit., 157; *The Christian Doctrine of Reconciliation*, 304–5.

179. *The Atonement and the Modern Mind*, 117.

180. See C. Wistar Hodge, 'Dr. Denney and the Doctrine of the Atonement', *Princeton Theological Review* xvi (1918), 623–641. G. B. Stevens in *The Christian Doctrine of Salvation* (Edinburgh: T. & T. Clark, 1905), 196, also thought that Denney's position had undergone a change from an earlier forensic view to a later, more liberal, view. But J. K. Mozley disagreed; see his *The Doctrine of the Atonement*, 181–2; and *Some Tendencies in British Theology*, 132–3.

181. See also B. B. Warfield, *Critical Reviews* (New York: OUP, 1932), 103 for a further Princetonian criticism of Denney's view of scriptural authority.

182. *The Christian Doctrine of Reconciliation*, 20.

183. Ibid. 233.

184. *LN*, 59, dated 17.10.1905; cf. *The Christian Doctrine of Reconciliation*, 109.

185. *The Christian Doctrine of Reconciliation*, 162, 235; cf. 239.

186. Ibid. 269.

187. *The Death of Christ*, 123.

188. G. F. Barbour, op. cit., 602.

189. *The Death of Christ*, 312.

CHAPTER TEN:
EPILOGUE

1. John Dickie, *Fifty Years of British Theology* (Edinburgh: T. & T. Clark, 1937), 93.
2. P. T. Forsyth, *The Principle of Authority* ([1913], London: Independent Press, 1957), 219.
3. See further A. P. F. Sell, *Theology in Turmoil. The roots, course and significance of the conservative-liberal debate in modern theology* (Grand Rapids: Baker Book House, 1986), ch. i.
4. See A. P. F. Sell, 'Dubious Establishment? A neglected ecclesiological testimony', *Mid-Stream* xxiv, (1985), 1–28.
5. For further reflections on this point see A. P. F. Sell, 'Christians, humanists and common ground', *Journal of Moral Education* i (1972), 177.
6. For a fuller discussion see A. P. F. Sell, 'The peril of reductionism in Christian thought', *Scottish Journal of Theology* xxvii (1974), 48–64.
7. P. T. Forsyth, op. cit. 77.
8. A. P. F. Sell, 'Transcendence, immanence and the supernatural', *Journal of Theology for Southern Africa*, 26, March 1979, 62.
9. P. T. Forsyth, *The Cruciality of the Cross* ([1909], London: Independent Press, 1957), 50.
10. C. D. Broad, 'Critical and speculative philosophy', in *Contemporary British Philosophy* i, (London: Allen & Unwin, 1924).

Index of Persons

INDEX OF PERSONS